FERTILE GROUND

The Impacts of Participatory Watershed Management

edited by

FIONA HINCHCLIFF, JOHN THOMPSON,
JULES PRETTY, IRENE GUIJT and PARMESH SHAH

IT PUBLICATIONS 1999

Intermediate Technology Publications Ltd,
103–105 Southampton Row, London WC1B 4HH, UK

© International Institute for Environment and Development 1999

ISBN 1 85339 389 4

Typeset by Dorwyn Ltd, Rowlands Castle, Hants
Printed by SRP Exeter

Contents

v

CHAPTER CONTENTS AT A GLANCE

Farmer innovation of technology	Farmers' groups	Farmer-to-farmer extension	Equity/ gender	Government programmes	Policies for participatory watershed development	Institutional change	Methodology of participatory evaluation
					■		
							■
■							
■			■			■	
■	■						
■	■	■					
■	■			■			
■		■					
■				■		■	■
	■			■	■	■	
				■		■	
			■	■		■	
	■			■		■	
				■		■	
	■			■	■	■	
				■	■	■	
■		■	■		■		
■	■	■				■	
■	■		■			■	
■		■	■			■	
	■					■	
	■		■				
■		■				■	
■	■						
						■	
	■			■		■	■
	■			■		■	■
					■		

Exchange rates at time of study

Currency	Pound sterling equivalent (1994)	US Dollar equivalent (1994)
Australian dollar	2.1	1.3
Indian rupee	48.3	31.4
Nepalese rupee	76.5	49.6
Pakistan rupee	47.1	30.5
Philippines peso	40.8	26.5

Foreword

THIS COLLECTION OF case-studies opens windows on an emerging approach to achieving conservation of water and soil through processes of agricultural development. While many of its agro-ecological and socio-economic elements have been known for many years, they have rarely been drawn together coherently. From this collection it is possible to see clearly a number of common features of positive rural change which underlie improvements made by self-help groups as diverse as large farmers in Australia to small-scale subsistence farmers on the margins of the Sahel. The evidence here points to the need for a change in the ways in which external institutions interact with rural people, moving away from a prescriptive approach to one of facilitating and catalysing.

These studies show that better husbandry of the land can result in greater security of food and water supplies, higher productivity, improved livelihoods, and greater sustainability of all these. They show that when mutual trust and credibility increase between and among farmers and their non-farm technical colleagues, information flows more easily between them. Once this occurs, the merging of local priorities and externally-perceived opportunities becomes possible and realistic. It seems that the need is not for ever-increasing amounts of new technology from research, but for more two-way and open channels of communication, so that local insights and knowledge can be incorporated in the shared planning, implementation and monitoring of improvements.

All the cases suggest that a basic premiss for the future must be that resource-poor farmers are more concerned with improving their soil's productive potential, sustaining production and improving food security than is any salaried employee of a government or non-governmental organization. Their lives, literally, depend on this. On realizing this, rural people's actions and reactions come into focus as being more rational than many have acknowledged in the past. Because farm families have multiple objectives, their views of reality often differ from the views and more limited objectives of specialist off-farm advisers who come from a varied range of single disciplines. Truly participatory approaches expose many unwarranted assumptions hidden inside many a professional's approach. 'Top-down' initiatives of the past have been based on the assumption that farm families should participate in outsiders' projects and programmes. Rural people's responses to this approach have been muted at best, and few lasting positive changes have occurred. But farmers' actions, in these studies and others, suggest that the converse approach – in which field staff participate with rural people in developing their own projects and programmes – is what farm families have been hoping for over many years. Their difficulty seems to have been finding appropriate, usable and effective advice.

It becomes evident that there are two largely untapped potentials that could markedly improve the effectiveness of agricultural development initiatives with small farmers. First, the self-recuperating capacities of soils, when adequately managed, is remarkable. Second, the latent skills, enthusiasms and capacities of rural people can be awakened when their confidence is strengthened to decide on and manage their affairs. This process becomes self-enhancing as the understanding, knowledge and skills of field staff are also built upon in response to positive interactions with farmers.

An academic debate rages about the relative values of 'natural scientists' and 'social scientists' in promoting and assisting agricultural development with small farmers. Effective field staff have always bridged that gap by combining sound technical knowledge with skills in facilitation and communication with community groups. Specialists in natural and social sciences are jointly valuable in supporting multi-faceted field staff and farmers with insights, knowledge and advice in interdisciplinary ways. The need for their skills in support of the new approach is greater, not less, than ever.

Contrary to common viewpoints, the catchment or watershed[1] is not always the most rational unit for all activities in rural development. Because neither catchments nor the groups who live among them are homogeneous, the nature of their problems and the possible solutions are varied and complex. Prescriptive external solutions have little chance of fitting more than one-third of cases at best, and may be inappropriate or unacceptable to the majority of farmers. Nevertheless, working with common interest groups on contiguous areas of land, whose boundaries may be administrative, social or physical, enables agency staff to provide assistance more efficiently than where individual farms are scattered across the countryside. It makes more likely the neighbour-to-neighbour transfer of information and favoured innovations, and gives the end-results more visual and psychological impact when they are concentrated together in defined areas.

---

[1] A catchment is an area from which rainfall drains into a river or reservoir, whereas a watershed is a line of high land where streams on one side flow into one river and streams on the other side flow into another (Oxford Dictionary). The case-studies presented here tend to take either a catchment or a watershed focus. While the terms differ in meaning, both provide an appropriate focus for participatory soil and water conservation, and the process taken and results obtained do not differ.

Thus it is not 'catchment management' as such that results in improvements in agriculture and livelihoods. Insistence on such a framework may run contrary to communities' needs and priorities and generate unnecessary antagonisms. Rather it is the integration of improved husbandry of land, of crops and of livestock with better interpersonal relations in the context of catchments that produces tangible benefits. These two aspects are complementary, and for lasting improvements in livelihoods to occur, improvements in both are necessary in the same time-frame, in the same place, and at both micro- and macro-scales.

Emerging from these case-studies are new challenges. What are the social, economic, political, environmental and institutional factors that currently hold back the more extensive and rapid spread of positive experiences like these? How can we amend the nature of our support to rural communities to mitigate these limiting factors and facilitate these positive changes in attitudes and in soil conditions? What changes in attitudes, in policies, in research agendas, in curricula for staff training, in institutional arrangements, in programme planning, in funding, etc. are needed, and how quickly can they be made?

In a world made gloomy by continuing population increase and the inadequate success of earlier efforts to improve people's land and livelihoods, this book provides evidence that significant changes are still possible, that we seem to have left the best till last, and that it is we, more than farmers, who may have to make the most marked adjustments if such positive changes are to occur on a worldwide scale.

Francis Shaxson

Preface

FOR CLOSE TO a century rural development policies and practice have taken the view that farmers mismanage soil and water. Farmers have been advised, lectured at, paid and forced to adopt new soil and water conservation measures and practices. Many have done so, and some environments and economies seem to have benefited for a time; but critical internal contradictions have often undermined these efforts. Financial and legal incentives bring only short-lived conservation, and farmers soon revert to their own practices. Many efforts have thus been remarkably unsuccessful, frequently resulting in more erosion.

Where soil and water conservation is successful and sustained, farmers are seen as the solution rather than the problem, and local knowledge and skills are put at the core of programmes. Local organizations are reinforced through participatory planning, an interactive and empowering approach to participation.

Recent evidence is indicating that these new encounters between professionals and farmers are producing considerable productive and sustainable benefits. There is a growing number of mostly small-scale projects that are sufficiently successful to suggest the need for application on a much wider scale. But until recently almost no evidence existed of the value of their efforts.

In 1992, the Sustainable Agriculture Programme of the International Institute for Environment and Development (IIED) launched the 'New Horizons' collaborative research programme. This provided support to diverse organizations engaged in participatory watershed development to assess the environmental, economic and social impacts of their work. The aim of these studies was to document and analyse the processes they followed, and to link these processes to their impacts.

This book presents the detailed findings of these 25 case-studies from Asia, Africa, Latin America and Australia, and draws out the many lessons and implications for the future of watershed development practice and policy. The first chapter of the book sets the scene with a brief history of soil and water conservation in the 20th century, amply demonstrating the necessity for participation if sustainability and equity are to be achieved. After a detailed chapter on the methodology used for the analysis of impacts in these 25 case-studies, the book is divided into four major sections. The first presents case-studies where farmers' capacity to experiment with, innovate, adapt and disseminate resource-conserving technologies has been a key element. The remainder of the sections are organized according to the type of institution promoting participatory watershed development: from governments, to NGOs, to initiatives where local capacity and innovation have been key. Each section is preceded by an overview, summarizing the major insights found in the sections. At the front of the book a matrix provides a more detailed overview of the key aspects covered by each chapter, and will help guide readers to those areas that are of most interest to them.

This collaborative research programme was made possible through support from the Swedish International Development Cooperation Agency (Sida), the Swiss Directorate for Development Cooperation and Humanitarian Aid (SDC), the Deutsche Gesellschaft für Technische Zusammenarbeit (GTZ), the Ford Foundation, the British Department for International Development (DFID, formerly ODA) and the Australian International Development Assistance Bureau (AIDAB – now called AusAid). Funding for the publication and distribution of this book was provided by the Directorate General for International Co-operation (DGIC), The Netherlands.

The fascinating findings and lessons presented here are entirely due to the many committed individuals, institutions and community groups, too numerous to mention, who have striven for participation and sustainability and who have painstakingly recorded and analysed the processes involved.

OVERVIEWS

1

Soil and Water Conservation: A Brief History of Coercion and Control

JULES PRETTY and PARMESH SHAH

Towards coercion with technologies

AGRICULTURE HAS HAD many 'revolutions' throughout history, from its advent some 10 000 years ago to the renowned 17th–19th century agricultural revolution in Europe. In the past century, rural environments in most parts of the world have also undergone massive transformations. In some ways, these have been the most far-reaching in their speed of spread of new technologies and the nature of their impacts upon social, economic and ecological systems.

Two guiding themes have dominated these agricultural transformations. One has been the need for increased food production to support growing populations. The other has been the desire to prevent the degradation of natural resources, perceived to be caused largely by growing numbers of people and their bad practices. Farmers have been encouraged to adopt a wide range of conservation practices and technologies, including soil and water conservation, to control soil erosion; grazing management schemes to control rangeland degradation; and exclusion of people from forests and other sites of high biodiversity to protect wildlife and plants.

Central to this process is the assumption that technologies are universal, and so are independent of social context. New technologies are assumed to be better than those from the past, and so to represent 'progress'. Such a process is usually depicted as linear, with the new and modern displacing the old and 'traditional', usually implying that what has gone before is not as good as what we have now.

The assumption of the universality of technologies has inevitably led to greater standardization. As farmers have been made to comply 'in their own best interests', they have done so only by completely changing their own livelihoods, simplifying their practices to incorporate new technologies. External institutions have acted as if they alone know best. Such universality of approach or technology leads to homogenization of environments, bringing with it the steady erosion of cultural and biological diversity. Where farmers used to use a range of biological and physical measures to control soil erosion, now they might only have terraces.

Throughout recent history, institutions concerned with encouraging soil and water conservation have had all the components of modernity. Farmers have been first encouraged, then later coerced, to adopt

1

technologies that are known to work. When these farmers fail to maintain – or others spontaneously to adopt – these measures, then interventions have shifted to the remoulding of local social and economic environments to suit the technologies.

The modernization of soil and water conservation in the USA, Africa and South Asia

Beginnings in the USA

The knowledge that soil erosion was both costly and damaging was first appreciated on a wide scale by agricultural authorities in the USA in the 19th century and in colonial Africa and India in the early part of the 20th century (Pretty and Shah, 1994; Hall, 1949; Bennett, 1939). Rural development policies and practice have generally taken the view that erosion occurs because farmers are poor managers of soil and water.

The style of intervention was first established in the USA, where there is still a marked contrast between the enduring success of indigenous soil and water conservation and the approaches adopted by soil conservation authorities. Native American farming cultures farmed with soil and water conservation measures for at least 1500 years in the Greater South West. Farmers of Anasazi, Hohokam, Pueblo, Zuni, Hopi and Papago cultures located fields where water ran off hills, built earthen diversion dams and channels to conduct water, used contour bunds, stone terracing and contour hedges of agave, sited silt traps to produce gully fields, grew crops in mounds and on ridges, and stored runoff in reservoirs (Rohn, 1963; UNEP, 1983; Fish and Paul, 1992).

These combined to produce complex, diverse and productive agricultural systems. At Point of Pines, for example, 2500ha of cultivated land with contour terraces, check dams and bordered gardens supported at least 3000 people for 500 years. And in New Mexico, bordered gardens connected by ditches to vast rain catchment areas supported a population density of 700 per km². None the less, these systems were ignored by the modern conservationists.

At first confined to the southern States, soil conservation spread across most parts of the country in the early to mid-1800s. The principal technology was terracing, but this was supplemented by a wide range of other resource-conserving technologies, including contour ploughing, cross ploughing, green manures and cover crops, drainage ditches, check dams and hillside stripping with hedgerows (Hall, 1949). These technologies were developed, tested and adapted to local conditions by farmers. Until the late 1800s, technologies were derived from 'the experiences of practical planters and farmers'.

But by the 1870s-1880s, things had begun to change. Terraces of various forms (broad base, bench, Nichols, Mangam, Chisholm and others) had become increasingly popular. Although there were objections, such as that terraces took too much land out of cultivation and harboured weeds, increasing numbers of advisers, researchers and extensionists began to make wider recommendations based on terraces alone. Researchers at experimental stations, who at first had published bulletins and papers based entirely on the observations and experiences of 'progressive' farmers, later came to advocate technologies developed solely on research stations. By the early 20th century, agricultural extension agencies and county agents 'built terraces for farmers and instructed them in terrace making and maintenance' (Hall, 1949).

By far the greatest boost to modern conservation ideology occurred when the 'dust bowl' struck the southern and southwestern states of Oklahoma, Arkansas, Kansas, Colorado, Texas, and New Mexico during the 1930s. In the previous two decades, farmers had been encouraged to move westwards by favourable homestead policies and the high price of wheat (Worster, 1979). In the 1910s, 30 000 farmers each year registered new land holdings in these states and in 1919 alone some 4.5 million hectares of grassland were ploughed up to grow wheat. By the time the dust storms began, much of the land had been farmed for only a generation. Eventually some 50 million hectares of farmland were said to be severely affected by erosion. Dust and earth blanketed houses and crops, and there were potent images of destruction where there had once been crops (Worster, 1979).

These images of erosion linked farmers' cropping and grazing practices to increased frequency of droughts. The message was clear. Farmers caused land degradation which could lead to national ruin. At the time, several influential writers suggested that whole civilizations had collapsed through neglect of the soil (Bennett, 1939; Jacks and Whyte, 1939). The head of the US Soil Conservation Service, Hugh H Bennett, spoke of environmental catastrophe by indicating that 'the ultimate consequence of unchecked soil erosion, when it sweeps over whole countries as it is doing today, must be national extinction' (in Beinart, 1984). Over a relatively short period, policy-makers came to treat the problem as so serious that widespread social and institutional action had to be taken.

As a result, a federal Soil Conservation Service (formerly the Soil Erosion Service) was established in 1935 as a body separate from the existing extension service. Its agents conducted a national inventory of erosion, so they could 'help the farmer do things correctly' (in Trimble, 1985). From the start, erosion was seen as a problem arising out of bad farming practices that had to be corrected. But to demonstrate the efficacy of the approach, the SCS needed large amounts of land to practise the new large-scale engineering measures. As few agreements came from private farmers, they selected Navajo reservations on which to experiment (Kelly, 1985).

The SCS constructed physical measures and enforced compulsory destocking of sheep and goats. College graduates did the technical work, and local Navajos worked as labourers. But the project provoked an intense negative reaction, not only to soil conservation but also to all government programmes. Anthropologists discovered that the local people were not against soil conservation but were opposed to the way it was being implemented (Kelly, 1985). They took exception to the locations of the measures, as these interfered with other activities. It was not a lack of interest that prevented them from maintaining or repairing the structures and earthen dams, but rather that the measures had been constructed with heavy equipment over which they had no access or control.

Conflict over budgeting and approach continued to hamper the SCS. Their approach was vigorously opposed by the extension service, whose agents at county level and in land grant colleges had a good knowledge of the diversity of local conditions. The SCS applied terracing technology widely, while local agents argued for locally adapted and appropriate technologies. But the dissenting voices were ignored. Sauer was one of the few who indicated that construction without maintenance did more harm than good: 'the present erosion crisis is the result primarily of the introduction of terracing, originally thought of as protection against erosion' (Sauer, 1934 in Trimble, 1985).

Transfer to Africa

The pattern of intervention was repeated by colonial authorities in Africa. Erosion was first recognized as a problem as early as the 1870s, though it was not until the early part of the 20th century that concern grew over farming as practised both by indigenous people and colonial farmers. At first, farmers were encouraged to adopt soil conservation practices through publicity bulletins extolling the virtues of contour ploughing and grass strips, by establishing demonstration plots, and via local legislation (Stocking, 1985; Gichuki, 1991). But few farmers adopted the technologies, even though groups were taken to demonstration farms to see the benefits of the new farming practices.

New grazing management systems of enforced enclosure of grazing lands developed in Texas were also implemented. Again potent images of erosion spurred these efforts. In Kenya, Huxley (1960) described 'gullies 15–20 feet deep . . . in places, the landscape seems as dead as the moon's' in the west, and elsewhere the 'land is gashed . . . scraped bare, pounded into dust by the hoofs of little cattle and greedy goats'. It was clear to officials that local people were to blame. They sought technical guidance from the USA, and brought back recommendations for large-scale conservation intervention. There were occasional dissenting voices. Writing in 1930, Sampson drew attention to indigenous methods of cultivation designed to check erosion, particularly mounding and ridge-and-furrowing systems on the contour. He indicated that local farmers 'fully realise the losses caused by

4

erosion and consequent soil exhaustion, and their methods are well worth studying not only for themselves, but as a guide to those who seek to improve on them' (Sampson, 1930). But these sentiments were rare.

When these new soil conservation efforts proved to be too costly to sustain, particularly where mechanization was required, administrators increased the use of local labour rather than adapt the technologies (Anderson, 1984). They also put together the components of good conservation practice into farm plans. These were laid out on a blueprint chart showing what every field was to grow for 10 years, with all contours marked, the locations for woodlots, paddocks and homestead, and where to plant cash and food crops.

All of this required the monitoring of farming practices to ensure compliance. The final stage of control was achieved by the compulsory resettlement of farmers to centralized linear settlements where they could be observed more easily. In Kenya, more than one million people were moved in the mid-1950s to some 850 new linear villages (Huxley, 1960). Officials, proud of the new neatness and order, commented that farms of one village in Zimbabwe (then Rhodesia), were 'all in lines and look very nice' (Alvord, in Beinart, 1984). Soil and water conservation had extended to the remoulding of all aspects of rural life.

Soil and water conservation in South Asia

As in the USA and colonial Africa, there is a long history of both recognizing and ignoring local conservation practices in South Asia. The earliest accounts show that in 1888 some 1200 hectares of ravines in Uttar Pradesh were treated with conservation measures to protect the adjoining town of Etawah from water erosion. This was followed by tree planting, and farmers were coerced into adopting zero-grazing for livestock. The programme was acclaimed as a success (PRAI, 1963).

At the same time, though, visitors were seeing local innovation and skills. Professor Voelcker, a consultant to the Royal Agricultural Society of England, visited India in 1889 and wrote in his report: 'Nowhere would one find better instances of keeping land scrupulously clean from weeds, of ingenuity in device of water raising appliances, of knowledge of soils and their capabilities as well as the exact time to sow and reap, as one would in Indian agriculture . . . Certain it is that I, at least, have never seen a more perfect picture of careful cultivation, combined with hard labour, perseverance and fertility of resources' (in Dogra, 1983).

By 1928 the Royal Commission on Agriculture had recognized soil erosion as a problem of special importance, and had noted work already in progress: 'In the United Provinces, the main remedy for soil erosion has been sought in the afforestation of the ravine tracts. In Bombay [now Maharashtra] State, the measures adopted to prevent soil erosion are terracing of land and the construction of earth and stone embankments.' The Famine Enquiry Commission of 1945 later indicated that the large-scale experiments conducted in Bombay had produced results sufficiently satisfactory to warrant contour bunding on a large scale. In Bombay, conservation work started in 1939 when the scheme for bunding and dry farming development was sanctioned.

In the years that followed, conservation structures were constructed solely by the State. Though these were initially effective, it was soon realized that the approach could not be extended because of the high cost of operation and maintenance. The lack of involvement of farmers was understood also to be a problem, but at the same time they were considered to be ignorant. Most technical literature emanated from the USA, and training opportunities for professionals were again on US Soil Conservation Service programmes.

The technocratic model of development of watersheds became the predominant approach at this stage and formed the basis for the formulation of five-year plans and allocation of resources for soil conservation. These began with the objective 'to govern, regulate and administer the use of land both under private and public ownership, so as to facilitate the optimum use of land resources in the interests of the present and future generations' (Planning Commission, 1964). But the plans consisted of technical and engineering solutions with repeated emphasis on the education of farmers who had to be made aware of the new technologies.

Problems with implementation and maintenance followed. When cultivators in Madhya Pradesh were reluctant to undertake earthwork it was entrusted by the department to contractors. The contour bunding was completed with bulldozers, with no attention paid to the interests of farmers. In Maharashtra, Gujarat and Mysore, farmers were said to have taken to large-scale contour bunding, but it later became clear that 'the aspects of conservation farming practices or follow-up are neglected. As a consequence . . . the project is not serving the purpose for which it was set up' (Planning Commission, 1964).

Soil conservation continued with a technocratic emphasis. Between 1963 and 1990, national initiatives spent Rs 4215 million (equal to $149 million at current prices) on soil conservation in river valley projects (Fernandez, 1993). But farmers did not perceive any benefits from the structures. Indeed, many levelled and destroyed the measures because of the loss of cropland to conservation and the increase in observed soil erosion.

The lack of compliance encouraged authorities to seek legal solutions. Several states passed laws to prevent 'wilful' destruction, and to allow specified 'improvements' to be made on farmers' fields and allocate the costs of these improvements between the farmers and the state. In some places, provisions were made for compulsory treatment of the fields of farmers refusing land treatment. This led in many cases to increased alienation with, for example, people uprooting plantations and destroying fencing and conservation measures.

Fundamental problems with recent soil and water conservation programmes

The 'complete' conservation technology package

Like other practices in agricultural development, most soil and water conservation programmes have begun with the notion that there are technologies that work, and it is just a matter of inducing or persuading farmers to adopt them. Yet few farmers are able to adopt whole packages of external technologies without considerable adjustments in their own practices and livelihood systems. To some, this may not be a problem; to the majority, it is a major impediment to adopting conservation technologies and practices.

The problem is that the imposed models look good at first, and then fade away. Alley cropping, an agroforestry system comprising rows of nitrogen-fixing trees or bushes separated by rows of cereals, has long been the focus of research (Kang *et al*, 1984; Lal, 1989). Many productive and sustainable systems, needing few or no external inputs, have been developed. They stop erosion, produce food and wood, and can be cropped over long periods. But the problem is that very few, if any, farmers have adopted these alley cropping systems as designed. Despite millions of dollars of research expenditure over many years, systems have been produced suitable only for research stations (Carter, 1995).

There has been some success, however, where farmers have been able to take one or two components of alley cropping, and then adapt them to their own farms. In Kenya, for example, farmers planted rows of leguminous trees next to field boundaries, or single rows through their fields; and in Rwanda, alleys planted by extension workers soon became dispersed through fields (Kerkhof, 1990).

But the prevailing view tends to be that farmers should adapt to the technology. Of the Agroforestry Outreach Project in Haiti, it was said that 'Farmer management of hedgerows does not conform to the extension program . . . Some farmers prune the hedgerows too early, others too late. Some hedges are not yet pruned by two years of age, when they have already reached heights of 4–5 metres. Other hedges are pruned too early, mainly because animals are let in or the tops are cut and carried to animals . . . Finally, it is very common for farmers to allow some of the trees in the hedgerow to grow to pole size' (Bannister and Nair, 1990). The language used clearly indicates that what farmers are doing is bad. Yet it could also be interpreted as good for sustainability: farmers were making their own adaptations according to their own needs.

7

Lack of maintenance by local people

Despite decades of effort, soil and water conservation programmes have had surprisingly little long-term success in preventing erosion. On paper, the quantitative achievements of some programmes can appear impressive. Throughout the world, terraces have been built, trees planted and farmers trained on a massive scale. In Africa, huge areas of land have been protected in the short term by conservation measures (Box 1.1).

Box 1.1:   Extent of large-scale soil conservation programmes in Africa

Burkina Faso	120 000 ha of graded bunds constructed 1962–1965
Ethiopia	1.5 million km of stone and soil terraces and bunds constructed on 300 000 ha, and 80 000 ha closed off from local people during the late 1970s to 1987
Lesotho	all the uplands were said to be protected by buffer stripping by 1960
Malawi (then Nyasaland)	118 000 km of bunds were constructed on 416 000 ha between 1945 and 1960
Malawi	288 000 ha terraced between 1968 and 1977
Rwanda/Burundi	750 000 ha terraced and planted with trees to 1960
Swaziland	112 000 km of grass strips laid out to 1950
Tanzania	125 000 ha of Kondoa completely destocked of cattle to 1979 to encourage hillside regeneration
Zambia (then North Rhodesia)	half the native land in Eastern Province was said to be protected by contour strips by 1950

Sources: Stocking, 1985; Marchal, 1986; Reij, 1988; IFAD, 1992

These have not, however, been long-term successes. In virtually all these sites, structures and practices have not persisted. Projects assume that maintenance will occur. Yet as farmers are treated at best as labourers for construction, they have few incentives to maintain structures or continue with practices that they neither own nor have had a say in designing. All too often, impressive new structures and practices slowly disappear, leaving little evidence of interventions and institutions.

This was recognized in the early days of the SCS in the USA. A 1941 study of some 520 terraced fields on 5000ha in the South found that most terraces had been 'improperly constructed' and poorly maintained (Carnes and Weld, 1941). The terraces had been constructed by the SCS, yet 83 per cent were not being maintained by the farmers on whose fields they were situated.

Sometimes successes are reversed almost immediately. In an evaluation of World Food Programme supported conservation in Ethiopia, the extent of the terracing was quoted as 'impressive', yet monitoring found 40 per cent of the terracing broken the year after construction (SIDA, 1984). The project had expected that local people would bear all the costs of maintenance. Another example comes from the Yatenga region of Burkina Faso, where 120 000 hectares of earth bunds constructed at high cost with machine graders in the early 1960s have now all but disappeared (Marchal, 1978, 1986). In the Majjia and Badéguicheri valleys of Niger, most of the 6000 hectares of earth bunds constructed between 1964 and 1980 are in an advanced state of degradation (Reij, 1988). In Sukumuland, Tanzania, where contour banks, terraces and hedges were forced upon farmers in the 1950s, almost no evidence remained of these conservation works by the early 1980s, and now 'erosion is extremely severe' (Stocking, 1985).

Graded and contour bunds developed for large-scale farming in the USA are still widely applied in programmes in India. Even under heavy subsidies most small farmers reject them (Kerr and Sanghi, 1992; and see Chapter 14, this book). These bunds leave corners in some fields, and so there is a risk of losing the piece of land to a neighbour. The central water course for drainage benefits only some farmers, damaging the land of others'. Contour farming is inconvenient when farmers use multi-row implements, and so is suitable only where the holding is large and tractors are available. Contour bunding without facilities for dealing with surplus water commonly breach, again concentrating water flow that quickly forms gullies. It is, therefore, not uncommon for entire bunds to be levelled as soon as project staff shift to the next village (Sanghi, 1987; Fernandez, 1993).

In Cape Verde, the state takes responsibility for erosion control by paying farmers to work on their own land. The result is that traditional practices are ignored as farmers take the money without influencing the project. Socalco terraces, for example, are built from top to bottom of steep slopes, with the result that foundations are often left hanging in the air (Haagsma, 1990). As Haagsma has put it, 'this does not stimulate . . . good cooperation between farmers and MDRP [the project]. It is difficult to eradicate the attitude "MDRP knows best".'

A major project in Niger was described by the implementing agency in this way: 'People's participation is the power behind the Keita project.

From decision-making – to planning – to action: local farmer-livestock owners have been consulted and actively taken part in every step' (FAO, 1992). Some 2.76 million work-days were paid for with World Food Programme rations, which served as 'incentives to participate in land reclamation and training courses offered by the project'. Yet no farmers apply the technologies to their own lands, and replicability is close to zero (IFAD, 1992).

In Ethiopia, where 1.5 million km of terracing were constructed during the 1980s with food for work, participation was 'either compulsory via peasant association campaigns or paid through food for work' (SIDA, 1984). A total of 34.3 million person-days of work was devoted to conservation, involving the 'cooperation of some 8000 Peasant Associations' (FAO, 1986, in Östberg and Christiansson, 1993). Apparently, 'farmers' participation was shown by their contributions of labour for infrastructure development', and the project expected these structures to be maintained because 'training . . . will help in sustaining activities when the donor pulls out. The privilege of being trained will keep the individuals responsible in the activities he (sic) was trained for' (reported in Oxfam, 1987).

Most soil and water conservation projects have paid, and continue to pay, local people in cash or food for their 'participation' (Kerr, 1994; and see Chapter 14, this book). But this is clearly self-defeating. According to Reij (1988): 'practice shows that where people are paid for soil and water conservation, the end of the project almost invariably leads to a stop in the construction of conservation works'.

More terracing, yet more erosion

As a result of programmes not involving farmers in conservation, many have actually increased the amount of soil eroding from farms. Local people whose land is being rehabilitated have found themselves participating for no other reason than to receive food or cash. Seldom are the structures maintained, and so conservation works deteriorate rapidly, accelerating erosion instead of reducing it. If performance is measured over long periods, the results are extraordinarily poor for the amount of effort and money expended (Shaxson *et al.*, 1989; Hudson *et al.*, 1991; Reij, 1991; Shaxson, 1996).

Poorly designed structures cause erosion. Yet throughout Africa, little account has been taken of how more terracing can lead to more erosion. In the early 20th century, erosion in Lesotho was not a serious problem in cultivated fields, as grassed field boundaries were well developed and maintained (Showers, 1989). Yet the authorities ignored this indigenous practice, and installed contour banks. Local people did not approve, because these reduced the size of fields, and were easily breached, so causing gullies to 'develop leading to more erosion. The administration attributed these gullies to 'unusual weather' (Showers and Malahleha, 1990).

Elsewhere in southern Africa, the first anti-erosion measures introduced in the early 1930s were large ridge terraces and bunds. But these imported measures permitted storm water to break through at vulnerable points. Careless construction made them susceptible to bursting, and locals came to believe that 'gully erosion was caused by the government' (Beinart, 1984).

Narrow-based terraces were introduced into Kenya from the USA in 1940 (Gichuki, 1991). For 15 years they were widely used. By 1947 some 4000 hectares were being protected each year, and this rate continued until 1956–57. But these terraces were found to fill up with sediments quickly, were impossible to maintain, and even began to aggravate erosion. And so by 1958, the number falling into disrepair was exceeding new construction. By 1961, some 20 000 hectares had fallen into disrepair. Eventually, the authorities recognized the problems and L H Brown, the chief agriculturist, issued a memorandum in 1961 saying that 'narrow-based terraces should be abandoned as policy . . . we should move to strips of vegetation, preferably grass' (in Wenner, 1992).

Bad contour ridging in the 1960s was worse than none at all in Zimbabwe (then Rhodesia), where farmers say the compulsory construction of ridges caused siltation of rivers. The ridges connected whole fields and drained in a single drainage line. During large storms, they concentrated water into powerful and fast moving bodies that caused great damage (Wilson, 1989). The same thing has occurred with cut-off drains in Kenya. Their function was to intercept and divert storm water, but many were constructed in a way that caused erosion. The same story was repeated in Swaziland in 1977–83, where the Rural Area Development Programme built terraces with heavy machinery (IFAD, 1992). These destroyed all previous practices, but none of the new ones were maintained.

In Oaxaca, Mexico, a large-scale government soil conservation programme is also establishing contour bunds based on the US models. It is an area noted in the 1970s and 1980s by various 'expert' missions as having 'massive soil erosion' and 'the world's worst soil erosion'. But recent evidence is suggesting that erosion has only become serious following the imposing of terraces and bunds (Blackler, 1994). Rill erosion has been recorded within one year of their establishment, and degradation has been so severe that less than 5 per cent of the bunded area is cropped.

Induced social disruption

The impact of these programmes has been to make many things worse. A failure to involve people in design and maintenance can create considerable long-term social impact. The enforced terracing and destocking in Kenya, coupled with the use of soil conservation as a punishment for those supporting the campaign for independence, helped to focus the opposition against both authority and soil conservation (Pretty and Shah, 1994; Gichuki, 1991). This

11

led, after independence, to the deliberate destruction of many structures because of their association with the colonial administration (Anderson, 1984).

In Rwanda prior to 1960, the massive terracing programme of the Belgian administration using forced labour created such negative feelings towards soil conservation that no further activities were possible until the late 1970s (Musema-Uwimana, 1983). In the Uluguru mountains of Tanzania, where ladder and step terraces were common, the Uluguru Land Usage Scheme introduced compulsory bench terracing in the 1950s – the scheme had to be abandoned after serious riots by local people (IFAD, 1992).

Elsewhere in Tanzania, the HADO project completely removed livestock from whole communities, with tens of thousands of animals removed from individual districts. Such a policy was possible only 'after mustering the cooperation of the ruling party and government machinery at village, district, regional and national levels. Inevitably some of the actions necessary to reverse soil degradation processes are a bitter pill to swallow'. Despite this, the project staff believed that 'the favourable results of destocking have sparked an interest in taking similar measures, particularly in the region's other districts' (Mndeme, 1992).

In Somalia, a large FAO-funded project constructed dams during the 1970s to check gullies, but because of poor construction, many collapsed or diverted the floods, so accelerating gully erosion instead of preventing it. This induced widespread disenchantment among local people for all conservation projects that followed (Reij, 1988). Such attitudes remain a critical constraint for many current soil conservation efforts.

Future challenges

By most performance measures, conventional conservation programmes have been remarkable failures. Little has changed over the course of this century. Large sums of money have been spent in the name of environmental protection encouraging and coercing farmers to adopt conservation measures. But poor implementation by outside technical teams means that few structures persist, so causing erosion rather than preventing it. The result has been widespread discrediting of conservation projects and programmes in the eyes of the rural people themselves. But the issue and costs of soil erosion will not go away. The challenge remains enormous.

As this book illustrates, there are many cases to show that resource-conserving technologies and practices can bring both environmental and economic benefits for farmers and communities. Importantly, these breakthroughs have come on farmers' fields and in rural communities, with agricultural professionals increasingly working with, and learning from, farmers.

It is to be hoped that the approaches described in this book represent the start of a new, more positive, chapter in the history of soil and water conservation.

2
Sustainability Indicators for Analysing the Impacts of Participatory Watershed Management Programmes

JOHN THOMPSON and IRENE GUIJT

Impact studies and self-evaluation

THE 25 CASE-STUDIES presented in this book provide insights into the economic, environmental and social effects of participatory watershed management programmes in a wide array of ecological and social contexts. For some of the team members involved in these studies, it was the first time that a comprehensive assessment of the impacts of their participatory activities had been conducted. Since many were technical officers and development practitioners – not trained researchers or academics – the process of carrying out the research proved to be as challenging and illuminating as the impact studies themselves. Thus, through their assessments the case-study teams reflected on their own organizational procedures and progress as they examined the impacts of their programmes on local livelihoods and environments.

To support the teams in their research, IIED suggested a framework of 'sustainability indicators' for assessing impacts and a participatory research process for applying it. This chapter presents details of that framework and that process. It begins with a brief overview of the participatory rural appraisal (PRA) methods that were used in many of the studies. This is followed by a description of the rationale behind the development of the framework. Details on the six sets of criteria and indicators included in the framework are presented as they relate to the biophysical, socioeconomic and institutional dimensions of land husbandry and organizational change. The chapter closes with a short reflection on the insights gained from using the participatory impact assessments.

Participatory rural appraisal

The development of rapid rural appraisal (RRA) in the 1980s and participatory rural appraisal (PRA) in the 1990s led to the creation of a rich menu of visualization, interviewing and team performance methods (Cornwall *et al.*, 1994; Chambers and Guijt, 1995; *RRA/PLA Notes*, 1988-present). These methods have proved valuable for understanding local people's needs, priorities and capacities relating to natural resource management, the processes of agricultural innovation and technology development, and the complexities of social systems and structures (Table 2.1) (Abbot and Guijt, 1997; Thompson, 1997; van Veldhuizen *et al.*, 1997). They also offer opportunities for mobilizing local people for joint action (Chambers, 1997).

One of the key strengths of PRA is the emphasis on visual analysis and sharing. In formal surveys, information is taken from a respondent by an enumerator or interviewer who converts what is said into words and symbols on a page. That information is frequently analysed and interpreted by investigators who are often located in urban centres many kilometres away from the study site. Thus, the research process is controlled by outside analysts, leaving local people little opportunity to assess critically or use the information generated by and with them. In contrast, participatory diagramming allows local people some measure of control over the research process. They are not only able to express ideas and opinions, but also to analyse the information critically, which can frequently lead to refinements of the diagrams and improvements in understanding. Local categories, criteria and symbols are used to represent complex concepts

Table 2.1: Participatory rural appraisal methods

Group and Team Performance Methods	Sampling Methods	Interviewing and Dialogue	Visualization and Diagramming Methods
o Team contracts o Team reviews and discussions o Interview guides and checklists o Rapid report writing o Energizers o DIY – taking part in local activities o Villager and shared presentations o Process notes and personal diaries	o Transect walks o Wealth ranking and well-being analysis o Social maps o Interview chains	o Semi-structured interviews o Direct observation o Focus groups o Key informants o Ethnohistories, oral histories and biographies o Traditional practices and beliefs o Local stories, proverbs and parables	o Participatory mapping and modelling o Social maps and wealth rankings o Seasonal calendars o Daily activity profiles o Timelines o Trend analyses o Matrix scoring o Preference or pairwise ranking o Venn diagrams o Network diagrams o Systems diagrams o Impact flow diagrams o Pie diagrams

and relationships in the diagramming techniques, which range from mapping and modelling to comparative analyses of local perceptions of seasonal and historical trends, and diagrammatic representations of household and livelihood systems. Rather than answering questions that are directed by the values of field staff or researchers, local women, men, and children are encouraged to explore their own versions of their worlds.

Ranking and scoring exercises provide an opportunity to understand some of the complexities involved in decision-making. They are particularly valuable in the generation of locally appropriate, socially differentiated criteria for selecting and evaluating particular varieties or technologies. Methods such as crop biographies, network and pathway diagramming and, more recently, systems diagramming, have added to a repertoire of methods which can be used effectively in facilitating an interchange between development professionals and rural people.

But PRA is much more than simply a 'toolbox' of interactive methods to be applied in the field. There is also strong emphasis on creating awareness among development professionals that their attitudes and behaviour towards local people have a significant effect on the outcomes and impacts of their work. Moreover, there is an equally clear focus on creating more supportive systems, procedures and working rules within development agencies to enable them to institutionalize and use the participatory approaches effectively on a large scale (not just a single community or catchment). When understood in this broader context of organizational learning and institutional change, and employed in a spirit of openness, mutual respect and shared responsibility, PRA becomes an extremely powerful approach for joint learning and action. Overall, the far-reaching institutional implications of scaling up and spreading a participatory approach by innovative development agencies and professionals (Blackburn, 1997; Scherler et al., 1997; Thompson, 1995) (Table 2.2).

Evidence presented in the case-studies suggests that, where there is an institutional commitment to create an environment that supports local priorities and preferences, PRA can act as a catalysing methodology for facilitating improvements in land husbandry. It can also help to build strong links between farmers and external support staff, encourage more open debate and discussion among local people about soil and water conservation and land management issues, and mobilize local resources and capacities. Given the flexibility and interactive nature of the approach, and the familiarity by most of the research teams with PRA methods, it was the principal methodology used in the impact studies.

Objectives of the impact studies

The cases reviewed in this book aimed to understand the economic, environmental and social impacts of participatory watershed management programmes. More specifically, the studies attempted to:

Table 2.2: Some organizational implications of participatory approaches

Core Principles of Participatory Approaches	Organizational Implications
A systemic learning process	o Value the learning process by creating time, and equipping staff with skills, to reflect on each new experience o Develop system for efficient and effective sharing between staff members o Allow staff members to make mistakes without punishment o Encourage learning at different levels in the organization through monitoring learning experiences and changes in attitude and work practice
Seeking diverse perspectives	o Equip staff with skills to value, see and analyse different social groups/individuals o Accept only fieldwork/plans that have sought and incorporated diverse perspectives
Context-specific	o Allow enough time to refine the basic framework of any policy or procedure to each geographic area/level at which staff operate o Ensure that staff incentives recognize heterogeneity between field sites o Reward staff for site-specific innovations
Group inquiry process	o Equip staff with skills to facilitate group discussions and encourage analysis, including conflict resolution skills o Equip staff with skills to recognize local power relations and how these influence group-based discussions
Facilitating external agents with key responsibility resting with local people	o Equip staff with awareness and skills to take a listening and encouraging role, rather than an implementing role
Leading to sustained learning and action	o Ensure that staff emphasize the motivation of local people and others involved to act independently of external support agency o Field staff to focus on building local planning capacity that can operate independently of external support

Source: Guijt, 1995

o quantify the impact of participatory watershed management programmes in different agroecological and socioeconomic conditions in
Africa, Asia, Australia and Latin America

16

○ draw out key insights for adapting and applying participatory approaches for watershed management and soil and water conservation in future
○ understand how to strengthen capacity among programme staff to facilitate participatory research and development processes
○ test and use participatory methods for impact analysis, and help to encourage more systematic self-evaluation within the normal working procedures of the collaborating agencies
○ identify key policies for institutionalizing and scaling-up participatory approaches in watershed management and soil and water conservation programmes.

Using PRA for impact analysis

Most of the case-study teams took the catchment or watershed as their basic unit for assessing change, as this was the level at which many of the key development interventions were aimed. The teams used a mixture of participatory and, in some cases, more formal methods to quantify these changes, such as resource maps, impact flow diagrams, household and focus group interviews, and trends analysis and timelines. The PRA methods, described in Table 2.3, were used to gather information from and with the people living and working in the research sites.

Timelines, trends diagrams, historical Venn (institutional) diagrams, network diagrams, farm sketches, flow diagrams (both systems and impact) and seasonal calendars were all invaluable for identifying key changes over space and time. Several methodological innovations occurred during the course of the impact studies. For instance, flow diagrams were used with both adopters and non-adopters of soil and water conservation measures to assess the differences in land management practices between the groups in Brazil (de Fretias). Historical matrices were used widely with different groups to explore long-term trends, including changes in land use management and conservation practices prior to and after the implementation of the participatory programmes (e.g. Bhuktan et al.; Igbokwe et al.). In Central America (Bunch and López), Kenya (Kiara et al.), India (Chatterji et al.; Krishna; Lobo and Palghadmal; Shah and Shah). In Nepal (Wagley) and elsewhere these analyses revealed a number of interesting relationships, including:

○ increased levels of conservation and agricultural productivity coinciding with increased population densities and agricultural intensification
○ crop diversity declining with the adoption of modern varieties of cereals, then rising after the launch of participatory programmes
○ increasing use of manure, compost and crop biomass to improve soil fertility as fertilizer prices increased

Table 2.3: PRA methods for impact analysis

Methods	Applications
Systems diagrams of watersheds and individual livelihoods	○ impact of participatory watershed programmes ○ changes in livelihoods before and after intervention
Participatory mapping	○ location of changes and adoption of new technologies ○ household listings ○ inventory of resources in watershed or catchment ○ uptake of technologies in neighbouring watersheds
Wealth ranking	○ analysis of differential access to, and control of, resources ○ identification of potential focus groups and key informants ○ inter- and intra-household distribution of costs and benefits
Resource maps: before and after	Changes in: ○ productivity of fields ○ land ownership/tenure arrangements ○ type and intensity of resource use ○ erosion and land degradation ○ adoption, adaptation and diffusion of technologies ○ surface water and groundwater availability
Venn diagrams and network diagrams	○ strength of interactions between catchment committee and other organizations inside and outside the catchment ○ frequency and coverage by government agencies and NGOs ○ training received by catchment committee members, number of farmer-to-farmer exchanges ○ federation of local groups ○ local perceptions of their institutions' and external agencies' support ○ linkages to neighbouring communities
Mobility maps	○ migration patterns ○ labour opportunities before and after impact
Timelines	○ development of village institutions ○ history of land use trends and changes ○ history of external interventions, shocks and stresses
Presentations and discussions with local groups	○ triangulation of findings ○ comparison of priorities and perspectives of different social groups
Focus group discussions	○ livelihood options, income and expenditure ○ changes in input costs, wage labour rates ○ investment in land management measures
Trend and historical analyses	○ impact of external institutions on local factors
Seasonal calendars	○ timing and amount of labour invested in land management ○ rainfall, cropping patterns
Matrix scorings and rankings	○ comparisons of technologies, practices and services ○ quantification of benefits according to locally generated criteria
Team contracts, reviews and discussions	○ more interdisciplinary teamwork and better group dynamics

Source: Thompson and Pretty, 1996

o soil and water conservation was widespread when imposed during the colonial era, declining during the post-independence period, then re-appearing after the participatory interventions

o improved conservation of common lands, such as grazing lands, shrub lands and communal forests, as conflicts over access and control of resources were resolved.

The maps and other diagrams, many of which were drawn on the ground and then recorded on large sheets of paper, were used as a focal point for the teams' discussions during the documentation phase after the field-work was completed. Based on this empirical material, each team analysed the impacts according to the set of commonly agreed general indicators. Team members took time to cross-check their information. They identified the more trustworthy evidence and rejected dubious data where there were concerns over the manner in which it was generated (such as in cases where local people's analyses may have been influenced by the statements or actions of team members or more dominant com-munity members).

A framework for impact analysis

Besides support through suggested methods, IIED provided a set of poss-ible indicators that would allow a more extensive assessment of impacts than the usual 'project efficiency' indicators. A framework of possible en-vironmental, economic and social indicators was developed from an extensive literature review and sent to all case-study teams to help guide their research. Not all teams followed this framework precisely. Many took it as the starting point for their impact studies and adapted it to suit their specific environmental and social contexts. Nevertheless, it provided a basis for comparing and contrasting the findings and for drawing out common lessons from the diverse experiences.

Six categories of change were included in the framework (Tables 2.4 to 2.9):

1. Sustained increases in agricultural productivity
2. Decreases in resource degradation
3. Increases in local resilience (i.e., livelihood security) and decreases in vulnerability
4. Increase in autonomy and capacity of local groups and organizations
5. Replication in non-programme sites (i.e., where no external interven-tion has occurred)
6. Changes in the operational procedures and institutional norms of ex-ternal support agencies and the attitudes and behaviour of development professionals.

The first two sets of indicators (Tables 2.4 and 2.5) deal with fairly standard, measurable, biophysical changes in agricultural production and soil erosion. They arise out of a working hypothesis that assumes that increased productivity and decreased land degradation will occur with the adoption and broad application of ecologically appropriate, socially acceptable and technically viable land management practices. The case-study teams found these to be the most straightforward indicators as they could use their own observations and secondary data to cross-check the information gathered through their participatory impact analyses. Despite the relative ease of analysis, some case-study teams were hampered by inadequate baseline data and had to make simultaneous assessments of pre- and post-intervention trends, changes and impacts.

The third set of criteria and indicators (Table 2.6) describes changes in the diversity, flexibility and robustness of local livelihood strategies. It focuses on the ability of local livelihoods to cope with various environmental and social shocks (e.g., a pest invasion, a flash-flood, devaluation of a currency, etc.) and stresses (e.g., increasing land prices, debt, a prolonged drought, etc.). It is based on the assumption that if local livelihood strategies become more diverse, adaptive and durable, then risk and uncertainty will decrease and sustainability will increase.

The importance of long-enduring, self-governing, local organizations is increasingly being seen as central to the sustainable management of natural resources, and is the focus of the fourth set of indicators (Table 2.7). It concentrates on changes in the cohesion, adaptability and self-reliance of local groups, attributes that are difficult to assess in quantitative, let alone qualitative terms. Its working hypothesis is that if local organizations, formal and informal alike, are supported and strengthened, then they will become more self-sufficient and better able to manage their own affairs. These indicators attempt to assess the strength and capacities of local organizations engaged in the collective management of soil and water resources, often in complex, risk-prone and diverse environments.

Table 2.4: Sustained increases in agricultural productivity

Change in yields	○ increase in yields at year t+1 (immediate benefits) ○ increase in yields at year t+5 (transition yields) ○ increase in yields at year t+10 (sustained impact) ○ economic value of yield increases at each time period
Change in costs	○ change in input costs ○ change in gross margins
Economic multipliers	○ change in labour wages rates ○ change in land prices (sale and rental) ○ change in migration rates and patterns
Farmers' support	○ proportion of farmers still conserving resources at t+5, t+10

Table 2.5: Decreases in resource degradation

Change in resource-conserving practices on private lands	o number of farms with physical, biological and cultural resource-conserving measures o km of terraces o area treated o number of trees, checkdams etc. o number of farms using green manuring, multiple cropping, integrated pest management etc.
Change in resource-conserving practices on common lands	o area treated o number of trees planted o biomass productivity on commons
Retained ecosystem functions	o groundwater recharge – increase in months wells are wet o proportion of watershed protected
Contribution of farmers to technology adaptation and multiplication	o local variations of a technology o number of local/individual tree nurseries o adaptation and incorporation of indigenous practices and technologies components into external practices and technologies
Decrease in resource degrading practices and external effects of pollution and contamination	o reduction in soil loss o reduction in pesticide and fertilizer use and increase in the use of organic fertilizers (e.g. manure, compost, crop residues, etc.)

Table 2.6: Increase in local resilience and decrease in vulnerability

Diversity of agricultural and wild products managed/farmed	o change in diversity index o proportion of land under monocropping versus intercropping
Change in health of local people	o increase in local food security o reduction in hazardous or harmful practices (e.g. uncontrolled pesticide use)
Access to credit	o access of poor groups with little or no collateral to rural credit or loans schemes o increase in local savings
Change in impact of shocks to local system	o impact of drought in years t+5, t+10 compared with before resource conservation and compared with neighbouring unprotected watersheds

Table 2.7: Increase in autonomy and capacity of local groups and organizations

Willingness of local people to participate	○ lack of financial inducements to participate ○ active involvement of people in planning
Building local capacity and skills	○ number of paraprofessionals trained and supported ○ number of new paraprofessionals trained by existing paraprofessionals (replication) ○ number of farmer-to-farmer extension trips
Effectiveness of local resource management groups	○ existing and/or new groups and organizations functioning ○ number and type of groups (proportion of population involved) ○ representativeness of groups (persons included/excluded; active members) ○ leadership elected or selected ○ number of group resource management works organized ○ attendance at group works ○ local organizations federated with others ○ financial contributions to group works or group savings ○ ability to form own management rules
Dependence on external resources	○ proportion of yield increases and economic benefits due to local regenerated resources compared with external resources (e.g. fertilizers, pesticides, hybrid seeds)

Replication is the focus of the fifth set of indicators (Table 2.8). Its underlying hypothesis assumes that if a demand-led and locally managed conservation process in a particular catchment is deemed successful by people in neighbouring communities, then it will spread to those areas spontaneously – without external intervention or advocacy. This is a crucial factor if wide conservation coverage is to occur with limited investment of public resources, particularly at a time when shrinking and budgets, structural reforms and liberalization of national economies has led to a significant reduction in state services.

The sixth and final set (Table 2.9) directed the attention of the case-study teams to the changes taking place within the key external support agency that was supporting the watershed programme. It is based on the assumption

Table 2.8: Replication in non-programme sites

Replication to neighbouring communities and villages	○ changes in adoption rates ○ independent adoption and adaptation ○ willingness to pay paraprofessionals
Federation of groups	○ creation of organizations or federations of users' groups across watersheds or catchments

that if the participatory resource management process is to be sustainable, then the external support agency must become less of an *implementer* and more of an *enabler*. That is, fundamental changes must occur in an agency's operational procedures and institutional working rules for it to become a people-centred, strategic, learning organization with the technical capacity and organizational culture capable of institutionalizing and scaling-up the new participatory approach effectively. Within this new culture of learning, it also involves changes in the attitudes and behaviour of individual professionals, including technical assistants, programme managers, engineers and other development practitioners, towards local people and other professionals with whom they work.

From the beginning of the participatory impact assessment activities, IIED and its partners took the view that all six types of change are essential elements of any *sustainable* land husbandry strategy that aims to work with and support the efforts of local land managers. During the course of the field research, this position was reconfirmed time and again. Case-study after case-study revealed that if one or more of these elements is missing then the likelihood of the practices and processes being sustainable is significantly diminished. If they are all present, then chances are high that the resource management practices and processes of innovation will be self-sustaining.

Table 2.9: Changes in the operational procedures and institutional norms of external support agencies and attitudes and behaviour of development professionals

New roles for professionals	○ use of participatory methods for planning, implementation and monitoring ○ professionals in the field (not in the office) ○ support for practices and projects developed and managed by local people ○ increased job satisfaction ○ publications by professionals on participatory work ○ number of PRA-trained professionals who are training others
Enabling policies in institution	○ support from the top for professionals in the field ○ willingness to permit participatory work to be treated equally with other modes of analysis/research etc. ○ flexibility of procedures and ability to accept slow progress at first ○ commitment to withdraw after set period
Increased links with other permanent agencies	○ intersectoral and/or interagency collaboration in participatory watershed planning and management
Commitment to developing local capacity	○ involvement of local people in analysis and problem diagnosis ○ number of farmer-to-farmer visits facilitated ○ capacity to train paraprofessionals

Lessons from the participatory impact assessments

The framework of sustainability indicators was adapted and applied by the case-study teams to assess the impacts of a wide variety of participatory watershed management and resource conservation programmes. For many, the idea of carrying out an in-depth impact study based on this elaborate framework created both challenges and opportunities. For example, before starting the research, some of the contributors had little or no direct experience of using participatory methods for impact assessment. Consequently, a number of the case-study teams had to be trained in the basic principles, core concepts and key methods of participatory research (e.g., West Hume, Australia (Campbell *et al.*) and Kenya (Kiara *et al.*)) before beginning their studies. The team training and preparation proved useful not only for the immediate studies, but also for strengthening capacity to undertake similar work in future.

Many of the teams' previous attempts at assessing impacts focused on only a rather limited set of biophysical and, to a lesser degree, socio-economic indicators (e.g. 'number of trees planted', 'kilometres of bunds constructed', 'changes in cereal yields', 'numbers of farmers trained', and so on). The challenge of using new types of criteria and indicators and an accompanying suite of interactive methods within a holistic research framework led them to recruit a diverse set of members with complementary skills and experience. Thus, the disciplines represented in the studies included agronomy, anthropology, crop science, ecology, engineering, forestry, geography, range management, sociology, soil conservation and veterinary science, among others. Together these researchers formed interdisciplinary teams capable of carrying out the multidimensional impact analyses. In the end, however, some of the research teams were more successful in their use of the framework of sustainability indicators than others. One common weakness among many of the teams was the lack of a trained economist to help guide the application of the indicators related to economic costs and benefits and the later analysis of the findings. As one reads the cases in this book, this shortcoming will become apparent and points to the need for more in-depth economic analyses to help broaden our understanding of the impacts of these programmes on people's economic well-being.

Despite these limitations, many of the organizations involved in the impact assessments welcomed the opportunity to conduct a new type of evaluation, one that was more interdisciplinary, interactive and comprehensive in scope than their previous attempts. One team (i.e. Bunch and López) had the unique chance to return to several locations four to 15 years after programme activities had ceased in order to assess the long-term impacts of the interventions in Honduras and Guatemala. This experience was more the exception than the rule, however, as the average

24

length of time over which most teams were able to assess the performance of their participatory programmes was seven years. Furthermore, few teams had access to high quality baseline information from which they could measure trends and changes from the past to the present and then project into the future. As a result, they were forced to use secondary information (e.g., official programme reports, government reports, consultants' studies, etc.) and consult with a wide range of knowledgeable local actors in order to understand pre- and post-intervention changes in land management, livelihood security and organizational learning.

Because most teams were able to assess impacts at only one point in time, the case-studies are really 'snapshots' of conditions found in the study sites when the participatory research was conducted. There was no opportunity for longer-term monitoring or follow-up research in most of the study sites. For researchers who were trying to understand the complexity, diversity and uncertainty of human-environment interactions, the time-bound nature of the case-studies proved frustrating as it left several important questions unanswered. For example, will the process of learning, innovation and adaptation that was sparked by these participatory initiatives continue after the external support agencies withdraw? Moreover, will the factors that stimulated the emergence of co-operation, reciprocity and collective action among different resource users in the study sites ensure their persistence over the longer term? Finally, how do changes in local people's property rights and their access to and control of resources affect their ability and willingness to adopt and adapt different resource-conserving technologies and land management practices?

While these and other important questions remain, the case-studies included here provide clear evidence that many of the most effective watershed management programmes have been successful because they have developed and applied participatory approaches that facilitated the active involvement of local land managers in diagnostic appraisal, planning, implementation and performance monitoring and evaluation. At the same time, they reveal that participatory methodologies alone do not explain this success. There have also been many important institutional and policy factors supporting the development and continuing evolution of these innovative approaches and the programmes that employ them. Many of these programmes have received long-term financial, technical and institutional assistance from committed foreign or national agencies. At the international level, flexible and sustained funding arrangements and significant investments in training and capacity strengthening by donors have enabled government departments and NGOs engaged in watershed management activities to experiment with new ways of working and to develop the skills and knowledge needed to use participatory approaches effectively. At the national level, there has been support from senior officials for approaches that focus as much on people as they do on natural resource management.

At the professional level, there has been a transformation of the role of field worker from that of an 'implementer' to one of 'enabler' or 'provider of occasions' for learning and action. And at the watershed or catchment level, there have been changes in local organizations and groups, which have increasingly taken greater responsibility for their own conservation and land management activities.

There is much that governments, NGOs and donors can learn from the case-studies presented in this book, particularly those who are still making use of public subsidies and financial incentives to encourage people to conserve natural resources. Innovative programmes that put people's participation and collective action at the core of watershed development are discovering that the improvements in land management and soil and water conservation can be significant. The challenge now is to ensure that these improvements are sustained.

RESOURCE-CONSERVING TECHNOLOGIES AND PRACTICES:
FARMER INNOVATION AND ADAPTATION

Overview

Resource-conserving Technologies and Practices: Farmer Innovation and Adaptations

Technologies are not sustainable; what needs to be made sustainable is the process of innovation itself. Bunch and López

THIS SECTION CONTAINS six case-studies which give important insights into resource-conserving technologies for watershed development, and processes whereby these are adapted and disseminated by farmers themselves. As these cases demonstrate, the process of technology development for soil and water conservation is not just about finding the right technologies: it is as much about creating the right institutional and social environment to allow the process to be dynamic, productive and sustainable.

Choice and durability of technology

It is first necessary to define what is meant by 'resource-conserving technologies'. These can be biological (agricultural systems, and/or specific crops), such as intercropping, the use of green manures, mulches, cover crops and so forth. Or they can be physical (structures for soil and water conservation engineering), ranging from boulder bunds, to contour ridges, to check-dams and terraces. These technologies tend to perform two important functions. They conserve existing on-farm resources, such as nutrients, predators, water or soil. Or they introduce new elements into the farming systems that add more of these resources, such as nitrogen-fixing crops, water-harvesting structures or new predators, and so substitute for some, or all, external resources (Pretty, 1995).

Common to all the cases presented here is the emphasis on locally adapted resource-conserving technologies that provide immediate returns to farmers, rather than the use of externally-driven and derived technologies.

However, an important lesson from these cases is that while there are very many technologies available that are successful in conserving soil and soil moisture, and in enhancing the fertility of the soil, there can be no single 'package' of technologies that can be applied across the board. Clearly, unless farmers are enabled to adopt and adapt technologies to suit their particular conditions and needs, many mistakes will be made (Igbokwe *et al.*; Fernandez). Again and again, these case-studies

29

underline how the diversity of farmers' conditions and their specific individual needs from a technology mean that no engineer, however highly trained, will be able to capture these without help from the farmers themselves.

For example, Fernandez (Chapter 7) describes the differences in the designs of boulder bunds proposed by technical 'experts' and those proposed by local people. While people wanted boulder bunds to be raised so as to provide protection from cattle and to restrict access, the technical staff had designed them solely to control erosion, and had therefore designed them as low and rounded structures, useless for keeping cattle out. Fernandez also describes how farmers may be happy to settle for a structure that is not technically perfect, but which means that good relations can be maintained with neighbouring farmers as the structures do not encroach on to their fields. Thus the 'multi-functionality' of technologies and farmers' strategies can be far from straightforward.

A key lesson from Bunch and López's study of three agricultural development efforts in Guatemala and Honduras, up to 15 years after the termination of outside intervention, is that specific technologies do not generally have long-term sustainability. Many technologies 'eventually fall by the wayside because changing circumstances, such as emerging markets, disease and pests, land tenure, soil fertility, labour availability and costs, and the adoption of new technologies have reduced or eliminated their usefulness'. In fact the authors assert that specific technologies have a half-life of only about six years. However, as long as farmers' capacities to access, adapt and develop new technologies have been strengthened, then sustainable livelihoods can be maintained.

Maintenance of soil and water conservation (SWC) structures is a major concern in many SWC programmes. What is fairly clear from these cases, especially the case described by Fernandez, is that if farmers are not involved in the design and development of these structures, there will be little commitment to maintain them.

Igbokwe and colleagues provide a useful summary of the factors that enhance farmers' adoption and refinement of technologies, including consideration of whether the benefits of technologies are continuous and are realized quickly; whether farmers are convinced the technology will improve their income or enhance crop productivity; whether there is financial support or availability of credit; whether they are organized into groups; and whether technologies are low-cost, simple and easy to understand, have high acceptability, and can be demonstrated convincingly.

The key to designing a sustainable soil conservation or agricultural programme does not consist, therefore, of choosing a group of technologies that will be sustainable. Rather, the key is choosing a very few technologies that will motivate farmers to become involved in the process of innovation, to search for new ideas, experiment with them, adopt those that prove useful and share the results with others (Bunch and López). The six cases in this section demonstrate this well.

Farmer-to-farmer extension of technologies

Two cases from the Philippines show how farmer-to-farmer extension is another important process for developing technologies appropriate to particular conditions, and for encouraging more farmers to adopt resource-conserving practices. Bhuktan *et al.* explain that since farmers were encouraged by farmer extensionists to use the available technologies according to their own land conditions, every farm was established somewhat differently – 'every farm has its own signature'. As with the experience in Honduras and Guatemala, farmers made many modifications over the years, and experimented with a wide variety of technologies. Both Bhuktan *et al.* and Balbarino and Alcober describe in detail the steps needed to support the process of farmer-to-farmer extension and participatory technology development. This important theme emerges again in the fourth section of this book.

New roles for professionals in technology development

As described in most of these cases, if the goal of participatory watershed development is to promote farmers' participation, experimentation, innovation and dissemination of SWC technologies, then the traditional role of the technical support professionals needs to alter. This is another recurring theme throughout this book.

As Balbarino and Alcober describe, technical project staff have assumed roles quite different from the traditional 'expert' or 'teacher' roles. There is now more guidance than direction; and more suggestions than instructions. Project staff have assumed the roles of *searchers* (of technology options); of *suppliers* (of materials for farmers to try out); of *consultants* (establishing trials of different soil and water conservation techniques); of *convenors* of meetings and formation of local groups; of farmers' *colleagues*, (establishing a close working relationship with farmers); and as *travel agents*, arranging cross-farm visits for farmers to see new innovations which they could try on their own farms.

It is clear that in the area of support, there is no uniform and definite solution that can be used in all situations with guaranteed outcomes. Again, an approach dealing with these issues must be based on achieving a process of continual learning and on-going change. This requires an open-ended and flexible strategy. It is impossible to predict the future needs and development of farmers. The conventional notion of a 'project' must be revised (Schorlemer).

31

3

Soil Recuperation in Central America: How Innovation was Sustained after Project Intervention

ROLAND BUNCH and GABINÒ LÓPEZ

Introduction

MUCH HAS BEEN said and written about the sustainability of agricultural development. But there have been few studies on programme impact after the outside intervention has ended. This chapter describes a study of three agricultural development efforts in Guatemala and Honduras and assesses impacts up to 15 years after the termination of outside intervention. The study was carried out by the Honduran organization COSECHA (Associación de Consejeros una Agricultura Sostenible, Ecológica y Humana).

The study assessed the impact that soil recuperation interventions have had over many years. The results show considerable increases in productivity after intervention, and indicate that while specific technologies do not generally have long-term sustainability, the process of agricultural innovation does. The study points to a need for future agricultural development programmes to design their work in such a way that villagers are given strong motivation to innovate.

The three areas studied

This chapter concentrates on the following three areas of Guatemala and Honduras:

The Cantarranas area. Between 1987 and 1993, the Cantarranas Integrated Agricultural Development Program, financed by Catholic Relief Services and managed by World Neighbors, worked in some 35 villages around the central Honduran town of Cantarranas (Bunch, 1990). Using in-row tillage and intercropped green manures as its cutting edge, it expanded into a general programme of agricultural development and preventive health.

Cantarranas lies at about 300m in elevation in a narrow valley about 40km long, between two parallel mountain ranges that rise to over 1800m. The programme worked almost entirely with small farmers with 2–5 hectare landholdings. These hillsides vary in slope, with an average of about 30 per cent. The forests have been seriously degraded. The climate of the Cantarranas area varies from hot and semi-arid, with frequent and severe droughts in the bottom of the valley, to a cool climate, with sufficient rainfall for six months each year.

The Guinope area. Between 1981 and 1989, a similar World Neighbors programme worked in 41 villages, most of which are included in the townships of Guinope, San Lucas, and San Antonio de Flores in south-eastern Honduras (Bunch, 1988). This programme also worked heavily in soil recuperation, basic grains, and diversification, as well as preventive health. The programme's lead technologies were drainage ditches (at 1/2 per cent slope) with live barriers and the use of chicken manure.

The Guinope area contains the same variations in altitude and rainfall as Cantarranas, but with less severe slopes. Nevertheless, an impenetrable subsoil underlies the 15cm to 50cm deep topsoil. When this thin layer of topsoil has eroded away, agriculture becomes impossible. Before 1981, emigration from the Guinope area was heavy; some residents referred to it as a 'dying town'.

The San Martin Jilotepeque area. The San Martin Integrated Development Programme was financed by Oxfam-UK and carried out by World Neighbors between the years 1972 and 1979 (Bunch, 1977). It was a highly integrated programme, working in everything from agriculture and health to road construction, functional literacy, and co-operative organization. The Programme used contour ditches and a side-dressing of nitrogen on maize as the initial technologies to motivate people.

The San Martin township lies just 50km west of Guatemala City. The southern half of the township, where the Programme worked in some 45 villages, varies in altitude from about 800m to 2000m, and has enough rainfall for a good maize crop in most years. The mainly Cakchiquel Indian population is extremely land poor, owning an average of less than 0.5ha of seriously depleted land per family.

Methodology for the impact study

The methodology used in the study varied from area to area. The most explicitly participatory work occurred in Guinope and Cantarranas. In these cases, team members knew the areas well, having worked in the programmes being studied. The four COSECHA personnel involved in the San Martin study were all Cakchiquel Indian farmers originally from the area, who had been trained in the programme and gradually progressed from programme participant to extensionist to programme director.

The methodology consisted of a combination of:

o observation of the plots in the study villages, including visual productivity estimates and the use of a checklist of questions about easily observed factors in the fields (the existence of contour live barriers, contour ditches, and fruit trees)

- individual open-ended interviews
- open-ended informal conversations held with people known to the study team
- participatory rural appraisal (PRA) methods with groups of villagers which included men, women, and children – these included mapping exercises, priority exercises, and participatory economic analyses of specific crops
- a review of programme documents, including evaluations made of programme impact.

COSECHA personnel made a list of all the 121 villages, and divided these into three roughly equal categories:

- those in which they judged the impact to have been best
- those in which the impact was moderate
- those in which the impact was relatively poor.

A composite list was then made, averaging the ratings in the three separate lists. One village was then selected from the best category, two from the middle category, and one from the poorer impact category. These villages were selected so as to provide an even geographic spread within the programme area, afford fairly good access during the wet season (when the study was carried out), and avoid contamination of the findings by subsequent work of other development agencies.

Findings of the impact study

Changes in technologies used

Different technologies had been given different emphases by each programme, and in different villages within each programme. Nevertheless, the figures displayed in the tables below give some idea of the relative sustainability of the technologies. For each technology, the number of farmers using the technology is shown at the time of programme initiation, programme termination, and at the time of the study (1994).

The villages studied in Guinope and Cantarranas are presented in decreasing order of previously judged quality of impact. That is, the first village listed is that chosen from the one-third of the villages with best impact, the next two from the group of average impact villages, and the fourth from the group of least impact. These results show that the overall level of continuing innovation, despite programme termination, is remarkable.

Changes in productivity

In Central America, maize is the basic staple. As it is very sensitive to soil fertility, maize productivity is a good indication of overall soil fertility, and

Table 3.1: Changes in adoption of resource-conserving technologies in three programmes in Central America during and after projects (no. of farmers with technologies)

	At Initiation	At Termination[1]	In 1994
Contour grass barriers			
San Martin	1	100	203
Guinope	0	44	33
Cantarranas	0	48	44
Contour or drainage ditches			
San Martin	1	136	162
Guinope	0	56	43
Cantarranas	0	39	34
Green manures			
San Martin	0	21	38
Guinope	0	0	2
Cantarranas	0	14	12
Crop rotation			
San Martin	0	6	10
Guinope	12	46	125
Cantarranas	0	97	119
No longer burn fields or forests			
San Martin	0	0	0
Guinope	2	83	117
Cantarranas	0	77	108
Organic matter as fertilizer			
San Martin	10	42	124
Guinope	4	100	213
Cantarranas	30	53	60

[1] Project termination dates were: San Martin 1979; Guinope 1989; Cantarranas 1991.

of productivity in general. Table 3.2 shows that major increases in productivity have been achieved after the programmes ended.

All averages of harvest data are rounded off to the nearest 100kg/ha in the tables. Most of the harvest data come from farmers, based on the number of bags they carry home during the harvest of the mature grain. These calculations, therefore, exclude grain lost to thievery, eating ears harvested early, and occasional ears given to labourers as partial recompense for their work.

The figures are especially dramatic in San Martin, where the time since programme termination is longest. Thus these figures are probably the most important in the entire study, clearly demonstrating that productivity has continued to improve after the programmes' termination. Although the increase in yields is not as dramatic as during the programmes' existence,

Table 3.2: Productivity of maize (in kg/ha) at project initiation, termination and at the time of the study

	Initiation	Termination	1994
San Martin			
San Antonio Correjo	400	2400	4800
Las Venturas	400	2800	5200
Xesuj	300	2000	3200
Pacoj	500	2800	4800
Guinope			
Pacayas	600	3200	4200
Manzaragua	600	2000	2000
Lavenderos	600	2000	2000
Cantarranas			
Guacamayas	800	nd	none
Joyos del Caballo	400	2000	2200
Guanacaste	800	1900	1900

Note: the lack of maize production in Guacamayas is due to the fact that farmers make more money from vegetables, and prefer to buy maize. Thus, the lack of maize is precisely because of the dramatic increases in yields and value of production achieved in this village since programme termination.

these figures leave no doubt that even though some practices have been abandoned, the productivity of the better villages (and all the villages in San Martin) has continued to rise after the programmes ended.

Table 3.3 shows the productivity of beans in the villages where they are grown.

Table 3.3: Productivity of edible beans (*Phaseolus vulgaris*) in kg/ha at project initiation, termination and at the time of the study

	Initiation	Termination	1994
San Martin			
San Antonio Correjo	200	1200	1800
Las Venturas	100	200	800
Xesuj	200	1200	2000
Guinope			
Lavenderos	100	800	800
Cantarranas			
Guacamayas	none	900	1500
Joyos del Caballo	500	1500	1500
Guanacaste	500	900	900

Further impacts

Other positive impacts in the project areas have also occurred:

o increased wage rates
o increased land values
o decreasing or reversed emigration from the project areas (Table 3.4)
o decreased resource degradation
o increased numbers of trees planted
o almost total elimination of the use of herbicides through hand weeding or green manures
o significant reduction in the use of chemical fertilizers with a variety of organic fertilizers now used
o increased crop diversity and practice of intercropping
o an increase in local savings, leading to a decreasing dependence on formal credit and increased investment in education, land improvement, and purchasing animals
o marked improvements in diets, including the consumption of more vegetables, native herbs, milk and cheese
o improved resilience and resistance to drought and climatic variability
o increased involvement in local groups, such as producers' associations, agricultural study groups, community improvement committees, or groups formed by whole villages to protect communal forests from loggers or corrupt municipal officials.

Less success has been achieved in reducing dependence on the use of insecticides and fungicides. Central America in general has been slow to find feasible alternatives for these chemicals. The programmes taught people the dangers of pesticides, the importance of integrated pest management, and encouraged them to try any others they could. But few effective alternatives have been found. Finding alternatives to insecticides is a major area for additional work.

The most disappointing finding is the lack of spontaneous technological spread *between* villages. Whereas spontaneous spread within villages does

Table 3.4: Impact of programmes on migration

Migration (no. of households)	Initiation	Termination	1994
San Martin:			
San Antonio Correjo	65	nd	4
Las Venturas	85	nd	4
Guinope: 3 villages	38	0	(2)*
Cantarranas: 3 villages	nd	10	(6)*

* These represent negative outmigration, or families moving back to rural areas.

occur, spread between villages is negligible. This might be attributable to the Guatemalan counter-insurgency campaign of the 1980s, which purposely turned villages against each other, and the Honduran villagers' aversion to walking from one village to another (there being no major village markets in the programme areas). Nevertheless, there is no evidence that the technology would have spread in the absence of these factors.

Local innovation

Local innovation is critical to villagers' becoming the 'subjects' of their own development. Within the study sites, the amount of continuing innovation has been remarkable. In San Martin, over 30 innovations have been adopted successfully since programme termination. These include the introduction of new crops (cauliflower, broccoli, and herbs), adoption of new green manures (velvetbean and *Tephrosia*), planting improved pastures (such as Kikuyu grass), and building stables for animals.

Probably the most important is that each village has developed at least one whole new system of production. In one village, a whole system of intensified cattle raising has been developed, in which improved pastures are planted to supplement the Napier grass barriers, legumes are being tried to increase protein, animals are stabled, pastures rotated, and cheese making increases the value of the milk before it is marketed. In other villages, much land has gone into coffee or fruit production. In Las Venturas, a system of sustainable forest management has become a major economic factor, where villagers are planting out seedlings to fill clearings, and are cutting a certain number of the largest trees each year.

In Honduras, innovations have occurred in virtually all the villages.

o In Guacamayas, new crops include avocados, lemons, potatoes, tomatoes, green beans, and cauliflower; farmers are also experimenting with new green manures (*Mucuna pruriens* and *Phaseolus coccineus*), organic vegetable production, and have developed a simple way of processing coffee pulp.

o In Guanacaste, people now grow fruit and cassava on a commercial scale for the first time, mainly because of their observed resistance to drought.

o In Lavanderos, chilli peppers, cabbage, carrots, beets, and strawberries are all common crops which did not exist in the village at programme termination.

o In Pacayas alone, people counted 16 innovations adopted since programme termination. These consist of four new crops (chilli peppers, beets, onions, and carrots); two green manures; two new species of short grass for use as contour barriers in vegetable fields; a zero-cash-cost chicken pen made entirely of king-grass planted on a rectangle;

marigolds used to control nematodes; the feeding of both lablab bean (*Dolichos lablab*) and velvetbean to cattle and chickens; numerous cases of nutrient recycling from fish ponds and animals to vegetables and field crops and back; the use of human waste through composting latrines; home-made sprinklers; and the use of Napier grass on cliff edges to stop further caving in.

Discussion

The persistence of specific technologies

The technologies that have proven sustainable over a 15-year period in San Martin Jilotepeque without significant abandonment are contour grass barriers, fertilization with organic matter and crop rotation. In central Honduras, however, the grass barriers were losing popularity after only five years, and the local green manure systems have not fared well – largely because they still need some improving. The cessation of agricultural burning has also continued to spread, and should continue to do so.

However, fertilization with organic matter is really not a single technology, but rather a range of quite varied technologies. Farmers in San Martin are using methods of organic fertilization that are quite different from those originally introduced. The ending of burning is not really a technology either, but rather the absence of a previous technology, which has been superseded by the use of alternative sources of organic nutrients. Therefore, only one technology – crop rotation – has really survived in its original form for at least 15 years.

Might this lack of technological sustainability be caused by poor selection of the technologies? It would appear not. These same technologies work well elsewhere. It is much more likely that most of the technologies have fallen by the wayside because changing circumstances, such as emerging markets, disease and insect pests, land tenure, soil fertility, labour availability and costs, and the adoption of new technologies, have reduced or eliminated their usefulness. Wheat growing, a major programme technology in San Martin (adopted by over 600 farmers), was lost completely because cauliflower and broccoli – also cash crops – paid much better. Broccoli and cauliflower, in turn, disappeared when farmers nearer the processing plant took over San Martin's market.

Similarly, when grass barriers that trap eroding soil build up a natural terrace (some four to six years after adoption), farmers stop cleaning out their contour ditches. As many villagers have explained, 'If my ditches never fill up with water any more, why should I keep cleaning them out?' Both in-row tillage and cover crops can make contour barriers irrelevant. This study has led us to believe that the half-life of well-chosen technologies for farmers is probably about six years.

The sustainability of the development process

The results clearly indicate that even though the vast majority of specific technologies disappeared, farmers' productivity continued to climb. In some of the best villages, yields are continuing to increase at rates comparable with those achieved during the programmes' presence. Thus, the sustainability of specific technologies may well be largely irrelevant. Much more relevant to farmers' well-being and productivity is the sustainability of the development process. That this process can lead to significant increases in people's well-being and can be carried on by the villagers themselves, is probably the most important single finding of this study.

Some might wonder if this continuing improvement was not the result of other outside programmes' work in the area. Yet no other programmes worked for any significant period of time on soil conservation or crop production in these villages during the ensuing years, except in minor ways in the cases of Pacayas and Pacoj. Another possibility would be that agricultural productivity was increasing during these years in any case, and the villages studied merely shared in a more general improvement. However, in villages near the studied villages, yields presently average less than 1.6t/ha (compared to Las Venturas' 5.2t/ha), and most of the last two decades' relatively small increase in yields is directly attributable to heavier use of expensive chemical fertilizers.

What has happened is that the process of agricultural innovation was greatly accelerated by the programmes to the point that it is capable of improving yields over the medium and long term. This increase in the intensity of the innovation process requires that villagers:

○ learn the rudiments of simple scientific experimentation
○ learn a minimum of very basic theoretical ideas about soils and agriculture, in order to orient their experiments in useful directions
○ learn to share with each other the results of their experiments
○ become motivated to do all of the above sustainably.

The key to designing a sustainable soil conservation or agricultural programme does not consist, therefore, of choosing a group of technologies that will be sustainable. Rather, the key is choosing a very few technologies that will motivate farmers to become involved in a process of innovation, to search for new ideas, experiment with them, adopt those that prove useful, and share the experimental results with others.

One of the striking features of soil conservation technologies is that they rarely accomplish any of the above. We have heard farmers say dozens of times, 'But I can't eat a grass barrier'. For farmers to accept soil conservation technologies and become involved in a sustainable process, the technologies must be combined with a technology that enhances yields. It is the increase in yields that convinces the farmers of the value of soil conservation.

Through such a process, subsidies in the form of food-for-work or direct financial incentives become irrelevant. If the yields have increased or costs decreased, artificial incentives are not needed. If the yields have not increased, no artificial incentive will make the technology's adoption sustainable.

Recommendations for sustainable technologies

Combine soil conservation or recuperation technologies with technologies that raise yields or reduce costs. Farmers adopt technologies that bring rapid, recognizable success. But soil conservation technologies cannot bring rapid increases in yield. For villagers to become motivated to maintain and/or improve soil conservation technologies, they must achieve such increases while adopting soil conservation measures.

Use intercropped green manures (or other green manures that can be produced on land with no opportunity cost) wherever possible. Most small farmers already use virtually all the organic matter they produce, and can seldom afford to buy more. Therefore, we must seek to increase the high-nitrogen biomass that can be produced on farm. One of the best-known ways to do this is to produce green manures or cover crops. These can usually be produced without spending cash and in ways that involve no opportunity cost – they can be intercropped, on wasteland, under trees, during periods of frost, or during the dry season. The best of these are multi-purpose crops – they can fix nitrogen, prevent soil erosion, increase soil fertility dramatically, control weeds, control nematodes, and/or provide both highly nutritious animal fodder and human food (Bunch, 1993; Flores, 1991–96).

Use simple, low-cost and appropriate technologies. These should give positive ecological impact, rapid recognizable results, and the possibility that the technology can serve as a basis for many other technological innovations.

Maintain flexibility in technological recommendations. Giving exact specifications and making only one recommendation for solving a problem reduces the space for villagers to experiment and make the technology their own.

Initiate the process with the smallest number of technologies consistent with achieving significant success. Since the objective of the initial technologies is not to introduce permanent innovations, but rather to get people involved in a process of self-generated innovation, there is no reason to introduce a large number of technologies, or even a 'technology package'. In time, as in the villages studied, the programme and the farmers themselves will expand the array of technological innovations being used. This is the only way to sustain a positive impact on agricultural productivity.

41

4

Continuous Adaptation for Soil and Water Conservation: The Case of PATECORE in Burkina Faso

DIETMAR SCHORLEMER

The process and scale of PATECORE's work

THE PROJET D'AMÉNAGEMENT de Terroirs et Conservation de Ressources (PATECORE) is a government project working on the Central Plateau in Burkina Faso to improve village land use and conservation. It is a collaborative effort between a consortium of various ministries (Agriculture, Environment and Tourism, and Livestock) and NGOs operating in the field of resource management, and is funded by the German Agency for Technical Co-operation (GTZ). It began in seven villages in 1988, and has since expanded to 242 of the 331 villages situated in the project area. This zone covers about 5000km² divided over nine departments in the provinces of Bam and Passoré. Rainfall is some 550 mm/year, but soil erosion can reach 200 t/ha/year.

There is much evidence of land degradation in the two provinces. Since its establishment in 1988, about 10 000ha of arable land have been improved with stone works (small dams, bunds and stonelines). It has been estimated that the average family was in cereal deficit by 645kg/year at the beginning of the project. By the mid-1990s, this had been turned around to an excess of 153kg per family.

PATECORE staff do not intervene directly in villages but work through existing local government and non-governmental institutions. The project involves local groups in the planning and implementation of soil and water conservation, with the objective being to develop the self-help capacity at local level. The project staff co-ordinate activities at provincial and district level and train village extensionists (VEs) in technical skills and planning methodology. The VEs facilitate analysis and planning in villages, so as to develop village resource plans. The villagers conduct analyses, plan and implement resource-conserving technologies based on their own needs. One land-use committee is set up in each village, and members are elected by the community.

The main technologies adopted have been permeable dams, stone bunds (*diguettes en pierres*), contour ploughing, tree planting, the establishment of protected zones for regeneration, composting and increased use of manures. Rocks are collected from outside the villages and transported in trucks provided by the project (although ways are being sought on how trucks, too, can be managed locally). The impact on yields was immediate. Within one growing season (1990) an increase of sorghum yields from 870 kg/ha to 1650 kg/ha was measured.

Instead of the classical approach of 'doing something for' women, PATECORE instead tried to integrate the concerns of women into the overall aims and targets of the project. Meetings were held with women to discuss their particular problems and perspectives linked to the use of and access to natural resources. This allowed them to be well prepared for defending their interests when participating in village-level decision-making.

Other major impacts include rapid replication to neighbouring communities (the project provides support to villages only at their request); decreased flood damage and soil erosion; stabilized yields; increased capacity of villagers to plan and implement changes on their own; and increased understanding between government agencies and NGOs that are able to work together with fewer prejudices and better co-ordinated activities.

The evolving approach of action research

The long-term objective of PATECORE is not limited to rearranging stones. It seeks to contribute substantially towards the rational use of natural resources in two ways. On the one hand, support is given to the extension of simple and replicable regeneration and conservation technologies. On the other hand, the project contributes to the improvement and readaptation of village-based natural resource management under the increasingly difficult circumstances of the Sudano-Sahel zone.

The main field of intervention of the project constitutes a dynamic and evolving system of both physical and human resources. Due to the continually adapting state of natural resources and changes in society (communities of resource users), resource management has also continually to change and improve. Being aware of these changing conditions, the project identified action research as being central to all activities.

The central aim is to achieve a process of continuous change. PATECORE wanted to avoid a distinct scientific or investigative research phase which conventionally precedes any activities. Instead, it opted to create a window of opportunity through a concrete activity from which the process would develop in response to local people and the impacts of action. The project's activities are never fixed, but are continually adapting in response to changes on the ground. We have no finalized solutions – we can only learn with local people.

The window of opportunity

The window of opportunity that was identified by the project was support to physical soil and water conservation (SWC) measures. After eight years of experience, this 'opportunity' has clearly withstood the test of time, as it has fulfilled certain favourable conditions that enabled large-scale implementation:

o The different SWC measures not only affected erosion and improved soils, but they have also had direct impact on a vital interest of the villagers, food security, considerably increasing yields and reducing risks of total crop failure in drought years.
o The measures are based on traditional techniques – they are improved traditional measures that are accessible to village men and women, and that do not require any imposed technology.
o The effectiveness of these improved techniques were pre-tested by pilot projects in the same area, and so required only minor adaptations to local conditions.

Two other conditions helped with the acceptability of the measures:

o After years of low rainfall, and almost 10 years of different projects in the area with many sensitization activities, people are aware of the condition of their natural resources;
o The local economy is based on subsistence agriculture and a self-sufficient food supply, neither of which is guaranteed. Any action that enhances food security is eagerly grasped.

Impacts of SWC activities and subsequent adaptations

The economic impacts of SWC measures are difficult to quantify. Nevertheless, research results indicate a remarkable increase in yields in the first year of the construction of the works. This increase depends on many factors, such as climatic variation, the type of measure and the agricultural practice used. According to the villagers' experiences, the advantages of SWC measures are especially important in dry years. It is significant to note that in this region farmers do not necessarily aim for optimization of yields, but rather for minimization of risk of famine, for which conservation measures are especially appreciated.

A good indicator of how measures are valued can be quite simply inferred from the massive number of villagers who are involved in creating the structures. Neither the project nor its partners (state agencies and NGOs) impose construction. In fact, the villagers decide, plan, organize and implement the physical measures themselves, with the technical support of external agencies. Within its task of support to the improvement of land management, the project offers a range of planning methods adapted to the village situation, and support for the improvement of village organization.

In terms of the social impact, the project was initially concerned that the improvements were benefiting only the better-off. This concern was based, among other things, on the fact that the measures were concentrated in the *'bas-fonds'*, the low-lying wetter depressions in the land. Access to the *bas-fonds* is generally limited to a small number of farmers. This tendency was reinforced by the project because the impacts of the measures were greater when carried out on a large scale with percolation dams in the *bas-fond* areas. Benefits in these areas were guaranteed, especially in years of low rainfall, even without the use of manure or fertilizer.

The development of different measures, and research into their impact, has shown that this favouring tendency can be reversed over time. This is a result, on the one hand, of adaptations by the project, including lighter measures that can be used outside the *bas-fond* areas and for different types of land use. It is also a result of an evolution at village level, with increasing interest from different types of land users in a range of types of land uses.

Nevertheless, there are always groups of socially-disadvantaged people in terms of access to SWC measures. These are notably women, especially the households headed by widows, households with older people, sedentary *Peulh* (traditional pastoralists), and other ethnic and social groups that are not well represented in normal village groups or associations.[1] To deal with this problem, PATECORE has therefore particularly favoured improvements on women's fields and stimulated the creation of village organizations for those social groups not represented in existing groups. The project has just finished planning a process for the support of village organizations that envisages a better representation of different social and ethnic groups within rural communities.

Other impacts that are particularly important for the project's development include a growing awareness among villagers about environmental problems and about the availability and appropriate use of existing resources. There is now growing adoption of sustainable agriculture techniques, such as mulching, reforestation and use of organic fertilizer, besides the physical SWC measures. The efforts of villagers in these areas are very promising.

Participation, responsibility and the involvement of villagers

For PATECORE, the measures that conserve water and protect and restore soils are an integral part of the support towards the improvement of village land management. The village land management approach aims to encourage villagers to engage with, and feel responsible for, the management of all of their natural resources. Based on existing management systems and shared experiences with the activities, the approach focuses on two key areas of management: planning and village organization.

---

[1] Village Associations are the counterparts of the external agencies, who address themselves to these local forms of organization.

The main areas of support to the improvement of village planning consist of five key points:

Spatial dimension. Developing a sense of spatial issues, notably through interpretation of aerial photographs, participatory mapping, research on the boundaries of village lands and the local resources within the area;

Analytical dimension. Conducting a joint inventory of resources (type, quality, quantity, potential) and appraisal of practices, uses and users;

Operational dimension. Identification of activities for better management of natural resources;

Temporal dimension. Developing a sense of time through the programming of management activities in the short term and the long term;

Normative dimension. Formulation and documentation of rules and community norms *vis-à-vis* the use of natural resources.

In terms of the support to the improvement of village organizations, the project aims to enhance local capacities in several areas by supporting existing structures. These are the:

○ capacity for consultation and collaboration between village associations, their capacities for dialogue and communication between village groups pursuing their own interests
○ capacity to manage and execute environmental activities
○ capacity to manage conflicts within and between villages.

PATECORE's role in all this is in terms of support, as it does not see itself as the main actor. The project merely participates in the realization of objectives set by villagers. It responds to community needs and help by proposing and negotiating the improvements that allow villagers to use their resources better and to organize better, and thus to achieve their own objectives.

This approach, which focuses on enhancing villagers' sense of responsibility and involvement, emerges from physical activities. For this reason the SWC measures play a very important role as the point of departure. The objectives set by villagers (both SWC measures and other activities that allow for a rational use of resources) often go beyond their existing capacities for planning and self-organization. A lack of skills is identified and expressed by villagers, thus creating an opportunity to increase the area of intervention and to initiate a process that involves stone-based measures and which moves to the integrated management of natural resources.

It is clear that in the area of support, there is no uniform and definite solution that can be used in all situations with guaranteed outcomes. Again, an approach dealing with these issues must be based on achieving a process of continual learning and ongoing change. This requires an open-ended and flexible strategy. An important aspect to note is that the social processes at the village level are not predictable. Therefore, it is also impossible to anticipate the future development of PATECORE and its activities. The conventional notion of a 'project' must be revised.

A challenge for the future: integration of pastoralists

One lesson that has been learnt is that enhancing the sense of responsibility of villagers regarding the value and use of resources can, in the local context, have a negative effect on pastoralists. Resources are scarce and better management of resources also means acquiring them. The first to acquire resources are sedentary farmers, who are the majority of the population. They are also increasingly organized. This means that the more or less latent conflicts between sedentary agriculturalists and more mobile groups are in danger of being aggravated. The problem of integrating pastoralists needs an innovative solution. Approaches to conflict resolution will be indispensable. The process of research-action will continue.

5

Participatory Technology Development in Southern India: Improving Rainfed Agriculture

KENNEDY N. IGBOKWE, ROMY SAN BUENAVENTURA, CARLOS BASILIO, SCOTT KILLOUGH, NEELKANT PANDHARE and RAMANCHANDRAPPA[1]

The project area

THE PROJECT IS located in Kamasamudram, Bangarpet, Kolar District in Karnataka State, Southern India, and is home to some 31 725 people. Most farmers have between 0.2 and 1.2 hectares. The major crops are ragi (a finger millet), groundnut and paddy with cereals as intercrops. Farmers with access to irrigation (tanks) grow mulberry and crops used to feed silk worms. Much of the rainfed agricultural lands are severely degraded. Rainfall in the area is erratic and low, averaging about 650mm annually.

In 1985, the NGO MYRADA initiated activities designed to lift farmers from poverty and stem environmental deterioration. The initial plan was to help thousands of mine workers facing destitution from the closure of the Kolar Gold Field. However, when the mining shutdown was avoided, MY-RADA refocused its efforts on the villages in the area, where poverty is widespread and the effects of drought occur regularly (Bhat, 1991).

Fifteen villages were initially chosen for intervention. In each, local people were organized into village development associations and self-help credit management groups (CMGs). These CMGs 'are small, homogeneous, voluntary and autonomous groups that mobilise savings and develop their own rules and regulations governing the purpose and size of loans, the rate of interest, schedules of recovery and sanctions' (Fernandez, 1993). Project activities in agriculture, health, training and mass education were also developed and by the early 1990s there were 117 *sanghas*, or self-help groups, in more than 82 villages.

In the first phase (1985–91), efforts centred on employment generation and infrastructure development. Villagers were also taught management skills necessary to sustain the development process. They were also given loans to establish income-generating ventures.

---

[1] The first four authors work for the International Institute of Rural Reconstruction in the Philippines, while Neelkant Pandhare and Ramanchandrappa are Agricultural Officers with MYRADA, India.

MYRADA and IIRR collaboration

MYRADA's focus shifted to watershed management in 1990. Three micro-watersheds in Ramakrishnapuram (R K Puram), Garudakempanahalli (G K Halli), and Srinivasanagara villages were identified as 'pilot areas'. Later, two more micro-watersheds in Lakennahalli and Balamande expressed interest in joining, bringing the total to five.

At this time, the International Institute of Rural Reconstruction (IIRR), Philippines, began to collaborate with MYRADA on participatory technology development for improvement in rainfed agriculture. These activities were funded by the Ford Foundation, New Delhi. A dryland technology research component was added to the watershed initiatives, with a special focus on increasing the growth of tree and fodder species to increase biomass production and reduce the effects of drought and erosion.

Responsibility for project implementation rests chiefly with MYRADA, from the carrying out of participatory planning with Participatory Rural Appraisal methods to the implementation of plans developed by the farmers. Monitoring is carried out at three levels: the first is a system of monitoring and self-assessment at the community (project village) level, carried out by the *sangha* and other self-help groups. The second, comprising one or more micro-watersheds, is the responsibility of a project staff member assigned to the sector. The third, at the project level, covers the entire project area and is carried out by the project manager.

The watersheds

o *R K Puram watershed* comprises 61 hectares, of which 20 are under dryland crops cultivated by 16 farm families. Ragi, the main crop, is grown on about 10 hectares of the micro-watershed, intercropped with castor, jowar, redgram and lablab. Groundnut is the next most important crop and is intercropped with mixed rows of redgram and lablab.
o *G K Halli watershed* encompasses 212.5 hectares belonging to 59 farm families from four villages. A pilot micro-watershed was selected covering 9.7 hectares cultivated by nine farmers. Ragi is the major crop grown in the micro-watershed, followed by groundnut.
o *Srinivasanagara micro-watershed* covers 32 hectares of barren, stony and very unproductive land. Only about 16.2 hectares are cultivated. Four hectares are wasteland and 12.1 hectares are forest land owned by the Forest Department. The village came into existence only in 1988 when 17 families were resettled from nine villages. These families belonged to seven different castes.
o *Lakennahalli watershed* covers 103.6 hectares belonging to 66 farm families. Some 94.5 hectares of this land is cultivable, the rest is wasteland. The selected micro-watershed encompasses 17.80 hectares, cultivated by

29 farmer co-operators. All the farms are located on the non-irrigable upper ridges of the watershed.

O *Balamande watershed* covers 43.7 hectares, and 31 farmers farm the mostly rolling terrain.

The project process

Objectives of the project

The project was designed to develop dryland agriculture technologies, using micro-watersheds as the unit of project planning and implementation, to address low soil fertility, fodder and fuel wood shortages, and to augment farmer income. Specifically, the project has aimed to demonstrate farmer-centred approaches for technology development, adaptation and refinement; promote the integration of traditional trees in the watershed village ecosystem; improve soil fertility by adding organic matter and increase on-farm fodder production; reduce erosion; increase farmer income; and promote information sharing.

Project implementing mechanism

From the beginning, it was recognized that between farmers and resource institutions there exists a great diversity of potentially useful ideas and technologies for the improvement of rainfed agriculture.

The basic idea of participatory technology development (PTD) is to combine indigenous knowledge and research-generated technology. The process is interactive: farmers, development workers and researchers work together. It involves identifying, generating, testing and adapting new or overlooked techniques to help solve local problems. Thus, farmers play a key role in the entire process (Figure 5.1).

The project has used a three-tier approach.

1. A basket of technologies is collected from research and development institutions, and farmers. This basket of technology blends indigenous, low-cost technology with research-generated technology. The approach puts the farmers first, as they choose the technologies they need. This has allowed farmers to choose from a range of available options and adapt and refine these to suit their situations (see Table 5.1).
2. The farmer-centred strategies are practised through participatory methodologies (such as Participatory Action Learning Methods – PALM). The participatory approach was critical for finding and testing traditional technologies and management systems. Participatory methods are used for problem identification, the development of local treatment plans and for monitoring impacts.

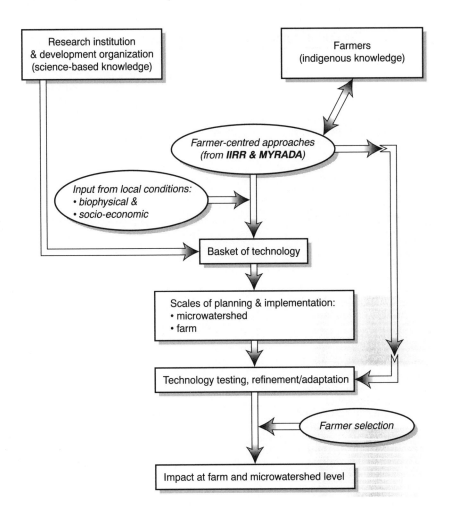

Figure 5.1:   Conceptual framework of the project

3. The project framework uses micro-watersheds as units of project planning and implementation. This small-scale focus promotes involvement of local organizations in decision-making and implementation and so should increase the likelihood that activities will be sustainable. This emphasis on the micro-watershed as the basic planning unit permits a focus on increasing biomass, reducing soil loss, increasing soil water retention and improving the on-farm microclimates.

Local institutions and functions

To encourage participation and ensure sustainability of the initiatives, Watershed Development Associations (WDA) were formed in the micro-

Table 5.1:   Basket of technologies and sources

Technologies	Farmers as source	MYRADA/ IIRR as source	Dept of Agriculture as source	University of Agricultural Sciences as source
Improving Farm Income				
i. traditional intercropping	✓		✓	
ii. planting fruit trees on rock on wasteland or unbunded fields	✓			
iii. agro-horticulture combination				✓
Improving the On-farm Microclimate and Increasing Biomass and Fodder Production				
i. planting of two metre cutting of *Gliricidia erythrina*		✓		
ii. establishment of *Cassia siamea* on the farm bunds		✓		
iii. planting *Sesbania grandiflora*		✓		
iv. planting *Stylosanthes hamata* and *Stylosanthes scraba*		✓		
v. establishment of community mini-forest and protected fodder bank		✓		
Increasing Soil Fertility				
i. green leaf manuring	✓	✓		
ii. application of farmyard manure	✓			
iii. crop rotations	✓			
iv. mulching	✓			
v. Composting	✓			✓
vi. return of crop residues		✓		
vii. silt application	✓			
Water Conservation				
i. boulder bunds		✓	✓	
ii. earthen bunds		✓	✓	
iii. gully checks		✓	✓	
iv. diversion drains		✓	✓	
v. check dams		✓	✓	
vi. small farm reservoirs		✓	✓	
vii. vegetative barriers (vetiver)				✓
viii. silt traps		✓	✓	
ix. rockwalls		✓	✓	
x. dead furrows				✓
xi. planting *Agave americana*	✓			

watershed villages. The WDAs have the broad task of planning and implementing watershed activities and resolving conflicts among their members.

Within the WDAs, the following structures and individuals were identified and established.

i)   Credit management groups (CMG): The main function of these groups is to monitor the activities of the WDA, especially financial matters. Because of its critical role, the CMG wields considerable influence in the WDA. (In some watersheds, CMGs were formed in the initial phase of the MYRADA intervention.)

ii) Watershed development committees (WDC) supervise and report on all activities. They report to the CMG, whose president or designate then reports to the project officer (for release of funds when necessary). The WDC is composed of some members of the CMG. The functions of the WDC differ from one watershed to another.

iii) Watershed promoters are farmers selected by WDA members to serve as links with project staff and to help carry out awareness-raising programmes.

iv) Farmer co-operators (FCs) are WDA members who own or cultivate land on the programme site, and whose land is the target of some intervention. Participation is entirely voluntary.

v)   Farmer instructors are selected from among FCs. They perform a more specialized or technical role than the other groups in the WDA. They influence and motivate other farmers; help to supervise technology testing and documentation; help to write project proposals for watershed activities; conduct informal extension and training; organize exposure trips; and help to monitor and evaluate the project.

The adoption and impact of resource-conserving technologies

The evaluation process

An internal evaluation was conducted by the project team using a combination of informal and structured techniques. To begin with, a workshop was held with project staff to determine possible evaluation indicators and methods of data collection. Workshop participants suggested a set of indicators for each project objective.

A participatory evaluation approach was used for less complicated information that the team felt could realistically be collected from farmers. Group discussions and interviews were held in each watershed. In Srinivasanagara micro-watershed, 14 and 12 farmers, all male, out of 17 farm families, attended the first and second meetings respectively. In Lakennahalli micro-watershed, 16 farmers attended the first meeting and 13 attended the second, all male, out of a total 29 farm families. During these

53

discussions it was observed that the information given by the farmers could easily be validated by themselves. They had very good knowledge of their neighbours' farms.

General level of technology adoption

The progress made on resource conservation practices introduced by the project are shown in Table 5.2. Detailed analysis of the level of adoption and impact are limited to only two micro-watersheds – Srinivasanagara and Lakennahalli.

Technologies for improving farm income

All farmers in Srinivasanagara and Lakennahalli micro-watersheds continued to use the centuries-old practice of intercropping. Many retained the

Table 5.2: Extent of Physical Accomplishment in Different Micro-watersheds

Resource-conserving Technologies	Srinivasa-nagara	Lakenna-halli	R K Puram	G K Halli	Balamande
Length of earthen bunds (m)	15 050	8375	2505	4769	24 010
Length of tree lines planted (m)	14 966	7500	1462	1911	24 010
Length of fodder grasses planted (m)	11 512	6269	2132	3150	11 130
Number of compost pits constructed	70	10	11	16	31
Number of nurseries constructed	–	–	–	–	1
Number of seedlings planted	29 151	27 750	8100	2470	14 560
Area treated for mini-forest development (ha)	2.73	6.8	0.51	0.2	0.71
Farmyard manure applied (cartloads)	8–10	10–15	6	–	8–10
Silt application	12	6	–	–	2

system but used improved cultivars (Table 5.1). Farmers have reported increased yield and reduced vulnerability in the market thanks to crop diversification. Some of these intercropping practices include: ragi intercropped with jowar (sorghum), cowpea, redgram and lablab; sunflower intercropped with redgram and lablab; and groundnut intercropped with jowar, redgram and other crops.

However, some traditional crops, intercropped with improved cultivars, were found to do better in some micro-watersheds than others, largely as a result of varying local conditions and practices. For instance, more farmers in Lakennahalli micro-watershed intercropped sunflower with redgram and lablab because they achieved better yields than farmers in Srinivasanagara, who instead intercropped sunflower with groundnut or chilli. Farmers regularly refined technologies to suit their needs.

Only farmers with patches of wasteland planted fruit trees on their farms. Miniforests were also established on wastelands in Srinivasanagara, but were limited mostly to community lands.

About one-fifth of farmers in Srinivasanagara adopted agro-horticulture technology, though none did in Lakennahalli. Agro-horticulture technology involves planting dryland fruit trees like ber, pomegranate, tamarind, mango and custard apple in combination with farm crops. Lack of irrigation and the small size of holdings were some of the reasons cited for non-adoption. Even though farmers recognized the importance of these technologies, they preferred to put their land into crop production.

Planting mulberry cuttings along the earthen bunds was not taken up by the farmers because of problems the bushes might cause for grazing animals.

Technologies for improving biomass and fodder production

About 15 species of mostly indigenous trees, including some with fodder value, were planted in the village hillocks of the Srinivasanagara and Lakennahalli micro-watersheds. These are *Derris indica* (pongamia), *Gliricidia sepium*, *Cassia siamea*, *Acacia auriculiformis*, *Mangifera indica* (mango), jackfruit, jacaranda, *Syzygium cummi*, *Delonix regia*, *Tamarindus indica*, *Wrightia tinctoria*, *Erythrina indica*, *Melia dubia* (fodder neem), *Ficus religiosa* and *Bauhinia purpuria*.

All farmers in both watersheds had planted *Cassia siamea* along their bunds. They observed that it could be grown easily and, compared to other tree species, posed less competition to crops. It is also non-browsable, good for fuelwood and provides leaves for composting. Farmers also used the wood for small agricultural implements.

Stylosanthes scraba and *Stylosanthes hamata* have been widely adopted by the farmers for animal fodder. In Srinivasanagara, all farmers grow them on bunds. In Lakennahalli, more than 60 per cent of farmers are growing these fodder trees.

55

In addition to these, farmers used other tree crops with fodder value such as neem. Neem has good fodder value, but since it is propagated by cuttings, it is difficult to spread. A tree of fodder neem is estimated to give about Rs.150–200 worth of fodder every month, once established. Ragi and jowar are popular for their crop residues.

Technologies for improving soil and water conservation

Most of the project's soil and water conservation techniques – boulder bunds and rock walls, gully checks and dams, and diversion drains – were adopted at the micro-watershed level. On the private lands, earthen bunds had 100 per cent adoption. Farmers observed that earthen bunds, if properly constructed, are effective in erosion control and water conservation. Fuel and fodder trees can also be grown on the bunds, though two or three loppings a year are essential from the second year onwards to retard root growth and possible moisture competition with crops.

As one farmer put it 'Unlike the rockwalls or boulder bunds, the soil and land area lost to bunding can be compensated by growing trees on it.'

Perhaps most importantly, the trees planted on the farm boundaries help modify the microclimate on the small farms, reducing moisture losses and improving the microbial activity.

Some 25 per cent of the farmers in Srinivasanagara micro-watershed adopted farm pond or farm reservoir technology for rainwater harvesting.

Vetiver grass was not adopted in any of the micro-watersheds because of lack of planting materials, although the farmers expressed doubt about its adaptability because of high moisture requirements during the early stage of establishment. Some farmers said they would try it if they had irrigation. About 35 per cent of farmers planted *Agave americana* in Srinivasanagara micro-watershed. In Lakennahalli, it was grown on common areas.

Technologies for improving soil fertility

All farmers in both micro-watersheds made use of a wide range of soil improvement technologies. Almost all practise crop rotation, stating that rotation improves and sustains their crop yield. All also apply manure and silt to their fields to enhance soil fertility. All in Lakennahalli practise green leaf manuring, but only a quarter do so in Srinivasanagara.

The adoption of composting, on the other hand, was complete in Srinivasanagara with an average of three pits per farmer. In Lakennahalli half the farmers have dug compost pits.

Return of crop residues to the soil was not adopted in Lakennahalli. Farmers reported that mulch attracted termites to planted crops. In Srinivasanagara, adoption was complete and farmers reported that termites have not been a problem. No farmer in Lakennahalli, however, adopted

56

mulching because animal grazing was a problem. They did, however, recognize its usefulness during the rainy season to slow runoff and promote infiltration.

The impacts of project interventions

Crop productivity

The yield of the main crops planted in Srinivasanagara micro-watershed increased by an average of 45 per cent between 1991–92 and 1993–94 (Table 5.3). Farmers who planted ragi as a major crop obtained an average yield of 423kg/hectare. The land area reclaimed for intensive crop production has also increased by an average of 21 per cent since 1991.

In Lakennahalli micro-watershed, crop yields increased by an average of 12 per cent. This area produced yields before the project of 850kg/hectare for ragi and 768kg/hectare for groundnut. The project's impact on productivity is encouraging (Table 5.4). It should be remembered that interventions in Lakennahalli started later, in 1992, and so the impact on crops and biomass productivity are understandably less than in Srinivasanagara.

Intercropping with improved cultivars has also boosted productivity. Jowar and redgram in Srinivasanagara have yielded 46.9 and 35.6kg/hectare, respectively, since the project began. Other intercrops planted include cowpea, niger, lablab and castor. These increases can be attributed to intercropping, the introduction of improved cultivars, and the various

Table 5.3: Average sampled yield of main crops (kg/ha) in Srinivasanagara micro-watershed

Crops	1991–92	1992–93	1993–94	Average change (%)
Ragi	385	321	558	+29%
Niger	444	642	657	+34%
Chilli	–	427	953	+123%
Horsegram	556	445	547	–2%
Groundnut	445	780	563	+24%
Jowar (sorghum)	988	474	1317	+62%

Table 5.4: Average sampled yield of main crops in Lakennahalli micro-watershed (kg/ha)

Crops	1991–92 (pre-project)	1992–93	1993–94	Average change (%)
Ragi	850	894	1115	+18%
Groundnut	768	625	823	+7%

regenerative practices adopted by the farmers, such as green manuring, composting and soil and water conservation practices. Most farmers attributed the poor crop performance to low rainfall.

On-farm biomass production

The amount of biomass collected for fuelwood in Srinivasanagara microwatershed increased by 25 per cent from 83kg in 1992–93 to 110kg in 1993–94, which lasted for 18 to 28 days for cooking (Table 5.5). In monetary terms, farmers each saved between Rs 166 and Rs 276 that would otherwise have been spent on fuelwood in the market. This is in addition to the farm wastes and crop residues that are used as cooking fuel. A final project evaluation in 1995 showed that farmers in Lakennahalli and Srinivasanagara are now obtaining enough fuelwood to serve them for 35 and 240 days (annually) respectively.

On-farm fodder production

Farmers in Srinivasanagara are also benefiting from the fodder trees and grasses introduced by the project. In the 1992–93 cropping season each farmer fed an average of three cows for about three days from the fodder grown on the farm. This increased to 11 days in 1992–93. An additional 10 sheep were fed for 60 days. This meant that a farmer could save between Rs 450 and Rs 1650 on green fodder annually.

Farm ecological conditions

In Srinivasanagara, farmers reported that prior to the project erosion was a severe problem, but by the time of the study the problem was perceived to

Table 5.5: Project impact on biomass production in Srinivasanagara microwatershed

Households	Kg fuelwood collected (1992–93)	Number of cooking days (1992–93)	Kg fuelwood collected (1993–94)	Number of cooking days (1993–94)
A	200	45	200	45
B	0	0	125	10
C	200	30	200	30
D	0	0	25	15
E	50	20	75	30
F	50	15	35	35
Average	83	18	110	28

be slight. Before the project all farmers in Lakennahalli felt that erosion was severe, but by the time of the study they considered the problem to be moderate (Box 5.1).

Box 5.1: Farmers' observations of bio-physical changes

In the group sessions, farmers in Srinivasanagara made a number of important remarks.

'Before the project, when it rained, the soils were washed away, except the stones. The presence or formation of gullies after the rain was noticeable. But, now they don't form any more because of the introduced erosion control measures', said one farmer.

'Before, if the land was ploughed and kept ready for sowing, the rain would wash away all loose soils. It was a severe problem for us. But now, the land is protected everywhere possible . . . so erosion has become minimal' said another farmer.

Achari, another farmer in the micro-watershed, put it this way: 'Three years back, gully formation in some areas was five feet deep or more, but now they have a depth of less than two feet.'

Farmers in both micro-watersheds feel that soil fertility has improved.

'Before, our land was barren and rocky . . . now the soil is easy to plough with fewer stones. Our yield has also increased', said a Srinivasanagara farmer.

'All we could see earlier were stones and pebbles; now there is some soil to be seen and felt', said another farmer.

'Ragi will not dry up even if there are no rains for a month', said a woman farmer.

It has been reported that when farmers first moved into Srinivasanagara, the land had little monetary value. Soil organic matter content increased from 0.37 per cent to 2.32 per cent after the end of the project (1995). The rocky and barren lands that characterized the project site in the beginning have been transformed and are now valued at over $300 per acre, according to farmers.

Regarding water availability for irrigation, only farmers in Lakennahalli felt there had been an improvement. This question, however, was more relevant to farmers in Lakennahalli, which has a community tank. The Lakennahalli tank was dredged and the silt applied to farmers' fields to improve soil fertility.

Farmers were also more aware of soil conservation: 'What we knew before was a few traditional practices taught by our parents. But, now we have more knowledge', said one Srinivasanagara farmer.

Social status

The farmers in Lakennahalli felt that the goal of community co-operation had been achieved to some extent between watershed members and non-members as a result of the project. Members reported that they felt there was a stronger relationship as a result of the project.

Farmers from Srinivasanagara watershed felt little improvement in their level of co-operation. This could be because the community is composed of seven different caste groups. Although their general perception on unity was low, they felt more united than before. 'Before, we just said hello, but now we work together and discuss farming problems . . . although some members do create problems in the group', said one farmer.

On the participation of women and youth in watershed activities, Lakennahalli farmers perceived a moderate involvement. Srinivasanagara's farmers, on the other hand, perceived a high participation of women, but very little for the youth. Their life aspirations have also changed for the better. Farmers in Lakennahalli and Srinivasanagara are moderately optimistic since joining the project. Before the project, farmers held out little hope of achieving their goals.

Problems encountered and lessons learned

Problems encountered during project implementation

A number of important problems had to be overcome during the project implementation. These included:

○ biophysical, such as low survival rate of young seedlings due to drought

○ political, such as interference from big landlords and their lack of co-operation during implementation of watershed tasks, and farmers' fear and reluctance to give correct figures of their land which was necessary for planning

○ economic, such as difficulties of the project beneficiaries meeting their 20 to 30 per cent counterpart project contribution (cash or labour), and migration of farmers to other places and/or selling their land to outsiders who were not interested in watershed activities.

Lessons learned

Important lessons were learned for watershed development.

○ In selecting micro-watersheds for interventions, priority should be given to areas where land is mostly owned by the co-operating farmers. The projects' results/impact can expect to be greater if self-help groups or other forms of people's organizations already exist.

o Participatory methodology (such as PRA) should be used before site selection to determine the conditions of the watershed as well as the interest, priorities and responses of the community.

o In identifying farmer instructors, it is important that the following criteria be met. Potential farmer instructors should be literate and trained in agriculture (formal training in agriculture is not critical); responsive to new ideas; committed and enthusiastic; and already convinced of the value of introducing trees and new technology into farms.

o Several factors enhance farmers' adoption and refinement of technologies, including whether the benefits are continuous and are realized quickly; if they are convinced the technology will improve their income or enhance crop productivity; if there is financial support or availability of credit; if they are organized into groups; and if technologies are low-cost, simple and easy to understand, have high acceptability, and can be demonstrated convincingly.

o Several factors prevent farmers' adoption and refinement of technologies, including if there is no follow-up by the project team or extension personnel; if there is no visible economic benefit; if a technology has failed for other farmers; and if other component technologies are not available.

Conclusion

In the course of its three years, the project has demonstrated that the three-tier approach, involving micro-watersheds, the basket of technologies and farmer-centred approaches using the knowledge utilization strategy, has encouraged farmers to participate in technology testing and refinement. This has allowed them to adapt and adopt technologies suitable to their specific environmental conditions. Thus, the project has helped farm families increase their food and biomass production, and income; modify the microclimate by reducing soil erosion and moisture loss, and improve soil fertility. The levels of optimism and co-operation among farmers have also increased.

6
Participatory Technology Development for Watershed Management in Leyte, The Philippines
EDWIN A. BALBARINO and DOLORES L. ALCOBER

Introduction

CONVENTIONAL ON-STATION research is mostly disciplinary or commodity-oriented, and emphasizes technology generation. While this approach works well under the homogeneous conditions typical of 'green revolution' types of agriculture, it fails almost completely under the much more complex, diverse, and risk-prone environment of upland agriculture.

In this upland agriculture, technologies generated on-station can be irrelevant in the context of the complex circumstances of farmers. Something has to be done to the research system to make technologies more relevant to, and readily adoptable by, upland farmers.

Thus a research and development institution, the Farm and Resource Management Institute (FARMI), was created in January 1987, based at the Visayas State College of Agriculture (ViSCA) with a resource-base orientation and an on-farm research thrust focused on upland rice- and corn-based agro-ecosystems.

The research and development site

The municipality of Matalom covers an area of about 12 000ha located about 160km south-west of Tacloban City. Some two-thirds of the farms are less than one hectare in size, mostly split into several field parcels. The soil is Maasin clay with a pH of 4.2–5.9, very low P and K, and relatively low organic matter. The area is 100–300m above sea level, and has an average annual rainfall of 2 000mm. Maximum rains occur between July and December, with dry months from February to April.

Farming is the primary means of livelihood for local people. About one-third of farmers are landowners while 38% are share tenants. To augment their income, some are engaged in fishing, off-farm activities, and selling labour. Swine and poultry raising are also common.

The area has problems common to other uplands in the Philippines. The red acid infertile soils, which cover about 73 per cent of the land area, represent the extensive and infertile uplands elsewhere. Matalom acid soils are found at the lower elevations (<200m asl) where slopes range mostly from 5 to 40 per cent. Soil acidity, inherent soil infertility, and soil erosion are among the factors that cause low and declining yields of the farmers' staple food crop (upland rice).

Adjacent to this is a contrasting sub-ecosystem: the smaller calcareous soil area representing the second most important fragile-upland agroecosystem of the Philippines. This sub-ecosystem is found in the areas of higher elevation (200–450m asl) where slopes are steeper, ranging from 25–60 per cent. Here, extremely poor soil fertility and excessive soil erosion are threatening the food security of the inhabitants.

In both sub-ecosystems, 'shifting cultivation' has been, and still is, the dominant method of farming. The challenge is for research to find suitable alternative land-use systems and production technologies that can produce enough food on a sustainable and equitable basis to feed the ever-increasing population and at the same time to conserve the local resource base and safeguard the environment.

The participatory watershed management programme

FARMI's participatory watershed management programme addresses con-straints in hillside and highland farming in Matalom. The general objective of the programme was to develop new solutions and disseminate innovative tech-nologies, in collaboration with the farmers, to rehabilitate the watershed and promote more productive and sustainable hillside/highland farming systems.

Under the soil and water conservation and agroforestry projects, the project sought to:

○ involve farmers in the search for alternative productive and sustainable land use systems
○ disseminate soil and water conservation and agroforestry technologies using farmer-to-farmer extension
○ promote the use of indigenous farmer organizations (*alayons*) in the establishment of contour farms.

A major focus was participatory technology development (PTD). PTD field-work is based on the premiss that farmers are knowledgeable and are active experimenters. Most of the studies started with participatory rural appraisal to make sure that farmers' views, knowledge, and preferences are fully tapped. Other methods for farmer participatory research (FPR) were also applied.

The project used the PTD approach for the development and extension of soil and water conservation and agroforestry technologies.

Getting started

As it is important to start with the farmers' technology, the project staff first learned from farmers about indigenous technologies for soil

63

conservation. A simple technique known as *kahon-kahon* – grass strips/ bunds – was found to be practised by some 35 per cent of the farmers in the upland areas where slopes ranged from 10–40 per cent.

Equipped with a better understanding of the strengths and weaknesses of the indigenous technology, researchers collaborated with farmers in looking for innovations to add to the existing technology so that farmers' other priorities could be accommodated.

The cross-farm visit

To start the planned soil and water conservation project formally, a four-day field trip was organized for 15 farmers and five project staff to visit two upland projects of the Mag-Uugmad Foundation Incorporated (MFI) in Cebu (see Chapter 18, this book). There the field trip participants were able to interact with local farmers and project managers, getting from them tips for successful soil conservation. They also observed the different contouring techniques used and the different grass and tree/shrub species planted in hedgerows. Most importantly, they personally witnessed the benefits of contour farming.

After the field trip, the participants were visited individually by the project leader and encouraged to start contouring their farms. The first to answer the challenge were the three field trip participants from Templanza, followed later by those from Altavista. The balding mountains and highly eroded fields testify to the enormous soil erosion losses in these villages. The residents of the calcareous barangays depend solely on hillside and highland farming for their livelihood, whereas their counterparts in the acidic villages have alternative sources of income such as fishing, small business, and other employment.

After the field trip, the field trip participants presented to their fellow barangay officials the upland farming technologies they had observed in Cebu. The barangay council then agreed to initiate the soil and water conservation project through *alayon* groups – the traditional labour exchange system (Box 6.1).

The *alayon* started in September 1991 with only four members. But the early days of the *alayon* were not encouraging. For several months, the group fluctuated in size, rising and falling as members had conflicts with other needs, such as having to work off-farm for labour.

By the end of the year, however, the group had 10 active members. *Alayon* members continued to assist in the dissemination of information about contouring in informal gatherings and in Sitio chapel meetings. Several more farmers wanted to join the *alayon* but found it difficult at the time because they were engaged in other activities, such as selling labour. Others requested planting materials (grasses and shrub/tree legume species) to plant to improve their own soil and water conservation.

Box 6.1: The *alayon*

The *alayon* is an indigenous co-operative institution. The main theme of its operation is co-operation without taking account of the amount that a member can contribute to the overall success of the group. Members with *carabaos* (buffaloes), for example, have to do the ploughing, which is a relatively heavier input than laying out contour lines with an A-frame or planting grasses. Four of the *alayon* members have *carabaos*.

There are no hard and fast rules for membership of the *alayon*. A group of neighbours, relatives or friends can form their own *alayon* group. The most important requirement is the interest of a farmer to learn and his willingness to work. There is no formal set of officers. In Matalom, only four of the 29 groups have elected their officers. In most cases, members just selected or agreed on someone to act as their group leader. There are mixed *alayon* groups of men, women and young people who perform similar tasks.

The system reduces the burden and amount of labour input. Instead of only one farmer working a farm, more people help to accomplish the farm tasks. It also allows sharing of resources among members, including draught animals, planting materials, etc. which make farm activities and land cultivation a lot easier. Furthermore, *alayon* also serves as a venue for interaction. Members exchange experiences and problems on farming. It also fosters friendship and builds teamwork within the group and in the community. Some *alayon* groups that help each other on the farm also work together in constructing tree nurseries, repair feeder roads, and other off-farm or non-farm activities.

To generate income for their group members, some *alayon* groups sell pooled labour, such as for ploughing, planting and weeding, to other farmers. The *alayon* is also instrumental in the formulation of some communal functions such as the establishment of communal grazing areas.

Farmer testing of technologies

While there were existing techniques of contouring available for adoption, the project's focus was on encouraging farmers to experiment with and adapt different techniques so as to fit them to their particular needs and preferences:

o Diking. This technique was developed by the *alayon* members themselves. It is done by piling the *guang* (soil clods) along the unploughed contour lines in much the same way as dikes in lowland fields are made.

65

The dike measures 0.6–0.9m high and about 0.5m wide. Although laborious, farmers found it barred the downflow of soil during heavy rains. A combination of leguminous shrub species and fodder grasses are planted on both sides of the dikes.

○ 'Slash and pile'. Cut grass and shrubs are piled along contour lines to serve as brush dams and as a source of organic matter when decomposed. Cuttings of madre de cacao (*Gliricidia sepium*) or ipil-ipil (*Leucaena leucocephala*) are stuck below the piled grasses to prevent them from collapsing. These alleys are ploughed only when the field is to be planted.

○ Contour hedgerows, established while the area is still fallowed. In this technique, furrows are made along the located contour lines and planted with grasses and leguminous shrubs/trees to form the hedgerows.

○ Direct planting of hedgerow materials such as *mura* (Vetiver grass), napier, ipil-ipil, and *Desmanthus vergatus*, on the located contour lines while the field still has standing crop(s). Similar to the preceding method, the hedgerows are improved during the next farm cultivation.

○ Levelling of the alleys is similar to bench terracing. Fertility is maintained by digging holes where dried animal manure mixed with soil is placed before corn or peanuts are planted.

Side by side with these different contouring techniques was the farmers' testing of different contour hedgerow materials. The materials included the traditional hedgerow species like ipil-ipil, mura grass, *Cajanus cajan*, mulberry, dapdap (*Erythrina*), madre de cacao, napier, and Guinea grass and introduced legumes (*Desmanthus vergatus, Desmodium rensonii, Flemingia congesta*).

The advantages and disadvantages of each method and material were made known to the farmers, but the choice was left to them. Both the contouring techniques and planting materials used are subject to farmers' evaluation, based on their values in controlling soil erosion, recovering soil fertility, and supplying livestock feeds, among others.

Sharing the results through farmer-to-farmer training

Farmer-to-farmer training in SWC and agroforestry (Box 6.2) endeavoured to make farmers themselves trainers of other farmers. This training was mainly focused on knowledge and skills in establishing farm contours and improved upland farming systems.

As part of the training, the farmers visited a demonstration farm to see the different grass and legume hedgerow species before they were brought to the training venue in Templanza. The training was done through farmer-to-farmer sharing of experiences. Three members of the original Templanza *alayon* served as the major trainers, while the others served as support trainers. Subjects taught included the construction of the A-Frame, location of contour lines, construction of contour bunds (dikes), planting of different hedgerow grasses and legumes, and intercropping corn with rice bean and Crotalaria.

At the end, a short informal evaluation of the training topics was done. The farmers were also asked about their plans after attending the training. Planting materials were distributed after each training session.

By March 1992, the farmers who had visited the upland projects in Cebu had trained eight farmers from barangay Hitoog, Matalom in the technology tried on their farms. In turn, the Hitoog farmers formed themselves into an *alayon* with 15 farmer-members. They were the first batch of farmers trained in soil and water conservation through the farmer-to-farmer extension approach. The approach spread, and by early 1994, 29 *alayon* groups had been formed and trained.

Box 6.2:   Conditions for successful farmer-to-farmer training

1. A good and articulate farmer-teacher who can effectively discuss the topic.
2. Financial support for the training such as expenses for snacks, small trainers' honoraria, petrol, etc.
3. Transportation for the trainees and planting materials.
4. Farmers' farms that are relatively improved for other farmers to observe the technologies at work.
5. Organization of the farmers into *alayon* groups. The *alayon* facilitates the implementation of what the farmers learned from the training.
6. The need for the technology. Farmers who need the technology and are ready to contour their farms are given priority to participate in the training.
7. Training aids (A-frame, visual aids, etc.)
8. Distribution of seeds/planting materials after the training.
9. A good co-ordinator/facilitator to manage cross-farm visits and training.
10. A good rapport among the project staff, the farmer-trainees and the trainers.

Economic, social and environmental project impacts

By March 1994 there were 29 farmer associations or *alayons* with 300 members continuously engaged in contouring activities. This indicates about a 50 per cent increase in the number of farmers participating in the soil and water conservation programme since 1992. Among the non-*alayon* farmers, the project noted more than a 100 per cent increase in the number of farmers adopting SWC practices from 1993 to 1994.

Changes in the trends of resource degradation

By mid-1994, there were 210 farms contoured by the *alayons* and 110 farms by farmers who do not belong to *alayon* associations. Of the 81 589 metres of hedgerows established, 70 per cent were established by *alayon* farmers. In terms of the number of contour strips, the non-*alayon* farmers developed 277 strips. Since the average farm size was one-half hectare, the total area contoured is estimated to be 150 hectares.

The contouring adopted by the farmers is a combination of physical and vegetative methods. The physical method includes the establishment of soil dikes/bunds and shallow canals along the contour lines where different species of grass and leguminous trees and shrubs are planted as hedgerows. More than 50 farmers used *mura* (Vetiver grass) as hedgerow foundation, although the majority (more than 75 per cent) have napier on their hedgerows.

In 1994, the project introduced agroforestry schemes into the farming system. The most widely adopted system was the planting of trees in the upper part of the contour farms. As of mid-1994, 150 farmers started integrating trees into their hillside and highland farms. The majority (60 per cent) of the 17 117 trees planted in the communal and individual contour farms thus far are mahogany trees. About a thousand trees were planted through co-operative tree planting. Perhaps the most important development taking place in Matalom now is local people's recognition of the importance of trees in their ecosystem.

The other major thrust of the project for the coming years is on the research and promotion of soil fertility enrichment technologies. At present, only very few have started using green manure.

Apart from the individual farms contoured, six of the 29 *alayon* groups have established communal farms. The same techniques in soil and water conservation were used in contouring the communal farms. These *alayon* groups borrowed seeds of peanut, mungbean, rice bean and red cowpea from the project for their communal farms. The borrowed seeds have been returned and are now dispersed to other groups. The communal farms were also planted with trees like mahogany, gmelina and fruit trees.

Retained ecosystem functions

Monitoring of groundwater recharge is being done by the project in areas where most of the contour farms are established. A study was started in August 1993 to gain an understanding of the hydrologic system characteristics, determine the effect of widespread implementation of different farming systems on hydrology and develop strategies for optimizing the benefits of the soil and water conservation scheme through critical analysis of field sites at various stages of development. The results are not yet available.

Contribution of farmers to technology adaptation and multiplication

As mentioned above, the project started from the farmers' own SWC technology (*kahon-kahon*). The technology is not without its problems, however. On bunds/strips covered by low-growing grasses, the field staff observed portions that are broken. The causes, according to farmers, are either heavy rains or animals. With a good understanding of the indigenous technology, researchers and farmers collaborated to seek innovations to improve their current practice, testing the technology and sharing the results of their tests.

Exactly a year after selected farmers from Matalom visited the upland projects in Cebu, some farmers in Templanza had successfully demonstrated the effectiveness of improved *kahon-kahon* contouring not only in checking soil erosion but also in providing feed for livestock and in recovering soil fertility.

The farmers were not only involved in testing and disseminating technology; they were also active in helping the community regenerate natural resources by establishing tree nurseries. There were six small tree nurseries established by the *alayon* groups, which also served as meeting places for *alayon* members.

Decrease in resource degrading practices and external effects of soil erosion

While the project received farmers' testimonies about positive soil changes occurring in the contoured farms, e.g., volume of soil trapped by the contour hedgerows/bunds, it is still in the process of collecting data for more conclusive findings, through an on-going study entitled 'Changes in Soil Properties in Various Farmers' Agroforestry Schemes Within the Watershed Development Project'. It seeks primarily to evaluate the effects of various agroforestry schemes/production systems within the watershed development on soil properties and erosion.

Interestingly, some farmers do not burn farm refuse anymore, e.g. corn husks. Traditionally, farmers burned their farm waste. Little by little, some farmers realized that these materials could contribute to the recovery of soil fertility if properly managed.

Changes in local resilience and vulnerability

Diversity of agricultural and wild products managed/farmed

The project has started a study aimed at optimizing plant diversity in farming and other managed vegetational systems of the area. This should result in the conservation of land, water and biodiversity and the improvement of the lives of rural peoples by providing a wide range of income options.

One major accomplishment of the project is the successful introduction of rice bean as an intercrop of maize. Traditionally, maize is planted as a mono-crop. The change in cropping systems started from a litre of rice bean seeds obtained from the Mag-Uugmad project in Cebu during the farmers' cross visit in September 1991. The seeds were given to two farmers for testing, but only one farmer was able to plant the seeds because the other farmer's seeds were eaten by rats. The result was so dramatic that farmers were convinced of its potential for increasing farm income and in contributing to soil fertility. The rice bean is planted two weeks after planting corn. As the corn is harvested, the rice bean starts to mature, with the standing corn stalks serving as natural trellis. Farmers found the crop to be higher yielding than mungbean.

The project is currently monitoring 300 farmers who are planting rice bean as corn intercrop, while a study on the costs and benefits of corn–rice bean intercropping is underway.

Access to credit

Two *alayon* groups are developing an indigenous savings and lending system locally called *bo-bo* (meaning 'to pour'). The system calls for all members to contribute an agreed amount per month to a revolving fund. The pooled money is open for borrowing by the members at 10 per cent interest per month. The money generated will be divided among the members at the end of the year or will be used to fund a project or activity. The system is also adopted as a management strategy to assemble its *alayon* members even in periods when there are no *alayon* activities.

Building self-reliance in groups and communities

Willingness of local people to participate

A common question asked by project visitors is about the financial inducements for farmers to participate in project activities. While the trainers are paid P50.00 each, equivalent to a day of farm labour, farmers do not receive any financial incentives to get involved in the project.

This is also true of farmer-initiated projects like the tree nurseries. Another interesting example is the construction of the training centre in the village of Templanza, which is the venue of the soil and water conservation trainings for farmers. The training centre was built by the *alayon* group with materials contributed by the members. The project contributed only the nails used in the construction.

Planting materials, such as seeds of legumes and vegetables, are lent to requesting farmers or farmer groups on the understanding that the same quantity will be returned to the project after harvest. The system is doing well so far. For trees, the seeds were given free for the *alayon* members/ farmers to produce the seedlings.

Every year, all the *alayon* groups are called to the annual planning and evaluation workshop. Each *alayon* sends a maximum of five members to participate in reporting the *alayon* accomplishments during the current year and in planning for activities and projects for the coming year. The meeting also provides a venue for the experimenting farmers to present their research findings to the project staff and farmers. Farmer leaders from other projects (e.g.. Mag-Uugmad Foundation Incorporated and World Neighbors, Cebu) are also invited to share their experiences with the Matalom farmers.

The annual review workshop is supplemented by quarterly meetings of all *alayon* leaders to review quarterly accomplishments, problems and solutions. Each *alayon* group also holds monthly meetings, attended by the project staff to discuss matters relating to *alayon* operations, projects or activities.

Building local capacity and skills

The farmer-to-farmer training team conducted 27 training events with 288 farmer–trainees. These training sessions included two with farmers from another town. Apart from the farmer–trainers, the *alayon* leaders also taught fellow *alayon* members other things they learned from the quarterly seminar meetings conducted at the FARMI field office.

One plan of the project is to develop a core of farmer–trainers to handle training on soil and water conservation and agroforestry, to meet the demand from other towns for such training. Recently, local government officials from six Western towns of Leyte met in ViSCA to discuss their agricultural pro-gramme plans. The need to protect their watershed became one of the priority programmes of mayors and local agricultural extension personnel. The water-shed development project in Matalom will eventually take the lead in dis-seminating upland technologies to upland farmers in these municipalities.

Replication to neighbouring communities and villages

The neighbouring town of Hindang, Leyte has adopted the *alayon* system in an effort to conserve the soil of their hillside farms planted to rootcrops. They also obtained hedgerow planting materials from Matalom.

Changes in operational procedures of support institutions

New roles for professionals

The project has strengthened the FARMI staff's understanding of the situation in Matalom, and of the importance of learning first from farmers before proceeding with any research and development activities. With this came the staff's appreciation of the fact that the shift from the traditional transfer of technology approach in upland development to farmer-first approach calls for the genuine involvement of farmers in the designing and testing of technologies for their own use.

This awareness enhanced the project staff's understanding of more farmer-focused approaches, such as building on farmers' knowledge, enhancing farmers' capability to experiment and encouraging active farmer participation from the start to the end of a project.

Through the participatory technology development approach, technical project staff have assumed roles quite different from the traditional 'expert' or 'teacher' roles. There was more guidance than direction; and more suggestions than instructions.

The project staff assumed the role of *searchers* (of technology options) and discussed with the farmers different contouring methods that they could try on their farms. As *suppliers*, they provided (in the early stage of the project) hedgerow planting materials for the farmers to try out on their farms. In testing the different soil and water conservation techniques and in putting up trials, the project staff served as *consultants*.

The staff always encourage the farmers to participate in finding solutions to the soil erosion problems in the area. In farmers' meetings to discuss problems and plans, the staff – with the help of farmer leaders and barangay officials – serve as *convenors*. As farmers' *colleagues*, staff endeavour to establish a close working relationship with farmers by working beside them during contouring works. The staff also acted as *travel agents*, arranging cross-farm visits for farmers to see innovations which they could try on their own farms.

An informal newsletter called *On-Farm Research Notes* is published by FARMI and circulated locally and internationally to share on-farm research experiences. Copies of the OFR Notes are sent to all academic units of ViSCA. Since relevant researchable areas appear from time to time in the newsletter, researchers appreciated this feedback mechanism and made use of it in guiding their research efforts.

Enabling policies in institution

FARMI adopted research management procedures for funding, screening, and approving research proposals that try to accommodate the felt needs of upland farmers. Actual field problems are studied by the technical team, while funding is made ready for the prompt conduct of the research. FARMI researchers do not receive honoraria as practised by projects with external funds. In this manner, monetary considerations are eliminated (or minimized) from the researcher's motivation to work in the hope that those who do are really sincere in their undertaking. However, the institute is ready to provide financial support to staff to attend seminars, conferences, and symposia to share research findings.

The project also tried to develop research methodologies suitable to the upland agro-ecosystem. The participatory technology development (PTD) approach was adapted and refined by the project. Farmers' participation in all areas of the project implementation were continuously sought through participatory rural appraisal and the farmer-to-farmer extension approach. The project also emphasizes team work in its research and development strategy. Activities are conducted by a multidisciplinary team working in an interdisciplinary manner.

Commitment to developing local capacity

The remaining years of the project will be devoted to strengthening the capacity of the local government to assist the community-based, small-farmer associations (the *alayons*) in planning and implementing sustainable cropping practices and natural resource conservation measures. This includes the building of capability of local organizations in formulating and implementing policy on resource management issues of community interest.

The project has made steps towards developing the capacity of upland farmers and farmer organizations to conduct small-scale field trials aimed at developing sustainable technologies suitable for the various agro-ecological zones of the Matalom watershed. Apart from being involved in the analysis and diagnosis of their problems, some farmers are now involved in the promotion of farm-proven technologies. Farms in more advanced stages of development have been visited by scientists, extension workers and researchers, students and more than 30 farmer groups.

Conclusions: linking process to impact

In summary, the process taken by the project was as follows. With farmers as the central figure in all phases, the programme started with a farmers' indigenous soil and water conservation technology: the contour grass strips. Innovations followed through on-farm tests and farmers' evaluations. Farmer participation in the programme was systematized by the formation of indigenous labour exchange groups called *alayons*. In farmer-to-farmer training, farmers trained other farmers in SWC.

In all this, the project staff has taken on a supportive role. Technical people have shed their 'expert' role to take on a more collegial give-and-take relationship with farmers. Institutions provide support and guidance, but do not exert undue influence on farmers' decision-making.

Impact may be perceived through the increasing number of *alayons* working on SWC, more non-*alayon* members adopting contour farming, more contoured farms, demand for farmer-to-farmer SWC trainings from neighbouring villages and municipalities, and diversification of *alayon* activities (establishment of tree parks, nurseries, income-generating activities).

However, it is felt that the most significant impacts have been:

o the local people's appreciation of their role in environmental protection and in responsible upland farming, and the initiatives that they are taking towards enacting this higher level of awareness

o researchers' recognition of their new roles as consultant and colleague to farmers, and the subtle institutional changes that may lead to policy formulations that are more relevant to PTD.

7

The Impact of Technology Adaptation on Productivity and Sustainability: MYRADA's Experiences in Southern India

ALOYSIUS P. FERNANDEZ

Introduction

MYRADA IS AN NGO which promotes sustainable rural development and institutional management systems for poverty reduction in Southern India. MYRADA's involvement with watershed management began in Gulbarga District, Karnataka State about nine years ago. The participative integrated development of watershed (PIDOW) project was a partnership of three: the government (through the Dry Land Development Board – DLDB), the Swiss Development Co-operation and MYRADA, with the primary objective of enabling local people to emerge as the fourth partner progressively to take on the management of the watershed resources. The programme aimed at increasing the productivity of natural resources on a sustainable and equitable basis. MYRADA's role was to ensure that the process of planning and implementation became a mechanism for the community to acquire the skills, confidence and organizational expertise to control and manage the watershed resources. The government was to provide technical and financial support. The initiatives in Gulbarga cover approximately 58 micro-watersheds, and are now being replicated and adapted in many other watersheds.

This chapter is divided into two sections. The first section examines the impact of MYRADA's approach to technology adaptation which uses indigenous technologies as a starting point. The first section demonstrates the importance of involving local people in the design of technology and the plans for catchment development. The second section examines the impact of this process on the productivity and sustainability of watersheds. Later in this book, in Chapter 22, we describe MYRADA's approach to credit, equity and the organization and sustainability of farmers' groups.

Differing perceptions of technology[1]

The need to manage water and soil has been the basis of traditional practices throughout the region; boulder and earthen bunds, silt traps, diversion

---

[1] The technologies dealt with in this section are restricted to physical 'treatment' structures, and not agricultural practices. While some vegetative measures are used by farmers for SWC, the focus here is on physical structures.

channels and interceptor structures of different materials including natural vegetation on fields have been constructed as far back as people can remember, and the process of innovation continues today (Box 7.1).

In most of MYRADA's programmes, these form the basis for the planning and technology development process. This strategy has worked well at most locations where watershed management programmes are supported solely by MYRADA. However, in Gulbarga the government (DLDB) is one of the major partners. Consequently there have been differences in perception about the role and effectiveness of indigenous technologies, with the DLDB promoting standard practices as regards treatment measures, the design of structures and the types of materials to be used.

Box 7.1:   The continuing process of technological innovation

In the upper reaches of the Limbu Thanda watershed, farmers perceive incidental soil erosion as an opportunity and have trapped the soil and silt in the wider areas in the valley by creating boulder dams. These structures are regularly maintained. The height of these dams is raised periodically as and when silt accumulates. These bunds are reported to improve the yields by 25 per cent.

Mr. Monu Naik, an enterprising farmer in Limbu Thanda built a boulder dam about 10 years ago. He kept raising the dam by one to two feet every year. As a result, he has been able to harvest 0.75 acre of excellent topsoil which supports a dry paddy crop during the main season and an additional crop of bengal gram using residual moisture. Even though the rain ceased in July, a good amount of moisture was seen below the surface. Encouraged by the impact of the indigenous technologies, he has built two more checks on the upstream side. In the last two years he has been able to harvest about 700 kg of paddy and about 75 kg of bengal gram. The productivity achieved is 2800 kg per hectare and is considerably higher than achieved on uplands.

Indigenous technology management has many features that distinguish it from the blueprint technical approaches followed by the government. Farmers tend to treat the lower catchment first and attempt to harness silt along waterways, creating a micro-environment where both soil and moisture are harvested to ensure a secure crop. In one watershed farmers actively discouraged soil conservation measures in the upper reaches, as they perceived that these measures would slow down the collection of silt in the traps lower down. They regarded soil erosion as an opportunity and not a problem. They were even willing to contribute in cash and kind (up to 60 per cent) to construct these silt traps. These silt deposits are often the only areas where farmers in drought-prone areas are ensured a crop. The silt harvesting also gives farmers an opportunity to cultivate paddy, which they prefer.

By contrast, the standard government approach is to treat the upper reaches first in order to control erosion and check water velocity, and to work from the ridge to the valley. This strategy takes into account the entire watershed, especially the upper and middle reaches where the poorer farmers mainly own land.

While both strategies make sense, a compromise is needed whereby the upper catchment is regenerated, with farmers allowed to take the initiative to harvest silt lower down. This is where the ability to co-operate, and the institutions required to support co-operation, assume importance.

Large areas on the upper reaches are on lands belonging to the Forest or Revenue Departments or are encroached upon; this is another reason why farmers hesitate to invest in these areas. The introduction of treatment measures has to cope with people's perceptions that tree planting on encroached land will encourage the Forest Department to claim them back. It is also necessary to negotiate interdepartmental agreements and establish rights for user groups which may conflict with traditional user rights or open access to the poor.

Management systems required on the upper reaches therefore are more difficult to develop and maintain and require a far more concerted effort on the part of the people, as well as the intervenors, than measures lower down – which are either on or bordering private lands over which the owner or neighbours exercise a degree of control. The degree of intervention required if people are to develop management systems appropriate to the upper reaches demands restructuring and policy changes at various levels, both within and outside the area.[2]

A significant result of MYRADA's approach towards co-operation has been the regeneration of fallow lands and wastelands owned by the Revenue Department in the upper and middle reaches. This has been a significant factor in conserving run-off and reducing soil erosion. Although this was not a traditional measure, the people responded spontaneously once the basis for co-operation was established and the titles to the land were clear.

MYRADA has also introduced the idea that indigenous measures already adopted by farmers should not only be respected but also compensated for. The government agreed, provided these treatment measures could be integrated with the overall plan. After a survey of these traditional measures in the Gulbarga Project area, the Soil and Water Conservation Department compensated farmers in 1989 – 90 for the conservation work they had done on their fields. This is in contrast to the prevalent practice of implementing a treatment plan even though it may require that

---

[2] See Chapter 22 for a description of the approach taken by MYRADA in the upper reaches.

existing structures are levelled or destroyed. This decision to pay farmers for their initiative raised the value of their conservation efforts in their eyes. They were more eager to discuss and follow up plans for the maintenance of these structures.

Participation in the design and type of SWC structures

The design of SWC structures raised a great deal of controversy between 'technical staff', namely engineers (both from government and MY-RADA), on the one hand, and staff involved with community organization on the other. The differences in design between what was proposed by people and what the technical staff considered to be technically sound related to boulder bunds and boulder checks on field boundaries. While people wanted boulder bunds, especially in fallow lands, to be raised in order to provide protection from cattle and to restrict access, the staff viewed these structures solely for erosion control, hence they designed them as low, rounded structures.

Where earthen field bunds were prone to be washed away at the lower boundary corners of fields, farmers constructed boulder bunds that allowed water to run through but conserved soil to a large extent. These boulder bunds tended to overhang the lower field belonging to the neighbour. This made them unstable, resulting in a few boulders toppling over occasionally. They were therefore judged by the engineers to be technically unsound. However, the farmers did not mind replacing a few boulders. They gave priority to good relations with neighbours, which would have been strained with a more stable bund that encroached on a neighbour's field.

This highlights differences in perception between experts and farmers. Experts felt that indigenous technologies were inadequate for achieving their single objective of erosion control and soil conservation. In most cases, however, indigenous technologies and technology adaptations carried out by the farmers aimed at achieving multiple objectives, such as concentration, harvesting, and conservation, as well as social factors.

Engineers working with both government and NGOs have been trained in the use of cement and concrete. However, these structures are expensive and have limited use in watershed management. Besides, wherever these structures were constructed in Gulbarga, the quality of the construction was below standard. This was noticed by local farmers. There is a major gap between the technical knowledge and capacity of technical staff to draw up blueprints of high quality, and the actual construction of structures, largely because these are implemented by contractors without adequate supervision, especially by local people (Box 7.2).

A joint evaluation carried out in Wadigera watershed in 1991 indicated that wrongly placed and designed gully checks, built without adequate consultation with farmers, led to flooding in some farmers' fields. This

Box 7.2:   Local supervision leads to sustainability

In Kadiri micro-watershed, the local self-help group (SHG)[3] decided to construct a weir and chose its location. It was designed by an engineer and constructed by a contractor. The SHG members supervised the laying of each stone and called on MYRADA engineers only when they suspected that the quality of materials used was poor. This weir has proved to be effective, resulting in large water storage. By comparison, a weir constructed solely by contractors lower down in the same watercourse is a failure.

resulted in fights within the local watershed management institution and eventually the farmers dismantled the checks. This shows the importance given by farmers to maintain institutional solidarity and minimization of conflicts in the design of technologies.

Types of SWC measures

The differing perceptions between experts and farmers on key objectives of conservation, concentration and harvesting continue to constrain the emergence of a participatory technology development process. The same is true for the materials chosen for the structures.

The government's policy provided only for earthen bunds. However, local people were more familiar with bunds made of boulders which were readily available in their fields. People already had a well established indigenous practice of using boulders for most physical structures. Boulder bunds are built from stones recovered from the land after each ploughing. These are also used to construct boundary bunds and are heaped in a corner for future use. Creating stable boulder bunds requires skills acquired by only a few farmers.

After negotiation between the Soil and Water Conservation Department and local people, people in each watershed were asked to work out norms of payment for the use of boulder bunds. The people responded immediately and worked out a system. As a result, boulder bunds were adopted in 1987 as part of the recommended practices of the Department.

Participation for increased cost-effectiveness

MYRADA's experience indicates that when people are involved in the process of planning and budgeting, unit costs are reduced. Costs tend to be

---

[3] See Chapter 22 for a full account of MYRADA's self-help groups.

highest when treatment plans are made by government or by external support organizations without the involvement of local people (Boxes 7.3 and 7.4).

Box 7.3: Conditions for the uptake of technology

There are many reasons why farmers do not take up conservation measures, prominent among which is the perception that the increase in productivity is not significant enough to reward the investment of cash and labour. Those measures that farmers perceive as having high potential, such as large silt traps, are too large to implement independently or to finance adequately. They are unlikely to be implemented unless there is intervention to motivate people to cooperate and to provide funds for these structures, partly as grants and partly as loans.

However, where farmers have participated effectively in exercises to plan and budget treatment of the watershed, and have been able to establish priorities among the various treatment measures, intervention has been more successful. Farmers involved in this way in Huthur, Talavadi and Bangarpet projects, for example, have also agreed to repay up to 50 per cent of the investment on their lands to the SHGs. Even farmers in drylands are willing to borrow up to 20 per cent of costs from SHGs to construct treatment measures, especially silt traps, where the combination of good soils and better moisture retention capacity assures them of a crop. These signs give MYRADA hope that, given the right mix of options, interventions, level of profit, linkages and management systems, farmers will increasingly opt to increase their investment of time and money on watershed management measures, thus increasing the basis for sustainability; if they have invested in treatment measures they have a stake in them.

There are two ways to mobilize people's involvement in, and contribution to, treatment measures:

○ The external institutions play a major role in budgeting, even if the planning process is participatory, and ask people to contribute towards costs as a pre-condition for support.

○ Communities play a major role in planning and budgeting.

In the first case the budgeted costs of structures are invariably higher than in the second case. People also tend to give lower contributions in both absolute and relative terms. People visualize their contribution as a cost and a pre-condition for investment. In the second case, when people are in control of planning and budgeting (with external support if requested), the budgeted costs tend to be lower and people's contribution is higher both in absolute and relative terms (Boxes 7.3 and 7.4). People view their contribution more as an investment in which they have a stake, which they will maintain, rather than as a cost. In this approach the community members also contribute to the common fund of the SHG.

Box 7.4: Comparing government and local budgets

In Kalamandargi mini-watershed, where MYRADA was the sole intervenor, plans and budgets for activities were drawn up by the people during a PRA exercise after a preparatory phase. People also supervised the implementation of the plan; they fine-tuned the wages due to each person on the basis of the distance each farmer had to transport boulders to construct bunds or other structures. MYRADA acted as a catalyst.

Comparing the unit cost budgeted by the community and the official government rates for the same structures and activities, the unit costs are lower by 23 to 64 per cent for community budgets. The community members also contributed 20 per cent of the total budgeted cost.

Economic, social and environmental impacts

Key impact indicators

Participatory watershed management programmes have the multiple objectives of productivity, sustainability and equity. The criteria for sustainability that have emerged over MYRADA's years of experience with watershed management are broader and more diversified than short-term increases in productivity. These are summarized in Box 7.5.

MYRADA's experiences show that the key objective is sustainability, especially where the poor and marginal groups are involved. Any sharp increase in productivity in the initial stages due to improved varieties of seeds and a large input of fertilizers at subsidized rates is not a significant achievement, unless it can be maintained over a longer period of time after the subsidies introduced by the project come to an end. Neither is increase in income and production of some large and well endowed farmers an indication of a successful watershed programme.

While the impact referred to in this chapter is restricted to increases in productivity of a few crops and biomass, impact should therefore also cover new skills acquired during the process and institutions of people that have emerged in the watershed. These are considered in Chapter 22 in this volume.

Box 7.5: Indicators for sustainability of watershed management programmes

Visible indicators:

○ marked and sustained improvement in productivity on fields, especially of small and marginal farmers

○ farmers and people noticing significant improvement in groundwater recharge and the understanding that this improvement is linked to improved management of the watershed surface

○ maintenance of structures (silt traps, gully plugs, stone and earthen bunds) and vegetative barriers

○ marked improvement in resilience of crops to long dry spells

○ increased investment for protective irrigation especially through shallow ponds along drainage systems

○ continuous improvement in management and regeneration of all lands in the watershed, including private fallows, and of all types of government and public lands with the multiple objectives of decreasing erosion, managing surface water effectively and increasing biomass for fuel, fodder, fibre, fertilizers and raw materials for cottage industries.

Skills and Institutions:

○ adequate skills to construct and maintain all the structures required to control or trap soil and water without external help

○ gradual extension of effective management by the People's Watershed Associations over all lands in the watershed, including communal lands, private fallow lands and private cultivated lands

○ ability of farmers to finance further treatment of the watershed and the repair of existing structures from their own group credit funds

○ ability of people's watershed institutions to resolve conflict among different groups in the watershed, and to respond to the needs of those groups whose interests are affected by watershed treatment. These include those farmers who are cultivating lands on upper reaches or steep slopes but which need to be protected, whose grazing areas are being affected by regeneration measures and the landless who have to cope with new management measures that may obstruct their hitherto free access to watershed resources

○ recognition by external support organizations that the people's watershed association is in control of all watershed activities and that no plans can be imposed or funds and services provided without its involvement at every stage of the process, from planning through implementation.

Impact on crop productivity and income

Wadigera micro-watershed in Gulbarga district was selected for the impact analysis. Wadigera was one of the first micro-watersheds in Gulbarga, with the programme beginning in 1987. By 1993 most external support was withdrawn. However, MYRADA staff continue to visit the self-help groups in the area and audit them periodically. Wadigera, being an early intervention, did suffer from the lack of experience in the process used for formation of people's institutions to manage and sustain the resources of a micro-watershed.

This section aims to assess the increases in farm productivity with regard to cereals, oilseeds, cash crops and fodder in Wadigera micro-watershed. The sources of information include joint appraisals by government and MYRADA while planning the programme, participatory appraisals with communities and self-help groups, a participatory joint evaluation of the programme in 1991 and data from secondary sources.

The process of watershed development and the adoption of hybrids

Many professionals hold the view that farmers will willingly accept the introduction of hybrids; all that is required is a demonstration. This may be true in certain areas where water availability is assured and both forward and backward linkages, such as marketing services, necessary inputs, credit, technology and skills, are established. However, it is not true for many parts of the country, including Wadigera. The key constraints to the introduction and spread of hybrids in Wadigera before 1987 included vulnerability of hybrid crops to long dry spells, lack of ready access to cash and credit for purchase of inputs, poor quality of hybrid seeds, poor transport and communication and lack of confidence that support by extension services would be effective and timely. Many of these constraints have been overcome by treatment and management measures introduced in the process of watershed development. But they have also been overcome by the whole nature of support given to farmers by the project.

The hybrids and other crops became less vulnerable to long dry spells as soil and water conservation measures were undertaken by farmers. The self-help groups (SHGs) in Wadigera built up a village common fund of Rupees 2.5 million, from which the members could draw loans for any purpose. This increased the amount of credit used to procure agricultural inputs, enabling farmers to use hybrid varieties. Regular monitoring by government officials and MYRADA also ensured a degree of standardization in seed quality. Transport and communication were improved by broadening several connecting roads with the help of community members doing *shramdaan* (voluntary labour) as a part of the watershed management programme. The SHGs developed linkages with reputable seed companies and banks. However, farmers continued to face problems of low prices for agricultural products just after the harvest, indicating the need to develop strategies for marketing and storage.

The regular visits of agricultural staff and the presence of MYRADA field staff living in the watershed have helped to increase the farmers' confidence in external institutions. They are confident that the external agencies will not 'touch and vanish' (as the Training & Visit – T&V – system is often referred to) but will remain in the area and can be called upon for support if required. During the joint evaluation of 1991, people testified that before the project, 'Government programmes were sporadic and not continuous, but now because of close relationship with MYRADA and government, farmers get constant guidance . . . and timely inputs'.

Since the start of the project farmers have switched to hybrid varieties of sorghum, groundnut and redgram, with resulting significant increases in productivity. For example, the productivity of hybrid sorghum was double that of local varieties in 1993–94. However, conservation measures have also caused the productivity of local varieties to increase.

The total increase in income due to the introduction of hybrids of sorghum, groundnut and redgram in 1993–94 as compared to 1987 for the entire Wadigera micro-watershed was Rupees 326 000.

Changes in cropping patterns and productivity

The areas under sugarcane and sunflower have increased significantly in the Wadigera micro-watershed.

Sugarcane. Sugarcane is not a new crop in Wadigera. However, before 1987 there was only enough water to cultivate 12 acres at the bottom of the valley. Significant changes in water availability first occurred in the lower part of the valley, and in 1993–94, 30 acres were bought under sugarcane irrigated by seven open wells. The amount of water required to irrigate one acre of sugarcane is about four to six million litres (including rainfall), spread over four irrigations. It is therefore reasonable to state that the treatment measures did have an impact on the recharge of the wells. The increased area under sugarcane was also influenced by better prices and marketing facilities in 1993.

Sunflower. Sunflower is a new crop that was introduced after 1987 because of its higher income potential compared with hybrid sorghum. The farmers were willing to take the risk because of the better moisture-holding capacity of soils after treatment.

In the 1993–94 *Kharif* season, 13.5 acres were under high-yielding varieties of sunflower. The average yield was reported to be 700kg per acre resulting in a total production of 9450kg. The net income from sunflower production was Rupees 108 675. As sunflower mainly replaced the local sorghum, this yielded an additional income for the watershed of Rupees 86 400.

Cost-effectiveness of investments made

The treatment works in Wadigera were undertaken by the Soil and Water Conservation Department. The total investment made by the government and MYRADA in the construction of structures was Rupees 612 519. Approximately Rupees 280 000, given as a grant for agricultural inputs, was converted into a revolving credit fund by the SHGs and hence is not considered here. This investment has led to a total increase in annual income from agriculture to Rupees 544 025. This indicates that the investments made in watershed management have been cost effective.

Farmers' perceptions of the impact of treatment measures on dryland crops

The study indicates that crops in the middle reaches and unirrigated crops even lower down in the valley are coping much better with stress conditions since treatment measures were undertaken. During a participatory evaluation exercise conducted in Kalmandargi micro-watershed, the farmers cultivating the middle and lower reaches indicated that the moisture-holding capacity during long dry spells had increased. A participatory exercise conducted in Ningchennala micro-watershed early in 1994 also indicated an increase in the productivity of dryland crops for both local and hybrid varieties. The reported increase in dryland crop productivity in Ningchennala in 1993 compared to 1990 is significant, averaging 100 per cent. The highest increases after treatment were recorded for sorghum (*jowar*) crops grown in red loamy soils of the uplands and in the black soils of the middle reaches.

While there is adequate evidence to indicate that the productivity of hybrids has increased, a significant increase in the productivity of local varieties on drylands is also noticeable. But the cause-effect relationship between increased production and the soil and water management measures is still debated. It is accepted by all farmers that there is an increase in the recharge of wells. The shift to new crops such as sugarcane, which require more water, also indicates a positive impact. The rate of groundwater recharge has also improved, allowing farmers to draw water for longer periods. Several wells that previously were dried up by December are now recharged till April. This change has occurred mainly in the lower reaches where the impact of water conservation measures is most likely to be experienced in a visible and measurable manner. The impact on fields between the ridge and valley is more difficult to assess and the change is also not so dramatic. The results are related to the ability of crops to withstand water stress and can be assessed only in comparison with similar situations in the same year. While this is possible, it makes it difficult to isolate the impact of treatment measures on dryland crop production. However, farmers claim repeatedly that treatment measures have had an impact on dryland crops.

Increase in fodder productivity

Although many watershed projects tend to focus on increases in agricultural productivity, people in drought-prone areas also give priority to increases in fodder and fuel production, especially during the first few years. Moreover, increases in fodder and fuel are significant in the short run and correspond to people's expectations of visible and tangible benefits. The increase in fodder and fuel production in Wadigera (and in other watersheds in Gulbarga) accrue mainly on protected plots on private fallow lands where the titles are clear. The watershed groups enter into an agreement with the landowners who are absent or employed elsewhere, or give low priority to cultivating that piece of land in comparison to their other fields. On regeneration, these protected plots not only contribute to soil and water management in the watershed, but also allow traditional trees and grasses to grow, flower, seed and spread.

A study was conducted in three micro-watersheds in Gulbarga project in May 1994, the driest part of the year, to assess the quantity of grass production and regeneration. The monsoon rainfall had also failed in that year. Three sample plots of 5m × 5m (25 sq.m.) were selected in each protected area and all these plots represented average growth. All the grass in the sample plots was cut and weighed to determine fodder yields.

An analysis of data collected from Wadigera and Maramanchi Thanda micro-watersheds indicates that the highest yields of fodder are from lands taken on agreement by self-help groups (an extract is shown in Table 7.1). In these cases, the SHG was entirely free to enter into an agreement about a particular plot. There was no pressure from the NGO or other intervenors on the grounds that regeneration of a particular plot is needed as part of the strategy to manage the watershed. The study indicates that the SHGs take the initiative to enter into agreements when:

○ the title is clear
○ the plot is close to the village
○ the project agrees to invest in the boulder wall
○ the soils are reasonably good
○ the owner has agreed not to graze his animals.

The main motivating factors are therefore productivity, easy access to the resource and control of the asset and produce.

Table 7.1   The effect of management structure on fodder production

Area	4 ha	4.86 ha (1989)
Location	Top of slope	Middle
Ownership status	Private land	Private land
Present management	Managed by the owner	Managed by self-help group
Degree of protection	Protected by boulder wall built by farmer	Fully protected by boulder wall
Saplings introduced	No planting, only regeneration	Few species introduced; mainly regeneration; ave. no. trees/ha = 2542
Grasses introduced	Nil	*Hamata scabra*
Grazing	Partly allowed – his animals	Not allowed
Division of produce	All to farmer	30% Sangha 70% owner
Grass harvested	1994: 60kg/ha	1994: 4560 kg/ha. Cut and distributed locally.

Farmers convert their private lands to protected areas because they own better agricultural lands elsewhere and have neglected these lands. They also expect the project to invest in protective measures. They do not manage these protected areas as well as the SHGs since they are the only beneficiaries and prefer to graze their cattle rather than allow grasses to regenerate. They find it difficult to cut grasses for fodder. The protective walls enable them to keep other cattle out and establish their boundaries.

The increased fodder availability in Wadigera has encouraged farmers to increase the number of milch animals. The men's SHG has given 18 loans for buffaloes and the women's SHG 10 loans during the one-and-a-half years. Milk supplied by Wadigera Milk Co-operative Society to the Karnataka Milk Federation (KMF) in 1992 was 14 965 litres, which increased to 17 885 litres in 1993. The total income earned by farmers from supplying milk to the Federation was about Rupees 107 310.

Impact on water availability and recharge

There are seven open wells in the lower reaches. As was mentioned above, before 1987 these wells provided adequate water for only 12 acres of sugarcane. Since 1987 there has been no year in which rainfall has been significantly above the average. Yet, the seven wells were able to irrigate 30 acres of sugarcane in 1993. This change was visible in 1991 when people indicated to the joint evaluation team that 'there was an improvement in sub-

87

soil water resulting in two agricultural crops' in the valley. They also linked the conservation measures to this increase in water availability. The farmers pointed out in 1991 'The introduction of boulder bunds, earthen bunds, nala bunds, trenches, small dams have increased the ground water level. Now the water is available also after January and till the rainy season'. They also indicated that the wells dried up before the construction of water conservation structures.

A distinction should be made between perceptions of farmers owning land in the upper, middle and lower reaches. The participatory evaluation exercises indicated that farmers with lands at the valley bottom realize the cause-effect relationship between treatment measures and water recharge in wells. However, those who cultivate fields in the middle and upper reaches do not yet see this connection. They tend to accord high priority to irrigation, and consequently to wells as sources of food security and income. There are no open wells in the middle and upper reaches, but there is a growing interest among these farmers to sink shallow open wells along the drainage line since a few old wells which had dried out are now recharged.

Farmers cultivating the middle reaches have reported that, after treatment, crops are able to withstand dry spells of up to three weeks, whereas previously acute stress situations were evident after a dry spell of 10 days. Farmers feel that the impact in terms of reduction in moisture stress for crops is not as dramatic as the recharge in wells (Box 7.6)

Impact on land prices

In Ningchennala micro-watershed the land prices have increased by 20 to 25 per cent in all areas, except in black soils in the uplands where the price increase is about 33 per cent. This is one of the very few watersheds where black soils of depths of up to 12 inches are found on the upper reaches. Farmers perceive that these black soils fetch higher prices as they are suitable for a wide variety of crops, and outputs of all crops can be increased with adequate water conservation measures. Sunflower, a new crop, which fetches a good price, is also grown on these soils. In contrast, land prices have increased by only 10 per cent in the untreated watersheds.

Conclusion

In conclusion, the impact analysis of the technology adaptation process indicates that farmers are still using and adapting a range of indigenous technologies, evolved over a long period of experimentation. From their perspective, incidental soil erosion is an opportunity and not a problem. They tend to treat the lower catchment first and focus on silt harvesting through silt traps. This is in contrast to standard technical packages which

```
┌─────────────────────────────────────────────────────────────┐
│                                                               │
│  Box 7.6:   Ground water improvement in Ningchennala micro-  │
│             watershed                                         │
│                                                               │
│  Shri Lavappa is the waterman who operates the pump attached  │
│  to the drinking water well. He reports that in 1990–91 he    │
│  could operate the pump for only one hour per day during the  │
│  summer months. However, in 1993 he was able to operate the   │
│  pump for one hour in the morning and for half an hour in the │
│  evening. Another well in front of the MYRADA sector office   │
│  ran dry during the summer but in 1993 water was available    │
│  throughout the year, even though there was no increase in    │
│  the rainfall.                                                │
│                                                               │
│  Many farmers have reported improvements in ground water re-  │
│  charge. Rathnappa has an open well in the middle reaches     │
│  which was dry in 1990. He has reported water availability in │
│  1993 in the well and has decided to remove accumulated silt  │
│  from the well. Bhimsha's well is located in the lower        │
│  reaches and had limited water in 1990. In 1993, he was able  │
│  to pump water for one hour daily and has cultivated one acre │
│  of vegetables. Manohar's well is located in the lower        │
│  reaches. It used to provide protective irrigation in 1991    │
│  but could be used for cultivating one acre of wheat in 1993. │
│  On seeing the improvement in his neighbours' wells,          │
│  Gundappa decided to dig an open well along the *nala* in     │
│  1994.                                                        │
│                                                               │
└─────────────────────────────────────────────────────────────┘
```

focus on treatment of upper reaches that require a high level of community action and co-operation. The farmers' approach to soil conservation aims to achieve the multiple objectives of concentration, harvesting and protection, as well as social cohesion. On the other hand, technical professionals had the limited objectives of erosion control. These differing perceptions inhibit the emergence of a participatory technology development process.

Where these issues have been resolved, and people are enabled to participate more fully, there have been multiple impacts on productivity and sustainability. There has been a reduction in moisture stress for crops and an increase in ground water recharge, leading to new investments in wells and improvements in existing wells. These improvements in the condition of the natural resources, combined with the conditions created by stable and committed external support have allowed an increased investment in higher-yielding hybrid varieties. In turn, this has led to productivity increases of up to 100 per cent. These increases have been matched by increases in fodder and biomass productivity on group managed lands. The costs of watershed management programmes were also shown to decrease significantly when the responsibilities of planning and budgeting were delegated to local people.

8

Participatory Upland Agro-ecosystem Management in Bicol, The Philippines

JIT P. BHUKTAN, CARLOS S. BASILIO, SCOTT I. KILLOUGH, MA. FRANCIA L. DE LOS REYES, SAMUEL C. OPERIO and RICO V. LOCABA[1]

Introduction

OVER THE YEARS, the International Institute of Rural Reconstruction (IIRR) has been testing and implementing – in partnership with local people – sustainable agriculture in upland and lowland communities under its regenerative agriculture programme. Although there has been some success, low farm productivity and poverty continued to be problems in upland villages.

In 1986, with support from World Neighbors and the Mag-Uugmad Foundation, IIRR started the Upland Farm Management Project (UFMP) in Sto. Domingo village of Albay Province, the Philippines. The UFMP set out to build sustainable, regenerative and ecologically sound farming systems: to help farm households diversify their sources of farm income: increase farm production and income; and increase the availability of fuelwood and fodder. The underlying intention was to use participatory approaches to test whether agricultural practices can rehabilitate upland agricultural environments.

Sto. Domingo is a small municipality in Albay lying at the foot of Mayon volcano. It is a poor area characterized by widespread malnutrition and unemployment. The villages have diverse ecological conditions, and an altitude ranging from 10 to 240 metres. The 448 upland households in the project area cultivate 521ha, and over 50 per cent of them are landless. These farmers are forced into insecure land tenure agreements, and also rely on fishing and wage labour. There are large farms owned by absentee or non-resident landowners.

The strategy of the Upland Farm Management Project

Building on an earlier project that had emphasized social organization, the UFMP intended that farmers should play a central role in technology

[1] The authors acknowledge the contributions of a wide range of individuals and institutions in the conduct and reporting of this impact study. We are grateful to IIED; World Neighbors; Ford Foundation – Philippines; German Agro-Action; and USAID, all of whom provided partial financial support for the work described here; Julian Gonsalves; IIRR-AFO at Sto. Domingo and its staff; Angie Ibus; and the leaders and people of Salvacion, Alimsog and San Andres-Santiago; Girlie Belen, Jovy Solano, Edna Millete, and Lhai Kasala.

testing, adaptation and extension. Five farmers were initially selected in Salvacion village on the basis of their ability to organize groups; capability and willingness to share the technologies with fellow farmers; good reputation in the village; honesty; capacity to accept criticism; and capacity to test and disseminate technologies. Their own farms served as demonstration sites.

These five farmers formed a *hunglunan* group (HG) or self-help workgroup. The group was trained in a series of upland farming technologies, with emphasis on the ecological effects of upland farming and the need for soil and water conservation. This original group of farmers was further trained in community organizing, extension and training other farmers. Each then formed extended HGs in their respective villages and acted as technical supervisors or leaders.

The original farmers were then designated as farmer-technicians (FTs) and given responsibility to provide technical guidance and assistance to farmer co-operators (FCs). The smooth functioning of the HGs as self-help groups minimized labour costs and saved farmer-cooperators' time. From the pilot site in Barangay Salvacion, the project was later extended to six more villages – Banao, Buhatan, Alimsog, Lower San Roque, Bagong San Roque and San Andres.

Initially, sloping agricultural land technology (SALT) was introduced, emphasizing soil and water conservation. Later, the concept of integrated farming was incorporated. This consists of livestock farming, soil fertility management, cropping systems, woodlot and orchard farming, and market/backyard gardening. Dissemination of these alternative technologies to farmers through farmer-to-farmer extension and other participatory approaches gradually helped them to spread through the communities.

Participatory planning

Planning is done in group meetings during the evenings, when farmers are free. At these meetings farmers' problems are identified and discussed. The most common causes of poor yield and low farm income are first identified. Then the project staff and/or FTs introduce the available soil and water conservation (SWC) technologies one at a time. Cross-visits are arranged for farmers to see some FTs' farms in nearby villages.

On these visits, FTs discuss the advantages and disadvantages of the technologies and answer all the visiting farmers' questions. FTs usually explain the yield, soil conditions, type of crops, before and after adoption. The visiting farmers then return to their own village for reflection. Then the FT or project staff ask one of them to volunteer in establishing a sample farm using the SWC structures. The participants and other farmers help to establish the farm. An A-frame is constructed from local materials, and calibrated by the FT. Contour canals, drainage canals, soil traps and check dams are constructed and hedgerow seeds and cuttings sown. Usually 10–20 people participate, depending upon soil hardness, presence of stones or deep-rooted weeds and steepness of the slope. After completing the sample farm, a gathering is convened to reflect on these practical experiences.

The self-help groups

To form their own *hunglunan* group, farmers encourage their friends and relatives to join. The group farmer-leader is selected or elected, depending upon the situation. The group makes its own rules and regulations. FTs often tell them about other groups and some advantages and disadvantages of their practices, but the group is responsible for deciding its own rules. They make their group plan jointly, and then develop individual farm plans.

The *hunglunan* work schedule for farm work is rotated among the members' farms. The group works on one of the member's farms once or twice a week, depending on their agreed schedule. IIRR provides P 500.00 in revolving funds to each of the HGs as start-up capital to procure farming tools and implements. In every HG activity, each member contributed P 1.00. The funds were later deposited in a bank to be used for joint projects or for meeting emergency needs of the members.

The role of IIRR

During monthly meetings, the FTs reported their progress and problems, and IIRR helped to find solutions using participatory group approaches. IIRR, with the help of the FTs, continually contacted new farmers in the villages and encouraged them to adopt SWC technologies and form groups. IIRR also organized cross-visits of participating farmers to boost their morale and promote them to FTs; providing them with opportunities for further improvement of their farm and farming practices. IIRR also conducted refresher and on-the-job training for FTs – on facilitation, presentation and organizational skills. FTs also convened monthly HG meetings in each village that were attended by IIRR staff and in which experiences, progress and problems were shared.

Methods for impact study

Although the UFMP has been regularly monitored, and the farm level activities are periodically evaluated by farmers themselves, the actual impacts of the project both at the farm and community level have not yet been studied. A participatory impact study of the project was conducted to examine changes using the indicators proposed by IIED (see Chapter 2).

Selection of villages and field team

A joint planning meeting of farmers and researchers selected three *barangays* (villages): Salvacion, an entirely upland area; San Andres for upland with lowland rice farming options; and Alimsog with upland farming and sea fishing options. These also had the most farmer co-operators, and represented the range of environmental, agricultural and cultural variations found in the area.

The study team was composed of researchers with social science, development management, environmental science, soil science, participatory research, animal science, forestry and agribusiness experience. There were also two farmer technicians and two or three farmer co-operators in each of the three villages studied.

Data gathering methods

During two joint planning workshops the research team, groups of farmer leaders and FTs designed the impact study as a participatory exercise to capture the project's impacts from the farmers' perspectives. The workshop participants agreed to combine the following methods:

o *PRA methods* were used for preparing maps and transects, defining the agroecology of the area, reconstructing locally-important historical events, analysing sources of income of farm households (with matrix scorings), inventorying the local agricultural components, and recording the process through which the project expanded in the villages.

o *Key informant panels*, consisting of between five and nine men and women, were organized in the evenings of the field study. A host of general information including changing social, economic, technological and environmental conditions was gathered and verified.

o *Focus group workshop*, consisting of between three and five farmers, discussed topics such as the economics of upland farming, changes taking place in the local forestry and water sources, local indicators for reduction in soil erosion and water losses, and local cropping patterns.

o *Individual observations and reflections* were made by study team members every day, and reflected in the evening. The important findings were used for setting the agendas for the focused group workshops and key informant panels, as well as in village sharing and reflection sessions.

o *General interviews* were conducted with one-third of all FCs, selected according to number of years of participation, gender, farm types, and extent of technology used. From among the project non-participants, those smallholder upland farmers who were engaged in upland farming since before the start of the project were also selected.

o *In-depth interviews:* eight highly experienced FCs were interviewed in detail to gather information about the methodologies used in the project.

○ *Village sharing and reflection sessions:* the findings of the field studies were shared with local people in a village-wide assembly. This gave back the information to the local people, informed them about the research findings, and so helped to validate the information.

Key impacts of the upland project

A. Changes in productivity

Changes in crop yield

Farmers consistently indicated that the overall crop yields of the contour farming households had increased. In addition, the cost of production had decreased, and farm net income increased. But the crop yields were not stable from year to year, in some years actually falling (Table 8.1).

There was a variable rate of increase in yield of the major upland crops such as maize, upland rice, peanut, sweet potato and cassava. The average yield of maize increased from 1.23 tonnes/ha in 1985 to 2.23 tonnes/ha in 1993. The average annual rate of change in maize yield was 4.2 per cent. The average yield of upland rice increased from 1251kg/ha in 1985 to 2110 kg/ha in 1993, an average annual rate of change of 7.63 per cent. The average yield of peanut increased from 27 to 31 cans/ha in 1993, an annual rate of increase of 1.65 per cent. The average yield of sweet potato grew from 730 to 1210 cans/ha, and for cassava from 680 to 1516 cans/ha.

Economic value of yield increases

The PRA time line data and the price change data from the key informant panels showed that prices of farm products increased over time. This indicated that the economic value of farm products was also increasing. The price of upland rice increased from P 5.00/kg in 1985 to P 13.50/kg in 1994, that of sweet potato from P 20/can to P 50/can, and that of peanut from

Table 8.1:   Average yields of crops in UFMP sites, Sto. Domingo, Albay

Crop	1985–86	1988–1990	1991–93	9 year average
Maize (kg/ha)	1251	1520	2110	1625
Upland rice (kg/ha)	743	945	1220	985
Peanut (can/ha)	27	31	33	31
Sweet potato (can/ha)	730	1020	1210	1010
Cassava (can/ha)	680	nd	1516	nd

1 can = 22–25kg

P 60/can to P 120/can. Two cases of farmer-adopters, using the technology for about six years, are presented in Box 8.1 to illustrate the changes in crop yield and their economic values.

Box 8.1:   Two case-studies of farmer adopters

Rosauro Baile's case (Salvacion, Sto. Domingo)

Rosauro practised monocropping for 16 years using chemical fertilizers intensively. He noticed declining soil productivity over the years due to severe soil erosion. More rocks surfaced on his land, making it more difficult to cultivate. He harvested about 350kg of maize from his 0.25ha farm (equal to 1400kg/ha). Labour costs in land preparation were P 180 (6 person-days at P 30/day). Planting and harvesting costs were P 150, and cost of seeds and fertilizers P 730. Rosauro earned a net income of P 320 at P 3/kg of corn.

In 1988, Rosauro established soil and water conservation structures in his farm and began to practise multiple cropping. The next year, he harvested 500kg of maize from 0.25ha (2000kg/ha). His fertilizer inputs decreased from 100kgs to 50kgs (200kg/ha). After four years, with the inclusion of the livestock component in his farm, maize yields have increased to 800kg (3200kg/ha). He now applies eight sacks of goat manure to the maize farm.

Demetrio Ballares' case (Bical, Salvacion, Sto. Domingo)

In 1986 Demet harvested 530kg of maize from his one hectare upland farm. In 1987, he joined a *hunglunan* group, and began to use sloping agricultural land technology and integrated farming. He planted maize, upland rice and peanut on his contour farm by allocating one-third of the area to each crop. He harvested 265kg of maize (795kg/ha), 350kg of upland rice (1050kgs/ha) and five cans of peanut (15 cans/ha).

In 1992, drought hit badly, and his rice yield decreased to 250kg for 1/3ha, but his maize yield increased slightly to 400kg (1200kg/ha). In 1993, Demet harvested 328kg of maize and 650kg of upland rice.

Changes in input use and costs

In general, farmers have been cutting their conventional input use and increasing their use of biological products. But despite the reduced use of external inputs, farmers were incurring higher input costs. The price of fertilizers (up from P 3 to P 7 per kg), pesticides (up 200–400 per cent), seeds, wage labour, and animal power all have increased since the mid-1980s. These were the main reasons why the overall cost of production still increased despite farmers' efforts in using low external inputs.

But farmers perceived that the cost of crop production was decreasing due to application of the UFM technologies. They indicated that after using contour farming, soils had become soft and easier to till. Many had stopped using hired labour and *carabaos* (water buffaloes). This work was now done by household members themselves. They did not, however, put a monetary value on their own labour.

Similarly, they put considerable efforts into growing hedgerows, pruning them and incorporating the residue into soil or spreading it over the land. They also put much time into preparing biopesticides, though again they did not consider the monetary value of all this work to be significant.

Changes in Land Prices

Land prices increased considerably in the project area. Land with established SWC structures commanded a remarkably higher price compared with similar land without structures. The price of non-contoured steep slope land increased from P 2500/ha to P 15 000/ha; and the price of similar land with contours increased from P 5000/ha in 1985 to P 30 000/ha in 1994. The price of the relatively flat non-contoured land increased from P 15 000/ha to P 40 000/ha, whereas the similar contoured land increased from P 30 000/ha in 1985 to P 75 000/ha in 1994 (Table 8.2). The higher price for contoured farmland was due to the improved soil fertility, higher crop productivity and lower risk of crop failure.

The rise in land price, especially in the uplands, had both advantages and disadvantages. It was tempting for landowners to sell the land and migrate elsewhere. Others had started gaining the status of credit-worthiness in the local credit market. Those who had earlier wanted to migrate due to hardship were now finding it worth staying.

Table 8.2: Changes in prices of different land types, 1985–94

Land types	Price in 1985 (thousand Peso/ha)	Price in 1994 (thousand Peso/ha)
Uplands: undulating slope		
non-contoured	15	40
contoured	30	75
Uplands: mild slope		
non-contoured	8	20
contoured	15	45
Uplands: steep slope		
non-contoured	2.5	15
contoured	5	30
Lowlands		
Irrigated	20	100
Non-irrigated	18	80

However, tenant operators were now facing increased uncertainty and risk. Landowners who had initially encouraged their tenants to establish contour farms now found the land more attractive. Many absentee land owners had started to make plans to eject them. So far they have already ejected at least 10 tenant FCs using various means, including law suits. These cases have still been strong dissuading factors for non-adoption of UFM technology by tenant farmers, who represent about 50 per cent of the local population and are mostly engaged in upland farming.

B. Changes in resource degradation

Changes in resource-conserving practices

After one year of project operation in 1986, the area covered by five households with SWC structures was 1.62ha, together with 1570m of contour canals, 100m of drainage canals, 21 checkdams and 166 soil traps. There were 1570m of hedgerows (Table 8.3). As of June 1994, there were 143 households with 78ha of contoured farms. There were 13 170 metres of contour canals, 3453m of drainage canals, 130 checkdams and 217 soil traps. The FCs found over the years that it was unnecessary to maintain contour canals as their farmlands levelled and soils were soft enough to absorb water, hence the decline in the number of contour canals, checkdams and soil traps from 1990 to 1994.

Changes in resource-conserving practices in common lands

Resource conservation on common lands was not an objective of the project. Farmers were, however, concerned about the degradation of natural resources in the surrounding hills. The part-time fishermen were concerned about increasing floods in rivers entering the Albay Gulf that adversely affected fish populations, especially if flood waters carried pesticides. The lowland farmers were primarily worried about landslides affecting their paddies.

Table 8.3: Changes in the number of soil and water conservation structures

Soil and water conservation structures	1986	1990	1994
Contour canals (km)	1.57	21.2	13.2
Drainage canals (km)	0.1	3.1	3.5
Check dams (no.)	21	212	130
Soil traps (no.)	166	298	217
Hedgerows (km)	1.57	11.7	37.5

Those residing and farming in the uplands were already facing increasing landslides and scarcity of fuelwood, increasing distance of pasture, decreasing availability of water in the rivers, creeks and springs for both humans and animals. The poor, however, could do nothing about rich people who were cutting trees in the hills without replanting. By 1984, most of the hilly lands owned by absentee landowners were covered with cogon grasses.

Some of the early *hunglunan* groups therefore decided to motivate the tenants in such areas, who were engaged in shifting farming, to join the project. The FCs gave free tree seedlings to several hill-dwellers. Later several of these farmers came to the FCs to buy multi-purpose tree species.

Some leading FCs in almost every project village collaborated with local government officials and school teachers for tree planting along village roads, around the school compound and in other public places. In Alimsog village, the FCs put tree barriers along both sides of a flooding river. Villagers were now able to supplement their income by supplying an increasing quantity of fuelwood and banana packing materials to nearby urban areas.

Retained ecosystem functions

Farmers reported that water discharge from rivers, streams, creeks and natural springs was still less than that of 15 to 20 years ago. However, the rate of decrease had slowed since early 1990s. Flooding in the local creeks had lessened somewhat. Landslides in the nearby hills had decreased. According to participating farmers, this was indicated by the clear water in the creeks in contrast to former muddy water.

In two communities (Alimsog and Bicol), the farmers reported that in the last two years some of the almost dried-up natural springs have started to discharge water. Other farmers observed that more birds were found in the nearby forest compared to 10 to 15 years ago and that this happened with the increase in trees.

Contribution of farmers to technology adaptation and multiplication

Since farmers were encouraged by FTs to use the available technologies according to their own land conditions, every farm was established somewhat differently. This happened despite farmers using almost the same components of the technologies (Figure 8.1). Farmers made many modifications over the years – both in the SWC structures and crop organization patterns (Box 8.2). For example, some of the structures, such as contour canals, soil traps and check dams were removed after the land became levelled, hedgerows established and matured, and woodlots at the upper parts and boundaries had grown up. Some of the inanimate structures were replaced by living plants.

Box 8.2:   A selection of farmer adaptations and innovations

o One farmer in San Andres planted pineapple across the non-contoured slope and along the contour. He found that pineapple planted along the contour grew faster with vigorous growth and was deep green in colour, and bore fruits faster and bigger than on the non-contoured slope. From then on, he planted pineapple only along the contour.

o Two farmers, Elias and Enteng, modified their soil traps. Elias made shallow soil traps but within one year, he realized that too much soil was deposited during heavy rains, so he increased the depth of his traps. Enteng, on the other hand, initially made deeper soil traps to reduce the frequency of collecting eroded soil. However, over the years, soil deposits decreased anyway.

o It is common for farmers to plant a small quantity of new seeds in the first year (such as ginger, corn, upland rice, onion); then to observe their growth rate, plant type and especially yields. Those that grow well with higher yields were then grown on a bigger area in the next season/year and this area gradually increased over time.

o One farmer planted a few cacao plants in the main strip of his contour farm and applied compost. Within six months, the cacao plants grew much faster and vigorously. He then tried a few cacao plants as a hedgerow together with napier grass. Cacao thrived well but napier suffered due to shade. So, he maintained only one strip for cacao and none in hedgerows.

o One farmer brought 10 grains of local maize from a neighbouring province. The variety had much better yields than the previous varieties he planted. He used all the grains from this crop as seed material in the next year. He has been growing this variety since without applying chemical fertilizers.

o Another farmer, who used to grow maize and upland rice with chemical fertilizers and pesticides, changed when a farmer from a distant village informed him that both of these crops could be grown without fertilizers. He planted maize in January by incorporating madre de cacao (*Gliricidia sepium*) and ipil-ipil (*Leucaena leucocephala*) leaves in the soil. The yield was slightly less than previously, but he gained a higher net income. He then tried the same practice in upland rice in the same field. There was no reduction in yield. From then on, he planted both crops without using fertilizers.

o In maize fields, one farmer applied leaves of madre de cacao, ipil-ipil, flamengia (*Flemingia macrophylla*) and rensonii (*Desmodium* sp.) in three or four maize rows. Maize plants in soils applied with madre de cacao and ipil-ipil grew vigorously, with deep green leaves and thick stalks bearing full and uniform grains in large ears. But the effects of flamengia and rensonii were not good. From then on, he applied madre de cacao and ipil-ipil as green manures, even in hybrid corn. He said that he was able to reduce chemical fertilizer use and yet harvest the same yield as other hybrid corn farmers.

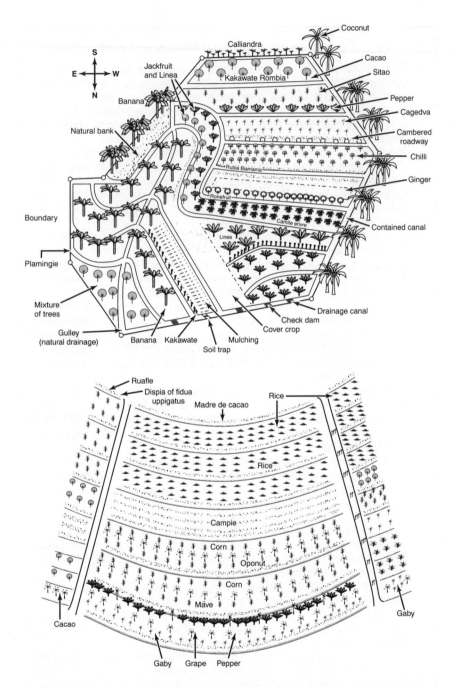

Figure 8.1: (and opposite) Every farm has its own signature: four of the upland farms treated with soil and water conservation and integrated farming system technologies

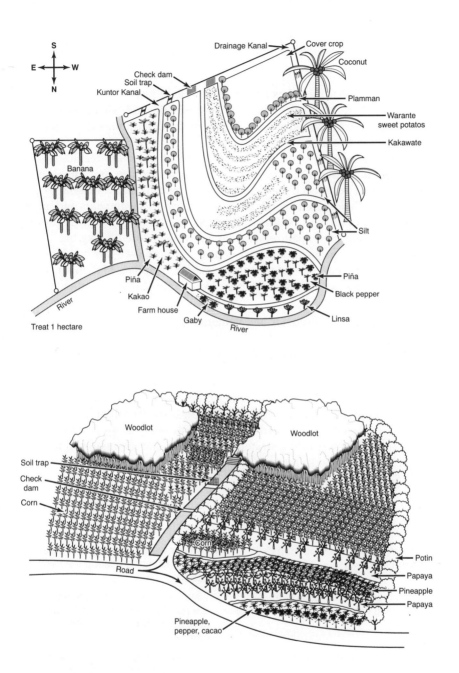

Decrease in resource-degrading practices and external effects of pollution and contamination

Farmers agree that there has been remarkable reduction in soil erosion in the areas where contour farms were established and where trees were planted. Farmers used indigenous indicators for determining the reduction in soil erosion (Table 8.4).

Farmers also agreed on the reduced use of chemical fertilizers and pesticides. Increased use of composting, green manures and animal manures resulted in reduced applications of chemical fertilizers. Some 97 per cent of households used chemical fertilizers two to seven years ago, at an average rate of 282kg (14–14-14 NPK) per ha. At the time of this study, only 62 per cent used fertilizers, and at an average dose of 73kg/ha.

In the case of pesticides, 65 per cent of farmers used various kinds of pesticides in the past (Follidol, Bordan, Endox, Thiodan, Malathion, Thiodan, and so on). As of June 1994, only 11 per cent still used pesticides.

C. Changes in local resilience and vulnerability

Diversity of agricultural and managed wild products

Monocropping was the dominant practice in the uplands prior to the start of the UFMP. Although several other crops were grown, these were seldom intercropped. Since crop diversification is so important in integrated farming, FCs were encouraged to intercrop as many crops as possible on their farms. This was also a strategy to enhance and maintain soil fertility and productivity and to prevent proliferation of pests and diseases.

Table 8.4: Indigenous indicators of reduced soil erosion

○ soil becoming softer over years	○ plants growing uniformly
○ changing colour of soils from dull brown to darker colour	○ contour walls becoming smoother without slumpage during the rainy season
○ land strips in the contour farm becoming flatter	○ water flowing out of field and water in the nearby creeks are fairly clear in contrast to muddy conditions in the past
○ stone pebbles on the soils no longer visible	○ decreased frequency of landslides and contour wall slumpages
○ the increase in the depth of top soils on the farm and decreased soil deposits in the contour canals, soil traps and check dams	

Farmers are now growing various combinations of the staple food crops; they are also growing one or more combinations of over 14 kinds of vegetable and spice crops; and one or more of over 12 kinds of fruit and nut trees and bushes. Farmers also grow various kinds of multi-purpose trees as hedgerows, in woodlots or as farm trees. These trees include madre de cacao, common and giant ipil-ipil (*Leucaena diversifolia*), Rensonii, Flamengia, Gmelina (*Gmelina arborea*), various Cassia and Acacia species. Narra (*Pterocarpus indicus*) and mahogany (*Swietenia macrophylla*) are also planted by some farmers, and growing bamboo for cash income is increasing. Napier grasses (and some vetivier and guinea grasses) are also grown, both as hedgerows and elsewhere as a feed garden for animal fodder (Box 8.3).

Box 8.3: A case of diversity: the farm of Pedro Baile

Pedro used to cultivate 0.25ha of his one hectare upland farm in 1985. He grew only maize and sweet potato. One year after adopting contour farming, he established hedgerows and also started planting chilli. By 1991, he had established SWC structures on half of his farm, and planted several types of field crops, fruit trees and other multi-purpose tree species. He now grew okra, eggplant, peanut, sweet pepper, cucumber, ginger and papaya, pineapple, cacao, and coffee, as well as upland rice, maize and chilli. In 1994, he contoured the rest of his farm, and planted additional root crops such as cassava and yams. More fruit trees were also planted.

Changes in the impact of shocks to the local system

Typhoon, drought and, at times, volcanic eruptions were the major shocks to the uplands in Sto. Domingo. In the past, one such natural calamity brought food crises among the poor. FCs have developed numerous coping strategies, including the adoption of dwarf (hybrid) varieties of crops; using living trees instead of posts for climbing crops; cutting the top of papaya before typhoon (so that the topless trees can regrow after the typhoon); growing hedgerows and boundary trees as wind-breaks to minimize crop damage, and intercropping.

The hedgerow, mulching and trees in the farms were also strategies for coping with drought. Increased vegetation in the hills reduced landslides and thereby floods in the local creeks. However, the floods in bigger rivers originating in distant villages still pose a threat during the rainy season.

D. Replication to non-programme sites

Replication to neighbouring communities and villages

Some *hunglunan* group members helped others do difficult farm work at lower cost. This convinced other farmers to reduce their cost of production by organizing their own *hunglunan* groups. This was the case when farmers from an adjacent municipality, Bacacay, organized their groups, and upland farm management technologies spread there. But the total technology package of UFM did not spread to many villages.

The multi-purpose plant species were, however, faster in spreading to both project and non-project villages. The research team consistently observed such species grown in non-project villages. Similarly, the new crops (cacao, ginger and yam) introduced in the project villages also spread to non-project villages.

Another observation of the team was the active involvement and participation of women in the project villages. One of the FTs was a woman who was able to convince other women farmers in her village to adopt the technology. At the time of the study, one of the *hunglunan* groups composed of women was active.

E. Changes in operational procedures of support institutions

Change in professionals' attitudes to rural people

Professionals in the field have different perceptions of rural people's capabilities. Their first impressions – that farmers who were not educated could not improve their standards of living – were proven wrong when they started work. At first, they wanted people to listen to them; they decided for the people. However, in the process, they learned to accommodate and include the ideas and opinions of the people in decision-making procedures. Participatory processes were central to these changes.

Field project staff felt satisfied with their jobs when they found that farmers were benefiting from the technology promoted by the project. Satisfaction was also felt by helping farmers realize their own potential. Farmers could now express themselves better, as they were more able to analyse their conditions.

Enabling policies in the support institution

Field personnel were encouraged by the support given by the Institute's management. Participation of the 'top people' in re-strategizing the project policies, often during semestral reviews and while planning daily activities also added to their job satisfaction.

The plans that were formulated through participatory processes were adjusted to the actual realities and conditions in the field. Flexibility was observed and practised.

Future implications

This study found positive changes in both crop productivity and real farm incomes among farmers. The project also introduced several sustainable agriculture practices, which were adapted and multiplied by farmers. As a result, rehabilitation of local agroecosystems is taking place. Some effective coping strategies have evolved, so contributing to local resilience and decreased ecological vulnerability.

Some *hunglunan* groups allow people to help themselves and each other in sharing the hardships of upland farm establishment and maintenance. HGs also help resource-poor upland farmers escape from the usual cash constraints on farm investment. But the greatest constraint is insecure land tenure. Some farmers have been ejected from their improved farms. This uncertainty was instrumental in the weakening of several groups. Insecure land tenure is the most forceful factor constraining the formation of new groups and thereby the spread and replication of the technology in the non-project villages.

The project has, however, shown that villagers can become agricultural paraprofessionals. Such paraprofessionals can effectively carry out farmer-to-farmer extension while promoting and improving the appropriateness of the new technologies. The project also demonstrated that given the clear-cut job responsibilities with needed flexibility and timely training, the job satisfaction of the field staff can be maintained.

The findings in general imply that facilitation of local people's participation in agroecological management for their own economic development should be central to development in fragile ecosystems. However, since this approach emphasizes private initiatives for private gains, structural changes such as people-beneficial policies, agrarian reform and their implementation must also be pursued with full political commitment.

ENABLING GOVERNMENT PROGRAMMES

Overview
Enabling Government Programmes

MOST OF THE chapters in this book describe impressive efforts in participatory land and water management, some of which have been sustained over many years. Nevertheless, many of these examples tend to be relatively small in scale and limited in geographic scope. Questions remain about whether most or all of these participatory programmes can operate on a large scale or over large geographic areas. Evidence from the case-studies suggests that the level of scaling-up required to achieve widespread coverage and sustained impacts will happen only if government agencies can create the enabling policies and institutional conditions needed to foster a climate of continuous learning and a process of organizational change. The good work of NGOs and local people's organizations can go some way towards promoting and applying these innovating practices and approaches, but, in most instances, only governments will have the human and technical resources necessary to establish and maintain national-level programmes.

This section presents fascinating accounts from Nepal, India, Southern Africa, Australia, Kenya and Brazil. They describe how government departments, learning from the ineffectiveness and inefficiency of past efforts, have opted to promote more participatory forms of watershed development and management. These chapters describe the steps taken, the struggles and challenges encountered, and the policies required to sustain the process.

The process of reorientation

The shift towards more participation appears to require a radical reorientation of government programmes in four main areas.

Changing attitudes and enhancing skills

A common theme is the key change needed in the attitudes and skills of professional staff. For many of these departments, the first step was to expose staff and policy-makers to participatory approaches and to allow them to interact closely with farmers. Some of the impacts of training staff in the Doon Valley Integrated Watershed Development Project, for example, included a break in the vertical hierarchy as well as in barriers to communication. Project staff were better able to link social with technical issues (Thapliyal *et al.*). In Brazil, extension agents now spend a longer period working in a well-defined area, rather than covering a large area with shorter visits. This improves rapport and working relationships with farming households, leading to higher job satisfaction among technical staff (de Freitas). Segerros describes for Southern Africa the powerful effect of bringing policy-makers and extensionists together in a workshop with farmers:

> Some of us were surprised by the way farmers conducted themselves in what was supposed to be an unfamiliar environment to them. They were able to really challenge researchers, policy-makers and other professionals in all aspects. Some of them proved to be more articulate and better teachers than the professional trainers.

Integration and interdisciplinarity

It is clear from all these cases that interdisciplinarity is needed for participatory watershed approaches. However, the practicalities of moving from what was often a purely technical focus are not straightforward. One approach is to merge key departments, although Krishna reflects on reality versus idealism in the creation of a new multidisciplinary department of Watershed Development and Soil Conservation in Rajasthan. Merging departments to create a new multidisciplinary department without shedding jobs meant immense pressures to step-up the scale of work to justify the numbers of staff involved. 'There was thus no room for the kind of leisurely experimentation which so many academics advise. This is a reality which those of us working in government have got used to accepting.' In other cases, the formation of district and state-level committees helps to bring different perspectives and disciplines together (Thapliyal *et al.*). As the initial planning in Kenya is conducted within the catchment by an interdisciplinary team working closely with all sectors of the community, the proposals for action based on a combination of locally articulated priorities and externally perceived opportunities are highly site specific. This is quite unlike the conventional approach, where pre-packaged messages were passed from the Ministry via senior extension officers and their juniors to farmers (Kiara *et al.*).

Creating space for flexibility and innovation

Another common theme is the fundamental importance of organizational flexibility and openness. Government departments must be able to respond effectively to often rapidly changing ecological and social conditions. They must be able to understand and deal with the different needs, priorities and capacities of a wide array of social actors (e.g., men and women farmers,

110

resource users and resource owners, etc.), and the economic and environmental risks and uncertainties they face. Furthermore, they must be able to help those different actors to select and employ land husbandry practices and technologies that enhance the diversity of physical and biological resources found in different environments.

The need for flexibility is an important requirement of all organizations involved in natural resource management – not just governments – but the implications for government departments can be particularly challenging. 'A vital corollary of this approach is that conventional targets become irrelevant. Each village may have an entirely different development agenda, reflecting unique priorities and requirements. Watershed management requires a great deal of in-built flexibility in planning, implementation and management' (Thapliyal *et al.*). In Nepal, this meant that policies were revised, and now provide clear and simple guidelines with enough flexibility for accommodating local requirements expressed during participatory planning. 'The field staff realize that if a particular programme requires some change in its operational procedures to ensure its success, that he or she has the liberty to make that change. Such flexibility in participatory planning procedures have provided plenty of opportunities to the professionals to incorporate their own innovative ideas into policy planning and has helped the project to adjust its approach in order to maximize returns' (Wagley). In the case of Kenya, all financial subsidies were stopped, and resources allocated instead to extension, training, tools and farmer-to-farmer exchanges (Kiara, *et al.*).

Transparency and accountability

One of the biggest challenges for government departments is often ensuring transparency and accountability in its activities. Yet this is crucial if full participation and a sense of ownership and commitment on the part of local people is to be achieved. As Krishna notes, the scope for 'that age-old malady, corruption . . . had been considerably reduced by a process of conducting all transactions in the open, and by UCs [Users' Committees] publicizing all plans and rendering all accounts fully to the village assembly in monthly meetings'.

Coping with change and uncertainty

Reorienting ways of working within government departments is not an easy process, and these chapters are testament to the challenges they face. In Australia, although the Landcare movement has had a profound impact on agricultural research and extension agencies and practices, these changes have required professionals to overcome fears of change in organizational norms, systems and procedures and to learn to give up some of

111

the power and authority they wield. 'Community empowerment can be threatening for people and institutions who fear it means losing their own power . . . Landcare has also increased the demand for on-farm technical advice, exposing cut-backs in extension resources . . . ' (Campbell and Woodhill).

In the case of Southern Africa, Segerros explains how government technical staff felt that PRA was not a relevant methodology for them to learn. It took a considerable amount of diplomatic discussion and preparation, along with an intensive 10-day field-based PRA training to convince the staff involved that the approach was relevant to their work. This encouraged them to then 'start talking about PRA openly.'

Some of these reversals within government departments have been made possible by sensitive and constant support from external donors. In the Kenya Catchment Approach example, the Swedish International Development Co-operation Agency (SIDA) has been an unfailing ally in the department's efforts to build the internal capacity needed to transform a national soil and water conservation programme (Kiara et al.). A large World Bank grant was the impetus for innovative, people-centred watershed management programmes of the Rajasthan State Government, India, (Krishna) and EPAGRI, Brazil (de Freitas).

The wider policy environment

However committed a government department may be to promoting participatory ways of working, conditions created by the wider policy environment can often constrain its efforts to scale-up and spread the new approaches and processes.

Subsidies for watershed development are one of the main policy instruments that can undermine participatory approaches, as Kerr et al. explain with reference to India. In many watershed programmes, subsidies lead farmers to adopt SWC techniques with no intention of maintaining them. They adopt the techniques solely on the basis of short-term financial gain, not long-term economic, environmental or social viability. Thus, the presence of subsidies makes it difficult for researchers and project managers to learn precisely what practices farmers will or will not find acceptable over the long term. The experiences in Rajasthan (Krishna, Chapter 11) demonstrate this well: 'Even after three years of development, people still say that, although they can relate large yield increases to the work, they will undertake work only if the Government provides some subsidy . . . In part, this is a reflection of poverty and of a diminishing concern for the land, but 40 years of wholly subsidized development programmes are equally responsible. A government programme that is not fully subsidized is looked at with suspicion: are they [staff] making off with some part of the money?'

112

A partnership of equals

The goal of many experiences described in this book is to establish an equal partnership between farming groups and government, where local groups set their own agenda and priorities and government provides institutional support and the necessary research and administrative structure. The Landcare movement in Australia has gone a long way towards achieving this goal, yet creating an equal partnership between government and local groups has remained elusive (Campbell and Woodhill). While the Landcare programme has 'empowered' the community by handing over tremendous responsibility to manage land, it has not provided resources in any way commensurate with the scale of the problem. One clear danger to be aware of in any government attempt to scale up participatory processes for watershed development is whether it is just 'a smokescreen for withdrawing resources and services, effectively transferring responsibility for, and ownership of, land degradation and its solutions to a community level, without allocating commensurate resources or decision-making authority?' Handing over responsibility is one thing, but 'responsibility without resources cannot lead to empowerment.' (Campbell and Woodhill).

It is not new for watershed management and soil and water conservation programmes to espouse the importance of people's participation. There is much scope for misuse of the term. It has been used to justify the extension of control of the state and to promote local capacity-strengthening and self-reliance; it has been used to rationalize external decisions and to devolve power and decision-making away from external agencies; it has been used to describe both data extraction and interactive analysis.

Kiara *et al.* summarize the potential prize of effective participation succinctly: 'If the objective of external intervention and support is to achieve sustainable development, then nothing less than interactive participation will suffice. All the evidence points towards long-term economic and environmental revitalization coming about when people's ideas and knowledge are sought, and power is given to them to make decisions independently of external agencies.'

9

Transforming Micro-catchments in Santa Catarina, Brazil

VALDEMAR HERCÍLIO DE FREITAS

The state of Santa Catarina

SANTA CATARINA IS a small state by Brazilian standards, covering about 96 000km². Located in southern Brazil, it is a state of small farms. Of the 235 000 farming households, 89 per cent have less than 50ha and 40 per cent of these are less than 10ha. Soils are very susceptible to erosion, and gradients lie between 20 and 45 per cent. Yet it manages to be the fifth largest food-producing state in the country, notably of garlic, apples, pigs, poultry, beans, tobacco, and onions[1]. Fodder maize, for pigs and poultry, covers about half the area of annual crops.

Land preparation for agricultural use traditionally involved much disturbance to soils by ploughing and harrowing, and was aggravated by increasing mechanization. This affected soil fertility, with crop productivity decreasing over time. For example, at colonization in the 1700s, maize production reached about 4800kg/ha and now averages around 3200kg/ha.

In July 1991, the steady transformation of agricultural practices received a huge impetus through a large World Bank funded microcatchment programme, the Projeto de Recuperaço, Conservaço e Manejo dos Recursos Naturais em Microbacias Hidrográficas (PRCMRN-MH). This chapter describes how the programme operates in Santa Catarina and assesses initial impacts since its inception, focusing on two microcatchments.

The birth of the programme

As in many parts of the world, soil and water conservation in Santa Catarina was based on traditional planning units: the community and the farm. These political or administrative units had boundaries totally unrelated to those determined by natural agents, especially rain. Mechanical practices, notably terracing, were most common.

---

[1] It is also a key producer of bananas, rice, wheat, maize, potatoes, tomatoes, cassava, and soya.

But from about 1978 onwards, the use of vegetation, such as green manuring, and low-tillage practices for erosion control started to receive more attention. EPAGRI (the State Agricultural Research and Extension Agency) achieved good results with the dissemination of various species of green manure. However, the actions were localized and dispersed, and lacked an integrated strategy with farmer-focused organizations, thus diluting the efforts of extension agents.

In 1984, EPAGRI's efforts to control erosion were seriously challenged by the disastrous consequences of two years of heavy floods. Following earlier experiences in the neighbouring state of Parana, it adopted the micro-catchment as the new planning unit for natural resource management. This concept highlighted off-farm impacts of on-farm practices.

After two years of small-scale initiatives in 17 municipalities, the National Program of River Micro-Catchments (PNMH) was created in 1986 by the Ministry of Agriculture. While this raised the numbers of participating municipalities to 68, it was only through World Bank funding in 1991 that large-scale efforts were made possible across the state. The Micro-catchment Programme of EPAGRI was born.

The Programme aims to increase the labour productivity and net profit of the farmers by regenerating and conserving soil productivity and controlling rural pollution (particularly of waterways from piggery effluents). Soil conservation is central to the strategy, with activities focusing on increasing vegetation cover, controlling surface run-off, and improving soil structure. EPAGRI also increasingly emphasizes improving soil fertility through the extensive use of green manures.

Eighty thousand producers in 520 of the 1680 mapped micro-catchments are to be involved in the work over a seven-year period. Activities will affect 200 of the 260 municipalities. Funding levels total about US$ 71 million, of which US$ 33 million is from the World Bank[2].

Assessing the impacts

Between 1991 and 1994, EPAGRI staff reached over 38 000 farmers in more than 255 micro-catchments through the PRCMRN-MH project. Over 11 000 property management plans were developed, more than 4300 tonnes of green manure seed distributed, about 1540 piggeries constructed, and over 1800 spring protection works completed. Research from two catchments showed that the increase in value over five years, from only three key agricultural products, was more than the total investment of PROSOLO[3] and of individual farmers over the five-year period.

---

[2] An additional US$38.6 million funding comes from the State of Santa Catarina.
[3] PROSOLO is a state-run one-year grant system, with strict conditions, for micro-catchment improvement activities.

Basic changes are continually monitored by the programme (Guijt, in press) in the number of:

○ new participating farmers
○ micro-catchment and property plans completed
○ motivation meetings, excursions, and training courses held
○ individual activities (per activity type, of which there are 14)
○ collective activities (per activity type, of which there are 10)
○ improved roads
○ water quality samples analysed
○ basic infrastructure (schools, protected wells, latrines, rubbish dumps, etc.)

While these types of data generate information on the quantitative objectives of the programme, they do not provide insights into the impacts and sustained value for local people, the local environment and economy. There is also no comparison with non-participating farmers. Thus it is difficult to assess whether participation in micro-catchment development is worth the effort. The *New Horizons* collaboration allowed for a more detailed assessment of impacts in two micro-catchments, Ribeirão das Pedras and Rio Macaco (see Table 9.1).

The impact data were generated through a series of community meetings, group meetings, and individual interviews. In both studies, the farm

Table 9.1:   Characteristics of Ribeirão das Pedras and Rio Macaco

	Ribeirão das Pedras	*Rio Macaco*
Municipality	Agrolândia	São Lourenço do Oeste
Area	about 1300ha	about 1000ha
Altitude	500 to 600 m	800 to 900 m
Average annual rainfall	1300mm	1800mm
Average annual temperature	17°C	17°C
Average annual relative humidity	81%	75%
Number of families	52	50
Average farm area	25ha	20ha
Soils	sedimentary rock basis, the majority Inceptsoils and Litic Soils, acid and with low natural fertility, clay texture	volcanic rock origin (mainly basalt); majority Inceptsols, Litic Soils, with some Oxisols

survey was a group-based discussion and farmers who did not participate in the micro-catchment activities were also interviewed.

The impact assessment in Ribeirão das Pedras[4], is based on views of 18 farming households adopting soil and water conservation technologies (referred to as 'the adopters') and six non-adopting households (referred to as the 'non-adopters'). Together, these represent almost half of the households in the catchment. In Rio Macaco[5], the impact assessment is based on the views of 16 adopters and four non-adopters. Together, these represent about 40 per cent of households in the micro-catchment.

Ten Years Of Change In Ribeirão Das Pedras and Rio Macaco

Land use

Over 10 years, adopters in Ribeirão das Pedras saw significant changes in land use, notably a 28 per cent increase in the area under annual crops and a 21 per cent increase in native pasture cover. Although exotic forest area increased, native woodland and brush decreased by 9 per cent. Much of this deforestation was caused by maize and native pasture expansion, due to increased pig farming and dairy cattle. Also, very steep areas are being abandoned for agricultural use and a lack of manual labour has stopped some cultivation. By comparison, the non-adopting farmers saw the area with annual crops drop by 9 per cent and native woodland by 15 per cent, with a large increase in pastures (28 per cent). Reasons cited were lack of manual labour in the farm due to young children, or children leaving home; health problems; and lack of investment capacity.

In Rio Macaco, the picture was different. Adopters saw a reduction in the area under annual crops and an increase in pasture. Native woodland cover remained the same. The most important development in the micro-catchment was the shift to new crops: vegetable production, fruit growing, and maté tea. Non-adopting farmers saw the greatest change in a decrease of cropped area, and small increases in exotic forest cover and native pasture. There was no diversification of land use among non-adopters.

Crops and productivity

Up to 1984 in Ribeirão das Pedras, most land was cultivated with maize, cassava, beans, and onions, with much turning over of the soil. Since then

---

4 Twenty-five men and two women participated in the community meeting which compared the current situation with that of 10 years ago. Twenty farmers then volunteered to work on the farm level survey. Women's input was sought with a meeting of the Mothers' Club.
5 Two meetings were held, one in each community, involving about 20 men farmers in total. The women had a separate meeting.

117

among adopters, land under maize increased from 36 per cent to 80 per cent of the total productive area, a doubling directly caused by increased pig farming[6], while non-adopters saw only a 40 per cent increase in land under maize. They also noted a decrease in the area under onions and beans, caused by high production costs and disease problems respectively.

From 1984 to 1994 in Ribeirão das Pedras, the productivity of traditional crops such as cassava and beans decreased, and onion yields remained the same for adopters. Maize yields increased greatly from 2050kg/ha to 4980kg/ha, even among non-adopting farmers (from 2320kg/ha to 3900kg/ha). The increase was greater among adopters, a result of greater investment in chemical and organic fertilizers and lime, together with the use of green manure and direct planting. Yield increases among the interviewed adopters represent about US$204 360[7] per year for the catchment. Without the changes brought by the catchment programme, this would have been only US$74 360 per year.

Rio Macaco saw a much smaller increase in maize area among adopters (from 67 per cent to 73 per cent). Soya was cultivated much less but most striking was the development of vegetable and fruit growing as a new source of income for some families. The situation for non-adopters has not changed. It shows a lack of diversification and a lack of capacity for change.

In Rio Macaco, productivity increase in maize was 49 per cent among adopters (from 2465 to 4880kg/ha), and 15 per cent among non-adopters (from 2460 to 2910kg/ha). Again, a range of changes in agricultural practices are the causes. The economic value of this increase among the 16 adopting farmers, represents US$100 000[8] at the catchment level. Without the changes, economic increases due to these yield increases would have totalled only US$20 000.

Livestock

Land degradation and low crop productivity prior to the programme caused a crisis in the Ribeirão das Pedras catchment, and a subsequent search for alternative income earners. This led to an almost four-fold increase in the number of sows and a more than five-fold increase in the number of shoats.[9] Among the adopters, even with fewer cows, there was an increase of about 150 per cent in the litres of milk sold. Non-adopters, by comparison, had 160 per cent more cows and a similar increase of milk sold, at 170 per cent of the 1984 figures. Also significant among non-adopters was a doubling of sales of beef cattle. This explains the large

---

[6] Pigs are fed on maize.
[7] About US$3930 with changes, and US$1430 without changes, for each of the 52 farmers in the catchment.
[8] About US$2000 with changes, and US$ 400 for each of the 50 farmers in the catchment.
[9] A collective term for sheep and goats.

increase in pasture area to the detriment of annual crops. Both these changes were stimulated by regional changes, the opening of a milk processing plant and extra incentives for pig farming from the existing cold storage plant.

In Rio Macaco, adopting farmers enjoyed a spectacular rise in milk sales: a relatively small 135 per cent increase in the number of cattle translated into a massive 820 per cent increase in litres of milk sold. The number of sows increased only slightly, with more shoats being acquired. On the other hand, among non-adopters, pig farming, cattle production and dairy cows plummeted. Only milk sales increased, despite fewer cows. The sale of milk, where cheese production was more common, has been greatly stimulated by the installation of a new milk processing plant in the region.

Income sources

A look at changes in income sources fails to provide any clear picture of the influence of micro-catchment activities. Regional economic influences, as described above (e.g. regional processing plants) seem more influential than local changes.

Adoption of Conservation Practices

The farmers in Ribeirão das Pedras explained that those who adopted the new soil management and conservation practices have not abandoned the 'non-adopters'; on the contrary, adoption rates are increasing. Seeing neighbours' fields has encouraged change among non-adopting farmers. Terracing, one practice adopted early on, was abandoned as it had been adopted in isolation without good management of the terraces, thus causing considerable damage in some cases.

In Rio Macaco, adoption rates are also growing for practices such as *murundu* (absorption) terraces, plant ridging, green manure, and direct planting. During the past 10 years, the area with terraces grew from 9 per cent to 62 per cent, the area under ridging from 6 per cent to 19 per cent, and only 19 per cent of the area remains untreated. There was a growth from only 8 per cent of the area covered with green manures to a remarkable 71 per cent.

Agricultural production system

Perhaps the biggest changes have occurred in the agricultural system itself. Table 9.2 shows the stages of transition of the agricultural system over the past decade in Ribeirão das Pedras. In 1984, soils were used intensively under cassava, maize, onion, beans and tobacco in Ribeirão das Pedras, and under soya, winter wheat, maize and beans in Rio Macaco. According to farmers in the first community, successive crops of cassava and beans contributed most towards land degradation. Maize was planted on top of burnt brush or maize stalks after ploughing. In both micro-catchments, soil was turned completely with ploughing and harrowing, practices which encourage soil erosion. Although there were some terraces, the absence of green manuring made them ineffective against erosion.

At the beginning of the project, farmers were encouraged to experiment with various types of green manure: turnip, lupin, crotalaria, vetch (*Vicia* sp.), oats (*Avena strigosa*), mucuna (*Stylozabium* sp.), spurry (*Spergula arvensis*) and nabo forrageiro (*Raphanus* sp.). By 1986, the farmers' findings had helped define the most appropriate system of green manuring, focusing on oats and vetch. Then in 1987, one farmer experimented with planting without turning over the soil, i.e. 'direct planting', using an animal-drawn machine with an adapted disk, and only one line. Based on this experiment, the farmers started to discuss the possibility of adapting conventional existing machinery to direct planting.

From 1988 to 1990, the farmers invested heavily in improving the machinery, with the help of technicians and blacksmiths from Agrolândia municipality. Direct planting machinery was developed by adapting animal-drawn seeders available in the market place. These tractor-based direct planting seeders, abandoned by wheat farmers in the State of Paraná, were bought cheaply, in a group for collective use, and adapted by the farmers themselves for direct planting of maize and onions. For example, they replaced the horizontal seed trays with vertical seed trays (of 2, 3, 4 and even 5 planting lines).

Table 9.2: Changes in agricultural production system 1984/5 to 1994

| | adopters | | non-adopters | |
	R. d. Pedras	Rio Macaco	R. d. Pedras	Rio Macaco
area left uncovered	82% → 17%	8% → 71%	85% → 73%	n.a.*
area with green manures	18% → 83%	n.a.	15% → 27%	14% → 3%
area with terraces/ ridging	n.a.	15% → 81%, or 9% → 62% (terr.) 6% → 19% (ridg.)	n.a.	16% → 10%
area under direct planting	0% → 80% (maize)	0% → 12%	0% → 20%	n.a.
area being harrowed or ploughed	100% → 20%	100% → 88%	100% → 79%	n.a.

* n.a. not available

Table 9.3: Key events in development of direct planting in Ribeirão das Pedras

1984/85	1986	1987	1988–90	1991/92	1993/94
Farmer study tours Creation of the micro-catchment committee	Green manure observation unit established Definition of the green manure system	Establishing first direct planting plot with animal-drawn machinery, by one experimenting farmer	Experimentation and machinery adaptation period by farmers Developing direct planting with animal/tractor-drawn machinery, designed by farmers, technicians and local blacksmiths Improving minimal cultivation and direct planting with small tractor	Start of direct planting system 5% adoption of direct planting Continued adoption	Great increase in area under direct planting Individual and group acquisition of machinery

Source: Giovani Farias, extension agent in Agrolândia

The definition of direct planting as a method of soil preparation took place after the machinery was bought with their own funds, and was adapted and improved. The whole process of adoption of the green manure went through experimentation to farm level. For green manure, various species were tested and the farmers adopted those that were better suited to their production system.

In Ribeirão das Pedras, several other changes were identified by the farmers:

o The use of chemical fertilizers increased by 48 per cent, but manure use was up by 95 per cent. Increased applications of lime were also noted, to correct soil acidity or eliminate toxic aluminium.

o Pesticide use, especially of herbicides, increased. Farmers justify their use due to lack of family labour, the large quantity of weeds and crop cover under green manuring, the need to create good germination conditions under direct planting and the short time for the development of the system. They firmly believe that it will be possible to reduce this use, at least for maize, in the near future (Figure 9.1).

o The area under terraces has dropped from 72 to 8ha, and under ridging from 13 to 2ha. This is caused by the shift to direct planting, obviating the need for engineering structures in Ribeirão das Pedras, which has gentler slopes than Rio Macaco.

o The survey revealed that about 30 hectares of trees were planted, or around 60 000 trees, basically pine and eucalyptus, especially in the steeper areas.

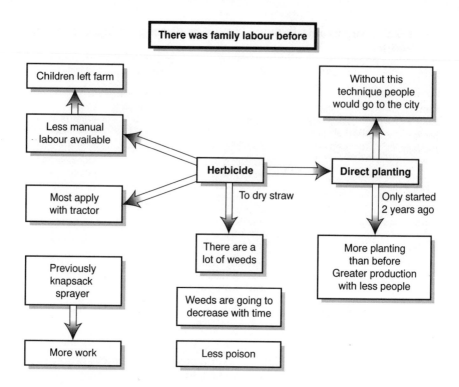

Figure 9.1: A farmer's view of the greater use of herbicide in planted areas

○ Farmers did not detect great alterations in the water level of the wells or even in the level of the river. Considering that 20 per cent of the cropped area is still kept without winter cover, the low percentage of reforested area, the reduction in the deforested area during the last ten years, and the widespread implementation of direct planting only two years ago, visible changes would be premature.

○ Although soil loss is not monitored, farmers were unanimous that it had dropped to very low levels. This was reflected in the improved condition of on-farm and access roads (due to less run-off from fields) and fewer expenses for upkeep.

○ Overall, about 91 per cent of the micro-catchment is adequately protected from the impact of rain, the greatest agent of erosion (includes 80 per cent of the total area under direct planting, area with native woodland, native pastures, under reforestation).

In Rio Macaco, other changes in the agricultural system included:

○ Adopting farmers have great interest in new land preparation practices, through direct planting with machines. But there are difficulties in identifying the type of machinery to be used, the high price of these machines, and the individualism of farmers, with each wanting to have his or her own equipment.

o The area where organic fertilizer is used had increased by 82 per cent, and that with lime by 133 per cent.

o In 1985, there were only 8.1km of *murundu* terraces, which has increased five-fold to 40.3km. *Murundus*, together with other land management practices, have greatly influenced the water flow in the micro-catchment.

o Changing land management practices appear to be reducing surface run-off and re-establishing underground water flow in the river channel. In January 1993, after rains of 70mm, the river level reached 1.9 metres. In May 1994, after a 102mm storm, the river level remained at 40cm.

o About 89 per cent of the micro-catchment area is protected, or at least the process of erosion has been checked (includes area with native woodland, pastures, exotic forest, area under green manure/direct planting/terraces/plant ridges).

Changes to Local Resilience and Local Vulnerability

Environment. The farmers of Ribeirão das Pedras noted many improvements. Deforestation of native vegetation has virtually stopped. Slash and burn agriculture occurs only in very small areas, and the brush is regenerating. Certain types of wildlife that had disappeared are showing signs of returning. Before, fewer trees were planted, the river level dropped after a drought, water quality in the wells was poor, less agricultural poison was used, and there were fewer flies. Nowadays, due to increased piggeries, while there are more flies, changes are generally positive. More trees are being planted, there are more cover crops and terraces are no longer needed, there is more water in the river and fish are coming back. Farmers stated that the soil retains humidity better under direct planting. A recent seven-week drought did not cost them any onion or tobacco seedlings. Farmers who did not adopt either the direct planting system or minimal cultivation, were unable to plant at the correct time because soils were dry and they lost the onion seedlings in the beds. Those who planted tobacco using the conventional system had to replant the seedlings.

In Rio Macaco, there are more fish in the rivers, some increase in wild-life, and the deforestation of native woodland has stopped. The greatest impact noticed by the community is a reduction in the quantity of black flies, which is associated with a cleaner river. The water level in the river does not rise after heavy rainfalls.

Health and food. Women in Ribeirão das Pedras noted several improvements. Diets are more varied, with more fruit, vegetables and fish being eaten. Although the use of poison has increased, it is being used with greater care. Although the amount of work has not decreased, it is less heavy now. Before, there was no end to weeding on the land.

In Rio Macaco, similar changes were noted. Due to increased income and the growing of wheat, diets are more varied. Flour is made and used, more foods are bought and can be kept uncooked (refrigeration), and fish are caught at the dams. Water is cleaner, piped water is now used for drinking, and there are more latrines. The incidence of worms is lower. In 1991, the Municipal Prefecture compared the contamination level of the River Macaco with another local river. It found that the total count of coliform bacteria in River Macaco was 70 per ml at 37°C, and in River São Lourenço it was 120. Today, all 24 pig breeders build manure heaps rather than dump faeces in the river.

Access to credit and financial help. Due to the high interest rates, many farmers in both study areas kept well away from rural credit through bank agencies. A popular alternative credit programme was the barter system, whereby the farmer paid for lime with produce. Also, the grants through PROSOLO are being used actively for soil conservation and reforestation. Other forms of support are provided in this transition phase through the donation of machinery and equipment for collective use via the PNMH and the prefecture. In the case of Rio Macaco it is important to note that despite the high cost of constructing a *murundu* terrace (seven bags of maize per hour), heavy machinery is in great demand due to its perceived benefits against erosion. The prefecture is sharing the costs by paying the equivalent of four bags of maize per hour.

Changes in local organization

Desire to participate. Farmers' participation was encouraged through community meetings and farm visits by extensionists. However, for the farmers, the milestone was a 1984 tour to see green manure experiences in the west of Santa Catarina, and to Paraná, to see community participation in micro-catchment development. After the tours, the micro-catchment committee was established as representative organization for the community. At the outset there was no financial incentive to stimulate participation. On the contrary, the participatory development of direct planting machinery led the farmers to invest their own resources.

In Rio Macaco after the project started in 1985, farmers participated in tours, kept up with demonstration units of green manure and adopted mechanical practices of soil conservation, but not intensively. The changes accelerated greatly in 1989, when very heavy rains caused a local disaster in the roads, fields, rivers, etc. For the farmers, the greatest incentive to participate now has been the municipal cost-sharing for building *murundu* terraces.

Local professionalism. In Ribeirão das Pedras, there are no para-professional, trained farmers. However, the accumulated experience in green manure and conservation systems of soil preparation is so high that farmers are acting as technology disseminators for their neighbours and other farmers in neighbouring regions. Of the 18 adopting farmers, six constantly receive tours. In the last few years, the micro-catchment received more than 40 tours from elsewhere. Among the interviewed families, 21 people had participated in tours to other farms and to other regions.

Before 1984, there was no organized group at micro-catchment level. Today, the micro-catchment committee[10] represents the community in any action. The committee is responsible for machinery and equipment for collective use, such as the harvester, sprayer, disk plough, manure spreader, animal-drawn machine for direct planting. Funds for repairs are generated through a use fee, and are managed by a caretaker. The committee also manages a communal grain drier, to deal with the increase in pig farming and increased productivity. Due to the improved quality of the stored grains, the maize from this micro-catchment is now preferred by traders. A third group, involving several communities, has a caterpillar tractor for collective use for heavy works. Several smaller groups with three to five members now operate in the micro-catchment, collectively using various bits of heavy machinery. Although the extensionist supports these groups, they all create and enforce their own rules.

There are no trained para-professionals in Rio Macaco either. Six adopting farmers have already received tours from other farmers' regions. There is no organized group that manages catchment affairs. The farmers acknowledge that they are individualists when it comes to crop cultivation and livestock.

Dependence on external resources. There has been a clear increase in the use of synthetic NPK fertilizers in Ribeirão das Pedras. On the other hand, the use of green manure and pig manure has also increased. Pesticide use in general has stayed at similar levels, with the exception of herbicides, which are now in greater demand due to the green manuring. The use of hybrid maize seeds has also increased. Although it is difficult to separate the effect of each input on increased maize productivity, the farmers assert that the use of green and animal manure increased productivity by at least 20 per cent. The winter vetch crop allowed a 50 per cent reduction in the use of urea as a source of nitrogen to top-dress maize. They also believe that a reduction in herbicide use, and even pesticide use, is only a matter of time.

In Rio Macaco, a similar increase in fertilizers, lime, green manure, and manure was noted. As the system of soil preparation is mainly

---

[10] It consists of six members who are elected every two years.

conventional, there is little use of herbicide. However, diversification into horticulture has led to greater use of pesticide. According to the farmers, the use of chicken manure can increase crop productivity by up to 50 per cent.

Replicability. Ribeirão das Pedras contributed most to the development of direct planting in the region. A municipal survey showed that in 1994, already 1500 hectares were under direct planting for a total annual crop area of 5500 hectares (or 27 per cent). In the micro-catchment, there are eight direct-planting machines and another 20 elsewhere in the municipality.

Rio Macaco has paved the way for more terracing in the region. *Murundu*-type terraces proved so effective that there are now about 500 hectares of terraces in the municipality, equivalent to 150km. The farm that pioneered the use of direct planting has received visits of 250 farmers from different parts of the municipality and more than 50 farmers for another detailed technical meeting.

Women's situation. Prior to the programme activities, women in both study areas did not participate much in community decisions, helping only at festivities and school meetings. In Ribeirão das Pedras, most of the children were leaving the area as income was low and it was not possible to split the land into viable farms. Now, there are several local groups, women are more active in community issues and have access to more guidance on child and health issues. They work less hard in the fields due to direct planting, but work more at harvest and with the grain drier due to increased harvests. They are better able to look after the home and vegetable garden, thus improving nutritional standards.

In Rio Macaco, all the children lived at home and there were mothers' and youth groups. Now, women are participating more at meetings, and the community has formed a guidance council which deals with local social development issues. Both the youth and mother's groups have stopped, as the youths have left the farm.

Changes within EPAGRI

The new role of professionals

Although the social, economic, and biophysical uniqueness of each micro-catchment influences the final process of watershed development, most follow a series of general steps as outlined below, seeking the greatest possible participation of rural families.

Preparation. EPAGRI senior technical staff organize a municipal-level meeting with local leaders, bankers, entrepreneurs, and technical experts.

This usually includes a tour to another micro-catchment. The group then identifies the micro-catchments in the municipality, and uses purely technical criteria to select four to be invited to join the PNMH programme. The nominated catchments are put before the municipal council, with farmer representatives, for final validation.

Micro-catchment motivation. EPAGRI considers this the most important phase. The extensionist responsible for the micro-catchment visits all the households for initial discussions. This includes a community meeting with leaders and/or families. The extensionist organizes a tour for about 40 families to visit another micro-catchment, a farm with an advanced soil management approach, and/or EPAGRI's training centre or research stations[11] to look at green manure units and soil preparation systems. Only then do the families in the nominated catchment vote whether or not to commit themselves to collaboration with PNMH. Work will proceed only if at least 70 per cent of the farmers of each micro-catchment consent to the partnership. During this phase, support is provided by EPAGRI's technical advisers at regional level.

Planning of activities. Soil and water conservation activities are planned for a four-year period. A so-called PIP (farm plan), is prepared for each participating property, generally by the extension agent, based on discussions with each farmer (almost always only men). The PIP describes present land use, natural aptitude, potential use, and conservation plans, in line with the agricultural objectives of each farmer. Activities that are eligible for financial support from PROSOLO are also identified.

Implementation. The conservation measures are implemented with the extension agent, usually only upon release of funds from PROSOLO. In most, but not all, micro-catchments, catchment committees are elected to guide overall implementation of activities, particularly those which require collective action and support. Individual activities include: piggery construction, toxic waste depot, green manure seeds, tree nursery, manure application, and calcium application. Collective activities include the construction of a water tank, a toxic waste depot, maize storage facility, or the hiring of various machines, such as a direct seeder, manure spreader, bulldozer, etc.

Extensionist's role and identity. The extension agent holds the key to success. The greatest difference with past EPAGRI work is that extension

---

[11] Over 100 experiments are being conducted by EPAGRI's research branch to seek solutions to problems identified in the micro-catchment process. EPAGRI's training centre in the west of the state has green manure units and conservation systems of soil preparation. In the 10-year period, more than 10 000 farmers have visited the centre.

agents now concentrate their efforts in a well-defined area for at least two years. As this allows for more contact with farming households and better rapport, job satisfaction is higher. The PIP process means that extension agents understand local agricultural realities in great detail. Results are faster and more clearly due to the efforts of the extension agent. Farmers and municipal authorities alike appreciate the role of the extension agent more. This has led to 101 of the 192 extension agents becoming direct employees of the municipality, an unforeseen employment generation impact. Recently, extension workers employed by EPAGRI have started identifying themselves as part of the municipal team. As EPAGRI staff can commit themselves to only two years per micro-catchment, this handing over of staff to local institutions will enhance the sustainability of the approach. Support is still provided by 16 regional-level EPAGRI agronomists.

Innovative partnerships. Scaling-up of activities has meant easier adoption in subsequent catchments due to off-site awareness of programme activities. But as extension staff maintain links with all catchments, they soon have limited time to invest in new catchments. Therefore, innovative partnerships are essential to ensure the spread of micro-catchment planning. As the micro-catchments concept has always been conceived as being the responsibility of the whole society, support is actively sought from the non-state sector. To this end, conscious efforts have been made to create linkages with the private sector, academic institutions, and municipal departments.

Farmers are being encouraged to act as promoters at micro-catchment level, taking over the task of the extension agent. EPAGRI's training programme has created a 'soil conservation, use and management' course for farmers to support this process. Students from agricultural colleges and faculties are participating in the elaboration of PIPs through paid internships.

The links with the private sector are particularly fascinating. The tobacco and poultry/pig industries (SINDIFUMO and SINDICARNE) are realizing that they can sustain their industry only if soil fertility is maintained. Chicken and pigs eat maize which must be grown sustainably, as must tobacco. EPAGRI has trained many staff employed by the two industries in soil management, who are training farmers. Also, SINDIFUMO and SINDICARNE now pay for about 50 of EPAGRI's extension staff to support the micro-catchment teams.

Other organizations are becoming involved with the project's execution. A development agency, CIDASC (Integrated Company for the Agricultural Development of Santa Catarina) became responsible for the forestry component. Monitoring, environment assessment, and protected areas are co-ordinated by FATMA, the Foundation for Technology and

Environment Support. Programme evaluation, according to a model approved by the World Bank, will be the responsibility of the Institute for State Planning.

Facing new challenges

EPAGRI recognizes that it faces many challenges to strengthen the work, improve the quality of the process and the outcome, and spread the impact (Guijt, in press). Questions it is asking include:

o How can the PIP process be more participatory? There is high dependency on the external agents to measure and plan.
o How can the involvement of external agents be phased out, or is this a pipe dream? This has not been thought through, despite the two-year per catchment objective.
o How to involve women farmers more? Although many women make essential contributions in the catchment work, very few participate in exchange visits or training and there are none on the catchment committees. There is no gender-differentiated data, other than one: three of the 192 EPAGRI extension staff are women.
o How to institutionalize participatory monitoring? Only a few quantitative impacts are being analysed in a handful of catchments. Studies such as these have not been conducted since.

10
Impacts of the Catchment Approach to Soil and Water Conservation: Experiences of the Ministry of Agriculture, Kenya

J.K. KIARA, L.S. MUNYIKOMBO, L.S. MWARASOMBA,
JULES PRETTY and JOHN THOMPSON

A brief history

KENYA HAS A long history of state intervention in both soil and water conservation and land management. Although erosion was first recognized as a problem as early as the 1870s, large-scale planned intervention was not undertaken by colonial authorities until the 1930s. The lack of adoption of new practices, combined with the widely publicized 'Dust Bowl' in the USA, encouraged the administration to take a vigorous campaigning approach (Anderson, 1984; Beinart, 1984; Bennett, 1939). Administrators travelling to the USA saw the devastation apparently caused by a combination of drought and mismanagement, and returned with recommendations for large-scale bunding and ridging, contour ploughing and planting, and new grazing management systems by enforced enclosure. The result was that the locally-adapted practices were largely ignored, even though they were more effective at coping with drought conditions.

The imposing of soil conservation measures on farmers had far-reaching consequences on conservation (see Chapter One, this volume), which became so tainted by the connotation of forced labour that no administrator or politician dared address it. After independence, this meant that further government involvement in soil conservation was impossible. For the remainder of the 1960s and into the early 1970s, soil conservation received little official attention, although it was still considered a major problem.

At the UN Conference on the Human Environment in Stockholm in 1972, Kenya's country report concluded that soil degradation was the main environmental threat facing the country, a statement based partly on an FAO study of that period (Lundgren, 1993). Soon after that event, in 1974, the national soil conservation programme (NSCP) was established within the then Ministry of Agriculture[1], with the financial support of the Swedish

---

[1] In 1993, the Ministry of Agriculture became the Ministry of Agriculture, Livestock Development and Marketing (MALDM). Unless referred to in a specific historical context, the Ministry will be referred to as MALDM. The authors would like to thank Maria Berlekom, H.G. Kimaru and Lill Lundgren for their valuable comments and information on the early history of the national soil conservation programme of MALDM.

International Development Authority (SIDA). During the first 15 years, the programme focused on working with farmers who were willing and able to accept technical assistance from Ministry agents. In turn, these farmers were expected to promote on-farm soil conservation through the use of a variety of physical and biological measures. The measures included construction of terraces, cut-off drains and retention ditches, treatment and control of gullies, river bank protection, rehabilitation of badly eroded lands, and promotion of agroforestry and other biological conservation practices.

The programme, which began working in pilot areas in four districts, expanded to 22 districts by 1976. Further expansion to all high and medium potential areas of the country occurred with the establishment of the Soil and Water Conservation Branch (SWCB) in the Ministry of Agriculture in 1977. A second round of reorganization took place in 1983 with the adoption of the World Bank-sponsored training and visit (T&V) system of extension, in which junior technical assistants were encouraged to maintain links with the farming community through direct interaction with individual 'contact farmers'. These staff passed the pre-designed extension 'messages' and technical 'packages' to the contact farmers. Special 'field days' were also arranged, in which new practices were demonstrated to groups of farmers.

The intention was for the messages and packages to diffuse through rural areas as the contact farmers shared their experiences with their neighbours. In practice, the results were mixed, especially as the contact farmers tended to be resource-rich, socially well connected, and male. Similar problems have been recorded with T&V extension elsewhere in Africa (Moris, 1990; Howell, 1988; Mullen, 1989). Although this approach emphasized that farmers were free to choose whether or not to adopt soil conserving measures, government found it necessary to induce farmers to participate through financial incentives. Cash payments were provided to encourage farmers to construct the more labour-intensive measures such as cut-off drains and artificial waterways.

With the aid of these subsidies and inducements, some 500 000 smallholder farms were conserved using a variety of physical and biological measures. In addition, 117 000 farmers, 7800 teachers and 4700 chiefs (local administrative officers) and sub-chiefs (local administrative assistants) attended 'field day' demonstrations aimed at promoting the adoption of resource-conserving technologies and practices. By 1987, however, the Ministry of Agriculture concluded that its current approach was unable to fulfil its goal of nation-wide conservation coverage, even though its early achievements were impressive. The Ministry found that new conservation skills and measures were scattered thinly across the country, leaving large parts of certain districts largely untreated. In addition, the adoption rates of the introduced conservation technologies and practices were disappointing

131

and the diffusion of these innovations remained sporadic and slow. Furthermore, the cost of maintaining high levels of public subsidies to promote and support soil and water conservation was proving to be financially unsustainable.

The catchment approach

The Government of Kenya recognized that the only way to achieve widespread conservation coverage was to mobilize people to embrace soil and water conserving practices on their own teams. The adoption of the catchment approach (or 'area of concentration') approach was an explicit attempt by the Soil and Water Conservation Branch of the Ministry of Agriculture to take a people-centred perspective, build upon the early success of the national soil conservation programme and avoid many of the contradictions encountered in conventional SWC and the T&V approach. At first, the catchment approach was seen as a way of concentrating resources and efforts within a specified catchment[2] (typically 200–500 hectares) for a limited period of time (generally one year), during which all farms are laid out and conserved. Small adjustments and maintenance would then be carried out by the community members themselves with the support of local extension agents. All financial subsidies were stopped, and resources were allocated instead to extension, training, tools and farmer field trips. It was then hoped that this would give better results than the formerly scattered efforts.

The concept of the catchment approach has changed over time, especially with the introduction of participatory methods in 1989 (Thompson, 1995). The intention was for local communities to be involved in the analysis of their own farming and conservation problems, and decisions and recommendations made with their active participation. Community mobilization would be achieved through close co-operation between farmers and planning teams, and the formation of catchment committees of local farmers, as well as through intensified publicity and training through field-days, *barazas* (public meetings), demonstrations and tours.

The aim of the Ministry of Agriculture's promotion of the catchment approach has been deliberately to reorient the extension system away from a focus on 'treatment' of soil and water conservation problems and towards responding to the resource management and livelihood security needs and priorities of rural people. The former head of the SWCB, H. G. Kimaru,

---

[2] The term 'catchment' is not used by the SWCB only in the strict hydrologic sense to mean a topographically defined area drained by a river/stream or system of connecting rivers/streams such that all outflow is discharged through a single outlet. Instead, it refers to an area, often defined by its settlement patterns and administrative boundaries, as well as its hydrologic features, in which all farms can be conserved within a single year.

described the difference in early 1990 in this way: 'We seek to develop a dialogue between the change agent and the farmer in order to ensure that new technologies can be focused towards solving the farmers' perceived problems (and not merely what the change agent may want to promote) . . . All of us should learn to recognise the central role of the farmer in development' (Kiara *et al.*, 1990).

At present, each divisional planning team (DPT), comprising the divisional soil conservation officer and two technical assistants, typically works in three to four catchments each year. Priority is given to catchments where local people or administrations have requested support, where erosion is serious, or where the Ministry has not worked before. Following the launch of the catchment and formation of the catchment conservation committee, a conservation plan is drawn up and all farms are laid out with new biological and/or physical structures. By the end of the year, the intention is for all farms to be conserved.

Inevitably, implementation has varied from site to site and over time. Many factors have been important, not least the local social and political context relating to property rights over land. Kenya is a country where access to and control of agricultural land remain hotly contested, and local sensitivities over land adjudication and consolidation processes can sometimes be extreme. The catchment approach has been most effective where security of tenure exists for local resource users and owners alike, thus creating a stable social climate in which co-operation and collective action for conservation and resource management can emerge and persist. Perhaps the most significant element leading to the broad success of the catchment approach has been the growing adoption of a flexible and dynamic methodology for appraisal, analysis and collaboration among extension agents of different government departments and NGOs, and between the government agents and the local people themselves.

Refining farmer participation

It is not new for soil conservation programmes to espouse the importance of people's participation. Indeed, the phrases 'people's participation' and 'popular participation' are now part of the normal language of most development agencies, including NGOs, government departments and development banks. Yet, it is not clear what exactly they mean by these expressions. Within the same project or programme, the term 'participation' is often interpreted in ways that appear utterly contradictory. It has been used to justify the extension of control of the state and to promote local capacity strengthening and self-reliance; it has been used to rationalize the primacy of external decisions and to devolve power and decision-making away from external agencies; it has also been used to describe both data extraction and interactive analysis.

In conventional rural development, participation has often centred on encouraging local people to exchange their labour in return for food (i.e., 'food for work'), cash or materials. Yet these material incentives distort perceptions, create dependencies, and give the misleading impression that local people are supportive of externally-driven initiatives (Raikes, 1988). This paternalism then undermines sustainability goals and produces results that do not persist once the project ceases. As little effort is made to build local skills, interests and capacity, local people have no stake in maintaining structures or practices once the flow of incentives stops.

If the objective of external intervention and support is to achieve sustainable development, then nothing less than interactive participation will suffice. All the evidence points towards long-term economic and environmental revitalization coming about when people's ideas and knowledge are sought, and power is given to them to make decisions independently of external agencies.

What defines *interactive* participation is the use of an explicit methodology for analysis and problem-solving. The SWCB has adapted a range of methods derived from participatory rural appraisal (PRA) and rapid rural appraisal (RRA) (Kiara *et al.*, 1990; Pretty, 1990; Pretty *et al.*, 1993; Thompson, 1995; Thompson and Pretty, 1996; MOA/MALDM, *passim*). These include a wide range of methods for improving interdisciplinary teamwork, fostering constructive dialogues between local people and government officers, and facilitating visualization and diagramming of complex processes and relationships (see Chapter Two, this volume).

Participatory methods imply shifts of initiative, responsibility and action to rural people themselves. These methods, when put together, constitute a system of participatory learning. These methods and principles are now used throughout the problem-analysis and planning phase of the catchment approach. Interdisciplinary teams drawn from various government departments at divisional level work for about a week in the catchment. These interdisciplinary teams often include officers from MALDM, as well as those from other departments and ministries, including Education, Environment, Fisheries, Forestry, Public Works, Water Development, Health and so on. They sometimes include staff of local and international NGOs who are actively working in the catchment.

This is sometimes called the rapid catchment analysis phase. As the methods are not yet widely known, the process usually begins with a day of orientation and introduction to the methods. This is followed by three days of intensive fieldwork, in which the teams work with farmers in the catchment, building up a rich picture of local skills, knowledge and perspectives on problems and concerns. On the final day, a public meeting, or *baraza*, is held during which findings are presented in visual form. Those present are able to comment, criticize and suggest changes.

Following these initial exchanges, a catchment conservation committee of farmers is elected as the institution responsible for co-ordinating local SWC implementation. The interdisciplinary team then prepares a catchment report to serve as a baseline document for planning, implementation, monitoring and evaluation. The catchment report forms the basis for the co-ordinated action by extension professionals based at divisional and district level. The planning team constructs a detailed map of the catchment and, with the committee, implements the soil and water conservation measures for each of the farms.

The catchment conservation committees

A central output from this process is the formation of the catchment conservation committee (CCC). These CCCs typically comprise 8 to 15 people, with a local technical officer as an *ex-officio* member. Sometimes these are elected to form an entirely new local institution. On other occasions, they are derived from existing traditional or formal institutions, such as elders' groups, co-operative societies, and so on. Their role is to provide a link between the local community and external agencies.

The CCCs receive support in the form of basic tools, equipment, and technical training and advice from Ministry staff. In turn, the catchment committee members assist their fellow farmers in planning and implementing various individual and group soil and water conservation activities. They are responsible for constructing and maintaining bulking plots for grasses and local nurseries for tree seedlings. They also become involved in supporting the planning teams in laying out and implementing SWC plans on each farm.

Their role, as a local institution, is another factor that defines the difference between the catchment approach and the former conventional approach. Local organizations are crucial for sustainable resource use and development. They develop and enforce their own rules, incentives and penalties to ensure behaviour conducive to privately and publicly efficient use of resources. They are able to make investments and take risks that individuals find hard to make. They are also a forum for negotiation, arbitration and conflict resolution, which arise from diverse individual and group interests.

It is ownership and commitment that has been achieved by divisional planning teams working closely with CCCs. In some cases, CCCs have continued to be active after implementation, initiating and co-ordinating activities well beyond soil and water conservation, including marketing of local produce, development of village tree nurseries, maintenance of local roads, etc. In others, they have become ineffective as soon as the planning teams have completed work and moved to new catchments.

CCCs are more likely to be effective if members have been freely elected and if they believe that they are working with, rather than for, the extension teams (MOA/MALDM, *passim*; Admassie, 1992). Where CCCs are selected, say by the chief or a local leader, it is most common for them to cease to function after intensive support from the government comes to an end.

The impacts of the catchment approach

The average annual number of farms fully conserved in Kenya with various SWC measures has risen with the implementation of the catchment approach from 60 000 in the late 1980s to some 100 000 in the mid-1990s (MOA/MALDM, *passim*). In addition, each year some 500 000–800 000 metres of cut-off drains and 50 000–100 000 metres of artificial waterways are constructed, while a further 1250–2700 gullies are controlled and 1780–3600 km of riverbanks are protected.

A number of recent evaluations of the catchment approach show that it brings significant benefits over the individual T&V Approach. One comparative analysis of two neighbouring catchments in Trans Nzoia found that crop yields, gross margins and returns per person-day had grown more rapidly on the farms in the community where the catchment approach has been used (Eckbom, 1992). There was increased demand for land, with values increasing between 1986 and 1991 by 62 per cent compared with 29 per cent and leasehold prices increasing in the catchment area and falling in the 'individual-farmers' area. Farming has also become more diverse in the catchment approach area, with a greater range of crops grown and more livestock kept.

The process of implementation of the catchment approach itself has varied according to the human resources available and differing interpretations of the degree of participation necessary to mobilize the catchment community. As a result, the impact on the adoption of new conserving technologies and practices has also varied. A multi-district impact study and self-evaluation carried out by over 20 officers of MALDM was the first to link the process of implementation with the impacts occurring in different catchments in various agroecological and sociocultural contexts. The MALDM investigating team used the framework of 'sustainability indicators' described in Chapter Two to assess the changes that had occurred as a result of the catchment approach with the local people of six catchments in Western, Rift Valley and Central Provinces.

The MALDM team discovered that the impacts varied according to the quality of the interaction between extension staff and local people. When participation in planning and implementation was interactive and interdisciplinary, the impacts were substantially greater than when participation was simply consultative (Table 10.1). In an interactively planned catchment, such as Siuna-Miruli in Bungoma District, an interdepartmental PRA is conducted to launch the catchment, which includes a *baraza* for presenting back findings and developing joint plans. The catchment conservation committee is freely elected, and includes both women and men. Farmers participate with the divisional planning team in planning and laying out the conservation measures on their farms, and a hand-over *baraza* is held after implementation. Afterwards, the committees tend to remain active and committed to maintenance and replication. They also take on new challenges beyond soil and water conservation.

In the conventionally planned catchments, such as Shiakunga in Kakamega District, the launch process begins with a *baraza*, which is held mainly for publicity purposes. The catchment committees are sometimes elected, but more frequently are selected by chiefs or local leaders. Women are rarely represented on the committees, and farmers are not involved directly in planning and layout. The committees tend to become inactive soon after intensive contact with extension staff ends.

As a result of this participatory evaluation, it has become clear that where there is mobilization of the community, support to strong local groups, committed local staff and collaboration with other departments in interdisciplinary planning and implementation of the catchment approach, there is increased agricultural productivity, diversification into new enterprises, reduction in resource degradation, enhancement of water resources, improvement in the activities of local groups and independent replication to neighbouring communities within two years. These improvements have occurred without payment or subsidy, and are therefore more likely to be sustained.

The implications for agricultural development are significant, as the productivity increases have been between 10 and 30 per cent where there has been interactive participation, compared with 5 per cent or less in other catchments. Few external resources, such as fertilizers and pesticides, are currently used by smallholder farmers in Kenya, because currency devaluations, inflation and weak marketing mechanisms have made their costs prohibitive and their supply erratic. Increased yields have been achieved largely with locally available resources and skills, coupled with support from an external institution now concerned with facilitating local efforts rather than directing them. Several studies have reported the benefits of increased yields following terracing (Tjernström, 1992; Figueiredo, 1986; Grönvall, 1987; Hunegnaw, 1987; Holmgren and Johansson, 1988; Lindgren, 1988), and reduced soil erosion (MOA, 1981), but few have reported impacts on whole communities.

Changes in operational procedures

None of these improvements could be achieved without significant changes in the operational procedures of SWCB and MALDM. There is widespread support within the branch at all levels for the use of participatory

Table 10.1: Comparison of the impacts of participatory rural appraisal and the catchment approach in six catchments in Kenya

Catchment name	Siuna-Miruli	Sinenden	Muroki	Gaturia	Getuya	Shiakunga
District	Bungoma	West Pokot	Trans Nzoia	Nyeri	Kirinyaga	Kakamega
Year of implementation	1991–2	1989–90	1988–89	1990–91	1991–92	1989–90
Launch process	PRA launch Baraza	No PRA Baraza	No PRA Baraza	No PRA Baraza	No PRA Baraza	No PRA Baraza
Organization and composition of the CCC	Elected women and men	Elected women and men	Elected men only	Elected men only	Elected and selected men only	Selected men only
DPT committed and active	Very active	Very active	Very active	Active	Active	Not active
Community mobilized by DPT	Yes	Yes	Yes	No	No	No
Other contributing factors to community mobilization	Hand-over Baraza	Provincial Field Day	—	—	—	—
Farmers involved in planning and layout	Yes	Yes	No	No	No	No (no DPT)
PRA study conducted, independently of CA	No	Yes	No	Yes	No	No
Conservation before CA	20%	40%	30%	60%	20%	10%
Conservation after CA (% farms concerved)	90%	90%	90%	80%	60%	10%
Maize yields*	+ + +	+ + +	+ + +	+ +	+	—
Fodder availablity*	+ +	+ +	+ +	+	+	0
Real wage labour rates*	+ +	ND	ND	ND	ND	ND
Trees numbers*	+	+ +	+	+	+ +	+
Diversity of crops grown*	+ +	+ +	+	+	+ (cash crops)	—
Multiple cropping*	+ +	+ +	+	+	+	0
Reappearance of springs; surface water availability	Yes	Yes	Yes	No	No	No
CCC active during implementation	Very active	Very active	Active	Active	Active	Not active

138

CCC active after implementation						
○ known by other farmers	Yes	Yes	Yes	Somewhat	Somewhat	No
○ active	Very active	Active	Not active	Not active	Not active	Not active
CCC developed own management rules	Yes	Yes	No	No	No	No
Replication to neighbouring catchments:						
○ aware of changes	Yes	Yes	Yes	Yes	Yes	No
○ adopting practices	Yes	Yes	Yes	No	No	No

Notes: * – relative changes (+ = increase; + + = significant increase; +++ = very significant; — no change/ no activity)

CA – Catchment Approach; CCC – Catchment Conservation Committee; DPT – Divisional Planning Team; ND – no data; PRA – Participatory Rural Appraisal

methods for planning and implementation, and for collaboration between different government departments. Recent efforts have aimed at drawing on the skills and resources of interested NGOs to join the branch in these activities and develop an effective participatory methodology for working with pastoralist groups to improve rangeland management in the arid and semi-arid lands. Senior officers who were trained in the participatory methods and procedures in one or more of a series of national participatory rural appraisal workshops organized by the branch since 1989 are now training their own staff members to employ them in their work.

At the end of each rapid catchment analysis phase, after the CCC has been elected and local priorities and conservation objectives have been set out, a detailed catchment report is written and distributed to all relevant institutions and individuals. This practice is now seen as a fundamental part of the process, helping to build a strong institutional memory within the branch and set high standards for future work. In this way, new institutional norms and conventions are created which emphasize interdisciplinary teamwork, interdepartmental collaboration, active farmer participation in all phases of analysis, planning and implementation, and thorough documentation of the process.

Farmers and extension workers alike have recognized how different the catchment approach is to past approaches (Box 10.1). Their comments reflect widespread perceptions of those involved in the participatory catchment planning and implementation process adopted by the SWCB. These statements reveal that the success of the catchment approach owes far more to its emphasis on improving a constructive dialogue between farmers and government agents than it does to introducing innovative conservation technologies and practices.

As the initial planning is conducted within the catchment by an interdisciplinary team working closely with all sectors of the community, the

Box 10.1: **Selection of comments from various actors on the perceived differences between the catchment approach and the former approaches to soil and water conservation**

Source of comments	*Comments on the catchment approach*
Farmers: on meeting interdisciplinary teams in their fields	○ 'It is nice that you are walking here in the fields even though it is hot, so that you can understand us.' ○ 'I have never seen this before. We are very happy to see so many government officers visiting us in this way.
Local extension workers: on the quality of the interaction with local people	○ 'One farmer was sceptical, but when we explained with the help of the map what we were doing he said this was very good. He was so pleased to see the different ministries working together.' ○ 'Now when I meet people from the catchment, they are anxious to know when we are going to be doing work.' ○ 'I came to realize these farmers know so much.' ○ 'Even when I was a student, I never used to interact like this with farmers.
Catchment Conservaton Committee chairmen: on being elected at a *baraza*	○ 'If you come back, next time you will find a changed catchment.' ○ 'Thank you very much for electing me chairman, and now we have these implements for soil conservation we are going to embark on serious business.'
Senior officials: on the wider benefits of the process	○ 'One success was uniting the community. They know there are resources they could exploit better, just by working together.' ○ 'Farmers realize that the Ministry does not have the money to solve all their problems, but they do like the fact that they can easily make contact with us now.'

proposals for action based on a combination of locally articulated priorities and externally perceived opportunities are highly site specific. This is quite unlike the conventional approach, where messages were passed from the Ministry via district officers and their juniors to farmers. In Kericho District, six catchments[3] in the tea-dairy zone were planned in parallel in May 1990 (Pretty, 1990; MOA/MALDM, *passim*). Existing plans suggested that the key problems and solutions would vary little between sites, the furthest of which were only 20 km apart. Following interactive participation and the use of participatory methods, communities discussed and ranked proposals in each of the *barazas*.

In five *barazas*, ten proposals were agreed, in the remainder only seven were discussed. Of these 57 proposals, 30 were different. Only six were common to three or more catchments. These were for roof catchments and tanks for drinking water, improved fodder production, local tree nurseries, better dairy marketing, improved access roads, and better SWC extension. More than half were specific to an individual catchment, such as better dip management, energy-saving stoves, livestock extension, more woodlots, and attention to disputes over land transfers within families. Even though not all proposals were directly concerned with SWC, action would indirectly benefit soil and water resources. Roof catchments, for example, store water on farm, allowing livestock to be zero-grazed rather than taken to riverine areas. Permanently housed livestock means an accessible source of manure for the farm and the protection of fragile lands from overgrazing. Local on-farm tree nurseries increase the availability of tree seedlings, and thus remove the transport costs and losses commonly incurred. Better access roads into inaccessible catchments means that marketing of milk is easier, so encouraging more zero-grazed livestock.

This further indicates that the catchment is an appropriate level for SWC planning. None the less, recommendations for action at a broader district-level can be made; for example, the popularity of the roof catchments proposals to ease the drinking water constraint for villagers and their livestock, dairy co-operatives and the pressing requirement for upgrading rural access roads demonstrate that these options would be important across at least the whole of Belgut Division in Kericho District.

The wider implications

As a government agency, the SWCB is unusual in that it has adopted participatory procedures to mobilize local communities for resource conservation. It has been successful because it has evolved methodologies for interactive participation. But the methodologies alone do not explain the

---

[3] These were Chemorir, Cheplanget, Cheronget, Kabaswet, Koiwelalach and Mindililwet, all in Belgut Division, and all within the tea-dairy (UM1) agroecological zone.

success. There have also been important institutional factors supportive of the changes required for the use of participatory methods. At the international level, these include long-term financial, institutional and technical support from the Swedish International Development Cooperation Agency (SIDA). This will continue to be essential if the catchment approach is to help stimulate the spread of resource-conserving technologies and practices into those areas where the SWCB has yet to venture, particularly in the more complex, diverse, risk-prone environments. At the national level, there has been support from senior officials for an approach that brings results for soil and water conservation and for local farmers. At the professional level, there has been a transformation of the normal role of extension worker from teacher to facilitator, with extension workers no longer concerned with passing messages to – hopefully compliant – farmers. And at the local level, there have been changes in communities, as they have increasingly taken greater responsibility for conservation activities through their own organizations and committees.

There is much that governments, NGOs and donors can learn from the SWCB, particularly those still making use of subsidies and financial incentives to promote improved land husbandry. The history of the conservation of soil and water resources in Kenya clearly demonstrates that sustainable development occurs through mobilization of communities, not through coercion and control.

11
Large-scale Government Programmes: Watershed Development in Rajasthan, India

Anirudh Krishna

Introduction

A MASSIVE GOVERNMENT initiative for integrated watershed development was started in early 1991 in India's north-western state of Rajasthan, when the state government created a new, multi-disciplinary Department of Watershed Development and Soil Conservation (WD&SC). By 1993, the new department was conducting work on more than 100 000 hectares annually, and department staff were working in collaboration with a large number of community organizations. A cadre of some 2000 staff had been trained in the multiple tasks of integrated watershed development, and a range of low-cost, area-specific technologies had been adopted by farmers.

What is special about this Rajasthan experience is a sense of organizational mission. This chapter describes the manner in which the organization came to define its mission. It highlights the organizational arrangements and institutional mechanisms that were developed to facilitate a successful achievement of this mission. The innovations that were developed have resulted in considerable success in several programme locations.

Rajasthan: why watershed development?

More than any other state in the country, Rajasthan depends on rainfall for meeting all its biomass needs. Of its total land area of 34 million hectares, 2.3mha are irrigated by wells and tubewells and only about 1.6mha are canal-irrigated. Since the sustainability of well and tubewell use is critically dependent on rainfall, almost all of the State is thus rainfall dependent.

Mean annual rainfall increases from 250mm in the western (arid) part of the state through 500mm in the central (semi-arid) part, to a high of about 1000mm in the south-east, and 90 per cent of precipitation occurs between July and September. Agriculture is the major occupation of almost 80 per cent of the population, with animal husbandry playing a critical role in protecting against the uncertainties inherent in rainfed crop production. The harvest is inadequate to meet local needs in three years out of every five. This is usually accompanied by severe fodder and drinking water shortages. In the arid areas, and parts of the semi-arid areas, groundwater is found at great depth and is high in dissolved salt content.

Watershed development is thus of critical importance for Rajasthan. However, apart from a few very small-scale projects implemented by scattered NGOs, no work of this type had been done prior to 1991. The state government had separate, specialized line agencies dealing with soil conservation, forestry, dryland crops, etc. Each of these agencies worked in isolation from all the others. There was hardly any involvement of local people in the field operations of any agency, except as day-wage labour. All field work was fully subsidized and planned from above. As a result, since there was little sense of ownership among local people, assets created by these projects were not maintained, and they deteriorated quite rapidly.

Performance of staff and of departments was judged by their ability to deliver on annual targets of area and expenditure. Apart from professional pride and peer appreciation, there was little organizational incentive for staff to strive for quality or sustainability.

Traditions among government development agencies were thus not ideally suited to provide any easy resolutions to the new department's quest for integration, participation and sustainability. On the other hand, since no other agency had the capacity to carry out the task in even a tiny part of the area that requires this type of treatment (nearly 25 million hectares), the state has to play the central role.

Making a start

Starting on a huge scale

The immediate impetus for the state government's decision to set up a new department was provided by the offer of large amounts of programme funds on soft terms (mostly grant) from the central government and from the World Bank.[1]

Work was to be taken up simultaneously on 250 watersheds located throughout the state.[2] Each watershed was to be worked on for a period of five to seven years, after which time no further funding would be available for that area. The programmes, designed as they were by the World Bank and the central government, were broadly pre-determined and were cast

---

[1] Rs 1360 million came from the central government (GOI) to finance projects under its National Watershed Development Programme for Rainfed Areas (NWDPRA) over the period 1991–95. An additional Rs 740 million was provided by the World Bank under its Integrated Watershed Development (Plains) Project, IWDP.

[2] The term 'watershed' in Rajasthan is taken to mean an area of between 1000 to 2000 hectares that drains at a common point. For planning purposes, each 'watershed' is divided into between five and eight micro-watersheds.

mostly in a top-down mode. However, there were some flexibilities, and it was here that the department looked to find space for innovation.

The Soil Conservation Wing of the Agriculture Department, with about 1000 staff, was to be merged into, and form the nucleus of, the new department. Staff from other line departments could be deputed in the numbers required. But as neither retrenchment nor redeployment of existing staff were feasible options, the new department would for several years have a preponderance of soil conservationists in its ranks. The need to justify the large initial staff base provided additional pressure to step up the pace. The numbers were such that we needed to treat about 100 000 hectares annually, which is ten times the area that had been covered in any previous year under soil conservation schemes.

There was thus no room for the kind of leisurely experimentation which so many academics advise (see Korten, 1980; Rondinelli, 1998). This is a reality which those of us working in government have got used to accepting.

Though speedy implementation was a definite imperative, no other guidance was available to the new department, and programme objectives were only broadly defined.

The problem was that both the state government and the funding agencies thought of watershed development mainly in technical terms, through the extension of new dryland technologies, such as soil conservation, water harvesting, improved agronomic practices, alternate cropping patterns, and fruit and fuelwood plantations. The *technical* dimensions of the task were emphasized at the expense of the *administrative* and, especially, the *social organization* dimensions. Thus, although 'participatory development' was an avowed goal of both the World Bank and the GOI programmes, there was no provision in either programme for any activity related to social organization.

Creating a common purpose

Having come into existence at the end of January 1991, the department had about four months of lead time before the monsoon season in which to gear itself up for first-year field implementation. There was thus little time available for a comprehensive strategy to be drafted. We had to plunge right in, get our hands dirty and refine our methods as we went along. This was, at the same time, both a drawback and an advantage. Since even the most senior officials had little prior conception of the innovations required, there was a general willingness to experiment. This, in the words of a visiting GOI official, enabled 'a widespread unleashing of the creative talent of field staff'.

A set of four three-day conferences was held by head office in February and March 1991. These were attended by the leaders of each field unit (there were 97) and their supervisors. The objectives and programming needs of the new task of watershed development were discussed in an open, semi-structured manner, with staff at each level being encouraged to give their views. Field officials were given a simple message: 'start with what you know, what you have resources for; what people want; do small-scale experiments of whatever you think might work'. It was agreed that no penalties would be enforced for experiments that failed. Supervisory staff would play a facilitative role, liaising with researchers, NGOs and field units in an effort to unearth and make available alternative best practices.

A range of new methods was devised innovatively and field-tested by staff acting on their own initiative. Methods that 'worked' were made available to other colleagues. At the end of the first-year planting season, extensive debriefing sessions were held. It emerged that significant progress had been made in developing area-specific technologies. Indigenous practices had been actively sought out, and, in many areas, local practices were found which had potential for wider application.

Early impacts

Considerable progress had been made during the first year, and a common vocabulary had emerged among department staff. Field results were encouraging and generated considerable enthusiasm among staff and local residents alike. A variety of practices had been experimented with. Tables 11.1 and 11.2 present some results for fodder production on common lands, and foodgrain production on privately-owned lands.

Tenfold increases in fodder yields from village common lands occurred in almost all locations. These early, visible results were important in demonstrating to staff and village residents alike that there were significant gains to be made from the new programme. Increases in grain yields on treated private lands also provided evidence of increasing productivity.

One problem area that still remained was the appropriate manner of social intervention. As the government, we had tried to overcome people's

Table 11.1: Fodder production on common lands (kg/ha)

Treatment	Eklingnath watershed	Kotri watershed
1. Control (no treatment)	25	35
2. Protection only (fencing)	75	65
3. *Agave* with V-ditch	210	385
4. *Vetiver* with V-ditch	167	460
5. *Cenchrus* with V-ditch	200	470
6. Chiselling at 2-metre intervals	259	406

Source: CTAE 1992

Table 11.2: **Foodgrain production on private lands (t/ha)**

Treatment	Sorghum Kotri watershed	Pearl Millet Barna watershed
1. Control (no treatment)	0.16	0.6
2. Field bunding	0.39	0.88
3. *Vetiver* barriers	0.46	0.93
4. *Cenchrus* barriers	n/a	0.72

Source: CTAE 1992

feelings of apathy and disinterest by going out freely among them. Staff participated in village discussions, which were held in order to arrive at a common understanding of the problem and to debate potential solutions. Some of us thought that showing a film would be a good way to start a discussion, but topical films were not easily available. The first film that we could get hold of was given to us by the World Bank. It was not about watershed development, or about Rajasthan. The film described farmers' experience with vetiver grass, but in Fiji no less! Still, this worked. People came to see the film and stayed to talk about the problems of dryland farming. They organized into users' committees and began to accept shared responsibility for implementation.

Still, field staff were plagued by more questions than we had answers to: how far should staff go in helping village residents to develop users' committees and use regulations for common lands? Was there a menu of models that could be discussed with the people of the area? I had thought that NGOs of the state could advise us on these points and perhaps provide some training to staff. We organized a series of workshops with NGOs. A parallel set of meetings were held with two social science research institutions. It was disappointing to find that researchers, NGOs and the government were all suspicious of each other. At this stage, each of them preferred to work separately, in spite of having a common concern.

Developing an integrated strategy

The results of first-year implementation were discussed in more participatory management meetings. Each level of staff participated in giving shape to the strategy that would guide the department's operations. The basic challenge was to integrate three elements:

o Technical: an integrated technology had to be developed combining elements from agriculture, forestry, animal husbandry, horticulture, and whatever other disciplines relate to an area's natural resources.
o Organizational: local residents from different caste and economic groups had to be integrated in order to take joint decisions.

147

○ Administrative: specialists from each of these disciplines had to be integrated into a team.

Most importantly, technology, administrative structure and local organization had to be integrated and compatible with each other. In addition to these requirements, each of these three dimensions had other characteristics that had to be addressed as we formulated our strategy. These are described below.

The technology dimension

Not only did the technology have to be multi-faceted, it also needed to be cheap and easily accessible by local residents. Two reasons pointed to this.

The first reason was the sheer scale of the task: over 25 million hectares in Rajasthan require some watershed development. The department could not, by any means imaginable, cover such a huge area in even 50 years of operation. Our mission, therefore, was to provide replicable demonstrations that could be adopted by residents of a wider area acting on their own account, and with little assistance from outside. The benefits of the new technology had to be clearly established and the techniques themselves had to be cheap.

The second reason was that our surveys indicated that, in order to be 'cheap,' a technique for soil and moisture conservation had to be labour intensive and require less than 40 man-days of work per hectare of land treated. This is equal to Rs 1000 per hectare spent on conservation alone; expenditure on improved production methods is extra. It is too much to expect that an investment of this small amount would permanently, once and for all, transform the face of low-input, high-risk subsistence agriculture. Instead, the technology needed to be renewable, which meant that not only would it have to be cheap, it would also have to be simple, drawing as far as possible on local skills and raw materials.

There was thus a primacy of the local over the central in the organization's search for appropriate technological solutions.

The dimension of social organization

It proved extremely difficult to motivate local people to come together in village organizations that could, through interaction with department staff, play a lead role in watershed development. At the very least, local organizations were essential for managing common lands, which comprise 40–50 per cent of land in each watershed and are the main reservoir of fuelwood and fodder.

Attitudes prevalent in the villages were not supportive of co-operative endeavour. There was widespread breakdown in traditional forms of social organization and the resulting vacuum had been insufficiently filled by the modern, party-politics-based systems. I have heard village people refer to the rifts created by party politics, to the breakdown of social and religious sanctions, to an expanding population that forces larger numbers of people to compete for ever-scarcer resources and to commercialization which widens the gap between the rich and the poor.

Many of these initial attitudes of local people were overcome when staff were able to deliver some early and visible results. People have seen too many examples of government projects that were launched with a fanfare, but which broke down mid-stream and produced indifferent results, or from which funds were skimmed off by officials and local notables.

We needed to restore faith before we could expect people to participate with enthusiasm in the new programmes. Since restoring faith needs situation-specific solutions and since social dynamics vary widely from village to village, there is an overwhelming need for decisions to be made at the points that are closest to the field reality.

The administrative dimension

Both the technology and the social organization dimensions pointed to the need for decentralizing authority to the field level. Since this is a major inversion in a bureaucracy that is steeped in a top-down tradition, it cannot be assumed that field staff would have the confidence to exercise enhanced authority. In most cases, they are afraid and need to be reassured.

The other major task for us consisted of integrating staff drawn from different line departments into a unified and cohesive team. 'Integrated' watershed development required not only that soil and water conservation treatments be installed, but also that improved production systems be introduced on treated lands (as one-off programme-funded demonstrations). Additional staff had to be drawn in from the Departments of Agriculture, Forest, Animal Husbandry and Horticulture.

An obvious administrative task concerned motivating staff. The use of pay- or promotion-related rewards and penalties is made impossible by civil service rules. Peer pressure was weak since staff are drawn from six different departments and, at least initially, had mixed loyalties. Yet, without high levels of motivation, staff could not be expected to act with the level of responsibility that was required in the new decentralized set-up.

Attempting new solutions

A series of important policy decisions, representing an iterative search for appropriate solutions, were taken during the first two years.

On the technology dimension, three major decisions were taken:

o Vegetative conservation methods were to be used in preference to mechanical methods. Although vetiver was preferred (primarily because we knew about it) and head office would arrange to get planting material to as many watersheds as possible, field units were free to experiment with other local species of conservation flora and report results to colleagues. The development of low-cost technical innovations was recognized through a newly-instituted system of departmental awards.

o Members of users' committees and educated, unemployed youths selected by the villages were invited to attend integrated, technical training of two months' duration. Increasingly, project activities were turned over to these 'para-professionals.'

o A technical manual was prepared and updated each year, describing the range of technical solutions that had been developed in the department and elsewhere. Staff were encouraged to develop yet more technical solutions (and to see their names in print).

Decisions relating to the social organization dimension included the following.

o We decided to work with users' committees, constituted through informal elections among area residents in each watershed. Users' committees (UCs) were expected to articulate local priorities for the development of common lands, to arrange for the protection of works, and to determine the criteria for sharing usufruct rights (for grass in the first and each subsequent year, and trees at the end of a longer period). Since we did not come across any existing organization in most villages, we had to enthuse local residents to create new ones.

No fixed formats were prescribed for the structure of UCs or for their procedures of work, though requirements for openness, accountability, and a representative character were stressed. All transactions were conducted in the open and on fixed days of the week. Members of UCs were paid for the hours put in by them.

The task of social mobilization was the most difficult one for us and required the greatest effort by the organization. At the end of two years, we did manage to work alongside effective local organizations in about half of our locations (with half again performing extremely well). UCs in several locations took over primary responsibility for implementation and after-care. The department shared the responsibility for planning and paid out programme funds.

o It was decided that local residents would have to contribute 10 per cent of the cost of work in the form of cash or labour. Field units were quite firm that local residents would be unwilling to contribute any higher proportion as they are not used to government programmes that are not fully subsidized. It was decided to begin with 10 per cent and to step it up as the benefits of the work became clearer and more widespread.

150

A concern for equity was addressed in two ways: by limiting programme expenditures to a fixed amount per participating family and by an insistence that all participants make labour contributions. Many large farmers nevertheless did avail themselves of programme benefits, but on the whole the strategy was more successful than if we had tried to debar large farmers entirely, thereby making enemies of them from day one.

Three decisions expedited progress on the administrative dimension[3]:

○ Tasks in any watershed were not subdivided by technical discipline. Each field-level staff member, from whichever discipline, was made responsible for one micro-watershed and for all the tasks of planning and implementation in that micro-watershed. They could draw upon other specialists in the field unit for technical advice, but could not absolve themselves of responsibility. Cross-disciplinary training was organized to equip field staff for undertaking broad-ranging tasks.

○ Five-year plans of development for every watershed were drawn up in the field through discussions between staff and area residents. Supervisory staff and head office had relatively little say in finalizing these plans. Further, five-year plans were not cast in concrete. First-year implementation was to be on a small scale, so that field officials and area residents could gain familiarity with new methods. Plans could be revised by field units whenever it was felt that new knowledge could be beneficially incorporated. To facilitate rapid, two-way communications between the field and head office, a system of link officers was instituted. Sixteen staff from head office were each allotted a part of the state to which they were responsible for passing problems and progress reports up from the field and suggested solutions down from head office.

○ A high-powered state-level steering committee was constituted. This is chaired by the Agriculture Secretary. Heads of all concerned line departments (Forests, Horticulture, Animal Husbandry, Rural Development) as well as representatives of the Finance and Personnel Departments are members. State and national-level research institutions are also represented. The committee is authorized to determine policy on behalf of the state government, thereby avoiding the delays and frustrations that might have arisen if each actor had to be contacted separately. Issues of co-ordination among line departments are also resolved 'across the table.'

---

[3] In our hurry to get on with the job (of implementation), we paid insufficient attention to process documentation. Beyond maintaining a record that was required to account for expenditure and to explain why certain techniques were preferred over others, many field officers did not keep any other written accounts of the action-research conducted by them. This is proving to be a source of considerable difficulty as the department searches for funds for future projects. Donor agencies, academics and senior bureaucrats want data; it does not help to ask them to visit the field and see things for themselves.

Principal impacts

Expenditure and coverage

These decisions resulted in a reasonably rapid rate of growth and the development of a large range of technical and social innovations for watershed development. However, given that staff had increased from about one thousand in 1991 to some 1800 in 1993, and about another one thousand para-professionals were additionally involved, the expansion in *quantity* of work is, by itself, not surprising. Since the organization's mission in each watershed was to work itself out of a job after developing low-cost technology and promoting the acquisition of skills by local people, other indicators are of equal importance.

The emergence of greater self-reliance among watershed residents also needs to be monitored, but is harder to measure. Cost of work per hectare of land treated is one important indicator. To an extent, diminishing staff costs also serve as a proxy for greater local self-reliance (Table 11.3).

These gross figures for the entire state hide wide disparities that exist between different watersheds and that depend on background and age-group of UC leadership, technical expertise and commitment of local para-professionals, 'people skills' and devotion to the task shown by department staff, etc.

Increased productivity

Encouraging field results, in terms of increased productivity, reduced soil and moisture loss, increases in local incomes, and enhanced supplies of grain, fodder and fuelwood, have continued to be observed as the department has expanded work to cover larger areas each year.

Productivity increases have also occurred on arable lands and grain yields have increased, in some places by as much as 100 to 150 per cent. Farmers in a sample of seven villages, who were interviewed during the evaluation exercise conducted for this study, reported that yields on their fields have doubled in the two to three years since treatment (Singh, pers. comm.).

Table 11.3: Changing costs of work per hectare

	Staff expenditure as a percentage of total annual outlay	Cost per hectare (Rs.)
1991–92	15.8%	4556
1992–93	13.5%	2968
1993–94	12.6%	2906

Source: WD&SC, Rajasthan

Table 11.4: Increase in Fodder Production (1991–93) (sun-dried grass: kg/ha)

	Kotri watershed			Barna watershed		
	1991	1992	1993	1991	1992	1993
Protection only (fencing)	65	550	880	300	490	510
Vetiver with V-ditch	460	1610	1652	686	1920	2050
Cenchrus with V-ditch 470	1390	1840	1133	2130	2250	—
Chiselling at 2-metre intervals	406	1730	1270	1166	2060	2200

Source: CTAE 1994

Farmers have been encouraged to try out newer and more drought-resistant varieties of rainfed crops, to experiment with new species of crops (including tree crops), to adopt better agronomic practices (contour cultivation, strip cropping, early ploughing, etc.), and to work with improved farm implements.

Notable successes have also occurred in the management of common lands (Box 11.1).

Box 11.1: Treatment on common lands

Silvi-pastoral plantation on common lands is another activity that local people have undertaken with growing enthusiasm, acting through their UCs. In the first year, village people were suspicious of any suggestion to take up such works on common lands. Their experience with previous government projects had led them to believe that if they allowed a government agency to fence the village commons, they would no longer have the right to enter the land and enjoy its produce. These suspicions diminished when it was discovered that the new project planned to work in a different way. Since all the work, including the vegetative fencing, was to be done by UCs, and since the grass produced each year was to be harvested by local people following whatever rules their UC decided, there was no loss of control to an outside agency. In the first year, 1991, village people were hesitant and watchful, but by 1993 over 30 000 hectares of common lands were being fenced and treated annually.

In addition to improved varieties of grass and legumes, over a million trees were planted on common lands to serve as a common pool of fuelwood. Tree species were selected by the UCs, who themselves contracted to raise the seedlings in decentralized village nurseries. Members of UCs, and the nursery raisers selected by them, were trained in various aspects of nursery and planting techniques. Careful attention to seed selection, nursery raising, land preparation and timely plantation have resulted in high survival rates.

While experimenting with and extending new techniques, a close link has been maintained between department staff and the research stations of the Rajasthan Agriculture University.

Remaining causes for concern

Although WD&SC has made a useful beginning in Rajasthan, there are a few aspects that are still a cause for concern, either because progress in these respects has been slow, or because the solutions found are not quite reassuring.

The question of subsidy

Even after three years of development, people still say that, although they can relate large yield increases to the work, they will undertake work only if the Government provides some subsidy. Farmers surveyed in June 1994 reported that they would be unwilling to take up even the most attractive practices (horticulture, agroforestry) if they had to personally contribute more than 25 to 40 per cent of the total cost.

In part, this is a reflection of poverty and of a diminishing concern for the land, but 40 years of wholly subsidized development programmes are equally responsible. A government programme that is not fully subsidized is looked at with suspicion: 'are they [staff] making off with some part of the money?' These doubts, hinting at that age-old malady, corruption, were largely exaggerated. The scope for corruption had been considerably reduced by a process of conducting all transactions in the open, and by UCs publicizing all plans and rendering all accounts fully to the village assembly in monthly meetings.

However, the questions when posed still needed to be answered. In the three years that I was director, we had to face such questions more than once from state legislators, district-level politicians and the press. The hostility of local, party-based politicians became more pronounced in some places where UCs had been doing comparably well and UC leaders had attracted a considerable following in the village.

Political support

The need for political support became more obvious as the work progressed and often became a bone of contention between two opposing groups in a village. Since not much else was going on in many of the villages where we worked, the UC became a readily visible target for carrying forth existing group rivalries. Politicians at various levels would be roped in to take sides in village conflicts; often, work would stop until allegations could be enquired into. Though we did make attempts to inform and educate

154

area legislators and arranged for cabinet ministers and party leaders to make visits to the field, these were at best makeshift solutions. Sustainable solutions could result only from linking up village-level UCs with higher-level political structures.

Legal and political status for UCs

UCs needed to gain legal status and become corporate bodies for legal purposes. Although they were managing all work that was done on common lands, the land itself continued to be vested, not with the UCs, but with government departments (Revenue and Forest) and village *panchayats*.[4] The departments and the *panchayat* were, in most cases, happy to hand over use-rights to UCs, but the transfer would be valid in law only when UCs were formally registered as co-operatives or companies, under the existing laws.

Each of these laws requires that UCs conform to some fairly standard organization structure, that they adopt standardized rules and procedures and that they open their books for government inspectors. So far, WD&SC has been unsuccessful in effecting any compromise acceptable both to the UCs and to the bodies that administer these laws. But some enduring arrangement will have to be found. This is especially important because most village people suggest that after the department's involvement is over, they would be unlikely themselves to make the effort required to keep these institutions alive (Singh, pers. comm.).

Linkages with NGOs

One source of support for UCs, in the post-project phase, could arise from networking with NGOs. I have already mentioned that in the first year, 1990–91, we tried, without much success, to establish links with NGOs of the state. However, in the later years, initiatives taken by staff at the field level proved to be more successful. Some of these initiatives were followed up by head office and have resulted in the formulation of a project proposal which envisages NGOs, WD&SC and UCs working collaboratively on a new set of projects. A new collaborative project funded in part by the Swiss Development Cooperation started operating in four watersheds in 1995.

---

[4] *Panchayats* are legally constituted bodies for a single village or a group of villages having a certain size of population. They are vested with some quasi-judicial powers and have also been responsible for some community development works. A valid question is: why did we not work with the *panchayats* themselves, instead of constructing new UCs? Jodha (1990) captures our feeling exactly: 'Despite their legal powers, the village *panchayats* are generally unable to enforce any regulation about CPRs [common property resources]. The dependence of *panchayats* on community votes, compelling them to avoid unpopular steps like enforcing CPR-user obligations, and their domination by the influential élite with little interest in CPRs, make these institutions ineffective.'

The watershed development programme has very little direct concern for the problems of the landless. Apart from the work done to develop common lands to provide fodder and fuelwood, there is a small provision in NWDPRA for grant-cum-loan-based assistance to landless persons to start small-scale village enterprises. This is neither sufficient, nor has the department done much about utilizing it effectively. Much more needs to be done.

Many of these problem areas reflect the limitations of a top-down programme, the pre-formatted provisions of which are unhelpful in dealing with many unanticipated, but nevertheless important, issues as they come up in the course of implementation.

Concluding observations

Prior to this programme, Rajasthan had little or no experience with large-scale, integrated watershed development interventions with small farmers in rainfed areas. Much has been learned about what to do and what not to do.

The integration of technology, social organization, and administrative arrangements has been crucial to programme progress. The department has tried to approximate, on a large scale, the methodology for integrated watershed development that academics have advised and that many NGOs have successfully implemented. The verb 'approximate' is used advisedly. There are many constraints – in structure, systems, processes, culture and traditions – faced by government agencies that limit optimal responses.

A need for integration is perhaps the most important requirement of large-scale government projects that are otherwise relatively less constrained – in terms of resources, technical manpower and policy support – when compared with NGOs and researchers. Although technical innovations are a very important contribution of the work in Rajasthan, good technical solutions, when unsupported by local institutional arrangements and administrative back-up, have rarely made for acceptable results. Technology is viewed here as one component of the overall strategy.

12
A New Approach for Government: The Doon Valley Integrated Watershed Management Project, Uttar Pradesh, India

K.C. Thapliyal, S.T.S. Lepcha and P. Kumar[1]

Introduction

Doon Valley is located in the foothills of the Himalayas. The biological diversity of the Himalayan ecosystem has coexisted with human cultural diversity since time immemorial. Populations were never high and human demands were minimal and well within the self-sustaining levels of the ecosystem. However, the extension of communications and the influx of a large number of people has led to the depletion of forest cover, over-grazing, bad land use and the construction of roads, particularly in areas susceptible to landslides, straining this delicate balance. Excessive runoff and accelerated soil erosion have become the order of the day, causing recurrent floods which have a devastating effect on agricultural land and property. The Himalayas form the source and main catchment area of all the major rivers of the Indo-Gangetic Plains. It is thus essential to treat catchment areas on a watershed basis, especially as the Himalayas are a young mountain ecosystem, and therefore very fragile.

The Doon Valley occupies 185 000 hectares spread around the town of Dehra Dun and includes parts of seven sub-watersheds. The elevation is between 500 and 2500 metres. The project area consists of four main zones:

o In the north and north-east are steep, south-facing slopes of the middle hills, with a maximum elevation of 2500m. The steeply sloping land of the middle hills is inherently unstable and susceptible to landslides.
o The upper parts of the valley are deeply incised, old alluvial terraces.
o The central valley of gently sloping pediments is crossed by broad belts of seasonal rivers.

---

[1] At the time of writing, the authors were working for the Watershed Management Directorate, Government of Uttar Pradesh, Dehradun, India. Although this paper was prepared by officers of the Government of Uttar Pradesh, the views expressed are personal and do not necessarily reflect the official policy of the Government of Uttar Pradesh, the Government of India or the European Commission.

○ In the eastern sector and along the southern watershed there are steeply dissected slopes with an average elevation of 500 to 1000m.

The majority of the population are subsistence farmers with low incomes.

Lessons from the past

After the devastating floods of August 1978 in North India, the Government of India (GOI) appointed a working group to formulate an action plan for flood control in the Indo-Gangetic Basin. Officials from the UP Forest Department prepared an integrated watershed management plan and its implementation was assisted by the World Bank under the *Himalayan Watershed Management Project* (HWMP).

The primary objective of the HWMP was to minimize, in selected areas, further deterioration of the Himalayan ecosystem, depletion of forest cover, overgrazing, bad land use and road development. In addition, efforts were to be made to improve agriculture productivity and enhance rural incomes.

Looking back at what this approach achieved, there were many problems encountered:

○ Because of the large area of operation, there was a greater focus on techno-economic issues than on social issues. The project had set a number of targets, and so village plans were prepared and designed specifically to meet these targets.
○ Furthermore, it was not considered useful to incorporate local knowledge into technical implementation activities. This caused a lesser acceptability of the technologies by local people.
○ As the approach did not take into account social organization, techno-economic changes could not keep pace with the changes in social/community groups, leading to unsustainable maintenance of common property resources.
○ The top-down approach, and the fact that projects were spread over large areas, meant that local people could not be involved from the initial stages in planning, implementation, monitoring and evaluation. They were not properly consulted at every stage and their involvement in the project did not motivate them to maintain their assets on a sustainable basis.
○ Staff were not well trained or oriented in sociological methodologies for consulting and collaborating with people from the initial stages. Neither did they have skills in organizational development.

A new approach

Based on these lessons, the Doon Valley Project is now focusing on a community participatory approach to integrated watershed management, emphasizing people's involvement in planning, implementation, monitoring and evaluation for sustainable maintenance of the project assets. For a government organization to work in partnership with the people is a novel experiment. In order to address the needs and the priorities of the people appropriately, and to motivate them towards self-mobilization, participatory rural appraisal (PRA) has been adopted, the centrality being consultation, collaboration and participatory learning processes. A vital corollary of this approach is that conventional targets become irrelevant. Each village may have an entirely different development agenda, reflecting unique priorities and requirements. Watershed management requires a great deal of in-built flexibility in planning, implementation and management.

PRA is used to develop village plans. In this interactive way, villagers draw up plans for their own development. Later on, these plans are used as the basis of annual plans for the project. In this context, the role of the Watershed Management Directorate (WMD) becomes very important. WMD is a multi-disciplinary agency of the Hill Development Department, Government of Uttar Pradesh, with staff deputed from line agencies and operating under a unified line of command. The aim is for watershed management to become a people's movement, with the project staff acting as facilitators.

Opening approaches

A number of criteria are used to select villages (such as the degree of erosion, forest cover, elevation, and socio-economic status); however, the degree of erosion and socio-economic status are the primary criteria used. Often hill villages are sited on a ridge, with village lands spanning more than one catchment. Keeping this in mind, project activities seek to target village watersheds that represent the areas of influence of each village (Figure 12.1). The ultimate aim is to cover the complete hill watersheds.

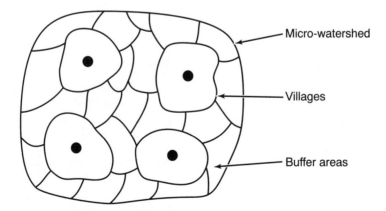

Figure 12.1:   Schematic diagram of honeycomb approach

159

The areas of micro-watersheds not used by villages are to be treated separately, with the active involvement of villages for sustainable maintenance. The initial approach of the project staff is to first identify with villagers an activity that is a priority to them. This can serve as an entry point to enable the project to develop rapport and build confidence with the community. For example, in Chowki village women identified the need for an embroidering and tailoring enterprise. Project staff made this their entry point and supported their sewing lessons and helped in establishing local marketing links. This assured a daily income for the women. Concurrently the women agreed to co-operate in developing fodder tree plantations on wastelands next to the village.

Sociological and technical training

Training staff and local people is the key mechanism for implementing and achieving sustainable development. The main types of training identified by the project include participatory planning, implementation, monitoring and evaluation; gender sensitization; and management analysis (e.g. human relations skills development). This training has been crucial in reorienting the approach of staff to work in a more participatory way. Examples of some of the transformations that have occurred as a result are shown in Table 12.1.

Table 12.1: The impact of training

Input	Who Trained	Output
Village ecosystem planning	Project staff	Understanding of Himalayan village ecosystem. Break in vertical hierarchy as well as inter and intra barrier of communications.
PRA training	Project staff	Attitudinal change towards people and people's attitude towards the project. Methodology of PRA generated in the working pattern of project staff. Local empowerment.
Villagers visit other areas of successful watershed management	Villagers	Changes in the perception of villagers regarding management of natural resources, organizational development and distribution of common property resources.
Study tour and exposure visits to other participatory watershed projects.	Project staff	Staff's confidence built in using participatory approaches

160

Training paraprofessionals

Villagers from an initial nucleus village are now being trained in various skills such as cutting and tailoring; vermiculture; gobargas plants; Lantana basket weaving; midwifery and participatory planning, monitoring and evaluation, with the help of local NGOs. In Chowki, 44 villagers have been trained so far.

Once trained, they in turn would cover the surrounding hamlets or villages, because there are not enough staff to cover all of these. They will act as an interface between villagers and WMD throughout the three years that WMD works in a village.

Community participation in research

Community participation in research projects is an essential ingredient for sustainable development. This approach has been started by the project with a number of NGOs/research institutions to solve area-specific problems. In these research projects, scientists will act as facilitators and the community-managed research will be easily acceptable to the community. Some of the specific problems identified for participatory research are:

○ recharging of springs
○ weed (Parthenium and Lantana) control
○ improving indigenous crops/farming practices
○ indigenous medicine for cattle
○ nursery practice in indigenous grasses, shrubs, medicinal plants, essential oils and aromatic plants
○ vermiculture, organic farming, compost making, proper use of compost, etc.

Impacts

The Doon Valley Project is still too young to measure the impacts in terms of meeting project objectives. However, some perceptible changes have been observed (see also Box 12.1):

○ project staff are linking sociological issues with technical issues – eg. PRA plans have been prepared by villagers with WMD staff as facilitators
○ a feeling of local empowerment in grassroots staff as well as villagers, especially women, due to their participation in preparation and implementation of village plans
○ breaking in hierarchy – staff becoming participative
○ generating curiosity from other agencies (governmental and nongovernmental). 29 participants from GOs/NGOs have been provided training in PRA planning

o bridge building with NGOs and line agencies. In order to link the non-project components with other NGOs and line agencies, district as well as state-level committees have been formed. We invite them to discuss the plans with project staff and villagers. In this triangular discussion, plans are chalked out to solve the problems of the villages

o congenial working atmosphere

o formation of user's groups. Assistance is provided in establishing savings and credit groups with revolving funds supported by contributions from villagers and the project.

Box 12.1: Villager's perceptions of some of the impacts

o reduced pressure on the forest, and grass is coming up naturally
o stall feeding has been encouraged
o cowdung collection is easier, and its use as manure has enhanced agricultural productivity
o impact on other villagers to initiate an interest in the protection of forests and community feelings
o less pressure on government for protection of forests
o benefits from the approach have strengthened people's confidence in WMD and in the government

---

Impacts on equity

Although there is a land-related bias in the project, the landless, poor and marginal farmers have not been forgotten. The project has provided opportunities to achieve economic sustainability through income-generating activities, skill formation and cultivation of high-income cash crops. Women are also an important focus of the work. Traditionally, women have been responsible for the cycling of biomass from the forests, fields and pastures to the homestead. They are the managers of the common resources of fuel, fodder, water and medicinal plants. Traditionally, however, most technical information from outside has been directed at men rather than women. This is ironic when one realizes that many men from Doon Valley spend much of their time in employment outside the villages. Advice on better methods of resource management has therefore not reached the women. The project has therefore facilitated a change from male-centred programmes towards a sharing of knowledge with rural women. Initially all project staff were male. This made it difficult to interact with women in the villages. Therefore young women were recruited from a nearby university to act as motivators with field staff. They have now been supplemented by village motivators, recruited from women in the villages. This has led to better community motivation and interaction with project staff, and has led

162

to the empowerment of local women, who have begun to take an active interest in development activities.

Limiting factors

As a whole, the Doon Valley Project is in a transitional phase towards the new approach of participatory rural development. The process has encountered a number of constraints which are being addressed by both staff and villagers:

○ 'Top-down' procedure of the existing system has to be rationalized in this new approach.
○ Very few planners and policy-makers insist on implementation of this new approach.
○ Project activities are land-based, which causes difficulties in assisting landless/small-marginal farmers.
○ Very little research and development of marketing facilities has been carried out at grassroots level.
○ Deconditioning of communities from past exposure to development methodologies.
○ Congruent social change is time consuming.
○ Low revolving fund for sustainable management of project assets.
○ Poor co-operation from line agencies.

As the approach described here is such a new one for a government organization, the organization is obviously experiencing a different work culture for sustainable development. The participatory process is itself a new concept which has to be studied, tested and corrective measures developed as required. This learning process in training, implementation, monitoring and evaluation has been started initially in three villages, and the process taken will also be evaluated.

Acknowledgements

The authors wish to thank their colleagues within WMD and the people of the Doon Valley villages who participated actively in the planning and implementation of project activities. Gratitude is due to the Delegation of the European Commission in New Delhi, Government of UP, Government of India, for financial and technical support for the Doon Valley Project and encouragement during implementation of the new approach. Thanks is also extended to Professor Neela Mukherjee, Jules N. Pretty, Girish Bhardwaj and other numerous NGOs (e.g. SIDH, HARC, NEEDS, HESCO, TARU, PRAYAS, SAMTA; PRIA, BMA, CHEA, INORA, WESA, AKRSP & MYRADA) as well as the T.A. team of W.S. Atkins Ltd., who have provided invaluable assistance.

13
The Impact of the Begnas Tal/Rupa Tal Watershed Management Project, Pokhara, Nepal
MOHAN P. WAGLEY[1]

The project setting

NEPAL HAS AN area of 147 181km² and is situated in the central Himalaya, an area that is young and ecologically fragile. This small mountain kingdom has several watersheds ranging from the big basin of the Kosi river to micro-watersheds of small streams and torrents. Two-thirds of the total population of Nepal live in these upland watersheds where agriculture is mostly at a subsistence level. Many watersheds have physically and biologically deteriorated due to the over-exploitation of natural resources.

Watershed management was first recognized as important by His Majesty's Government of Nepal (HMG) in 1974. Since then, many watershed management projects have been developed and a separate Department of Soil Conservation and Watershed Management established to tackle erosion in an integrated manner.

The Begnas Tal/Rupa Tal (BTRT) Watershed Management Project was started in 1984 as a joint effort of HMG and CARE International. It was initiated to address the problems of resource degradation and decreasing productivity of the watershed, so as to improve the lives of its 40 000 inhabitants. It is seen as a pioneer project, in which communities are empowered to carry out resource conservation and management activities.

The project is located 10km east of Pokhara in Kaski District in Nepal's Western development region, and covers some 173km². The project area represents a typical mid-hill location, with steep hills surrounding the lakes and rivers at altitudes from 600 to 1120 metres.

The project area has steep north-facing slopes ranging from 40° to 65° and gentle south facing dip slopes of 35° to 40° degrees. Farmers cultivate slopes of more than 45°. The aspect and steepness favours cultivation on south-facing slopes, with north-facing slopes often left under forest. Soils are mostly loam or clay loam with low nitrogen content, low to moderate potassium levels and adequate amounts of phosphorous. Organic matter is high only in dense forest, and is entirely absent in degraded land.

---

[1] At the time of the study, the author was working as planning officer, Department of Soil Conservation, Babar Mahal, Kathmandu, Nepal.

The climate is humid sub-tropical, marked by a monsoonal rainfall pattern. The annual average rainfall is 3580 mm, which occurs mostly between May and September.

The cultivated land is generally scattered over numerous plots. The main crops produced are paddy rice, millet, maize, wheat, potato, pulses and oil seed. Terraces of irrigated and rainfed lowlands are generally well built and maintained. Non-irrigated upland fields are intensively cultivated. Fodder trees and grass are maintained at the edges of some of the upland fields. Irrigated and rainfed lowlands are used for production of paddy, wheat, potato and other seasonal crops. Livestock is one of the most important economic activities, as well as being main the source of manure and draught power for ploughing.

In 1994, there were some 40 430 people living in the project area, mostly in settlements located on south-facing slopes. The annual increase in population of the project area is estimated as 2.9 per cent per annum (Krishna *et al.* 1978).

The conservation development efforts of BTRT

The goal of the project was to stabilize the physical environment and increase productivity through sustainable community management of its human and natural resources. To achieve this goal, the project has focused on the following activities:

○ conservation farming to increase farm productivity through soil conservation and farm management practices
○ community forestry to improve the quality and increase the level of community forest management on private and community land
○ agroforestry to improve the productivity of marginal land by introducing multi-purpose fruit and tree species in agro-forestry practices
○ conservation engineering to rehabilitate the physical environment of critical soil erosion sites and undertake water management activities using soft engineering and bio-engineering practices
○ community organization, conservation training and extension to facilitate community participation in the planning, implementation and maintenance of the project activities.

The first phase of the project focused on testing conservation technology, selecting conservation farmers and developing the local institutional context. The second phase was devised to enhance the productivity of the watershed and consequently improve the welfare of local people.

Institutional and organizational process

Local resource management groups were formed at the beginning of the first phase of the project. Farmers were selected to be conservation farmers

165

and their farms to act as demonstration sites. Project efforts to increase agricultural production were concentrated on their farms. Several other project activities were conducted through the formation of user groups for mobilizing people's participation. When the first phase of the project ended, the working strategy was changed slightly. The original concept of user groups was incorporated into community development conservation committees (CDCCs). The aim in this phase was both to strengthen local capacities and organize communities to manage their own resources.

The community development conservation committees (CDCCs)

The CDCC is a non-political development organization consisting of a group of people sharing common priorities for their community's development. These CDCCs were created to ensure an active focus for community participation. They are concerned with addressing local problems and identifying local needs and are efficient at mobilizing local resources.

All CDCCs have their own management rules. A meeting of the CDCC executive members is generally held once a month. Each member of a CDCC pays Rs. 5 per month as membership fees. Some CDCCs have set penalties and fines to be paid by a livestock owner when his livestock damages the crops or plants of other villagers.

The CDCCs that have enough money deposited in a bank provide loans to their members in emergencies. Between Rs. 100 and Rs. 1000 is lent at an interest rate of 2 per cent per month. No asset has to be presented as collateral but the debt must be cleared within two months. Poor local farmers benefit the most from this loan programme.

The CDCC of each village records the farmers' needs and demands and passes them to the project site and headquarters offices. These demands and needs are discussed at the CDCC board meetings, to which professionals from the project's site and central offices are invited. After sorting out the genuine needs for project activities the CDCC board send them to the district development committee for final approval. This process of planning, identifying, and finalizing project activities is carried out at the village level every year.

Members of these groups also motivate other individual farmers to adopt conservation farming practices. A number of innovations have been introduced and propagated in the project area through CDCCs. There are now 94 CDCCs functioning in the project area, each representing one cluster of villages (Table 13.1).

The user group

To implement an activity, a small user group is formed and its members work voluntarily under the guidance and supervision of the CDCC. Local

Table 13.1:   Number of CDCCs and their savings

VDCs	Number of CDCCs	Number of household members	Savings 000s NRs
Hanspur	25	800	72.63
Lekhnath	4	107	23.50
Kalika	15	601	64.09
Rakhi	8	363	14.68
Majthana	14	504	82.10
Begnas	18	341	55.49
Rupakot	10	n/a	n/a
Total	94	2716	312.49

Source: Field Survey and Project Documents.

extension workers, and farmer assistants will help the local community to form user groups.

Once a user group is formed, the design, the estimate, the user contribution and the project's support calculated by professionals will be reviewed and discussed by the user group members. When the project and the user groups are satisfied then a formal agreement is made between the project and the user group for implementing the work under specified terms and conditions. Monitoring and maintenance are also carried out by the users themselves. If necessary, the project provides financial support for the skilled labour and material support to the user groups that are not locally available.

The number of user groups has steadily increased since the start of the project (Table 13.2)

Table 13.2:   Approximate number of farmer households (HH) or user groups (UG) involved in resource conservation work

Activities	Number of HH and UG members		Total (nos.)
	1986–91	1992–94	
Multiple cropping	791 HH	1596 HH	2387 HH
Green manuring	116 HH	253 HH	369 HH
Private planting of fodder/fuelwood	1979 HH	2355 HH	4334 HH
Private planting of fruit	1442 HH	1950 HH	3392 HH
Conservation planting	40 UG	96 UG	136 UG
Other conservation activities	113 UG	203 UG	316 UG
Homestead gardening	n/a	1077 HH	1077 HH
Agroforestry	n/a	479 HH	479 HH

Source: Field Survey

Impact study methodology

A study to assess the impacts of the approach to date was conducted through:

○ direct investigation of the project area
○ information collected from the farmers and the members of the user and conservation groups of the project area
○ information collected from project professional staff and local leaders
○ review of related documents.

Changes in productivity

Changes in crop yields

Almost all farmers interviewed reported changes in the quality of agricultural and forest resources. The average changes in crop yields are shown in Table 13.3. There have been significant increases in rice and maize yields, with the greatest changes occurring in the uplands.

Farmers identified several reasons for increased crop yields. One was the introduction of new varieties of seeds. Once the project became involved, farmers were taken to visit other locations and to see the success of other farmers with their own eyes. A few farmers who participated in training received improved varieties of paddy, wheat and maize and introduced them into their own farms. Now almost 70 per cent of farmers plant improved varieties of paddy, wheat and maize.

Table 13.3: Changes in yield of crops in the project area

Land Type	Crop	Yield before project (t/ha)	Yield after 7 years of project (t/ha)
Non-irrigated upland	Rice	0.5	1.7
	Wheat	n/a	1.15
	Maize	0.5	0.52
	Millet	1.29	1.01
Irrigated upland	Rice	2.1	3.05
	Wheat	n/a	2.31
	Maize	1.21	1.54
	Millet	1.11	1.13
Valley bottom	Rice	2.7	3.35
	Wheat	n/a	1.34
	Maize	n/a	2.13
	Millet	n/a	n/a

Source: Field Survey

Almost all participating farmers also indicated that stall feeding, changes in cropping patterns, the intensive use and management of crop land, water management and protection of land from soil erosion were other key areas in which the project intervened to make possible the increases in land productivity and crop yields.

Another important factor was the introduction of agroforestry technologies. Farmers who participated in the project's agroforestry activities are now benefiting economically, with banana, coffee, pineapple, orange and guava all generating income. Farmers grow these crops on land that they once left fallow. Farmers have on average increased their incomes from agroforestry from a range of 2000–7300 NRs/year to 7050–25 700 NRs/year. Generally, the total annual income per family in the hills of Nepal per year ranges from Rs 2400 to Rs 12 000.[2]

Changes in resource degradation

The total area of the watershed under the project is 17 300ha. A rough estimate of the watershed area that has been treated by project activities is around 2700ha, which is about 15.6 per cent of the total watershed area. This includes abused and heavily degraded forests, gullies, landslide and severely eroded and unproductive marginal farm lands.

Changes in resource conservation practices on private lands

Over-exploitation of forest resources and abuse of marginal lands for agricultural purposes are the causes of resource degradation, which in turn leads to erosion and adverse effects in downstream areas. To the extent possible, farmers in the project area have been practising sound conservation measures in order to avoid depleting the resource base. Farmers stated that the project has added some novel conservation measures in addition to those that they have always practised.

Terracing, mixed cropping, and relay cropping are some of the resource conservation measures that farmers have adopted on their private land. These practices have been adopted primarily due to internal initiatives taken within the local communities. Farmers have also started retaining scattered fodder trees and local grass on the ridges and bunds of privately owned agricultural and barren hill slopes as sound conservation practices. The average number of fodder trees grown per hectare of land is estimated to be 40 in the project area.

---

[2] The exchange rates at the time of the study were:
1 UK Pound (£) – 72.00 (N.Rs)
1 US Dollar ($) – 52.00 (N.Rs)

About 871ha of privately owned land in the project area is protected by physical and biological resource conservation measures – this has grown from 10ha in 1989.

About 130 000 tree seedlings of fodder, fuelwood and timber species have been distributed to farmers and planted on private land. Similarly, around 10 000 coffee plants, 12 000 orange and 5500 banana seedlings have been distributed to farmers and planted on private land.

No engineering structures have been constructed on private land. Such structures as check-dams, spurs, embankments etc., have been constructed on community land in order to check erosion and landslides.

Farmers have stated that the biomass resources on their private land have increased since the project has intervened. A few farmers mentioned that since they have planted fodder trees on their private land they have adopted stall feeding, which has protected the biomass resources on their private land and has increased the amount of compost and farmyard manure. As a result, the productivity of their land has also increased.

Changes in resource conservation practices on common lands

Significant changes in resource conservation practices on common land have occurred since the project intervened in the watershed. Before the project, forests, grassland, shrubland and water were under increasing pressure from the demands of human and livestock populations. It was felt that the watershed was slowly degrading (BTRT, 1992).

Local farmers are now aware of the importance of conserving resources on common lands. Since the inception of the project, the traditional competition and conflict among farmers to fulfil individual needs and interests in resource utilization has vanished. Farmers are now inclined to use common resources in a sustainable way. The project has secured farmers' access to enough forest resources to meet their needs equitably and has ensured all farmers' rights to participate in decision-making and in managing community forests.

A heightened sense of responsibility and consciousness of forest resource conservation practices on common lands is found in the project area. There are about 94 common resource conservation groups active in the project area, of which 13 are composed exclusively of women and six of other minorities. Various forest user groups and conservation committees have been formed, and operational plans for the community forests have been prepared and accepted by the communities. A large number of such plans have been handed over to the communities. In some areas the communities have started harvesting forest resources and the harvested resources are equitably distributed among the users according to the operational plan.

Resource conservation is practised on about 1784ha of common land through the involvement and efforts of the community. This area includes common areas protected by engineering activities and those areas treated through biological and ecological activities. About 1010ha of common land is treated by conservation and management of natural forest resources. Around 320ha is treated by planting and by protecting degraded land and finally about 454ha of common land is treated by engineering activities.

Treatment of common land by planting trees has also been effective in the conservation of soil, plant and water resources. The area covered by community plantation has grown from 23 to 320ha between 1986 and 1994.

Estimates of biomass on fodder, fuelwood and timber production in community-managed natural forests have been calculated using the data from sample management plans, prepared for handing over forests to user groups. The estimated figures for production of fodder, fuelwood and timber per hectare of community natural forests are 1.23 tonne/ha, 40 tonne/ha and 0.36 m³/ha respectively.

No conservation activities were taking place on common land before the intervention of the project.

Retained ecosystem functions

The project has not monitored the status of soil erosion in the watershed regularly and thus there are no comparative studies on changes in soil loss. However, farmers in general believe that the protection and planting of degraded land in the watershed have helped reduce soil erosion. Similarly, the adoption of conservation farming on marginal land has helped control soil loss.

Construction of various engineering structures, such as check-dams, embankments and spurs have also retarded the rate of erosion and rate of expansion of gullies and landslides in the watershed. It is estimated that about 454ha of erosion-prone lands have been protected using engineering soil conservation activities.

Contribution of farmers to technology adaptation and multiplication

Project intervention has modified, but not totally ignored, indigenous resource conservation practices. In fact, the project has identified the indigenous practices which, when incorporated into an external technological framework, yield better results than the indigenous practices do alone.

Some examples of where indigenous components and the project's external technologies have been successfully combined include:

○ incorporation of traditional rainfed cropping into agro-forestry practices, such as the unification of moisture conservation and fertility improvement practices and the indigenous farming system

171

○ the consolidation of indigenous knowledge about forest management and community forest management
○ the blending of multiple and relay cropping of high-yield varieties of seeds and traditional knowledge.

It was observed that the greater the degree of blending of local knowledge and practices into external technology, the more of that technology the farmers accepted.

Most of the project activities have been wholeheartedly adopted – farmers were especially interested in the activities that helped to increase their farm income as well as conserve resources. Households exchanged seeds and seedlings of cereals, vegetables and fruit trees. Agroforestry and homestead gardening and vegetable farming are being gradually adopted by farmers, as the required seedlings and plants are introduced and produced in their own farms.

In addition, roughly one in every five households has planted banana, orange, coffee and pineapple plants in their homestead garden. The number of farmers who have adopted new practices through demonstration, extension and field observations is given in Table 13.4.

Almost all nurseries of the project area have been handed over to the communities. These nurseries produce seedlings of fruits and other trees which they sell to farmers and other private and government organizations. Five farmers have established their own private nurseries, producing coffee and orange seedlings and some vegetable plants.

Changes in local resilience and vulnerability

Diversity of agricultural and wild products

A major breakthrough of the project was its ability to demonstrate that diversification of crops lowers risks. After the project introduced its improved farming system to the watershed, the diversity of species on farm

Table 13.4: Activities adopted by neighbour farmers in the watershed (cumulative)

Activities	Number of farmers					
	1989	1990	1991	1992	1993	1994
Improved cropping	8	32	284	295	n/a	338
Agro-forestry	n/a	15	1217	1520	1910	2386
Homestead gardening	n/a	n/a	1103	2635	3305	4405

Source: Field Survey and Project Document.

172

lands increased, especially on the homesteads of conservation farmers. On these farms, the high diversity of crops has minimized the risk of crop failure and enabled farmers to earn an income throughout the year. On one 0.35ha farm, for example, 42 different species of fruit and fodder trees were planted and millet was also cultivated. However, it is more common for an average farmer to grow about six different varieties of fruit trees, five varieties of fodder trees and local grasses, and to cultivate cereal crops seasonally.

Diversity in forest species and wild animals is reported to have increased since degraded land was planted as community forests and since abandoned natural forests were handed over to the community to manage. Farmers claim that the degraded forests near each village cluster changed into dense forests after forest management became the responsibility of the community. In some places, people dare not enter such forests because they have become dense and wild animals are common. The killing of cattle and dogs by wild animals has been reported every year. Five years ago one child was reported to have been eaten by a leopard in a dense community forest.

Change in the health of local people

Agricultural production per unit area of land has increased because of the introduction and adoption of new agricultural technologies. But farmers stated that the high rates of population growth and inflation have made it difficult for them to support themselves despite the increases in agricultural production.

However, a study evaluating the impact of the kitchen gardening programme indicates that the farmers' interest in vegetable production has increased considerably at almost all project sites. Knowledge of the importance of vegetables for preventing Vitamin A deficiencies, especially night blindness, have increased among participating farmers, mothers and user group members. The study claims that the number of cases of vitamin A deficiency has decreased radically in the project area.

Some families stated that since they have adopted the homestead vegetable gardens they now eat vegetables regularly in all seasons, while they used to eat green vegetables only in the summer. Radish, rye, cauliflower, garlic and onion are now in high demand.

Changes in self-dependence of groups and communities

Building local capacity and skills

One aspect of the project is to build the capacities and skills of the local communities so that members will be able to assume responsibility for future resource conservation. To achieve this goal, the project has conducted and supported various training and workshops. The number of paraprofessionals trained since the start of the second phase of the project is shown in Table 13.5. Some of the trained paraprofessionals were also selected to be resource persons for new paraprofessional training programmes in subsequent years.

These new paraprofessionals are in demand. Local inhabitants are increasingly willing to pay for their services. People are willing to pay Rs. 140 to have one pit latrine constructed and Rs. 100 to have a smokeless stove constructed and installed; masons and plumbers are paid Rs. 70 per day worked and animal health workers charge Rs. 100 per visit, plus the cost of medicine.

Various opportunities for inter-project excursions and observation tours among farmers were also provided. In the second phase of the project, many study tours were conducted for the farmers: 335 farmers on forest management, 278 farmers on plantation management, 27 farmers on fruit tree management, 120 farmers on agriculture production and cropping patterns and 36 farmers on gully and erosion control. All excursions were within the project area to allow observation of each other's activities.

Effectiveness of local resource management groups

In their initial stages, the project gives cash to the user groups to pay for the skilled labour required. The user groups are also given inducements to participate. In an area where the majority of people are poor subsistence farmers, verbal exhortations to participate are ineffective. In such areas, at least at the initial stage, subsidies and financial incentives are essential. It is only at the later stages that the participatory groups become self-sufficient and capable of managing and organizing activities themselves.

Replication to non-programme sites

Almost all local people indicated that increasing numbers of farmers in neighbouring communities are adopting conservation technologies.

Table 13.5: Types of training and number of paraprofessionals trained

Type of Training	Number of paraprofessionals trained (1989–1994)
Masonry	23
Pit latrine construction	21
Smokeless stove construction	29
Drinking water maintenance	34
Bee keeping	51
Animal health and veterinary	29

Source: Project Document.

Neighbours are interested in the agriculture and agroforestry activities that the project has shown to be effective. Households exchange cereal and vegetable seeds. Neighbouring farmers purchase fruit saplings and vegetable seeds without any support from the project. Systems of conservation farming, particularly agro-forestry, are gradually being adopted by adjoining farmers through their own efforts.

Changes in the operational procedures of support institutions

The operational procedures of the project have changed considerably over time. In the beginning, the project implemented its activities directly through its professional staff, without considering whether or not the beneficiaries supported or wished to participate in those activities. Investment in maintenance and follow-up activities and supervision of on-going programmes became increasingly expensive for the project, and the farmers were reluctant to assume responsibility. Faced with these problems, the project switched from its conventional implementation procedure to a participatory approach. At this stage, the project runs all its activities with people's participation and the activities are later adopted by the people themselves.

Role of professionals

The success of the project depends upon the attitude and skills of the professionals. The professionals at the site offices are qualified not only to implement technological schemes but also to handle the general concerns of the rural people. The professionals also play the roles of social and extension workers in order to motivate the rural farmers to participate in resource conservation tasks.

The staff stationed at the district and central headquarters have continually supported the field professionals. Moral support, advice and backstopping are often provided to the field workers. The opinions and concerns of the field professional are well considered and their problems in the field are taken care of by top-level professionals at headquarters.

Enabling policies

In the past, operational procedures and policy guidelines for participatory approaches were inadequate and thus the inputs from users and beneficiaries were negligible. The technology applied did not take into account the people's perceptions of their problems and the solutions to them. Following its initial unsatisfactory experiences, the project made a major and clear shift in its policy in the second phase.

Institutions dealing with the project have modified their working policies so as to embrace the participatory approach. Policies now provide clear and simple guidelines with enough flexibility for accommodating local requirements expressed during participatory planning. The basic principles of the policy changes are transparency in decision-making, flexibility in operational procedures and strong motivation. The participatory approach is now mandatory for all activities and for all stages of planning, implementing and monitoring.

Field professionals are very willing to work with rural farmers and their attitudes are flexible. The field staff realize that if a particular programme requires some change in its operational procedures to ensure its success, that he or she has the liberty to make that change. Such flexibility in participatory planning procedures have provided plenty of opportunities to the professionals to incorporate their own innovative ideas into policy planning and has helped the project to adjust its approach in order to maximize returns.

Field-level professional staff are self-trained in the local-level participatory approach. Professionals who have had many years of local experience are used as resource persons in order to train other individuals.

Increased links with other line agencies

Appropriate linkages have been developed with line agencies operating the development activities in the project area, mainly at the district-level offices of forest, agriculture, irrigation and drinking water. The district development committee is the overall co-ordinator of all the development programmes in the district. All line agencies responsible for development programmes are the members of this committee. The committee organizes the line agencies.

The project also makes frequent contact with all the concerned line agencies individually for programme implementation and follow-up. For example, the project has kept in regular contact with the district forest office for the preparation and handing-over of community forest management plans, identification and formation of user groups and any other forestry-related matters. Similarly, the agriculture development office advises the project on agriculture. The line of co-ordination and linkages among the development line agencies has been extended up to regional level in order to resolve the cross-sector policy issues in co-ordination and integration. No co-ordination mechanism is developed at central level.

Conclusions

The project strategy of experimenting and demonstrating various innovations of improved conservation practices in the form of conservation farming is one of the reasons for enhancing the farmer's enthusiasm for adopting the improved practices. Almost all types of farming practices have been adopted by the innovative farmers, and process of replication of the technologies in adjoining farms has been gaining momentum without any project support.

The process of programme planning, implementation and maintenance is based at the grassroots level and the decision-making process is transparent and participatory. Almost all ethnic and minority groups are included in the CDCCs and their participation at all stages is effective. Users' contributions in all engineering activities, in the form of labour, have developed a feeling of ownership and involvement that has helped generate participatory approaches in the follow-up and maintenance of complete works.

Various village-level training, excursions, and observation tours from farm to farm are some of the important aspects of the project, which have helped build the local capabilities and self-confidence in the farmers' communities for successful implementation of the programme. The project area has become one of the main demonstration areas for community resource conservation activities for the whole country.

14

Subsidies in Watershed Development Projects in India: Distortions and Opportunities

JOHN M. KERR, N.K. SANGHI AND G. SRIRAMAPPA

Development is increasingly understood to be a process whereby people learn to take charge of their own lives and solve their own problems. Helping people solve their problems by giving them things and doing things for them makes them more dependent and less willing to solve their own problems. This cannot be called development; on the contrary, it is the very opposite of development.

Bunch 1982.

HEAVY SUBSIDIES ARE a standard component of virtually all agricultural and rural development projects in India. It is difficult to find examples of government or non-governmental projects that do not include substantial funding from the sponsoring agency. Such funding can take several forms: helping to pay for labour, agricultural inputs, machinery services or technical expertise. Sometimes assistance is provided to help rural people carry out work on their own, and sometimes the work is done for them.

This chapter discusses the effects of subsidies on watershed development projects, particularly in India, although the arguments presented are relevant throughout the world. In this chapter we do not argue against government support for agriculture and poverty alleviation. Rather, we aim to show that some unintended, negative consequences of heavy subsidies in watershed management programmes actually undermine watershed development objectives. The cause of the problem is that often watershed subsidies are intended simultaneously to support improved land management and rural employment generation. This is a lot to demand of a single policy intervention. We argue that watershed programmes could be more successful if these subsidies were reduced or eliminated, and the objectives of support for agriculture and poverty alleviation were achieved through alternative means. We conclude by suggesting alternative approaches that avoid subsidies or minimize their potentially destructive impacts.

Government support for agriculture and human welfare

Subsidies and payments to rural people have a long history in India. Employment generation for famine relief, for example, dates back several centuries. In contemporary times, many state governments sponsor employment programmes that provide important welfare benefits. Whether for constructing irrigation canals or promoting watershed development, employment generation can easily be built into a range of rural development projects and produce tangible benefits, such as combating hunger and stabilizing rural income.

Subsidies are also often seen as a useful way to convince farmers to try something that subsequently they will adopt with their own resources. This faith in the 'demonstration effect' is common among agricultural researchers worldwide, who believe that the technologies they develop will be adopted if farmers are shown their merits. The success of the Green Revolution contributed to this sentiment in India. In the Green Revolution, scientists' discoveries on agricultural research stations led farmers literally to replace traditional farming systems, resulting in spectacular productivity increases.

Agricultural demonstrations in India take several forms. Those conducted on farmers' fields normally involve subsidies. Researchers often select a farmer who receives free inputs if he donates a field to be used as a demonstration plot. Researchers then select a technical model to test on the plot. On a larger scale, watershed programmes often supply farmers with partially or fully subsidized inputs in exchange for allowing watershed works to be implemented in their fields, or to demonstrate to farmers the complementary effects of improved inputs and cultivation practices.

Some soil and water conservation (SWC) projects in India operate in areas where agriculture imposes external costs, or externalities, in downstream locations. The classic case is when erosion on farm land leads to siltation of reservoirs or other downstream infrastructure, decreasing their life span at a high cost to the national economy. Several publications of the Central Soil and Water Conservation Research and Training Institute in Dehra Dun display a photograph of a bridge in the Dun Valley that was nearly engulfed by half a century of upstream erosion (CSWCRTI, 1989). Images such as this leave a powerful impression of the need for government to help pay for erosion control measures on farms, even though such externalities are not present in every case.

Subsidies were also built into early SWC programmes because of official perceptions that farmers were ignorant and would manage their land properly only under coercion or persuasion. In some cases officials designed programmes that forced farmers to comply. But farmers resisted compulsory programmes; often destroying measures introduced against their wishes after the soil conservation officials leave (Pretty and Shah, Chapter 1, this volume; Fernandez, 1993).

Today, many people view compulsory programmes as unacceptably authoritarian in nature. They seek another way to encourage farmers to adopt soil conservation practices. Paying farmers for work done on their fields offers a more socially acceptable way to try to achieve conservation objectives.

In recent years subsidies have assumed great political importance. This is partly because India, unlike many other developing countries, is a functioning democracy. The rural vote is always hotly contested in Indian elections, with politicians often resorting to vote-buying schemes such as loan forgiveness and a wide range of subsidies to attract the rural constituency.[1]

The combined result of these efforts to create employment, demonstrate technology, combat externalities, guide 'ignorant' farmers, and gain political influence, is that most people in India do not question subsidies for agricultural development projects. Farmers have learned from experience that they may always expect subsidies, and the rest of society accepts – apparently without question – the idea that it should share the cost of measures intended to help farmers. There is little debate about why these subsidies are justified or what objectives they achieve. Here we argue that subsidies can hinder attempts to increase agricultural productivity and conserve natural resources.

When are subsidies appropriate and when are they not?

Economic policies should be used to accomplish objectives that the free market does not achieve on its own. For example, they are needed when the market sends signals to people to produce, consume or invest in ways that are economically optimal for the individual but not economically optimal for society as a whole. In the language of economics, under these circumstances the private costs and returns of an activity do not equal the social costs and returns. This situation is referred to as a market failure (Box 14.1). A policy intervention such as a tax, subsidy, or a change in the laws that govern the market, can correct the market failure by realigning private and social returns of the economic activity in question. Direct government intervention can also be used to provide goods and services that the market does not provide.

Policy-makers have many possible economic tools for correcting market failures. These include granting subsidies, levying taxes, assigning and specifying property rights, improving credit and insurance markets, and many others. The important point is that subsidies are just one of many policy tools. Depending on the market failure at hand, a subsidy may or may not be the most appropriate policy tool.

In economic terms, introducing a subsidy is justified if two broad conditions apply:

○ There must be a market failure (see Box 14.1)

---

[1] This situation is similar to that in Europe, North America, and Japan, where subsidies are politically important and often cause major distortions to the economy. In non-democratic societies, subsidies are politically important where leaders fear being forcibly removed from office rather than voted out.

○ A subsidy must be the best way to correct the market failure, i.e. the one that solves the problem as directly and inexpensively as possible, with minimal side effects.

A policy tool that is not directly targeted to the cause of a problem might fail to solve it, or even worsen it (Box 14.2).

Box 14.1: Types of market failure

Examples of market failure, when market prices signal people to carry out activities that are not in society's economic interests, abound in natural resource management and have a variety of causes.

Gadgil (1992) describes how forest product firms with short-term concessionary rights to forest land overharvested forests because they had no stake in their future productivity. Similarly, farmers collectively overexploit groundwater in semi-arid regions because there are no property rights governing access to groundwater, and because electricity price subsidies encourage overuse (Kerr, *et al.*, 1997).

Village irrigation tanks are poorly managed because traditional institutions for collective action have deteriorated. Pender (1993) found that many poor farmers wished to invest in wells but could not do so due to credit constraints. Farmers in dryland conditions apply less than optimal amounts of fertilizer because of the risk that their investment will be wasted if rainfall is insufficient. In all of these cases of market failure – externalities, short time horizons, unspecified property rights, credit constraints, risk, and others – the market fails to encourage the best pattern of natural resource management, and some policy intervention is needed to make the market work better.

A subsidy should address the causes of problems, not their symptoms. A subsidy is an appropriate tool, for example, if the problem is that farmers do not invest in watershed development because the benefits go to the national economy but not to the investing farmer. In this case a subsidy can raise private returns to match social returns. On the other hand, if the problem is that a farmer cannot invest in planting trees or digging a well because he lacks access to credit, the policy should be to provide credit. A subsidy might encourage the investment in trees or wells, but it is wasteful because a less expensive policy could have achieved the same objective.

In other words, in some cases subsidies are the best policy tool, but in other cases they are not. And they have four major drawbacks:

○ They cannot be extended to everyone, because funds are limited.
○ They are wasteful in cases where another policy could be used to accomplish the desired objectives.
○ They may be difficult to remove once put in place.
○ They may cause unwanted side effects.

Box 14.2: The consequences of poorly targeted policy

In India and several other countries, policy-makers alarmed by the loss of tree cover introduced laws against cutting and marketing trees, on both public and private land. On private land this legislation had a serious side effect: farmers planted fewer trees because they feared that they would not be able to sell them (Chambers *et al.*, 1989a; Murray, 1994). The policy that was chosen was not direct enough in addressing the problem of deforestation on public land. It also had the side effect of discouraging farmers from increasing tree cover on private land. A better policy would have helped farmers plant trees and market tree products while controlling the problem of logging in public forests.

How subsidies affect incentives

As stated above, a subsidy is a payment or service that raises the net private returns from an activity; an incentive is something that motivates or stimulates a person to act.[2] Financial subsidies are intended to increase financial incentives, but other types of incentives can be social, moral, psychological or political. There are different types of subsidies and these have different effects on a range of incentives or motivations.

Financial subsidies

Most people think of finance when they think of subsidies. The intention of a financial subsidy is to raise the incentive for people to pursue the subsidized activity. Subsidizing production of oilseeds encourages farmers to plant more of them, and subsidizing construction of contour bunds encourages farmers to build them. The economics of subsidies appears to be very simple: by making the subsidized item less expensive or more remunerative, more people will be willing to pay for more of it.

Paradoxically, financial subsidies can reduce financial incentives for people to invest their resources in subsidized activities. If a soil conservation programme subsidizes construction of conservation ditches in one

---

[2] Sometimes subsidy and incentive are used synonymously, but not here.

village, for example, then farmers in a neighbouring village who are considering investing in conservation ditches have an incentive to postpone the investment in the hope that the programme will soon operate in their village as well. The farmer whose conservation ditch was subsidized this year has an incentive to postpone repairing or rebuilding it in the hope that a future conservation programme will pay for it. Numerous SWC programmes throughout the world have faced this experience.

Subsidies also discriminate against products and practices that are not subsidized. If a subsidy reduces the cost of a commodity or technology or a certain way of doing things, it creates a disincentive to use substitute products or technologies. Electricity subsidies, for example, can reduce the incentive to search for alternatives such as solar-powered pumps. Over time, this can impede scientific progress and stifle indigenous knowledge because it reduces payoffs for innovating and finding less expensive, more efficient ways to do things. In the case of watershed management, subsidies for certain conservation techniques reduce incentives to try other, less expensive ones.

Financial subsidies also create opportunities for corruption because they put officials and influential beneficiaries in a position to mismanage funds and other programme benefits. In a worldwide review of food-for-work programmes, corruption occurred more often than not (Jackson, 1982).

Psychological and moral disincentives

Financial subsidies risk causing even more damage to psychological, social or moral incentives than to financial incentives. The experiences of innumerable agricultural development projects around the world demonstrate the psychological effects of cash and kind subsidies. Too often, villagers who receive free machines, irrigation wells or other items do not maintain or manage them properly. They value the services of free items, but they do not treat them as they would treat something they paid for themselves. These free items, or give-aways, never seem last as long as comparable items purchased by farmers with their own money. If the machine breaks, they look to the agency that provided it to repair or replace it.

Rural development agencies everywhere are now finding it difficult to operate without subsidies because villagers accustomed to give-aways act as though they are morally entitled to handouts, but not morally responsible for trying to solve their own problems. In this sense financial subsidies create *disincentives* that retard development.

Subsidized services

Development projects that provide services rather than funds offer another form of subsidy. Some subsidized services play an important role in the economic development and well-being of any country, and their potential benefits should not be discounted. Education is the best example. In rural development efforts, assistance that enables people to do things they could not (or believe they could not) do, can have a powerful, beneficial effect.

Not surprisingly, however, subsidized services that are not carefully designed can have the same negative effects on incentives as financial subsidies. For example, if a project relies on outside technical experts to perform such activities as maintaining accounts, managing marketing efforts, or organizing and mobilizing people to perform some work that benefits the community, these activities are likely to cease once the project has ended. Instead of working for themselves, villagers wait for outsiders to do things for them as they have become accustomed to relying on someone else to do the work, and hence have not developed the necessary skills. In the extreme case, external agencies even discourage villagers from thinking for themselves, suggesting solutions to villagers' problems and offering to subsidize them. This leads villagers to say, 'Tell us what we need,' instead of, 'We need this. What do we need to do to achieve it?' (Barbara Adolph, ICRISAT, pers. comm.).

The key principle here, then, is that subsidized technical assistance should be targeted as much as possible towards helping people do things for themselves as opposed to doing things for them. This is an obvious and often-quoted principle, but it is easy to forget. Sometimes the line between the two is fine, and to avoid crossing it requires great effort. This is because it is usually easier to do something for people than to teach them to do it themselves.

How subsidies can undermine watershed management projects

Many Indian government SWC programmes operate through heavily subsidized SWC packages. In these programmes, farmers have little say in the choice of technologies to be used on their fields, but they receive benefits ranging from several days of employment to free fertilizer, seeds and other inputs. The people responsible for implementing the work have little or no say in the project design, and they are evaluated by government auditors on the basis of the level of expenditure and the area covered by the physical structures they construct (government watershed officials, pers. comm.).[3]

This approach and its results are very similar to those of the compulsory programmes of old. Many farmers adopt the technology not because they like it, but to obtain free inputs or employment. Sometimes the implementing agency, under pressure to achieve quantitative targets, convinces any resisting farmers to accept the work by increasing the subsidy payment

---

[3] Most of the watershed projects referred to in this paper are deliberately left unnamed.

(government watershed official, pers. comm.). In this way all parties are satisfied: farmers receive substantial benefits and officials achieve their quotas. The drawback is that farmers' fields are littered with mechanical structures or vegetative barriers that they do not necessarily want. The structures are removed or left to deteriorate once the project staff depart.

Subsidized technology

Scientists and project managers who are confident in the technologies they develop often design top-down projects with minimal input from farmers. But even if a technology is scientifically sound, it may not suit the needs of farmers, who often have multiple objectives and constraints that cause their preferences to differ from those of scientists (Kerr and Sanghi, 1992; Chambers *et al.*, 1989b; Pimbert, 1991).[4] But if subsidies are high enough – often in India they reach 75 per cent, 90 per cent, or even 100 per cent – then farmers might accept them for reasons unrelated to the characteristics of the technology.

Experience shows that farmers are very particular when it comes to accepting new agricultural technology, particularly in unproductive, risky dryland environments. Achieving progress in agricultural development in these areas means understanding the subtle factors that contribute to farmers' decisions. Scientists and project managers should encourage farmers to test new technologies and consider how to adapt them to suit their needs. Clearly, the complicated task of sorting out the many determinants of farmers' acceptance of new technologies becomes even more difficult when large subsidies tilt the balance in favour of adoption (Box 14.3). Of course, the decision to adopt under these circumstances is likely to be reversed once subsidies are removed, and farmers' suspicions that scientists and programme managers do not understand their needs will be reinforced.

The problem becomes more damaging once farmers become accustomed to heavily subsidized projects that deliver unsuitable technology. In this case farmers anticipate the benefits of subsidies but do not expect anything else of value. In India, many farmers do not take government projects seriously, and they are upset if they do not receive give-aways (Sanghi, 1987). Under these circumstances, heavily subsidized projects are doomed before they begin. Moreover, new projects that attempt to operate without financial subsidies are not welcome: farmers evaluate them in advance on the basis of what give-aways they offer rather than on their merits (Bunch, 1982; Valdes, 1994).

---

[4] Kerr and Sanghi (1992) explain in detail how differences in Indian farmers' and scientists' priorities cause them to prefer very different approaches to soil and water conservation.

> **Box 14.3: Subsidized technology in Indian soil and water conservation**
>
> Many soil and water conservation programmes in India subsidize certain pre-approved technologies such as earthen bunds or vegetative barriers. These subsidies make farmers more likely to accept subsidized techniques and less likely to search for less expensive alternative conservation measures. In this way, subsidies inhibit farmers' creativity and slow the development of indigenous knowledge.
>
> An extreme example of this problem is found in hilly, rocky parts of India where the soil is very shallow. One watershed programme operating in such an area subsidized the use of vegetative bunds but not stone bunds; another programme in a similar agroclimatic region subsidized earthen bunds but not stone bunds. In the former case the vegetative barriers could not grow because the stony soil prevented the roots from penetrating. In the latter case, the soil was so shallow that removing it to build earthen bunds would have seriously damaged agricultural productivity.
>
> In both of these areas there was a rich tradition of farmers' own investments in indigenous SWC measures, particularly stone bunds and enclosure walls. In the former area, the project subsidized labour for planting cactus hedges so heavily that it became a highly profitable activity. Farmers responded by planting cactuses next to their existing stone walls. The cactuses served as no more than decoration, but they met the farmers' primary objective of earning subsidy payments.

Subsidized inputs

In some watershed projects and on-farm research demonstrations, farmers who adopt SWC practices receive free inputs, such as seeds and fertilizer. The idea behind these give-aways is to demonstrate that improved inputs in combination with SWC measures will result in high yields. Some farmers, however, accept the inputs but then sell them or use them on their irrigated plots rather than on dryland watershed plots (Y. Mohan Rao, ICRISAT, pers. comm.). As a result, the project fails to achieve the desired demonstration effect, and project officials and scientists obtain no information about farmers' reactions to the technology that might suggest ways to make it more acceptable to them.

Subsidized labour

Some projects subsidize labour devoted to watershed works. In both government and NGO projects, 90 per cent or 100 per cent labour subsidies are common. In fact these subsidies exceed 100 per cent, because they use the legal minimum daily wage of Rs 22, whereas the market wage in the dry season falls to below Rs 20 in many rural areas. Therefore 90 per cent of the legal minimum wage actually can be more than the market wage. Not surprisingly, many people eagerly participate in these programmes regardless of what they think of the technology. Formal and informal surveys (Box 14.4) of farmers in various watersheds find that they perceive employment to be the most important project benefit (ICRISAT data, 1994, unpublished).

Box 14.4: Do rural people want conservation measures or employment?

A group of researchers carried out an informal survey of soil conservation practices in a village in Maharashtra. One of the researchers was from the government and the rest were from elsewhere. When the villagers met the government researcher, they uniformly praised the large government soil conservation programme undertaken 15 years earlier and expressed satisfaction with the contour bunds that it introduced. On the second day of the survey the government official was not present, and the villagers admitted that they did not like the contour bunds but would happily accept them as a means of gaining lean season employment. Once again, subsidies obstructed officials and researchers from gaining information that could help them to improve technologies and project design.

Source: Personal communication with farmers

Subsidies and replicability

Development agencies often list replicability in non-project areas among the objectives of their work. Official documents for large Indian watershed development projects, for example, cite replicability as an important objective (World Bank, 1990; Government of India, 1991). The same documents go on to explain that the projects cover 50 per cent to 100 per cent of the cost of the technologies that they introduce, with farmers contributing whatever is left. These documents contain little or no discussion of the relationship between subsidies and replicability. They justify subsidies as supporting the demonstration effect, but there is no serious discussion of how subsidies will be phased out. For true replicability, however, phasing out subsidies is critical because funds are not available to provide them except in a limited area and for a limited period.

Because subsidies cannot be made available to everyone – certainly not to all of India's hundreds of millions of farmers – it is probably better not to introduce them in the first place. A watershed project initiated without subsidies obviously faces a more accurate test of replicability than any project supported by subsidies.

Paying for participation

Participatory watershed projects are intended to overcome the problems faced by top-down projects. Participatory planning between farmers and watershed officials is expected to ensure that the technologies selected are both technically sound and acceptable to farmers. Experience shows that this approach is very sound, but if it includes high subsidies, especially subsidies for labour, participation actually can worsen the problem of encouraging farmers to accept useless technology. Two examples illustrate this point (Box 14.5).

Box 14.5:   The consequences of subsidized participation

A programme in Andhra Pradesh aimed to encourage farmers to build bunds on their land. The project paid the farmers to carry out the work on their own land and allowed them to choose their own technology. Two soil scientists visiting the project in 1993 noticed that on some fields earthen bunds were far larger than necessary, and that they actually did more harm than good by taking scarce topsoil from the field. They also noticed that a large stone structure on the boundary of one field served no apparent purpose. Further investigation suggested that the lure of guaranteed employment led the farmers to build large bunds regardless of their purpose.

The second case concerns a participatory watershed planning exercise held in a drought-prone area of Andhra Pradesh. Under the project, villagers were to be hired to carry out work jointly planned by villagers and project officials. When the villagers were asked to present their plan, they said that enlarging the massive irrigation tank bund was their top priority, even though the tank had filled only three times in the previous 10 years. Subsequent investigation revealed that the farmers did not really think that the bund needed to be raised, but they knew that such a large project would employ them throughout the dry season, relieving them from having to migrate to Hyderabad or Madras.

These two examples are probably replicated on a daily basis in heavily subsidized, participatory projects in India. The essence of the problem is that subsidies distort incentives so that farmers select the technology made most attractive by the give-away rather than the one they think is best on its own merits. Project officials too trusting of farmers' wisdom are likely to be fooled in such cases.

True participation means working together toward a common objective. This will not be possible if the very design of projects creates incentives to mislead and deceive. Subsidies can create such incentives.

Promoting watershed development without an over-reliance on subsidies

If subsidies, particularly high subsidies that create employment or target specific inputs or technologies, can create so many problems in watershed development projects, what should be done? First, subsidies should be avoided where there is no obvious justification. Second, where subsidies are justified they should be designed and implemented in such a way as to minimize distortions to incentives.

Designing subsidies with minimal distortions to incentives

In India, high subsidies in watershed programmes are a fact of life, and it will be difficult to remove or greatly reduce them immediately. This is partly because of a 'culture' of high subsidies where no one questions their usefulness, but also because high subsidies are written into national legislation that will not be changed overnight. This means that it is very important to devise ways to reduce the harmful impact of subsidies on watershed programmes.

One way to reduce the harmful effect of subsidies is to require matching labour contributions by landowners on whose land conservation structures are built. The idea is as follows. Farmers may choose their own conservation technology and must build half of a given structure with their own labour (either family or hired). They may then request the conservation programme to construct the second half, according to the design specified by the farmer. The conservation programme would hire the workers under the programme to do so; these workers would be paid only after the farmer certifies that the work is acceptable to him. This approach has several advantages. First, it helps ensure that the technology suits the farmer's wishes and is built according to standards that satisfy him. Second, the farmer never receives any payment, reducing the chances that he will participate in the programme for unexpected reasons.

This approach also offers the important side benefits of helping to organize landless workers and teaching them skills that will increase their self-sufficiency. In particular, labourers may form an association to provide conservation construction services. Payments from the watershed project would be made directly to the association and distributed to its members. Assistance could be provided to the association to develop their business skills and perhaps develop spin-off activities such as revolving credit programmes. More generally, this idea follows the principle of using rural development programmes as leverage to create benefits for disadvantaged groups such as the poor, lower castes and women.

Contributing an input or a technology to a group of families instead of to an individual family is an important step in this direction, particularly if one family's receipt of benefits depends on other families' adherence to agreements made under the programme. This is a well-known principle that contributes to the success of Bangladesh's Grameen Bank, where loans are made to groups of five people, and if one of them does not repay, all five lose access to further credit. Another variation on this principle is known in India as rotational credit, in which loans are provided in sequence to different people in a group. Under this system, the second loan is made only after the first is repaid, and so on. Such schemes could be devised under subsidized watershed programmes in India.

However, it is preferable to avoid subsidies entirely where they are not justified economically, rather than try to cope with strategic behaviour by those who receive subsidies. The rest of this section suggests ways to promote watershed development with no subsidies at all.

Institutional innovation to manage local externalities

As stated above, subsidies for watershed management are justified when its private and social returns diverge. Recent evidence from numerous tropical countries, however, suggests that in most cases the benefits of soil and water conservation practices accrue mainly to the farmer who adopts them. The externalities that do exist are usually highly localized: soil erosion in most places does not deposit silt in downstream hydroelectric dams, but rather in neighbouring farms or ponds within the same microwatershed. Similarly, the low application rates of pesticides and fertilizer mean that runoff of poisonous chemicals is not a major problem. If there are no externalities then there is no argument in favour of subsidies; if externalities are small then only small subsidies are justified. In this case, if anyone should pay upstream farmers to adopt soil conservation it is their downstream neighbours, not taxpayers at large.

The idea of 'payments' by one group of farmers to another is not as revolutionary as it first sounds. In fact, it is an old and well known idea among economists (Coase, 1960). 'Payment' need not mean cash or even kind transactions, but rather some kind of formal or informal compensation mechanism from one group to another (Box 14.6). Such arrangements are sometimes found in common property resource management systems, whereby a group that benefits from a collective management arrangement secures co-operation from a group that does not.

If watershed externalities tend to be small and localized, two principles emerge. First, watershed managers should begin by assuming that there is no need for financial subsidies. If subsidies are justified they may be offered, but justification should not be assumed. Second, external assistance should focus on helping people organize themselves to solve their own

> **Box 14.6: Spreading the benefits of natural resource management**
>
> A classic example from India is the famous Sukhomajri watershed project, in which landless families received rights to irrigation water in exchange for protecting the irrigation tank catchment area. These families could then sell their water share or use it on leased land (Patel-Weynand, 1997). More recently, the National Tree Growers' Co-operative has adopted a similar approach, giving all households a share in the returns to protecting trees in common forests. Another example from India concerns current efforts in Andhra Pradesh to convert irrigation tanks to percolation tanks (Gangi Reddy *et al.*, 1994; and Chapter 17, this book). Under certain circumstances there can be substantial benefits from tank conversion, but they are not evenly distributed, so possibly some people who stand to lose have an incentive to sabotage the effort. Success in tank conversion projects therefore requires organizing all the people affected by the tank to ensure that the benefits are distributed in a way that satisfies all of them. No external finance is needed.

problems, and to facilitate access to credit, secure tenure, and other factors needed to guide private incentives toward socially productive activities.

Supporting community organizations

Informal village groups can potentially serve as a focal point for efforts to resolve local disputes and mobilize farmers into action. Experience in India suggests that participation in local groups can build villagers' confidence to work collectively, to establish thrift funds to generate capital, to consider new investment opportunities, and generally to become more active (James Mascarenhas, OUTREACH, pers. comm.; Parthasarathy, 1994). Active local groups can stimulate psychological incentives that previously were stifled by cultural or political constraints. These potential strengths of local groups have nothing to do with external finance. In fact, they present an alternative, more sustainable way to improve the welfare of rural people (see, for example, the chapters in the penultimate section of this book).

Farmer-to-farmer extension is an offshoot of community organization. Once villagers organize, skilled farmers can serve as extension agents to spread information to their neighbours. They may have more credibility than traditional extension workers because they face the same circumstances as the people they serve. Farmer-to-farmer extension has had favourable results in many countries.

Two principles from these experiences are worth highlighting. First, every community is different, so there can be no single blueprint for designing community organizations. Second, external funds donated to community organizations should be forthcoming only to groups that have already established themselves and demonstrated that they are serious. The funds should be small and should support costs of organizing, gathering information and spreading awareness; they should not finance giveaways.

Conclusions

In summary, there are good reasons to believe that subsidies are undermining Indian watershed development efforts. This is especially so where subsidies are very high and are tied to employment or to specific technologies that require subsequent maintenance to be useful. In many watershed programmes, subsidies lead farmers to adopt SWC techniques with no intention of maintaining them, and they make it difficult for researchers and project managers to learn what practices farmers accept or do not accept.

Many people in India believe that watershed development should be subsidized simply because so many Indian farmers are very poor and need assistance. However, projects in many countries with similarly poor farmers have removed or substantially reduced subsidies, with favourable results. These countries include Kenya, Lesotho, Niger, Haiti, Cape Verde, the Dominican Republic and the Philippines, to name a few (Lutz, *et al.*, 1994; IFAD, 1992; Critchley, 1991; Fujisaka, 1989). In some cases they found that removing subsidies made no difference; in others they found that it improved efforts to encourage conservation. Programmes under SPEECH in Tamil Nadu (Chapter 24, this book), Oxfam in Andhra Pradesh, and others have shown that this approach can work in India as well.

Evidence from around the world suggests that farmers will invest in conservation practices when it is profitable for them to do so (Lutz, *et al.*, 1994; Tiffen, *et al.*, 1994). This suggests that farmers do not need subsidies so much as they need less expensive, more profitable technologies; policies that encourage them to take a long-term perspective in caring for their land, greater awareness of the costs of degradation, and encouragement to organize themselves to invest in conservation (Pretty, 1995).

Even if these enabling conditions are created, there will remain poor people who need assistance to improve their livelihoods. But poor people can be helped in other ways that waste less money and do not distort incentives to invest in conserving natural resources. There is no need to tie poverty relief measures to natural resource conservation efforts.

Likewise, there are alternative ways for the government to support rainfed agriculture. Gulati (1990) found that Indian agriculture is subject to net taxation even though many inputs are heavily subsidized. This is because price and trade policies reduce output prices and inhibit demand by more than enough to overcome the benefits to farmers of input subsidies. One obvious way to promote investment in more productive agriculture, therefore, is to alter price policies to raise farmers' profits.

Reducing subsidies substantially will be difficult in India. Farmers are accustomed to high subsidies and will oppose efforts to remove them. Also, projects that try to reduce subsidies unilaterally will face difficulties if nearby projects continue to offer large give-aways. For these reasons, removing or substantially reducing subsidies will be very challenging. A concerted effort is needed to eliminate the give-away mentality if conservation efforts are to have long-lasting and widespread success.

Acknowledgements

John Pender, Chris Reij, Roland Bunch, Jules Pretty, David Seckler, Barbara Adolf, Doug Clark, Tim Kelley and JK Kiara all offered helpful comments on this paper.

15
The Policy Landscape and Prospects of Landcare

ANDREW CAMPBELL AND JIM WOODHILL

Introduction

LANDCARE IS AN unstructured, but widely recognized and supported, movement of about 3000 voluntary community land conservation groups in Australia (see Chapters 26 and 27, this book). Landcare groups operate co-operatively at a local or district level, usually with an initial focus on land degradation problems. Groups usually involve less than 100 members (often 20–30), covering areas ranging from a few thousand hectares to several million hectares. Landcare groups determine their own priorities, their own boundaries, their own membership, and their own activities and procedures. In this process they deal with a great diversity of bio-physical, socio-economic and legislative-administrative environments across the continent of Australia. This chapter describes this 'policy landscape', which has both helped and hindered the development of Landcare as we know it today. We reflect critically on the prospects for the Landcare ethos to spread, given the right support from policy.

An evolving policy landscape

A colonial agriculture in an old, brown land

Australia is an ancient land with a short history of European settlement. The nineteenth century saw increasing soil degradation owing to overgrazing, overcropping and the devastating impact of the rabbit (Barr and Cary, 1992). Then the introduction of high-yielding wheat varieties, superphosphate, and dry fallow heralded new prosperity for wheat farmers. These proved to be short-lived, and the erosion decades of the 1930s and 1940s spawned the first widespread community concern about land degradation and the establishment of soil conservation agencies by state governments. Improved crop varieties, clover ley rotations, soil conservation works, and biological rabbit control dramatically reduced erosion. The wool boom of the early 1950s created pastoral fortunes. Agriculture was the mainstay of the Australian economy (Barr and Cary, 1992).

However, since then more insidious and intractable problems have emerged, earning agriculture the description of 'mining in slow motion' . Soil erosion, salinity, acidification, soil structure decline, waterlogging and water repellency affect up to 16 million hectares of agricultural land (Beale and Fray, 1990; Cocks, 1992; LWRRDC, cited by Farley, 1996). Fresh water resources are fewer and degrading. Half the forests and about 35 per cent of the woodlands have been cleared or severely modified. The extinction rate of native flora and fauna is high and rising (ABARE, 1992, Campbell, 1994a, Cocks, 1992). These phenomena suggest that a truly Australian agriculture, adapted to its unique environment, remains a long way off.

Rural decline is severe (Lawrence and Williams, 1990). The number of farms continues to decrease, with the average age of farmers about 60 and increasing. About one-third of rural towns are in decline. Rural poverty is more widespread, more chronic, and causes greater social and health problems than urban poverty (Bryant, 1992). The Australian Bureau of Agricultural and Resource Economics (ABARE) estimates that farm business profit on Australia's 77 800 broadacre farms[1] declined by 350 per cent between 1989 and 1991, to an average loss of US$12 600 per farm (ABARE, 1991). ABARE forecast average farm business losses for subsequent years (Fisher, 1993), compounding difficulties for those carrying debt. The average broadacre farm in June 1992 owed more than US$70 000 and paid US$8500 in interest (ABARE, 1992).

The historical evolution of agricultural systems suggests that farmers' response to their environment depends not so much on local ecological constraints as on their society (Bayliss-Smith, 1982). Australian mythology is spiced with images of self-reliant farming communities carving out an existence in harsh circumstances and banding together during droughts, floods, fires, plagues and price collapses. Rural life is associated with strong moral certainties, its honesty and its healthy relationship with nature. While these images have some foundation, many farmers have long since removed their rose-tinted glasses. For them, the rural way of life is 'bloody hard work for little reward and much stress'. Environmental degradation from introduced European agriculture is also changing the image of farmers as the best custodians of agricultural land, to that of exploiters.

However, rural communities in Australia are yet to accept their decline as a foregone conclusion. They are neither ignorant about, nor indifferent to, their impact on the environment. Their willingness to do something constructive fuelled the emergence of the Landcare movement during the 1980s.

The emergence of Landcare

Australian farmers started to form voluntary groups to tackle problems such as salinity, wind erosion and pest animals and plants at a district scale in the late 1970s, notably in Western Australia and Victoria, encouraged by

---

[1] Broadacre farms include dryland crops, sheep for meat/wool, and beef (about 70 per cent of the gross value of Australian agricultural production).

state soil conservation agencies. In 1986, the Victorian government introduced a broader, community-based programme through which funds could be obtained by voluntary land conservation groups, which it registered under the name 'LandCare'[2].

In 1988, an historic partnership was forged between the National Farmers Federation (NFF) and the Australian Conservation Foundation (ACF), who jointly proposed a National Land Management Program (Farley and Toyne, 1989). The Australian government acted on this initiative, announcing that the 1990s would be the 'Decade of Landcare' with US$250 million funding. Despite tough economic conditions in rural communities, the explosive growth of the Landcare movement has continued, with about 3000 groups today, involving about one-third of Australian farming families (Scarsbrick, 1996; Campbell 1994a;). In July 1991, surveys showed that 22 per cent of people had heard of landcare. By September 1995, this was a remarkable 69 per cent (Scarsbrick, 1996).

So what's new about Landcare?

Landcare is fundamentally different from traditional government-directed land conservation activities in several ways.

○ It is not government-directed. Although government funding guidelines and staff influence the direction and effectiveness of Landcare group activities, most groups set their own agenda and priorities.
○ Landcare operates at the collective level (district/catchment/ community), rather than the individual farm. This has proven a more appropriate scale for co-ordinating technical information and practical resources to tackle environmental challenges that extend across farm boundaries. As Landcare groups tend to be neighbourhood groups rather than commodity production groups (involving similar farmers scattered over larger areas), they have the potential to represent community interests in general.
○ Landcare groups evolve organically, tending to broaden their concerns over time. Initial interests may be one land degradation issue, which spreads to several related environmental issues, to improving farming systems generally, and finally ending with the integration of social and economic concerns into group activities. The beauty of the Landcare group model is that the linkages between land degradation problems, between conservation and production, and between environmental problems and social and economic issues, become clear and encourage

---

[2] 'Landcare' with a small 'c' is the name of the government programme adopted in 1989. The broader notion of a land conservation ethic is often referred to as 'land care'. Landcare Australia Ltd is another version, a non-profit public company established to raise public awareness and raise funds for community action.

integrated solutions. But people can be overawed by the scale and complexity of these issues. To avoid a sense of powerlessness, facilitation support and group processes are critical.

The institutional setting

While Landcare in Australia is lauded as a community-driven initiative, the institutional support that local groups receive must not be overlooked. Indeed, the success of Landcare can, to a large extent, be attributed to effective matching of institutional support and government funding with local needs. Various support mechanisms aim to:

○ establish and support local Landcare groups
○ support integrated catchment management initiatives across river systems
○ provide research and administrative infrastructure.

The evolving partnership in Australia between community and government provides valuable lessons for other countries in search of policy support for local environmental action. But this is no perfect relationship. Indeed, many frustrations of Landcare revolve around inappropriate institutional structures and the slow speed of institutional change.

However, significant improvements have occurred in the last decade. It has become well accepted that: a) natural resource issues require an integrated, systemic and co-ordinated response, and b) active community participation is essential. The expert-oriented, 'technology transfer' model of agricultural extension has generally been replaced by models that value local knowledge and local learning processes.

Halfway through the Decade of Landcare, a relatively effective set of institutional structures have evolved (see Figure 15.1). The main institutional structures are: landcare groups, the Commonwealth Government, the National Landcare Programme (NLP), state and local governments, catchment management groups, and education and research institutions. There is constant debate about how these can be improved. Currently high on the agenda is improving co-ordination at the regional scale (see below).

Landcare groups

The heart of the Landcare movement is, of course, the local Landcare group. They are viewed by government as the basic mechanism for both raising community awareness and building capacity. The area covered per group is either based on its sense of where their community stops and starts or on a pre-existing organization that the group has evolved from (e.g. foot-rot districts, bushfire brigade districts, football team, tennis club) (Baker, forthcoming; Carr, 1994). These autonomous groups co-operate with

197

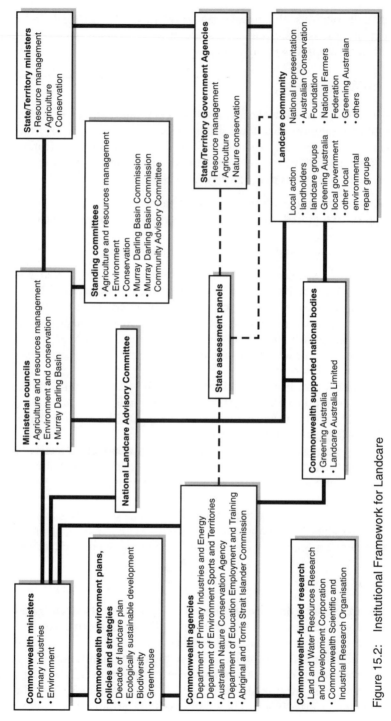

Figure 15.2: Institutional Framework for Landcare

government structures and staff, receiving most technical advice from the state and funding from the Commonwealth Government. Most groups are legally incorporated for insurance reasons and for ease of funding. The groups often form links with schools, local government, other community organizations and local businesses.

Dealing with a federal system

National institutional arrangements include policy-making ministerial councils, advisory bodies to these councils and ministers, and Commonwealth Government departments and the funding programmes administered by these departments (see Figure 15.1). Other government and non-governmental organizations also influence natural resource management policy.

This framework must be understood in relation to Australia's federal system of government. Under the Australian constitution, land management is largely the responsibility of the states. While the Commonwealth Government is responsible for a national approach to land degradation, land management policies must be implemented through the state governments and their agencies. Given their origins as formerly autonomous English colonies only a century ago, each state has different land management legislation and support structures[3].

The Commonwealth Government has two avenues to influence land management. It can implement a national funding programme for specific action at the state level, or seek agreement between all the state governments on a strategic direction and formalize this as a national strategy. On contentious issues where state governments feel their powers are threatened by the Commonwealth, establishing agreements for a uniform national response is increasingly difficult. Nevertheless, Australia has developed many national environmental strategies over the last decade, the main one being the National Strategy for Ecologically Sustainable Development. Others have been developed for biodiversity, greenhouse effect, water quality, coastal decline, and forest use. Landcare is part of the Commonwealth's overall approach to natural resource management, with funding commitments and a strategic role as the cornerstone for implementing environmental strategies.

Australians, particularly farmers, espouse a very strong ethic of private property rights. For this and other practical reasons, regulatory approaches to sustainable land management are considered to be counter productive. The focus of funds and strategies has been on creating a national 'Landcare ethic' and ensuring that land managers have the appropriate knowledge, skills, and technologies to manage their own land sustainably.

---

[3] There is no guarantee that the Australian states will take a consistent or even co-ordinated approach to any issue. In fact that would be the exception, rather than the rule. Doug Cocks of the CSIRO has defined a state border as 'a line on the ground impermeable to the flow of ideas'.

The National Landcare Programme

In 1992, a review of natural resource management programmes in the Commonwealth Department of Primary Industries and Energy (DPIE) led to the formation of the National Landcare Program (NLP).

A major emphasis of NLP has been to develop the capacity for self-reliant sustainable management of natural resources at the local and regional level. Considerable effort and funding has gone into farm and catchment planning, and improving farmers' knowledge and skills. The NLP has not yet funded much implementation of restoration or protection works. This partly reflects a government position that individual land users should bear the direct costs of managing their own land sustainably. It is also based on the sheer scale of necessary funding. However, this approach is coming under pressure as rural Australia continues with its economic crisis and the governments see that they cannot wash their hands of this responsibility.

Support for Landcare can be judged by funding levels. In the early 1980s, funding for soil, water and vegetation conservation amounted to less than Aus$5 million per year. For the Decade of Landcare, The Prime Minister pledged an annual Aus$34 million[4]. By 1993–94 annual Landcare-related funding by the DPIE had climbed to Aus$103 million, and in 1995–96 to Aus$110.4 million[5]. An entirely new scenario has developed recently through the allocation of Aus$1.2 billion over the next five years for national vegetation strategies alone.

The gap between existing funding and what is required remains vast. One estimate puts annual land degradation costs at Aus$1.4 billion (ABARE, cited by Farley, 1996). This does not include annual loss of production due to land degradation, which is in the billions of dollars. If the amount that land users spend is calculated (though difficult to estimate, it is probably equal to government expenditure), then Aus$200–300 million annually is spent on soil and water conservation in Australia. This is the same budget as for 8.5 km of Melbourne freeway or the purchase of one jumbo jet (Campbell 1992).

The role of state governments

State governments provide crucial technical advice and support to Landcare groups. Technical advice is usually available for agriculture, soil conservation, water resources, nature conservation, and forestry. In each state, one agency takes the lead on interacting with, advising and supporting

---

[4] About US$27 million (exchange rate Aus$1 = US$ 0.79).
[5] But this must be seen in perspective: only Aus$16.4 million of this will go to community landcare activities and of this only Aus$7.9 million will go directly to landcare groups for on-ground works (Hadler 1996).

200

Landcare groups. Staff undertaking this group support role are usually funded through the NLP.

However, concerns exist that some state agencies are using too much NLP funding for technical and single disciplinary information, and that insufficient funds go directly to groups. Some state funding for land conservation has been replaced with NLP funding, thus diluting the overall impact. Some criticise state agencies for fearing the political power of individual Landcare groups and wanting to control the movement. This is essentially a reluctance of government agencies to pass financial resources or decision-making powers to community forums. Yet there is also little doubt that the rapid growth in Landcare groups has placed huge and often unserviceable demands on state-level natural resource management agencies.

On the positive side, there are many extremely dedicated and competent agency staff working to support Landcare and they have had an enormous impact. Landcare groups generally feel very positive about the state-level assistance they receive. The capacity of agency staff to work with groups and in a more integrated and multi-disciplinary way has undoubtedly increased dramatically since the late 1980s. Most states provide facilitation training, essentially communication skills, for staff.

The potential of local government

Local government could potentially be a major player in Landcare. It has very significant powers over land use, thus playing a make-or-break role in providing land management (dis)incentives for farmers. Although few rural local government authorities have paid attention to natural resource management, there are signs that this will change dramatically in the second half of the Decade of Landcare. In 1994, a Natural Resource Facilitator was placed within the Australian Local Government Association to stimulate innovative responses. These include: appointment of environmental officers and dunecare co-ordinators, development of total catchment management plans, developing environmental employment opportunities, rate rebates to landholders, provision of machinery to Landcare groups, managing open spaces, and roadside remnant vegetation management (Robinson, 1996).

Catchment management

Most state governments have now introduced some form of catchment management for the major river catchments in their state. These tend to be co-ordinating bodies with both community and government representation. Their role is to establish an overall natural resource management plan and co-ordinate the efforts of the different players, including local

201

Landcare groups. Funding now favours those Landcare projects that fit into a larger regional or catchment-scale plan.

Response from Education and Research

Scientific research and education institutions, such as the Commonwealth Scientific and Industrial Research Organisation (CSIRO) make major contributions to the Landcare effort by providing know-how. Landcare has both demanded and provided an opportunity for more on-farm research, and increasing numbers of researchers work with Landcare groups. Yet much scope remains to improve the integration and applicability of research efforts.

At the local level, primary and secondary schools have been active Landcare participants. Many schools have nurseries that provide trees for Landcare group revegetation projects. They also involve students in environmental monitoring through various 'watch' programmes such as Saltwatch, Frogwatch, and Waterwatch. At university level, many students have researched various aspects of Landcare groups, providing benefits for the group and the students alike.

Evaluating Landcare

Landcare groups have grown quickly, during a farm financial crisis and with limited funding from the NLP (up to US$10 000 per group per year). The two evaluations of Landcare groups in this volume cannot do justice to the diversity of the Australian Landcare movement. Yet they raise issues that are consistent with other quantitative and qualitative assessments of Landcare. Campbell (1992; 1994a) reviewed the distribution, composition, activities and potential of Landcare groups in Australia and found that:

○ Landcare groups can potentially solve problems at a district scale which cannot be tackled effectively on individual properties, especially water-related issues; nature conservation; and management of vertebrate pests and weeds.
○ Landcare groups create a collective social pressure for more sustainable farming systems (Cock, 1992), supporting existing efforts of individual farmers and encouraging others to become more involved; individualism of farmers has limited the exchange of information, particularly quantities, to learn how others achieve their results. With most broadacre farms making a loss, farmers are very motivated to learn the skills, insights and techniques of the better managers. Landcare groups are starting to meet this need, which should increase aggregate productivity at the catchment scale.

o Landcare groups generate commitment to the goal of sustainability at an individual and community scale, and play an increasingly important role in gathering and managing information, and in raising awareness.

o Landcare groups have stimulated new technological developments, and their faster and wider dissemination (Curtis *et al.*, 1992).

o Landcare groups recreate social support networks and community spirit, sharing the stress of rural decline and generating constructive reactions (Carr, 1994).

o Landcare groups provide a useful structure, at an ecologically and socially sensible scale, for more efficient and effective use of government, private and community resources.

So far, so good. Landcare in Australia has been an inspirational and visionary project. But the task of achieving economically viable and environmentally sustainable watershed management is enormous. How can the phenomenal small-scale changes of sustainable land management be transformed into large-scale action and biophysical change over coming decades? Growing criticism leads us to consider new initiatives that are needed to carry the impetus of Landcare into the 21st century, particularly those that look at the structure of rural society.

Landcare and community empowerment?

It is common practice to talk of Landcare in terms of empowering the community as it has handed tremendous responsibility to manage land back to local communities and individuals. But it has not, despite the NLP, provided resources in any way commensurate with the scale of the problem. Responsibility without resources cannot lead to empowerment, especially when global economic forces are creating desperate economic situations for rural communities. Landcare is, to date, based on a somewhat naïve conception of 'empowerment' that ignores these non-local forces. Figure 15.2 shows how rural society is shaped by an interplay of local initiatives, government policy and global market forces.

'Empowerment', which has tended to be interpreted in a technical and local sense, is inadequate in dealing with the political and economic *status quo* that sets the structural framework within which participatory watershed development happens. The economic study of the West Hume Landcare group (Chapter 27) illustrates well the huge impact that structural factors, such as farm size and debt, have on farmers' capacity to invest in sustainable practices and accept the related risks. The potential for empowerment and biophysical impact is shaped by the financial situation of rural people, the enterprises they undertake, demography, community attitudes, social and physical infrastructure, access to goods and services, and the capacity of local people and organizations.

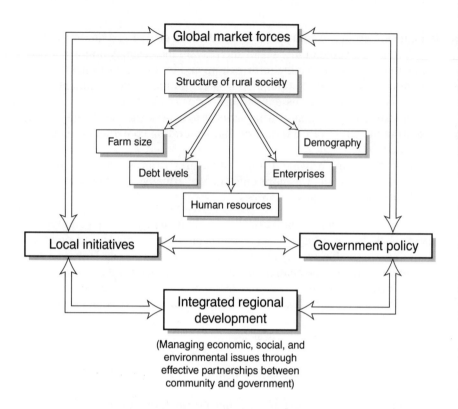

Figure 15.2: The context in which Landcare groups operate

Communities experience social, cultural, institutional and technical constraints (Campbell, 1992, 1994a) that limit what they can achieve. These include limited and declining human resources in rural areas; a lack of technically sound, practical and profitable advice; non-participatory institutional cultures within research and extension agencies; and the overwhelmingly technocratic training of professionals (Reeve *et al.*, 1988). Underlying these constraints, the essentially colonial structure of Australian agriculture, producing raw products that are marketed abroad, means that Australian farmers are vulnerable to declining terms of trade, without the shelter of subsidies received by their OECD counterparts.

It is difficult to see how a remote rural community in Australia can be autonomous when it relies on producing undifferentiated, raw agricultural commodities for distorted global markets, in an essentially *laissez-faire* economic and political context. It will depend on a national commitment to integrated regional rural development.

Nevertheless, integrated regional development does not descend from national initiatives alone. Seeing the gap between what Landcare activities can achieve and what local people would like in an ideal world is often a watershed in the evolution of the group. It can be either empowering or overwhelming, depending on the personalities and knowledge of people in the group and the quality of their facilitation support. When Landcare groups learn more about their resource problems and understand sources of technical and financial assistance, they often feel much less intimidated by 'the system' and more in charge of their destiny. Landcare group activity also excels at revealing the richness of local human resources, which can enhance a sense of local solidarity and resilience in the face of external threats. This is a key influence of Landcare groups: helping people realize that they are all in the same boat so they might as well paddle in the same direction.

The incremental improvements achieved by group and individual projects can easily be swamped by other influences. Australia is not only the driest, flattest and most poorly drained continent, it also has the most variable climate and is a minnow in the sea of global agricultural trade. A long dry spell or a collapse in commodity prices, such as in the early 1990s, increases pressure on farmers and the land which could overwhelm the fledgling efforts of Landcare groups.

Major structural adjustment in rural Australia is both inevitable and necessary. But will change be governed by global market forces with scant regard for environmental issues and social well-being, or can creative and imaginative ways be found to ensure more positive forms of change? Sher and Sher (1994) suggest that Australian rural policy is effectively neutral as to whether food and fibre is produced by 100 000 families, as is the case today, or 100 agribusiness corporations, which is more consistent with the predominant political-economic paradigm of *laissez-faire* economic rationalism. Long-term trends are towards a continued exodus of farmers, increasing farm size and corporatization. So for government to take a neutral policy stance is essentially to bless current trends, and to accept the environmental and social consequences.

But what are the alternatives?

Investment and integrated regional development

Environmental, social and economic issues are inextricably intertwined in rural communities. Land users can take land conservation seriously only if they have a larger than average farm, are better than average managers, and are free of debt (see Chapter 27, this volume). Being debt free is particularly difficult for young farmers with school-going children and rapid farm development investment. These farmers are the lifeblood of rural Australia. Their disappearance has desperate consequences for the social fabric of rural towns, agricultural service industries, and regional employment. Rising interest rates, poor commodity prices or a rise in the Australian dollar due to speculation in international currency markets can tip the balance, forcing these young families from the land. And these are the people whom, from a sustainability perspective, we can least afford to lose. Economic rationalists fail to consider the costs of losing people from the land. Those who remain undergo stress which often leads to unsustainable pressure on the land.

It is irresponsible, if not negligent, of governments to transfer responsibility for land degradation to the community level without commensurate resources. Further, governments have a responsibility to redress issues that have been directly caused or encouraged by their own policies, such as tax deductions for clearing land, lease conditions that made clearing compulsory, inappropriate land tenure administration and water pricing policies, ill-advised soldier settlement schemes and so on.

Government investment is essential if the potential of Landcare is to be realized. Key is how to make the bush a more attractive alternative to the cities as a place to live and work. More, younger, and better trained people can develop more sustainable farming systems and rural communities. These people need access to health, education and social services comparable to those available in urban areas. Greater investment is needed in research, not just to refine the *status quo* but to seek radical alternatives. Natural resource management professionals and land users also require a substantial degree of (re)training. Given the long-term decline in farmers' terms of trade and the inefficiencies inherent in subsidized farm gate prices, rural communities need assistance to add value to their produce, to get involved in off-farm and off-shore processing and marketing of their produce, and to change the image of Australian primary produce to emphasize uniqueness, low external inputs, and high quality.

But agriculture alone cannot revitalise rural Australia. With limits to urban growth, there are compelling reasons for Australia actively to encourage a movement back to the bush, driven not only by lifestyle concerns but also by job opportunities in, for example, knowledge-based industries, and complementary improvements in infrastructure such as transport, communications and services.

A rural revitalization strategy along these lines might best be implemented through a regional development approach, which operates between local communities and Landcare groups and state governments. The regional level still allows for sufficient intimacy and meaningful participation yet allows for strategic resource allocation. Regions can be coherent in terms of their biophysical endowment, their social composition, potentially allowing a better match between social institutions, environmental issues and economic aspirations.

Globalization and life politics

In Australia, as in many countries (cf. this volume), there are wonderful examples of what local people can achieve on their own. However, beyond

Degraded hill slope in San Martin Jilotepeque, Guatemala, prior to
introduction of conservation and green manuring practices (photo
taken during January)   *Roland Bunch*

Same hillslope after the land husbandry practices have been in use for
seven years (photo taken during same time of year)   *Roland Bunch*

In-row tillage is one of a number of farmer-developed technologies to make an impact on land husbandry practices in Honduras
Jules Pretty

(Close up) – Nitrogen-rich soil improved through a combination of in-row tillage and green manuring in Honduras   *Jules Pretty*

Degraded landscape of Paraikuluim, Tamil Nadu, India, before the
introduction of soil and water conservation measures (1991)
Jules Pretty

Same landscape three years later after the land husbandry prctices had
been introduced (photo taken during same time of year – 1994)
Jules Pretty

The Paraikulum Women's Group initiated many of the land
management improvements in their catchment in Tamil Nadu, India
Jules Pretty

A farmer-constructed stone checkdam designed to slow run-off, trap
topsoil and reduce soil erosion in a *nullah* (gully) in Paraikulum (1991)
Jules Pretty

The impact of the stone checkdam three years later (1994). Note the
increased grass cover and reduction in the size of the *nullah*
Jules Pretty

The impact of terracing built by local farmers on the steep hillslopes of
Sinenden Catchment, West Pokot District, Kenya   *John Thompson*

Farmers showing symbols of conservation measures
adopted after the introduction of the Catchment Approach
in Murang'a District, Kenya   *John Thompson*

Farmers describe the soil conservation practices they have adopted to officers of the Soil and Water Conservation Branch in Murang'a District, Kenya   *John Thompson*

The West Hume Landcare Group discusses salinity problems and
fertility management during a Soils Field Day, February 1995
Judy Frankenberg

Landcare Group volunteers working on erosion control structures in
Burrumbuttock Creek, Boxwood, May 1995   *Judy Frankenberg*

the local level is a global system of economic and political forces that all too often conspire to place farmers in a situation where they are forced into degrading the natural resource base just to meet the most basic of living requirements (see Figure 15.2).

Local participatory initiatives arise as local people try to cope as best they can with forces over which they have little influence. As such, these initiatives have often maintained a very local focus. The very limited time and resources available often preclude the individuals working at this level from engaging in broader-scale political change. Global commodity prices in no way reflect the depletion of the natural resource-base capital, and are the most significant constraint on the development of a truly sustainable agriculture in Australia. How can the larger national and global institutions be influenced and how can the philosophy of participatory action influence this bigger agenda (see Box 15.1)?

The Australian landcare movement has no national association as yet. The political bidding has been left to organizations such as the National Farmers' Federation and the Australian Conservation Foundation, or government-appointed advisory committees such as NLAC. In part this reflects a very jaundiced view that local people have of political processes. The challenge remains to build new appreciation of what political action means and to establish 'life-politics' through which local people can influence national and global agendas constructively.

Giddens (1992) reminds us that in today's world we are living with 'high-consequence risks' such as ecological decay or disaster, and that 'these are risks that no one living on earth can escape'. Without being naïve about the global situation, the experiences in this volume give some hope for being able to influence the global agenda. They reveal a well founded philosophy, rich set of methods, and firm basis of experience on local-level participatory development. The main stumbling block remains with institutional support and linkages, whether at the regional, national, or international level. This suggests a new phase for the participatory movement and the need to find better ways for local people to be able to have their say and exert influence at these higher levels.

Anthony Giddens (1992; 9) writes:

It becomes more and more apparent that lifestyle choices, within the settings of local–global interrelations, raise moral issues which cannot simply be pushed to one side. Such issues call for forms of political engagement which the new social movements both presage and serve to help initiate. 'Life politics' – concerned with human self-actualisation, both on the level of the individual and collectively – emerges from the shadow which 'emancipatory politics' has cast.

There are two sides to the 'landcare coin'. Landcare can sound like the answer to land degradation in Australia, and it can sound like a farce.

Box 15.1: Landcare and institutions

Landcare has had a profound impact on agricultural research and extension institutions and processes in Australia. It is accepted that land users have much to offer through their participation in research, extension, land-use planning and policy-making, that many activities that used to be done by government agencies can be better done by community groups with appropriate resources. Government technical staff can be used more effectively and efficiently if much of the logistics and local organization is done by Landcare group co-ordinators like Paul Ayers in Lower Balgarup and Judy Frankenberg in West Hume. Similarly, agency staff can be reasonably confident that their message is relevant if they are responding to issues raised by Landcare groups, rather than their own perception of the issues. The emphasis on farm and catchment planning processes in Landcare also places pressure on technical advisers to make sure their advice is integrated with that of other specialists, not given in isolation.

While Landcare has changed the state agencies, all is not rosy. Campbell (1992; 1994a,b), Carr (1994) and Woodhill (1992) have noted institutional cultures within government agencies that make a mockery of the 'bottom-up', 'community-based' rhetoric. They note patronizing attitudes, manipulation of groups to suit agency agendas and outright competition for resources. Community empowerment can be threatening for people and institutions who fear it means losing their own power (Woodhill, 1992). Landcare has also increased the demand for on-farm technical advice, exposing cutbacks in extension resources, and increasing cynicism within rural communities about the sincerity of governments' professed concerns for rural sustainability. There is an emerging view that governments have been able to use Landcare funding as a smokescreen for withdrawing resources and services, effectively transferring responsibility for, and ownership of, land degradation and its solutions to a community level, without allocating commensurate resources or decision-making authority.

However, Landcare has unquestionably provided a vehicle for people to work together on something that is constructive, positive and personally rewarding. The future of landcare may well rest in greater acknowledgment that, through Landcare, people have created a social movement that has much deeper reasons for existence than just the technical task of land conservation.

16
Regional Initiatives in Southern Africa to Put Farmers First in Soil Conservation
MIKAEL SEGERROS

Introduction

Overview of the Region

THE REGION OF the Southern African Development Community (SADC) covers about seven million km² and has a population of almost 130 million. The community was created to facilitate collaboration and economic development of the countries in Southern Africa. It has 12 member states, namely Angola, Botswana, Lesotho, Malawi, Mauritius, Mozambique, Namibia, South Africa, Swaziland, Tanzania, Zambia and Zimbabwe.

This region is endowed with rich natural resources, such as all kinds of minerals, land of good agricultural potential, fisheries, forests and wildlife. Despite good agricultural potential, substantial amounts of food have had to be imported to the region in recent years. One important reason for this deficit was a drought that was unprecedented in living memory. However, it must also be admitted that food production has not been able to keep up with a population increase of about 3.2 per cent per annum.

It is believed that almost all land in the region is affected by land degradation in one way or another and with more or less severity. After decades of largely unsustainable development, the lives and livelihoods of many people and communities throughout Southern Africa are threatened by environmental degradation, escalating deforestation, soil degradation, declining biological diversity and over-exploitation of wildlife fisheries and rangelands.

Brief history

During the course of the 20th century there have been many programmes aimed at stopping land degradation. In general, these have been dominated by experts with the opinion that there was nothing to learn from the methods and techniques being practised by local farmers. As the problem of soil erosion was perceived to be very urgent, a top to bottom approach evolved, with farmers forced by authorities through fines, threats of arrest and other forms of coercion to erect physical soil conservation structures. Under these circumstances there is no wonder that a strong resentment against soil conservation took root among local farmers. This bad taste linked to soil conservation remains today.

During the 1980s, there began to emerge a new understanding. In an attempt to counter the growing problems of land degradation and declining yields, SADC countries began to promote the more active involvement of farmers in planning and decision-making. By the early 1990s, the following ideas had gained ground:

○ the promotion and facilitation of the active participation of the land users during all stages of a project is the most positive decisive factor in rural development
○ the benefits of building on existing indigenous farm management and soil conservation technologies
○ avoiding complicated and costly farm management and soil conservation approaches so as to reduce government involvement and expenditure
○ a priority should be given to biological control measures over mechanical and physical structures.

This shift in thinking led gradually to two major changes in the organization of extension within farm management systems in the region. First, the farmers' role became, at least in theory, central in the formulation and implementation of soil and water conservation strategies. Learning from farmers started to be seen to be as important as teaching them. This meant that the extension agent and the researchers began to see the farming system in the same way as the farmer: as an integrated whole.

Second, assumptions about the roles of local institutions and the exercise of local authority has had to change. Post-colonial governments generally tended to down-play the importance of local institutions in influencing local land use planning and conservation, believing that these tasks were better handled by relevant line ministries. But now governments are learning how to work more effectively with local land managers, local systems of authority and local institutions in an attempt to design more appropriate and ultimately more sustainable land-use programmes and projects.

The SADC Environment and Land Management Sector (SADC-ELMS)

The SADC Environment and Land Management Sector Coordination Unit (SADC-ELMS) is based in Maseru, Lesotho. The programme aims to help the governments of SADC member countries:

○ to improve their performance in relation to the sustainable management of natural resources, particularly soil and water
○ to identify actual or potential conflicts of interest that may arise out of environmental degradation and to reconcile such conflicts
○ to develop policies and promote practices for the sustainable productive management of natural resources based upon partnership between government and communities of farmers and other land users

o to support institutions in member countries in their efforts to increase their competence in sustainable resource management and to integrate the various disciplines and contributions of such institutions.

The SADC-ELMS tries to stimulate impact down to grassroots level by emphasizing people's participation, the economics of sustainable resource management, techniques and approaches for good land husbandry, integrated land use planning, and awareness-creation among youth. There is an important focus on training and capacity building at all levels.

The training and capacity building process

SADC-ELMS has been promoting the importance of participation and farmers' knowledge in a continuous process of training and capacity building. These have included one-off workshops, as well as regular training courses.

Participatory methods for medium-level technical staff

Despite several successful workshops on popular participation and conservation project design in the 1980s, we found that little had been done to implement the recommendations. When, for example, the methodology of PRA was brought up for discussion, it was initially rejected as obscure and irrelevant.

By using stealth, however, a 10-day PRA/RRA exercise was organized for local-level extension staff. The idea was to test whether participatory methods that had worked well for the Ministry of Agriculture in Kenya could be applied in Southern Africa. The technical staff who participated in this training were very satisfied and wanted to see more of it. This gave us the courage to start talking about PRA openly.

In 1992, a regional PRA workshop was held in Lesotho. The site was selected because of a local project already using some participatory approaches.[1] The major objectives were to start selling the idea of PRA in the region, and identify people who could promote the methodologies widely. Government officers from nine SADC member countries attended.

We gained many insights from the workshop and from what followed, including:

o Of the 40 participants, there were 10 who have been able actively to promote PRA in their countries. We have learnt that spreading effects depends both on personalities and on the openness in the departments where the participants are working.

---

[1] The FISC – Farm Improvement through Soil Conservation project, which later became the PTC II – Production Through Conservation programme.

211

○ Although most appreciated the approach, participants should have been more supported in the form of material and moral back-up after the workshop to help with implementation.

Participatory methods for higher-level decision makers

The next workshop was organized in Zambia in 1993. This time we tried to mobilize support from the bosses of the previous participants, and so this workshop was aimed at high-level directors and chiefs in government responsible for management of natural resources.

The participants applied the PRA methods in villages near to Livingstone. Most were amazed at the depth of knowledge of the rural people. As a result, they accepted and gave their support for the PRA approach. They recommended that national workshops should be held for the training of trainers.

From here on we have no longer organized any PRA courses. Instead, we have sought to integrate PRA into other courses, workshops and activities.

Water harvesting

The recent drought, the worst in a century, clearly highlighted the need for better management and utilization of the region's water resources. Many governments and donors tend to emphasize large-scale development of rivers or ground water resources. However, only about 40 per cent of the total rainfall reaches rivers and underground reservoirs. Opportunities therefore exist to harness some of the remaining 60 per cent more directly for farmers. Being aware of the rainwater-harvesting techniques available, SADC-ELMS organized a practical workshop to increase awareness in the region.

The basic aim was to provide examples of sustainable water supplies for rural communities based on local water sources. For these supplies to be sustainable, many social, economic and environmental aspects have also to be taken into consideration, besides purely technical issues.

Again, we learnt that attempts like this at regional level are useful to raise ideas. However, to have a sustained impact, follow-up at national level is necessary.

Two regular courses

The Integrating Conservation into Farming Systems training is well established and has its roots in a course developed by the Malawi government in the late 1980s. This course is arranged jointly by the ELMS Unit and the Land Husbandry Training Centre (LHTC), Malawi. It includes an appreciation of why land degradation occurs and, in consultation with farmers and other land users, works on techniques that will reverse the trend of increasing land degradation, and increase productivity.

The Land Husbandry course is jointly run by the SADC–ELMS unit and Sokoine University of Agriculture in Tanzania. The overall aim of the training is to encourage a reassessment of commonly held approaches in soil conservation and to examine ways of working with farmers to increase production and minimize land degradation. The course is mostly field based and intends to place the participants in challenging situations within different agro-ecological and socio-economic settings.

Innovative Rural Action Learning Areas (IRALAs)

The concept of IRALAs

One of the fundamental problems with rural development up to now is that it has been all too common for governments, NGOs and donors to try to impose external ideas on local people. Even though the intention was good, it has taken initiative away from farmers – the very people directly responsible for managing the land.

With IRALAs we attempt to work the other way around:

> the land users shall feed decision makers, professionals, trainers and donors with ideas, techniques and approaches which have actually worked for them.

The main feature is to *discover* and *share* existing local experience. How to do this is something we are learning during the project. The project concept in itself implies a learning and adoption process. The IRALAs initiative has the following focus:

○ discovering what the farmers are actually doing in the region
○ monitoring and assessment of communities and individuals applying successful natural recourse management
○ visualization and dissemination of information from these areas
○ sharing knowledge and experience for promotion of existing and new successful schemes
○ feeding experience into policies and training/learning programmes as a means towards successful natural resource management.

Once the IRALA is identified, it is compared with other IRALAs. The second step is to identify the factors that have led to success; is it because of the personality of the farmer, or is it because of the location and natural conditions of the farm, or community? This analysis is done by researchers, extensionists and farmers.

213

While analysing the success we also seek reasons for non-success. If a certain farmer or community is successful why are others not? Why does the neighbour or adjacent areas not take up some of the innovations and ideas of the IRALAs? In this way, we hope to define what a successful farmer looks like under different conditions – there could be similarities between a successful farmer or community in Dodoma, Tanzania and Kanye, Botswana. This knowledge can then be used in policies, research, extension and training programmes, and in various campaigns.

In order to use this knowledge we have to find mechanisms for wide dispersion in the region. What we learn from the IRALA is shared between villagers and villages, e.g through study trips, informal farmer exchange and farmers training. The next loop is at district level where officers and farmers collaborate on training programmes, local training material, local research etc. At national level study trips are undertaken, training institutions are being influenced, and researchers and policy-makers are visiting the IRALAs to learn what to emphasize.

We are also learning and exchanging ideas among different countries in the region. The different IRALAs are nuclei in an SADC network where exchange of information is happening between the countries. Regional training material is being produced, exchange of information takes place in workshops where the IRALA farmers participate together with government officers, NGOs and researchers.

Activities within IRALAs

The IRALAs currently consist of the following activities.

Inventory. A national institution identifies successful areas in the country. The researchers will use the extension system, documents, farmers interviews and other means for this first activity.

National workshops. In a two-day workshop, researchers, extensionists and farmers from the successful areas come together and present their findings. An important question at this event is, from what point of view do we judge success? The farmers', researchers', donors' or governments'? This is debated and indicators for success are defined as bases for further activities. Out of the identified successful cases in the country the two or three best are chosen using agreed criteria.

In-depth analysis. The best IRALAs in the country are carefully analysed, so as to find out the conditions (policy environment, natural conditions, social and cultural set-up, external factors, institutions, local leadership) that have led to the progress.

Monitoring. This is important to ensure that we know what happens in the IRALAs in the long term. Conditions might change for the better or for the worse.

Publication. Many mechanisms will be used to publicize the results, including reports, videos, posters, books, pamphlets, journals and so on.

Impacts of IRALAs

It is too early to draw any definite conclusions from the IRALAs experience. The planned in-depth analyses will require monitoring of the selected areas over a considerable period. However, a number of lessons have begun to emerge.

On policy-makers. The exercise has served as an eye-opener for many policy-makers. In Malawi, IRALAs received attention from the highest possible level – the State President, His Excellency Bakili Muluzi. Support from the top is crucial for success among the grassroots.

On professionals' attitudes. We have seen a clear change of attitudes among professionals in these workshops. Some of us were surprised by the way farmers conducted themselves in what was supposed to be an unfamiliar environment to them. They were able to really challenge researchers, policy-makers and other professionals in all aspects. Some of them proved to be more articulate and better teachers than the professional trainers.

On academics' attitudes. Also for the IRALAs researchers, this exercise has been an eye-opener to many. However, we must really ensure that the exercise does not become too academic. Extensionists and academics often have a different way of thinking. The end result must not be a book for our publication records. Instead we hope that IRALAs can be a live project which actually can contribute to better conditions for the farmers in the SADC region.

The research so far is qualitative and might also be quite subjective. We will be criticized for this and also be accused of having an 'unscientific' approach. We have already experienced this, though it might be that many of us are still too hooked into old attitudes.

On farmers' achievements on the ground. So far, about 150 uniquely successful farmers have been identified who have started innovative, economically-viable and environmentally-sustainable activities. While most farmers are barely making a living, some IRALAs farmers have raised their yields by 200–300 per cent within a few years. In most, if not all,

215

cases production is their primary concern, and conservation merely a means to achieve it.

Almost without exception, successful farmers practise mixed farming. Many of them have also embarked on alternative ventures, as a risk aversion strategy – often small-scale enterprises, like shops or mills, or specialized activities such as breeding of livestock or niche crops. As put by one Malawian farmer, 'diversification is a higher degree of farming'. Research and extension personnel are thus challenged to heed this holistic view of farmers, and seek to stimulate such initiatives elsewhere.

Some experienced professionals dealing with rural development were very surprised when it was discovered what some farmers were already doing. It has been proven that there are farmers who can out-do the best soil conservationists and irrigation engineers. And they have followed through the whole process from the idea through to design, implementation and utilization.

On understanding community dynamics. Community dynamics is another area that needs further investigation. Some innovative farmers are appreciated by their communities, who emulate them. In several cases, IRALAs farmers have succeeded in organizing their neighbours into farmers' associations or other groups. Others are regarded with suspicion, as threatening the authority of formal or traditional structure – and hence blocked.

On the role of extension. It is often argued that the advice from extensionists is ignored because their knowledge and interest does not measure up to those of the top farmers. The IRALAs' experience, however, shows that most successful farmers are very responsive to extension advice. Mechanisms must be created, and attitudes developed, to enable a greater openness between both sets of actors.

On the way ahead for supporting farmers. In spite of the encouraging progress to date, the IRALAs' experience is only beginning. Should it end with the completion of the in-depth analyses, little will have been achieved besides a change in attitude among those who have been involved to date. It may have been proven that scientists, agronomists, extensionists and farmers can all learn from one another, and work together for a common purpose; but that is not enough.

To be meaningful, the lessons from IRALAs must be applied in practice. The experience gained must be fed into training programmes around the region – in colleges, universities and farmers' training centres. It must be incorporated into the policy-making, project planning, research and extension implementation processes, for the benefit of all farmers. The dissemination of information combined with new practices will be a vital aspect of IRALAs in future.

NGO-LED TRANSFORMATIONS

Overview
NGO-led Transformations

Natural resource management involves complex social interactions that are not immediately obvious to outsiders, yet can be encouraged by a supportive external organization . . . an impartial agent who resolves conflicts and witnesses agreements. Reddy *et al.*

THE WORLD OF soil and water conservation has been shaped by many innovations that can be attributed to non-governmental organizations. In this process, they have had to strike a fine balance between their narrow soil and water conservation mandate and diverse local priorities. To achieve this, NGOs have forced a rethinking, not only of the nature of technologies but importantly, of the roles of local communities and government, funding arrangements, and the very processes of social and environmental change.

This section discusses five experiences that have been initiated and managed by NGOs. Their collective message for catchment development is encouraging and simple.

Changing roles over time

Participatory watershed development involves the sequential adoption of changes in land use and social organization over time. This complex process of social and environmental change requires several inputs: information, collaboration, shared understanding and agreement, land tenure, money, seedlings, tools, planning skills, etc. Each of the NGOs described here played a unique role, roles that changed over time as different stages of technology development and implementation called for different inputs.

For example, Chaitanya, in Andhra Pradesh, India, has helped villagers convert irrigation tanks to percolation tanks (Reddy *et al.*) by:

○ awareness-raising of solutions through exposure visits to other villages
○ encouragement of doubters
○ conflict resolution
○ appealing to government to issue conversion permits.

The role of the NGOs involved in the Filippino experience (Cerna *et al.*) saw several changes from the process being initiated by one NGO, World Neighbors, who then facilitated the formation of a new local organization,

Mag-uugmad Foundation, Inc (MFI). MFI, in turn, handed over the farmer-based extension system to the farmers themselves.

But these are only some of the many necessary functions, which also include information provision, technological skills, funding, legislation and advocacy. Only in rare cases can one organization, such as an NGO, fulfil all these functions. Therefore strategic and healthy alliances are necessary for success and for widespread impacts.

Complexity of organizational linkages

A striking feature of the NGO experiences described in this volume is the complexity of linkages with other organizations and agencies. NGOs do not act alone. They seek alliances to deal with the wide range of tasks that participatory watershed development calls for. Furthermore, NGOs do not have the legitimacy and infrastructure of government agencies. Instead, their role is to show that there are alternative viable approaches to catchment development, and to provide support for competence building.

Chatterji *et al.* paint a rich picture of the complexity and diversity of organizational linkages that have made the work of the Society for the Protection for Watershed Development (SPWD) a success. Its contact with the grassroots level is through the village youth clubs. These clubs are federated under the umbrella of *Sevabrata*, which in turn, is supported by PRADAN, another NGO that mediates with funders. Finally, there is SPWD itself. Currently, the catchment activities are spreading to other parts of the region that require different, more locally appropriate partners, notably local co-operatives, *panchayats* (local councils), and state agencies.

In another example, the Social Centre (SC) recognized the importance of many institutions and their interactions, and involved them all: seven groups directly related to programme implementation (some internal to the community and others based outside), and several other groups instrumental to the work but not directly involved in programme implementation (Lobo and Palghadmal).

Guijt and Sidersky describe the difficulties of achieving results when there are no viable organizations with whom to build strategic alliances, as is the case in Northeast Brazil. At first they worked in partnership with a single institution – the Rural Worker's Trade Union. Now, however, to ensure long-term sustainability of their work, they need to expand the network to include a wide range of other partners. This means not only strengthening the capacities of their own NGO and community groups, but also those of new partners, including the state agricultural extension agency.

Central need for mediation

Within the changing roles and organizational complexity, one NGO role stands out as essential: that of mediation. Mediation is needed in relation to: finding and passing on technological information, communication between different social groups in the community, resolving internal and external conflicts, linking different communities to share experiences, negotiating with external organizations and agencies, and so on.

Lobo and Palghadmal describe this role in a nutshell: 'SC's policy was not directly to fund any projects, but to act as a "broker" or advocate between the people, government departments and banks. People were empowered by introducing them to local institutional actors, not only to use the assistance available but also to increase their independent capacity to make claims on the system.' Chaitanya, operating in Andhra Pradesh, India, served as 'a neutral broker among those interested in tank management . . . [and] played a conflict resolution role in many villages, which are aligned into small groups according to caste, political parties, etc.' (Reddy *et al.*). For AS-PTA in northeast Brazil, it is not conflict but technical information that needs mediating as there are virtually no links between farmers, farmers' organizations, and the formal agricultural research sector. AS-PTA seeks the technical information that, with modification, can help farmers remove key agricultural bottlenecks.

Mediation is accomplished through various means, such as exchange visits to farmers, communities, and/or organizations; or PRA-based analysis of bottlenecks and remedies. For example, SPWD led farmer visits to another NGO, Society for Hill Resource Management School, which highlighted alternative technologies at a crucial point for spreading the impact of the catchment work. MFI's farmer-based extension system rests on farmer-to-farmer visits. Clearly, NGOs will need to well and truly master communication skills and knowledge of key information sources, and pass this on to their partners. To illustrate this, MFI assesses farmers who want to become instructors against several criteria, including 'good communication skills'.

Maintaining a social focus

Linked to the role of mediator has been the NGO role of 'guardian of equity'. As the absence of social equity characterizes most of the catchments described in this volume, the challenge has been how to use the catchment development process to bridge that gap. As Lobo and Palghadmal describe: 'the SC prioritized and focused primarily on the economically backward sections of society', and refused to compromise for the more powerful in Kasare who were clearly jeopardizing the new, more equal, decision-making structures.

In other examples, a focus on social equity has been maintained by monitoring the impact of the catchment work for different groups and/or making explicit the equity principle of the catchment process. Chaitanya describes how much dialogue was needed to find a solution which benefited

221

all stakeholders, including the landless. SPWD aimed for a similarly equitable impact, with the output of the pooled private wastelands shared equally between landowners, labourers and the village. But they also monitored their work and found that the first technologies did not sufficiently benefit the poorer farmers with upland plots. Technologies were adapted to ensure the catchment work would ensure widespread benefits.

Critical start-up support

Besides mediation and benefit monitoring, NGOs have often played a vital role in starting up the catchment work. Changes to land use systems are risky for the many extremely low income farmers suffering the effects of land degradation. To cushion the impact of these risks, incentives however minimal, are often important. These have not been, in any of the NGO cases, in the form of payment to farmers for implementation of conservation measures. Rather, they ranged from subsidies on seedlings, to provision of essential information, or ensuring opt-out clauses for risky collaborations (see Reddy *et al.*)

While MFI staff rely strongly on farmer-based extension, they must overcome several problems, including the tight time schedule of most farmers, the lack of basic inputs and length of time before benefits become apparent. They have found that providing some financial support for start-up costs and compensating farmer instructors for their time is as essential as providing information and organizational development skills. For AS-PTA, start-up support is not given to farmers, but rather to the local partner, the Rural Workers' Union representatives, in the form of day-rates for the time they spend training farmers in contour planting, agroforestry, etc.

Flexibility throughout the process

The context-specific nature of catchments, socially as well as environmentally, requires collective, adaptive learning and planning on the part of NGOs: 'the overriding feature in evolving the technologies [is] flexibility and a willingness to learn' (Chatterji *et al.*). SPWD, for example, had to accept that their original focus on income generation was not a local priority and so they changed to one genuinely desired, that of drought alleviation. Later, they also adapted the original technology to find a second version that suited smaller farmers better. AS-PTA has established 'permanent planning' with the farmers, as each year throws up new challenges requiring new solutions. MFI uses the principle of continual change to encourage farmer group formation: as more farmers join a group, problems occur and the group decides to break into smaller, more manageable groups.

17

Converting Irrigation Tanks Into Percolation Tanks in South India: A Case-study of Social Organization Leading to Equitable Development

P. GANGI REDDY, G. SRIRAMAPPA, J.C. KATYAL, N.K. SANGHI, JOHN M. KERR AND RAMESH CHAKRAVORTHY[1]

Introduction

IRRIGATION TANKS CAN provide a stable source of water for agriculture in unpredictable environments, such as southern India. There are over 100 000 irrigation tanks in Andhra Pradesh, Karnataka, and Tamil Nadu, and most were built in the 18th and 19th centuries (Palanisami and Ramasamy, 1997). They are ponds that capture and store runoff water behind a large bund during the rainy season to supply water to lower-lying fields through sluice gates. They range from one to over 100 hectares, with most tank beds covering about 20–50 ha.

Recent years have seen a significant decline in the use of irrigation tanks. Tank construction stagnated after India's independence in 1947 when government resources focused on large canal irrigation projects. Farmers also lost interest in irrigation tanks when mechanical pumps and widespread electrification made irrigation wells increasingly attractive. In Karnataka, for example, the number of electrified irrigation pump sets rose from about 11 000 in 1957 to over 900 000 in 1993 (KEB, 1994). In Tamil Nadu, the area irrigated by wells rose from 20 per cent to 45 per cent of all irrigated area from 1960 to 1983, while the tank-irrigated area fell from 38 per cent to 20 per cent in the same period (Palanisami and Ramasamy, 1997). Traditional tank management systems declined as state government agencies took over irrigation co-ordination, without building effective new institutional irrigation arrangements.

Many tanks fell into disrepair, with collapsed tank bunds, silted feeder channels and tank beds, and faulty sluice gates. As a result, many tanks no longer capture and distribute water optimally. When tanks fill only partially, they either irrigate only part of the command area continually or the whole area for only part of a season. In either scenario, supplementary

[1] P. Gangi Reddy, Chaitanya; G. Sriramappa, Oxfam-India; J.C. Katyal, CRIDA; N.K. Sanghi, ICAR; John M. Kerr, Winrock/ICRISAT; and R. Chakravorthy, Society for Wasteland Development.

irrigation from wells becomes a necessity. In especially dry years, many tanks remain empty and farmers grow nothing as their waterlogged land can carry only irrigated crops. The average water level in most tanks has fallen and their irrigation capacity is increasingly unpredictable. Tanks have thus changed from a source of stability to one of instability[2] (Palanisami and Ramasamy, 1997).

Recently, efforts have been made to rehabilitate irrigation tanks. One government approach has been to provide external funds to improve the infrastructure and to encourage community maintenance. However, as farmers' disinterest in tanks is one of the reasons behind their decline, there is no certainty that they will invest time and money to continue maintaining the tanks.

Farmers responded with an alternative, entirely indigenous innovation. Instead of rehabilitating traditional tanks, they have converted irrigation tanks into percolation tanks. Percolation tanks resemble irrigation tanks but have no sluice gate. Instead, water escapes from the tank by seeping, or percolating, into the ground to augment groundwater aquifers. Many percolation structures have been constructed under watershed projects in semi-arid regions. But farmers in southern Andhra Pradesh have also started converting existing irrigation tanks to percolation tanks independently of government initiatives. Hydrologists previously did not advocate conversion of existing tanks. This is because new percolation tanks are superior to converted tanks unless efforts are made to desilt the existing tanks. Otherwise water in the converted tanks percolates only at a relatively slow rate. However, now that farmers are leading the way to tank conversion, hydrologists acknowledge that the approach is technically acceptable, if not optimal (Athawale, pers. comm.).

This chapter focuses on the merits and problems of farmer-led conversions of irrigation tanks. It also discusses the social conditions necessary for the conversion to benefit all those involved, and reflects on the role of support agencies in facilitating the process. Although the innovation was led by farmers, government or non-governmental organizations can play a role by helping to resolve conflicts and acting as guarantor to any agreements made between different interest groups within the village. We draw on experiences in Anantapur District, Andhra Pradesh. The work was initiated by villagers and has drawn the interest and stimulated collaboration of five NGOs and two government agencies: Chaitanya, Oxfam-India, Afpro, the Society for the Promotion of Wasteland Development (SPWD), Action for World Solidarity (ASW), the Central Research Institute for Dryland Agriculture (CRIDA), and the Indian Council for Agricultural Research (ICAR).

---

[2] For a more detailed history of tank irrigation in south India, see Von Oppen and Subba Rao, 1980, and Ludden, 1979.

Winners and losers from tank conversion

A tank is converted from surface irrigation to percolation simply by closing the sluice gate. The percolated water flows underground below the command area, where it is lifted by motorized pumps through irrigation wells. The advantage of this system is that a percolation tank can increase the supply of irrigation water even when it does not fill, whereas irrigation tanks provide surface water only when completely full. Percolation also supports the use of wells for irrigation, which are increasingly favoured by farmers.

However, the benefits of percolation tanks will not necessarily spread equitably through the community. The immediate beneficiaries are those farmers who own wells, the wealthy minority. Nevertheless, experience shows that percolation tanks can be managed in ways that improve well-being across the board. This will be described in more detail below. A possible disadvantage of tank conversion, which affects everyone, is that perennial water bodies provide breeding grounds for mosquitoes and water-borne diseases.

In most villages there are different groups of people who will be affected by tank conversion[3] in unique ways. These include:

- o farmers with well-irrigated land in the tank command area
- o farmers with land in the tank command area, but with no well
- o farmers who own land in the tank bed area
- o farmers who cultivate land illegally in the tank bed
- o the 'water man' who manages the sluice gate in the tank irrigation system
- o fishermen who raise fish in the tank
- o other farmers and other landless people.

Well-owning farmers in the command area

Well owners are the obvious, immediate winners from conversion. Percolation increases the amount of water that they can extract through their wells, allowing them to irrigate a larger area and for a longer period. Well owners can also benefit by selling excess water to neighbouring farmers who have no wells.

Farmers in the command area without wells

Farmers without wells lose access to surface irrigation. The impact of this depends on the reliability of the existing tank in providing surface

---

[3] Some people belong to more than one of the categories, so they might have competing interests in how the tank is managed.

irrigation. Since many, if not most, tanks are providing progressively less surface irrigation water, farmers without wells have less to lose from tank conversion than they would have in the past (Table 17.1).

The loss of surface water for these farmers is compensated by the increased availability of water in nearby wells. By buying water from their neighbours, farmers without wells can have relatively assured access to irrigation, albeit at a price. For them, the merits of tank conversion depend on the relative returns from assured but costly well irrigation compared to free but erratic tank irrigation (see discussion below).

Farmers with land in the tank bed

Land in tank beds is increasingly being cultivated. Once the tank empties, farmers can cultivate this highly fertile land. With widespread declining water levels, these farmers have grown accustomed to the tank emptying quickly each year, allowing them to grow a crop on residual moisture.

Tank bed farmers seemingly gain nothing from conversion to percolation tanks. With closed sluices, tanks remain full longer and the growing period shortens. Many tanks would be perennially full after conversion, making tank bed cultivation impossible. But whether tank bed farmers actually lose from tank conversion, however, varies between legal title holders and encroachers.

In recent years, political populism has motivated land distribution programmes. Government land that has been privatized in these programmes includes land on the edge of the tank bed, or its foreshore (Jodha, 1991). Title-holding tank bed farmers can legally obstruct the conversion to a percolation tank and may demand compensation.

But in many tanks, farmers have encroached illegally on the fringes of the tank bed. Most common are farmers who own land near the tank bed

Table 17.1: Likelihood of Surface Irrigation During the Decade Before Conversion in Anantapur District

Name of the tank	Percentage of command area receiving surface irrigation when rainfall was:			Number of months of surface irrigation when rainfall was:		
	Low	Medium	High	Low	Medium	High
Adeppalli	20	50	90	1	2.5	4
Adeppalli Thanda	25	45	90	1	2.5	4
Peddanapalli	30	60	100	1.5	3	4.5
Kammayagaripalli	25	70	90	1	2	3.5
Jammikunta	0	25	70	0.5	2	4
Jagarajapalli	30	60	100	2	3.5	5

Note: About 50 per cent of years are 'medium rainfall', 25 per cent are low rainfall, and 25 per cent are high rainfall. Most crops require about 3.5 months of irrigation.

226

and gradually extend their boundaries into the bed. Other farmers simply establish new plots within the tank bed. Rising population pressure has aggravated land scarcity, fuelling this encroachment. The general decline of local irrigation tank management systems has also reduced villagers' willingness or ability to prevent encroachment.

Since encroachers have no land rights, they cannot legally prevent tank conversion. However, most illegal encroachers are probably relatively powerful, enabling them to influence the village record keeper to allow encroachment. In this case, they might be able to prevent conversion, or at least to demand compensation.

The water man

Traditionally, the water man was employed by farmers in the command area to manage the flow of water from the tank by controlling the sluice gate. Although the water man is often relatively poor and landless, he usually has considerable influence over tank users because he controls when they get water. When the tank is converted, the water man's task becomes obsolete. Unless a new job is created for him, he is an unequivocal loser.

Fishermen

Fishermen are affected ambiguously by tank conversion. On the one hand, as water remains longer in the tank, fish can grow larger and fetch a higher market price. In tanks without fish prior to conversion, fishermen clearly gain. However, harvesting costs may rise due to conversion. First, some fishermen place traps in the open sluice, catching fish as the moving water draws them to the sluice. Closing the sluice would make this impossible. Second, fish are easier to catch as water recedes at the end of the season. If conversion causes a tank to be full perennially, fish will be more difficult to catch. Therefore, whether fishermen gain or lose depends on the relative magnitude of the gains due to the longer season and the losses due to the increased harvest costs.

Other farmers and landless people

Farmers outside the command and bed areas, and landless people other than fishermen, are unaffected by tank conversion unless special arrangements are made to include them. In some cases, employment might be created due to an increase in the net irrigated area created by tank conversion. Cattle owners benefit from tank conversion as they can water their cattle for a longer period. Whether or not this makes much difference depends on whether watering points had been available throughout the year prior to tank conversion.

Ensuring that everyone gains

Many people clearly risk losing from tank conversion and will be hesitant to support it. Tank conversion can succeed only if ways are found to ensure that no one loses from the process.

There are two ways to think about spreading the gains from tank conversion: first, the simplest way is to consider everyone who is directly affected by tank conversion: farmers in the command and bed areas, fishermen, and the water man. Second, and more ambitiously, it involves considering villagers who are not affected directly by tank conversion, including landowners outside the tank system and landless people other than the water man.

Ensuring that everyone gains who is affected directly by the tank

Farmers without wells. The largest group of potential losers is the group of farmers in the command area who do not own wells. Gaining their support is critical in the tank conversion process. Helping farmers without wells forms both a major motivation for tank conversion and a precondition for making it work. Without careful attention to the non-well-owning farmers, tank conversion might simply benefit the wealthier well owners more, at the expense of their less wealthy neighbours, obviating any socio-economic justification for tank conversion.

The success of tank conversion depends critically on the market for well water. Under the percolation tank system, irrigation water is extracted solely through private wells. Farmers who own wells benefit from the extra irrigation water for their own land or to sell to others. If the water price is low enough, farmers without wells also benefit by gaining access to a reliable supply of water.

Many factors influence the efficient operation of water markets and the consequent benefits for farmers without wells. These include:

○ the volume of water supply. Many conversions will result in a larger water supply, which implies a fall in the price of water.
○ the density of wells in the command area. More wells mean more sellers, more competition, and hence lower water prices. More wells also enable farmers without wells to find a nearby water supplier easily, keeping conveyance costs low.
○ the cost of energy to extract water. Currently, in southern India where tanks are numerous, owners of electric irrigation pumps pay a small annual fee to pump as much water as they want. The only additional cost is maintenance and a small amount of labour.
○ the difference in yields between the *rabi* (dry) season and the *kharif* (rainy) season. Yields are higher in the *rabi* season because there is

sunshine virtually every day. Tank conversion conserves water and increases the likelihood that farmers can cultivate a *rabi* crop. This affects the bargaining positions of farmers with and without wells alike. For example, it encourages well owners to offer low water prices to buyers, in exchange for closing the sluice and improving the chances that they will be able to irrigate a *rabi* crop. Water buyers, on the other hand, will be willing to pay more in the *rabi* than the *kharif* season.

A survey of 80 tanks, including 20 that had been successfully converted, was conducted jointly by Chaitanya and ICAR in early 1994. In the percolation tanks surveyed, water prices are linked to the level of water in the tank (see Box 17.1). Early in the season, while the tank is full of water, buyers pay Rs 5 per hour of irrigation. As the tank water level falls, the price becomes Rs 10 per hour. Once the tank is empty, the price rises to Rs 12 per hour. Prior to conversion, well owners charged Rs 15 per hour throughout the season, though sales normally began only after the tank emptied.

Box 17.1:   Water pricing in Jagarajapalli

In Jagarajapalli, farmers have gradually developed a pricing system for water transfers. In the beginning, well-less farmers agreed to pay the electricity and motor repair costs of well owners in exchange for irrigation water. This system worked well until major repairs were needed and disagreement arose. Now they have a system of payment for each irrigation moment. As water-intensive crops, like paddy, became more expensive to grow, farmers shifted toward water-conserving crops, such as sunflower, *ragi*, and maize.

Essential in these arrangements is that farmers without wells are not completely at the mercy of well owners: they can enforce their property rights to water in the tank and maintain substantial bargaining power. Before closing the sluice gate, they can enter into an agreement with well owners regarding irrigation water prices and quantities. They can also close the gate on a temporary basis, thus retaining the option to open it if well owners fail to co-operate. Even if the sluice gate is closed permanently, farmers without wells can extract irrigation water from the tank by siphon. This simply requires extending a tube from the tank over the bund and down to the fields. Therefore, well owners who want tank conversion have no choice but to sell water at a rate acceptable to their neighbours (see Box 17.2).

Farmers in the tank bed. The situation of farmers in the tank bed is more problematic and requires a case-by-case solution. Treatment for illegal and legal encroachers would probably be similar, as eviction is unpopular and legally cumbersome. There are several options for farmers in the tank bed to benefit from tank conversion:

○ If farmers in the tank command area stand to gain enough, they may agree to compensate the tank bed farmers directly, with land and assured irrigation water.
○ The government may compensate tank bed farmers, having privatized these lands in the first place.
○ If only part of the encroacher's land is submerged by closing the sluice gate, then total land area decreases may be compensated sufficiently by productivity increases on the remaining land. Alternatively, a wall can be constructed around the lower part of the plot to keep water out.

The last two solutions require agreement from the tank command farmers, since they may interfere with the supply of water to the command area.

The water man. Markets for groundwater require that all the users of a given well rotate their water use. As the number of water users grows, rotation systems become more complicated. Water buyers and sellers could hire the water man to manage this process. However, if water rotation schedules stay simple, then other ways will be needed to compensate the water man for his loss.

Creating additional winners

Besides the potential rise in demand for labour due to more intensive agriculture, tank conversion offers other benefits for landless people. One system would be to grant fishing rights in the tank to landless people. Currently the fishing rights are owned by the *panchayat* (for smaller tanks) or the state government (for larger tanks). Landless people would benefit by receiving fishing rights in *panchayat* tanks, which could provide a decent living (see Box 17.3). *Panchayats* in most tanks will not lose from this process, as most tanks currently contain insufficient water to be leased out for fishing rights.

Box 17.3: Accidently discovering the value of fish

The first known tank conversion in Anantapur District, Andhra Pradesh, occurred by accident in 1987. In Jagarajapalli village, the sluice gate of one tank was closed by farmers over a dispute about water allocation. Those at the top of the command area, the front-enders, took all the water, leaving nothing for the tail-enders at the bottom of the command area. The tail-enders, having nothing to lose, blocked the sluice gate, and the front-enders took the case to court. After five years the judge decreed that the sluice should be re-opened. By that time, however, all the farmers preferred the closed gate. Also, the extra water in the tank made fish production possible, which yielded about Rs 30–40 000 per year for the village.

The role of support organizations in tank conversion

Chaitanya is an NGO helping villagers convert irrigation tanks to percolation tanks. In most cases, villagers approach Chaitanya with a request for help. Chaitanya offers no financial or administrative assistance, serving only as a neutral broker among those interested in tank management. To date it has played several roles.

Awareness raising. On the basis of the Jagarajapalli experience (see Box 17.1), in 1993 Chaitanya organized an exposure visit for farmers from Adeppalli, Adeppalli Thanda, and Thummalakunta. After discussions with their counterparts, the visiting farmers, including the wary well-less farmers, were confident about experimenting with tank conversion in their own villages.

Encouragement. In Adeppalli and Adeppalli Thanda, well owners and well-less farmers agreed to close the sluice on a temporary basis to give the well-less farmers a chance to gain confidence in the move. Chaitanya played a critical role in both cases, assuring well-less farmers that the measure was temporary and could be reversed if they were harmed by it.

Conflict resolution. Chaitanya also played a conflict resolution role in many villages, which are aligned into small groups according to caste, political parties, etc. Assistance from a neutral, outside observer can be important in facilitating agreements among the different groups, each of which can undermine the process. Without trust, the process will fail. Worse yet, if tank conversion proceeds without clear agreements, then disputes are guaranteed, tank conversion can be reversed, and distrust increased.

Liaison with government. Many villagers are concerned that the government will not allow them to close a sluice. Chaitanya can assist the tank conversion process simply by appealing to the government to permit this.

However, Chaitanya found several circumstances in which conversion is unlikely, despite skilful external intervention. The most important of these is low well density which reduces the scope for efficient water markets. A second case is persistent social rivalry that could not be overcome by Chaitanya's intervention. Practical reasons, such as unsuitable hydrological circumstances and defective tank construction may also prevent tank conversion.

Preliminary assessment of the net benefits of tank conversion

The first tank conversion in Anantapur took place in 1987, and the second in 1993. After that, over 20 tanks were converted in rapid succession. This short history of tank conversion precludes a detailed analysis of the total costs and benefits.

Conversion appears to be very attractive, but we need more experience over a longer period to be sure. Table 17.2 shows the increase in irrigated area for four tanks converted in 1993. Rainfall in 1993 and 1994 was very similar, suggesting that the difference in irrigated area is attributable primarily to tank conversion. More sustained measurement would be needed to confirm this.

Cropping patterns are also changing, which will increase incomes. Prior to tank conversion, command area farmers grew water-conserving crops in the *kharif* season and left the land fallow in the *rabi* season. *Ragi*, sunflower, maize and green chillies were common *kharif* crops. Following conversion, in *kharif* they grow water-intensive crops such as onion, mulberry and paddy, and grow a second crop in the *rabi* season.

Table 17.2: Initial quantification of tank conversion benefits (1993–94)

Tank Name	% increase in irrigated area	% increase in number of farmers receiving irrigation	% decrease in water price
Kammayagaripalli	26	66	25
Peddanapalli	120	74	25
Nallarallapalli	61	78	25
Addeppalli	42	70	25

Policies to facilitate tank conversion

Several policy issues emerge from the experience with tank conversion to date. These include steps to facilitate tank conversion and recommendations for government action.

State approval. Some villages were ready to close their sluice but feared government disapproval. This suggests that the government could stimulate conversion simply by releasing a policy statement endorsing optional tank conversion everywhere.

Overcome tax revenue loss. Local governments oppose tank conversion as they will lose tax revenue through the decline of tank surface irrigation, on which they collect water-user charges. Changing this tax revenue policy, or providing local government bodies with alternative sources of income would overcome their resistance.

Stop tank bed land allocation. Tank bed farming obstructs efficient management of the tank system and makes conversion very difficult, yet is stimulated by the government land distribution policy. A reassessment of this policy, away from tank bed land allocation, would limit this obstacle.

Maintenance of old structures. Poor tank maintenance is a problem throughout the traditional tank irrigation regions of southern India, so it is naïve to assume that villagers will maintain new tanks appropriately. Starting with tank conversion gives villagers the chance to show that they can maintain tanks properly. Only if they demonstrate this successfully should construction of new tanks or major investment in rehabilitation of old tanks be considered.

Targeted well construction. Another large government programme gives grants to low-caste people for well construction. By targeting well construction in areas of potential tank conversion, it would increase the likelihood of digging a successful well, and would stimulate competition among sellers in water markets in tank command areas.

Silt removal or new tanks. Another issue in tank conversion is silt removal versus new tank construction. New tanks, of course, have no silt in them, while old tanks tend to be quite heavily silted, inhibiting seepage and reducing water use efficiency. However, the advantages of converting existing tanks probably outweigh the disadvantages associated with siltation. The government can consider investing in desiltation to support irrigation in semi-arid regions.

Silt removal for equity. If the government does invest in tank desiltation, giving the silt to landless people can encourage equity in irrigation development. Currently much desiltation is sub-contracted to a private tractor owner. Landless people may gain employment by (un)loading the tractor, but nothing else. But if they were to receive 'silt rights', they could organize a tractor for removal and sales, or auction the rights to others. Either scenario would mean an income transfer from current tractor owners, generally wealthy farmers, to currently landless people.

Conclusion

It is too soon to tell if converting irrigation tanks to percolation tanks will be attractive on a widespread basis. Our experience has been limited, and we do not know how farmers will react as agroclimatic and socioeconomic circumstances change. Higher or lower rainfall could change the perspective of one or more group of farmers, and changes in the price of electricity could make conversion unprofitable.

Still, there are important lessons to be learned from the experience to date with tank conversion. One is the critical role of process in promoting collective action to manage common property resources. A support organization like Chaitanya can work behind the scenes to increase communication and build trust among villagers. This helps them to focus on potential gains from successful collective action rather than on the potential losses, should it fail.

Perhaps an even more important lesson concerns the role of the 'fallback position' of each group. Tank conversion works despite the potential losses faced by several parties because, ultimately, all parties have the power to enforce the agreement. The most vivid example of this is well-less farmers, who depend on well-owners for water, but who can always revert to surface irrigation if faced with exploitation. A critical question for other common property debates is whether the mutual ability to enforce agreements is unique to the percolation tank system, or can be applied to management regimes for other natural resources.

Another lesson concerns groundwater property rights. In India, it is well known that the open access nature of groundwater is largely responsible for its unsustainable and inequitable extraction. In the percolation tank system, however, well owners and non-owners alike have a keen perception of who owns the water. Farmers understand that as long as there is water in the tank, water extracted from wells ultimately belongs to all farmers in the command area. This encourages well owners to sell water to well-less farmers at a low price. This suggests that specifying groundwater property rights in a way that assigns rights and responsibilities more widely could be a powerful tool to encourage more sustainable and equitable groundwater development.

234

Finally, Chaitanya's experience has important implications for government agencies and NGOs who seek to promote better natural resource management at the village level. In particular, natural resource management involves complex social interactions that are not immediately obvious to outsiders, yet can be encouraged by a supportive external organization. Villagers can devise their own community resource management schemes, but may need supportive laws and, in many cases, an impartial agent who resolves conflicts and witnesses agreements.

18
Farmer-based Extension for Watershed Development: The Case of Mag-uugmad, The Philippines

LAPULAPU L. CERNA, LEONARDO A. MONEVA, WILFREDO M. LISTONES and EFREN C. GERARDINO

Introduction

CEBU IS A mountainous island situated in the central part of the Philippine archipelago. The upland areas of Cebu, including its critical watersheds, are severely denuded. This situation was precipitated by the expansion of farming communities within the watershed areas, the conversion of inappropriate lowland farming practices into ecologically fragile sites and the extraction of resources from the remaining forest. These problems were compounded by the government's neglect of the upland areas as manifested by inadequate social services, inequitable resource access policies and weak enforcement of conservation laws, among others.

It was only a decade ago that the government and a few NGOs started addressing the problems, but their initiatives proved to be 'too little, too late'. Policy changes came about when resource degradation was already on the edge of irreversibility. In many cases, well-funded development programmes failed because the implementation processes were incompatible with the social dynamics of the community. Mag-uugmad Foundation Inc. (MFI) learned from these mistakes and worked towards a farmer-centred and process-oriented development approach.

Mag-uugmad Foundation Inc. is an indigenous NGO formed in June 1988 by encouraging staff and farmer leaders to expand and sustain the soil and water conservation programme initiated by World Neighbors in three watershed areas of Cebu in 1981. It was founded in the belief that the rehabilitation and sustainable development of the uplands are moral obligations of the very people who depend on these resources for a living, the farmers themselves. The promotion of soil and water conservation (SWC) through farmer-based extension is the main process used by MFI, with the following objectives:

○ to reverse the environmental degradation in the watershed area
○ to develop farming technologies suited to small farmers' resources, skills and management capacity
○ to demonstrate the ability of local farmers to teach their neighbours better ways of farming and facilitate the technology adaptation process

○ to improve farm productivity and increase income
○ to enhance the well-being of the family and the community

Mag-uugmad's development approach

MFI has developed an approach that integrates three key aspects:

○ an integrated range of technologies developed and adapted in the watershed
○ farmer-based extension
○ institutional mechanisms that can sustain the process.

These key aspects are described in the following sections.

Integrated technology development and adaptation

MFI does not only focus narrowly on soil and water conservation, but also emphasizes soil fertility management and improvement, erosion control, water conservation, improving cropping and production systems and diversifying farm-based livelihood opportunities.

The technical approach combines structural and vegetative techniques to contain soil erosion. Structural techniques include bench terraces, contour bunding, contour and drainage canals, rock walls, silt traps and gully check dams. Vegetative techniques include contour hedgerows, trees planted along farm boundaries, woodlots and experimentation with cover crops. In addition, farmers have introduced water conveyance and storage systems on their farms. They have constructed retention canals to increase water absorption and diversion canals to divert excess rainwater. This water flows to a ground catchment where it is stored for future use.

Soil fertility management involves replenishing nutrient losses through recycling crop residues, organic matter build-up from hedgerow prunings, composted manure in combination with inorganic fertilizers, and crop rotation using legumes. These technologies are integrated with farm productivity improvement technologies such as crop relay, crop rotation and intercropping practices.

Any technology, however workable it appears to be, will always pass through the filter of farmers' criteria (immediate economic gains, low cost, low labour requirement, compatibility with skills and farm resources, etc.) before they decide to adopt it. MFI therefore now emphasizes a selective and sequential technology adaptation process that evolved over three stages.

1. Only a few technologies were adopted by farmers at the start, with farmers preferring simple structural barriers (contour bunds, canals, checkdams, etc.) to control erosion and hedgerows for fodder production.

2. During the second stage, after the farms were relatively stabilized, farmers focused on soil fertility management technologies (composting, green manure, recycling of crop residues, etc.).
3. As the soil fertility was gradually restored, the farmers started to experiment with high-value crops. During this stage, crop diversification and the search for a more productive cropping system were the main interests of the farmers.

Currently, research and extension deal more with some specific concerns affecting productivity such as pest control, water management and long-term production systems.

Farmer-based extension system

Through the farmer-based extension system (FBES), farmer extensionists share their learning about SWC and farming systems with other farmers. Farmer extensionists also assist fellow farmers in identifying key farm problems, implementing appropriate technologies and facilitating the formation of *alayons* or farmers' workgroups. This farmer-based extension system evolved from the initial experiences of the SWC programme. The initial SWC technologies were readily adopted by farmers because their need for a steady supply of fodder was immediately addressed by such components as hedgerows and cover crops. World Neighbors, the project initiator, developed farmer extensionists among the community to assist in the implementation of a rapidly expanding programme. These farmer extensionists – then called farmer instructors (FI) – were selected from among the most successful farmer adopters in the community. However, in the early years of the project, the farmers merely served as 'extension aides' to the implementing staff.

As the programme expanded, the number of farmer instructors increased correspondingly. During this period, World Neighbors focused on strengthening the capabilities of the FIs and gradually turned over the extension programme to the farmers, while closely monitoring and mentoring them.

The SWC programme was eventually entrusted to MFI in preparation for World Neighbors' withdrawal. A formal management structure at the farmers' level was created to consolidate the institutional development process and develop mechanisms for scaling-up the process. As a result, technology adaptation advanced faster from farmer to farmer, from *alayon* to *alayon* and from village to village. Today, MFI's effort is geared towards the complete handover of FBES management to mature and capable people's organizations.

The FBES approach has six major components:

Farmer extensionists or instructors. The farmers selected as farmer instructors go through a long process of training, starting from experimenting and adapting some technologies, to being a fully-fledged farmer instructor. A farmer is considered an outstanding adopter if he or she is an active experimenter in the *alayon* and his or her model farm shows diverse but integrated technologies appropriate to the local setting. The farmer instructor trainee (FIT) is selected from among the outstanding adopters. The criteria and the process of selection of the FITs are decided by farmers. The FIT undergoes one-year on-the-job training through an understudy scheme. After a year, the FIT's performance is evaluated by Mag-uugmad based on the criteria agreed. Once the FIT passes the evaluation, he or she is then considered an FI on probation and serves for another three months before being evaluated and enlisted as a fully-fledged farmer instructor. At this stage, the FIT becomes a part-time staff member of Mag-uugmad.

To be a farmer instructor the candidate must have a deep understanding of the principles and practices of SWC; apply and experiment with various technologies and maintain them on their own farm; be willing and have the time to share ideas and experiences with other farmers; have good communication skills; and be credible in the community.

The 'alayon'. The *alayon* is a traditional form of co-operation in the village, wherein farmers group themselves informally and work on each other's farms on a rotational basis. Ideally each *alayon* is composed of five to eight farmers. MFI actively uses *alayons* as an institutional mechanism for technology experimentation. The *alayon* also serves as a forum for group learning, problem-solving and the promotion of equity among farmers. This mutual sharing of labour hastens the pace of the technology adoption, especially technologies that are labour intensive.

Participatory farm planning. Participatory farm planning (PFP) is a process whereby *alayon* members or informal groups of farmers support each other in preparing their respective farm plans. The PFP process is a sequence involving developing a vision and assessment of the household economy for the next three years; appraisal of current land use, cropping system, market trends and technologies; analysis of key farm problems; developing technology domain and options; preparation of the farm plan including farm sketches, key activities and performance indicators; and presentation of the farm plan to the family for review and decision-making. The family actively participates in the assessment and projection of the household economy and the finalization of the farm plan.

The model farm. The model farm belonging to the farmer extensionists displays the various SWC technologies, cropping systems and land-use patterns appropriate to the local conditions. It differs from a demonstration plot as it is not just a showcase but a product of a long process of technology adaptation by the farmer. The model farm serves as a living example of the technologies promoted by the FIs, without which training and cross-visits would not be productive. It also increases the farmer's credibility as an extensionist, experimenter and source of information.

Small-scale experimentation. Farmer extensionists conduct their own experiments to ascertain the appropriateness of new technologies before these are communicated to other farmers. Farmers learn of new technologies mostly from cross visits to successful farmers and technology resource centres, but they do not adopt the technologies on a wide scale without testing them first. Experimental plots aid the farmer in extension work. Neighbours may monitor the experiment and adopt the technology over a period of time. The role of women farmers in conducting the trials is important, as they are more keen about monitoring.

Training and cross-visits. Training and cross-visits are especially helpful to farmers from distant villages where SWC model farms do not exist, and the *alayon* is not yet present. The training and extension methodologies proven to be effective are farm tours, farm practicals, sharing experiences and other participatory methods. Farmer-to-farmer training is adaptable to the farmers' natural learning process, promotes analysis, discussion and depth of understanding and encourages farmers to adapt and apply the lessons learned.

Scaling-up farmer-based approaches

The *alayons* are a major mechanism for spreading the farmer-based SWC programmes. The FIs work closely with three to five *alayons*, or a total of some 20 to 25 farmers. Four or five FIs working in adjacent villages are organized into a working unit under the direction of the senior farmer instructor (SFI). The SFIs from the three sections of the watershed are formed into a collective under the supervision of the site manager, who is also a farmer. In addition to being implementors of FBES, FIs continue to be farmers, adopters, *alayon* members and extension volunteers.

New *alayons* tend to be formed either through 'cell-division' or through 'leap-frogging'. In the case of 'cell-division' the *alayon* expands from within, as more and more farmers learn about the advantages and the implementation process of the new technologies. As more farmers join the *alayon*, it takes much longer to complete one cycle of the rotated schedules of experiments, so the group decides to break into smaller and more manageable *alayons* and the same process of growth and division starts again.

In the case of the 'leap-frog', new farmer instructors facilitate the formation of other *alayons*. The new *alayons* produce potential farmer extensionists who will in turn be assigned to the next village to form and assist another *alayon*. This wavelike progression from one *alayon* to another has hastened the spread of technology adaptation in the watershed.

The FBES is managed primarily by the farmers themselves. Maguugmad deliberately limits its role to the facilitation, support, training and upgrading of farmers' extension skills. This role delineation ensures that the leadership and management capabilities of the farmers are enhanced and their sense of ownership of the programme is gradually reinforced.

MFI has identified areas where farmers' limitations are inhibiting implementation of extension tasks and its assistance is designed to overcome some of these. For example, farmers lack access to technology resource centres and research results are published in a language and form incomprehensible to farmers. MFI assists farmers on their visits to resource centres and provides research, documentation, translation and publication support.

However, other constraints that are yet to be overcome include:

○ If land tenure is insecure and unstable, farmers hesitate to experiment with labour-intensive technologies which give benefits only over a long term.
○ Conflicts between neighbours and meddling by politicians may inhibit extension work.
○ The presence of other 'development' projects whose processes are incompatible with FBES but who provide large funds, can be tempting for the poor farmers in the short run.

Economic, social and environmental impacts

PRA was used to examine the impact of MFI's approach, taking the case of one village within the watershed. Field inquiries and farmers' workshops were conducted to evaluate the farmer-based extension system. Maguugmad's recently concluded strategic planning session also contributed important information.

Resources and livelihoods before MFI intervention

Tabayag village is one of six villages within the upper catchment of the Argao River watershed. The village has an estimated land area of about 1350 hectares, which is approximately 55 per cent of the total area of the catchment. Seventy-five per cent of total land area of the village is usable. The remaining portion is classified as timberland and allocated to the social forestry programme of the government. Of the total land area, about 50 per cent is devoted to coconut and fruit trees, 25 per cent is allotted to open cultivation, 15 per cent is forested and 10 per cent is idle grasslands. Presently, the village has 168 households with a total population of around 1000.

Tabayag village was trapped in a poverty-resource degradation cycle when the SWC programme was introduced a decade ago. The socio-

241

economic situation was characterized by inadequate education, insecurity of land tenure, inaccessibility, unfair product prices, high cost of farm inputs, decreasing yields, low income, debt, food shortages, malnutrition and poor health. Low productivity was the result of soil erosion, nutrient depletion, water shortage and an unfavourable micro-climate. The loss in productivity was accentuated by other socio-economic problems, such as lack of farm inputs, seasonal out-migration, crime and damage by stray animals.

The farming system in the village was characterized by high dependence on external inputs, erosion and nutrient depletion and excessive monoculture. This resulted in low productivity and led to food shortages for households. These food shortages in turn led to farmers being dependent on extractive livelihood activities in the community forest. This kind of survival strategy caused the rapid destruction of the forest resources, which eventually resulted in water shortage, soil erosion and an unfavourable micro-climate; the same conditions that brought about the decrease in food production resulting in food shortages and low income. This compelled the farmers to look for off-farm jobs like small-scale mining and plantation work in far flung places, thus leaving their farms unattended or poorly managed, resulting in further resource degradation and low income from agricultural lands. Other external factors, such as poor accessibility, exploitative market forces and credit system, the inadequacy of the government to provide agricultural extension services, insecurity of land tenure and lack of social services, aggravated the situation.

Changes in food and livelihood security

The process of technology development and adaptation resulted in optimum utilization of the local resources. The *lagunas*, parcels of land left idle after years of overgrazing, were gradually rehabilitated, thus expanding the production areas. Before the project was initiated, most of the village could be farmed only during the first cropping season and the average production was significantly below the food requirements for a household. After a decade of project implementation, the majority of farmers produce for two cropping cycles and some are even farming for the whole year. This increase in production intensity has resulted in food security for most households (Box 18.1). There has also been an increase in income derived from cash crops and other farm-based livelihoods.

Resource conservation

Private lands. Most farms in the watershed are now using a combination of physical and biological measures, complemented by soil fertility improvement technologies. SWC technologies are adopted by farmers not only to

242

Box 18.1: A farmer's story

The case of Sergio Arobo illustrates the impact of the MFI programme. He is one of the poorest farmers in the village. In 1984, the yield from his 1.25 hectare farm was barely able to meet the food needs of the household for three months. Most members of the household had to work as labourers throughout the year in order to survive. In 1985, Sergio joined the *alayon* and started to experiment and adapt with various SWC technologies. After three years of sustained technology adaptation, the Arobo household attained self-sufficiency in food production. Five years later, in 1990, Sergio's farm was generating an average annual income of 15 000 pesos. This income is generated from a diverse on-farm production system. Forty per cent of the income is derived from poultry and livestock, 20 per cent from vegetable production, 25 per cent from coconut and coffee, and 15 per cent from hedgerow seeds. For the first time in their lives, the Arobos attained food security and income adequate to meet the basic needs of the household.

stabilize openly cultivated farms but also to create favourable conditions for the establishment of agro-forestry practices on farms and the enrichment of existing coconut farms. Farm productivity is being increased further through crop relay, crop rotation, and intercropping practices. Some farmers are starting to adopt alternative pest management through botanical pesticides.

Sustained farmer experimentation and adaptation has lead to diversification of farm-based livelihood options for most farmers. Farmers have derived additional income from the sale of seeds of hedgerow species. Pruned branches of fodder hedgerows and trees are processed into charcoal and fuelwood for sale. Livestock production (goats, swine, cattle) has been integrated into the farming system, augmenting the income of the farmers and helping to restore soil fertility.

Common lands. A decade ago the cultivated areas were almost devoid of effective vegetative cover and most households were earning their livelihoods from resource-degrading activities such as selling fuelwood, charcoal and timber from the nearby forest. This forest had a predominant secondary growth due to poor natural regeneration. Currently, most farms are stabilized by soil conservation measures and are adequately covered by vegetation for most of the year. The increase in farm production and income has also enabled the farmers to undertake long-term resource-conserving practices such as tree-based farming, enabling them to reduce their dependence on the forest for survival.

In less than a decade, the community forest has regenerated naturally. This has resulted in multiple environmental and ecological benefits such as a favourable micro-climate, beneficial fauna and increased water yield.

Resilience

Diversity of agricultural and other products farmed. The major crops grown are corn and vegetables. Corn is produced mainly for household consumption and is normally grown during the *panuig* or the first cropping season (April-August). If the crop yield falls short of a year's food requirement, corn production is repeated in the *pangulilang* or the second cropping season (September-January). The farmers cultivate a variety of seasonal cash crops such as bell pepper, pole bean, mungbean, tomato, ginger, tobacco, cut flowers, cauliflower and other high value crops. Bananas, taro and papaya are the common perennials. Farmers also grow such permanent crops as coconut, mango, jackfruit, coffee, cocoa, and other multipurpose trees.

The diversification into agro-forestry systems has led to an increased supply of fodder, supporting an increased diversity in livestock production and a significant increase in income.

Increased capacity to withstand external shocks. Farmers have countered market fluctuations by growing a variety of crops at the same time. Efficient water management has decreased fluctuations in yields due to erratic weather patterns. Boundary trees and farm hedgerows have minimized the damage caused by strong winds. Diversification of livelihood options has enabled the farmers to overcome natural calamities and crop failures in many cases.

The resilience of the livelihood strategies used by the farmers became evident when Typhoon Reming struck the village in 1987. The crop damage was almost total, yet the villagers did not seek relief assistance from external sources. They herded their goats and cattle to the town's livestock yard and purchased food supplies. In less than a week, community life was back to normal.

Replication to neighbouring communities and villages

The replicability of the farmer-based extension approach catalysed by MFI is evident in its spread beyond the boundary of Cabalawan, where the programme originated. The programme started in 1981 with five farmer participants. It took two years for the programme to make a breakthrough in other parts of Barangay Tabayag. In 1985, there were 27 adopters grouped in three *alayons*. In the same year, FBES initiated a planned expansion of the programme outside the village. During the next two years, about 90 farmers from the neighbouring villages of Kapyuan and Tigib started experimentating with SWC technologies.

From 1987 onwards, the technologies spread naturally from farmer to farmer in three more villages within the watershed. The village also served as a venue for Mag-uugmad's farmer-to-farmer training. It is estimated that more than 1500 farmers from 10 neighbouring provinces have participated in farmer-to-farmer extension activities and training programmes facilitated by the farmers from Tabayag village.

Building self-reliance in groups and communities

Equity. The *alayons* have helped to promote equity among farmers. The mutual sharing of labour and resources, regardless of one's situation in life, benefited the poorer sections of the community. The accumulation of economic gains from increased farm productivity and the sustained use of the *alayon* as an institution for group action has reduced the inequity among members.

The community wealth ranking exercise conducted during the PRA showed significant improvements in the economic well-being of the households in the village. In 1981 only 10 per cent of the households had an annual food surplus, 20 per cent had barely adequate food and 70 per cent suffered chronic food shortages. Today, 20 per cent of the households have an annual food surplus, 60 per cent are able to meet most of their food needs and only 20 per cent have chronic food shortages. The reduced vulnerability has enabled many households to experiment with diversified production technologies and take risks, investing more in farm-based activities.

Political empowerment. The *alayons* also laid the foundations for establishing people's organizations (PO). The group dynamics among the *alayon* members has fostered cohesion and solidarity and provided an enabling environment for the evolution of new and accountable leadership within the PO. As more farmers joined the *alayons* and eventually the PO, their participation in the political process and the power base has increased significantly. This participation and increased power has now been translated into significant electoral gains. The key PO leaders have won a majority of seats in the Barangay council, the basic unit of local government. The access to political institutions has resulted in multiplier benefits for the village, such as new access roads, construction of a health centre and improved linkages with government agencies for other services such as livestock breeding and land tenure improvement. The improvement in social infrastructure and services has accelerated gains in productivity and income.

The role of the support institution

MFI is now committed to a long-term process of institution building and technology adaptation. Unlike conventional approaches where research is divorced from extension, MFI uses farmer-based approaches enabling a continuum of extension-adaptation-research-extension activities, resulting in a participatory technology development process.

MFI has consciously decided not to give any financial incentives to farmers for adopting technologies, as is generally prevalent in the area. It encourages farmers to select appropriate technologies from a range of options. The technology adaptation process takes into account the knowledge, skills and resources of local farmers through participatory farm planning and group discussions during the *alayon* activities. The FBES approach needs limited external resources and professional support to implement.

The increase in the number of farmer instructors from the community has enabled MFI to develop an organizational structure that is more organic and increasingly less dependent on external professionals. MFI has consciously promoted co-management with communities. The development of a local people's organization has enabled MFI to delegate many functions locally without reducing the effectiveness of the overall process.

Reflecting on the process

Soil and water conservation is essential to the development of a populated and farmed watershed. But to be implemented effectively, SWC technologies should be promoted as a package of options, rather than ready-made solutions to be prescribed. The key elements of the success of the farmer-based extension system include the following:

○ the participatory process for selecting farmer instructors – by the farmers on the basis of qualifications they themselves define
○ the on-the-job training using the understudy scheme before a farmer becomes a fully-fledged farmer instructor
○ the combination of model farms, training and cross-visits, small-scale experiments, participatory farm planning and the *alayon*
○ the complementary support on the part of MFI, which aims to address the weaknesses and constraints of farmers
○ the management process, with its simple structure, co-management with farmers, planned phase-out, etc.

This approach has helped to promote a more productive, resource-conserving, resilient, equitable, replicable, empowering and thus sustainable development of a populated and farmed watershed.

19

Kasare – A Saga of a People's Faith: A Case-study of Participatory Watershed Management

CRISPINO LOBO and THOMAS PALGHADMAL

Introduction

UNTIL RECENTLY DROUGHT spelt despair, hardship and dislocation in Kasare, a small village in the drought-prone district of Ahmednagar in Maharashtra State, India. Agricultural operations were abandoned, cattle and bullocks sold at distress prices, houses closed and people migrated to towns in search of a livelihood. Today, however, despite receiving only 300mm of rain in the 1993 monsoon and 200mm in 1994, not only are there no signs of panic but the area under irrigation has actually increased by 233 per cent and 550 per cent in the case of perennially and seasonally irrigated farms respectively.

In 1989, the villagers supported by the Social Centre[1], launched a major effort to regenerate their environment along watershed lines following a ridge-to-valley perspective. Kasare today comes across as a village of hope and confidence, a people who have learnt to cope with the vagaries of nature, not by exploiting their natural resources but by husbanding and mobilizing them in a manner that is both sustainable and beneficial to the community.

The methodology

Since people are the key actors in a natural resources management effort, we followed both a quantitative and qualitative approach to assess the impacts of the watershed development (WSD) programme that began in April 1989. The following methods were used:

○ analysis of a baseline survey (149 families) done in May 1986.
○ a detailed socio-economic survey and analysis of 10 per cent of households (15 families) in November 1994
○ scrutiny and analysis of village records and secondary data available from various government departments

---

[1] An NGO founded in 1968 in the district of Ahmednagar by Hermann Bacher, a Jesuit priest. It is a voluntary agency established to support small and marginal farmers to access existing facilities and capacities in both the private and government sectors.

○ a participatory appraisal of the WSD programme, its activities, implementation, costs and impacts at the village level during several sessions
○ a qualitative assessment of people's perceptions and assessment of the WSD programme, and its impact using the life story approach.[2] The life stories of 22 individuals were gathered (November 1994), although here only two narratives are included.

A life story is a person's narration in his or her own words of how he or she sees and views the world around him or her – events, persons and situations affecting him or her, or likely to – and his or her assessment, valuation and response to the same. The life story approach seeks to gain an insight into a person's nature, behaviour, expectations, thinking and hopes, so as to understand the dynamics of both the person's as well as his or her group's behaviour.

As an instrument it focuses on selected individuals who are representative of the various socio-economic groups involved in the programme. Life stories enable us to see the poor as people and give a human ambience to otherwise bare statistics and clinical analysis.

Kasare: some facts and problems

Kasare is a hot dusty village with highly eroded and desiccated hills and stony wastes. Surrounded by a range of hills, until recently barren, it receives on average only 550mm of rain during the monsoons. Mean temperatures range from 42°C in the summer to 13°C in the winter. The soil is largely rocky and of poor quality except in the lower valley areas.

Village lands cover 827ha, of which 129ha belong to the Forest Department. Cultivable land comprises 544ha, and wasteland as well as land put to other uses comes to 154ha. The bulk of land (78 per cent) has a slope and soil depth that ranges from 3–15 per cent and 0–22.5cm, respectively.

The total population of the village consists of 1030 persons in 156 households in which men outnumber women by 22 per cent. The literacy rate is 59 per cent. There are 52 pastoralist/nomadic families (33 per cent), 64 families belonging to the Scheduled tribes or castes (41 per cent) and 40 families (26 per cent) belong to the Forward Castes.

There are 261 landowners and five landless families. The bulk are small land-holders most of whom were rain-dependent before the WSD, with 95 per cent of the farmland rainfed. Prior to WSD, the main agricultural crops

---

[2] This approach was developed and extensively used by the German Commission of Justice and Peace as a sensitization tool (Kochendorfer-Lucius, G and K. Osner: *Development has got a Face: Interpretations of Life Stories on People's Economy*) and as an analytical tool by Lobo C. and Kochendorfer-Lucius, K in *The Rain Decided to Help Us* (World Bank, EDI Training Material – 1996).

were coarse cereals like pearl millet and sorghum, which were intercropped with kidney bean, pigeon pea and gram.

Since output was poor and holdings small, most farmers would either join the agricultural labour force where wages were slim, or migrate to towns in search of work. In the drought of 1972, the village was abandoned. Until recently at least 150 able-bodied men were regularly based in towns. In summer, drinking water had to be brought from long distances. Existence was often at subsistence level and precarious.

Some of the main problems bedevilling Kasare prior to WSD were:

○ extensive land degradation and improper land utilization
○ improper agricultural practices and poor output
○ excessive dependence on the monsoons for agricultural purposes
○ absence of adequate green cover and meagre biomass availability for household, agricultural and artisanal purposes
○ lack of drinking water and protective irrigation in summer
○ forced migration in search of a livelihood after monsoons
○ poor health and nutrition status of women and especially children
○ fragile ecosystem that was very vulnerable to drought, which is a frequent occurrence in the Ahmednagar District.

The process of promotion and participation

The Social Centre (SC) came into contact with Kasare in 1984 when a few villagers approached it to assist them in starting a small lift irrigation scheme. This intervention of the SC greatly built the confidence of the people in the SC. Furthermore, seeing the poverty of the people and their basic unity, the SC decided to include this village in its action plans.

At that time SC's policy was not to fund any projects direct, but to act as a 'broker' or advocate between the people, government departments and banks. People were empowered by introducing them to local institutional actors, not only to use the assistance available but also to increase their independent capacity to make claims on the system.

Furthermore, the SC prioritized and focused primarily on the economically backward sections of society. It opted to use a group formation approach, and accordingly a Women's Group (Mahila Mandal) and a Youth Group (Tarun Mandal) were organized in 1988.

The drought of 1986–87 had a marked impact on the people and affected the village economy badly. The meagre assets acquired under previous development schemes made hardly any appreciable impact on income levels, and, in fact, quite a few became liabilities; for instance, cattle had to be sold at distress prices as wells became dry.

Both the SC and the people thus realized that unless a comprehensive and integrated approach was taken towards the question of poverty and

249

low agricultural output, no real development could take place. They began to look at their surroundings anew and accepted that only by conserving rainwater, however meagre, and regenerating their environment could they address their basic need for biomass and a stable and adequate income flow. The SC introduced them to the concept of WSD, and the need to begin from the ridge downwards, with an emphasis on soil conservation.

In May 1988 a trip was organized to a neighbouring village (Adgaon) where WSD work was being implemented successfully. The people were very impressed and decided they wanted to do something similar. They furthermore agreed to the conditions of the SC, namely, a ban on free grazing in the treated area, no felling of trees and provision of some voluntary labour. They agreed to impose this discipline by themselves.

A village watershed committee (VWC) was established in which the youth group was predominant and a small micro-watershed of 35ha was selected. Work began in 1989, and a multi-sectoral, integrated programme was launched. This involved not only environmental regeneration, but also the production, financial and social systems of the village economy. However, with the VWC controlling the money and decisions, the elderly started resisting the watershed work. It was a tussle for power. The social atmosphere became strained and the SC decided to stop working in Kasare. A week later, under pressure from the villagers, the elders yielded and approached the SC to restart the work. They gave a written undertaking of co-operation.

In 1993, the village was included in the government water conservation programme and the government undertook the construction of several conservation structures in the village, such as percolation tanks and *nala* bunds. In 1994, the government launched a watershed development programme, inviting the participation of NGOs. The VWC and the SC took up the offer and Kasare today, apart from people's own contributions, is financed partly by government through the SC and partly by the SC itself.

Today only about 200ha remain to be treated, the rest having been treated already either by the farmers themselves or by the programme.

The role of institutional and informal group actors: an interface

Two types of groups or institutions operate in Kasare – those directly related to programme implementation such as those that are village-based like the VWC, the *gram panchayat*, the forest protection committee (FPC); and those from outside like the Social Centre, government departments and other agencies. There are also those not directly related to programme implementation, like the thrift and credit unions, dairy co-operative society, women's group, youth group, choral group and sports group.

250

All these groups have close relationships and interactions with one another. All the major groups are represented on the VWC. Furthermore, all these groups have developed a stake in the well-being of the programme and also in each other's stability. The programme has ensured that substantial funds flow into the village economy and this in turn is reflected in enhanced turnover of each of the unions. Moreover, since effective programme implementation requires social harmony, it is in the interest of all to ensure that all benefit fairly and each group's interests are protected and furthered. The key role each of these credit union and groups play is reflected in the flow of bank credit into the village. From 1985 to 1991 a sum of Rs.1 043 000 by way of medium-term loans flowed into the village. From 1992–93 this flow has drastically reduced to less than Rs.25 000, a drop of 98 per cent. The reason for this is that people's credit needs are now mostly met from their own credit unions and their own savings.

Environmental regeneration

Of a total area of 827ha, 747ha needed treatment. A watershed approach with a ridge to valley perspective and an emphasis on soil conservation and biomass regeneration was adopted. This included afforestation; pasture development; soil conservation measures (contour trenching, contour stone bunding, contour/farm bunds, gully plugs); and water conservation (*nala* bunds, check dams, percolation tanks).

By February 1994, a total area of 402ha had been fully treated. In terms of cost, for the natural resources regeneration activities (this includes voluntary labour and related contributions by the people), the SC contributed 37 per cent of costs, the government 55 per cent and the people 8 per cent. In terms of contribution to total programme costs (inclusive of loans taken and contributions of the people), the SC's contribution came to 36 per cent, the government's 45 per cent and the people's 19 per cent.

Impact of watershed development

We used the data of 1989 (pre-WSD) as our baseline to compare 1994 data.

Agricultural and biomass resources

Despite a rainfall of only 300mm in 1993 (500mm in 1989) not only has there been no decrease in the net cropped area but a doubling in cereal output (Table 19.1). Similarly, the perennially irrigated area has gone up by 233 per cent and the seasonally irrigated by 550 per cent. In one place where no sugarcane was previously seen, around 12ha now support the crop.[3]

Farmers have also established orchards (none previously) and are increasingly switching over to other crops such as sunflower, soybean and especially vegetables, which are now exported to Ahmednagar and Bombay.

Drip irrigation has been introduced in the village, as has improved agricultural equipment. One tractor has been purchased by means of a loan. The period of agricultural employment has gone up considerably. There is an increase of 150 per cent in the number of families who are agriculturally employed throughout the year and 100 per cent in those who have eight months' work.

The nature of livestock is also changing. Scrub cattle, which numbered 250 head in 1989, are now down to 127 (a decline of 49 per cent). Crossbred cattle have gone up to 50 (none previously). Goats have been sold off in large numbers (a decline of 65 per cent) and are expected to be further reduced in the years ahead.

Where there were hardly any trees or harvestable fodder, the hills now support some green cover and are covered with grass. In 1993, 420 cartloads of fodder were used by 105 families.

The groundwater table has seen a dramatic rise in level. While formerly there were 40 wells, there are now 74 wells (85% per cent). Of these, the number of perennial wells has gone up by 150 per cent and seasonal ones (eight months) by 62 per cent. Electric pumps have increased by 527 per cent and oil engines by 200 per cent.

Impact on other economic indicators

The agricultural wage rate has gone up by 50 per cent in the case of men and 33 per cent in the case of women. Fertilizer use has increased 20 per cent in the case of organic manures (dung) and 1400 per cent in the case of chemical fertilizers. Similarly, pesticide use in liquid form has increased 1400 per cent and 233 per cent in the case of powders.

Land prices have shown a marked appreciation. In the case of rainfed farms with light soils, the prices have appreciated by 200 per cent while those with heavy soils by only 88 per cent. This is because the latter are on the plateau, which involves a hard climb to access. Seasonally and perennially irrigated lands have appreciated by 200 per cent.

There has been a marked impact on both in- and out-migration. Formerly during the summer months about 200 labourers would go daily to

---

[3] Sugarcane, being a water-consuming crop, poses a danger. Some farmers took up growing the cane because of irresistible incentives offered by a nearby sugar factory in terms of both inputs and purchase price. The SC is trying to convince these farmers to switch over to other high value non-consumptive crops and feels confident that in two to three years the farmers will abandon the crop. This is because there just is not enough rain to support large sugarcane stands and vegetable growing is now becoming a lucrative alternative.

Table 19.1:   Impacts on agricultural output (1989–94)

	Pre watershed (1989–90)		Current status (1993–94)		Percentage change	
	Area (ha)	Output (quintal)	Area (ha)	Output (quintal)	Area	Output
Amount of rainfall	c500mm		c300mm			
AGRICULTURE						
Net cropped area	540	1500*	540	3000*	Nil	+100
Kharif crops (pearl millet)	400	1000	400	2000	Nil	+100
Rabi crops	140	500	240	1000	+71	+100
Horticulture (*Ber*, mango, custard apple, sweet lime)	Nil	–	5**	–	NP***	–
NET IRRIGATED AREA						
Perennial	6	–	20	–	+233	–
Seasonal (1&2 crops)	20	–	130	1	+550	–
Total net irrigated area (ha)	26	–	150	–	+477	–

Notes:
*Includes food grains (pearl millet, sorghum, wheat) only
**Another 10ha was to be planted in the next rains
***NP = none previously

surrounding villages in search of work. That has now stopped completely and in fact a labour shortage is being experienced on project works themselves. Moreover, there has been an 87 per cent decline in the yearly migration to Bombay and 25 per cent of those who had migrated more or less permanently to Bombay have returned. Similarly, covenanted agricultural labourers who were working outside the village have declined by 85 per cent.

The village proper is being quickly emptied of people as more leave the village to live on their farms. There has been a 300 per cent increase in the movement to the fields.

The purchase of consumables has also increased, with radios, televisions, bicycles, motorbikes, trucks and tractors all becoming more common in the village. Forty-five new cement houses have been constructed, some of which are in the fields themselves.

Efforts have also been made concerning non-farm activities. As vegetable production has increased two farmers have become commission agents (middle-men), sending the crop to Bombay and other places. A poultry farm has been set up and the women's group is actively considering undertaking small business activities such as dressmaking and other small household requirements. Fifteen women have been trained in tailoring. Fishery has also been started in the standing water bodies. This activity has been given to a landless family.

The thrift and credit unions have seen a large increase in turnover. Of the five unions operating in the village, four were established after the watershed programme had begun. While ceilings on individual loans ranged from Rs.200 to Rs.1000 in the early years, they have now increased ranging from Rs.2000 to Rs.7000 (an increase of 900 per cent and 600 per cent respectively). Furthermore in the case of both the men's and women's credit groups, there has been an increase of 92 per cent and 150 per cent respectively in the monthly share contribution pre- and post-programme initiation. Over a five-year period (1989–94) the turnover of the men's credit union increased by 68 per cent over the previous comparable period (1984–89). The women's credit union over a five-year period (1987–92) had an average annual turnover of Rs.30 000 whereas in the year 1992–94 the average annual turnover was Rs.131 000, an increase of 337 per cent. As of October 1994, the total turnover of all five credit unions beginning in February 1989 totalled Rs.901 000 making an annual average turnover of Rs.150 166 over six years.

Thus we see that the watershed programme has significantly benefited the village economy.

Impact on natural resources

Stream flow and water harvesting bodies. In 1989, the rains were good (500mm) and water flowed in the main stream up to March 1990. It dried up in the summer. Nevertheless, of four percolation tanks (PT) only one had water throughout the year and three dried up by January. Despite poor rains in 1994 (less than 200mm), of six PTs in November 1995, one was full (five metres standing water), three were half full (two metres average water column) and one was dry. Of the six checkdams (none in 1989–90), three were full (three metres water column) and two were half full (one metre water column). The full dams were expected to last the year. Fisheries have been introduced in one PT and in two of the checkdams.

What is noteworthy is that because of erratic and poor rainfall in 1994 (the highest recorded rainfall in a day was 22mm) there was no runoff in the streams. The PT and the checkdams were thus filled by seepage and percolating water, which began in September while the rains began in July.

254

Impact on human resources

There has been a marked improvement in the status of women. The dairy co-operative is run by women and this responsibility has not only increased their assertiveness (leading to quite a few problems with the menfolk) but also enhanced their financial standing. All girls now go to school; there is 100 per cent immunization and 90 per cent of child-bearing women have been sterilized. Most women now regularly visit the primary health centre which is seven kilometres away. Women have also formed two credit unions and two of them are on the VWC.

There is only one landless family dependent on agricultural wages, headed by a widow. The VWC has built a house for them; one of the sons is on the VWC and the other has been given fishing rights. The other landless families are artisans and are, in fact, as well off as the small irrigated farmers since they still benefit from the old *Balutedar* system (grains, fodder, agricultural produce given by the villagers in lieu of traditional services rendered to the village). One of the families actually sells its surplus grain. While the farmers are adversely affected by drought, these artisans get their grain quota irrespectively. Furthermore, as a result of increased agricultural activity and enhanced income, the expansion of the local economy has resulted in a heavy demand for their skills and services (masonry, smithy, etc.).

As a result of close interaction with government departments, not only has the village benefited through access to various schemes (recently a tar approach road has been sanctioned as well as two cement storage tanks) but villagers now deal directly with government departments and banks.

The social and cultural life has improved significantly. A sports club, a dance group and a choral group have been started. A new temple has been completed from people's contributions and for the last two years a week-long religious festival has been held, together with a bullock race for which attractive prizes have been instituted, reflecting the surplus income capacity of the people as well as the desire for greater unity of the people.

Politically, the village is more united than before as a result of the joint efforts that went into making the watershed programme a success. There are no political parties in the village and all decisions are taken consensually.

Kasare and beyond

From the very beginning of the watershed programme, the Social Centre made it clear to the people that they would withdraw within a few years. Hence they consciously and deliberately devolved increasing responsibility for programme management on to the VWC. This was not without its difficulties, but is now yielding dividends.

255

Box 19.1: Giving the people a voice: life stories
Banshi Dagadu Datte: (small farmer)

I am a 45-year-old farmer. I have a total of 4.38 acres of which one acre only is irrigated. When we were young my father used to farm the land, of which he had 18 acres, all of which were rainfed. Of these, 11 acres were on the plateau and seven acres were of poor quality in the foothills. At that time we would get only 9–10 sacks of pearl millet and sorghum as our farm was rainfed. We had scrub cows and a pair of bullocks. We were very poor.

My father withdrew me from school when I was 12 or 13 years old as he wanted help on the farm. From 1967 to 1969 I worked in the fields, but as we were rain-dependent we couldn't live off the produce. When I was 15 years old I went to Bombay together with those of my village who had gone earlier. In Bombay. I worked as a coolie with one of the clearing agents in the docks. I stayed on in Bombay up to 1985, and after resigning with full compensation I returned to my village where I bought a plot for a house in Kasare. My farm was dry and in 1989 I dug a well (20 ft. deep, 15 ft. diameter) myself. I struck water, which today irrigates 1–1.25 acres. At that time the water was insufficient and I got only three sacks of grain from this land in 1989. Now it is sufficient despite the drought. This is due to the watershed programme.

Near my well there are two wells that were formerly dry but now irrigate throughout the year. Four new wells have been dug nearby – all of them having water. In summer at least one acre is irrigated. Crops such as tomatoes and vegetables are grown. For the last two years, vegetables have been sent to Bombay. When the rain was good, a truck would go daily to Bombay. Now a truck goes every three days.

There are two micro-watersheds in our village, one of which has three PTs and 13 *nala* bunds while the other has three PTs and nine *nala* bunds. In the former all the contour bunding works have been done, together with trenching and afforestation on forest land. As a result, the rains have become better and our streams have water throughout the year. The water in the wells has increased and we can now produce two crops a year.

At least half the farmers are experiencing an increase in yields. Since we have done work from the top, erosion has stopped and since every drop of rain is trapped and forced to percolate, the wells and check-dams are filled through seepage. Drinking water is no longer a problem.

Shri Rabha Devka Datir: (small farmer)

I am Rabha Devka Datir, 65. I have six acres of land, out of which one acre is seasonally irrigated and five acres rainfed. Of this, two acres are on the plateau and three in the valley. My land is part of the land that was purchased by my grandfather. We nine brothers were given a share in the land and also in the well, which is about 13.5m deep. If we deepen the well, we believe that we shall get more water. There are two electric pumps on the well, one of which is owned by myself and my brothers.

If there is good water in the well, then we can grow onion, potato, chilli and other vegetables. We get Rs.1000–2000 from these vegetables. If there are good rains, from the non-irrigated land we get seven to eight quintals of grains and if we do not get good rains then we get only two to three quintals. In such a situation we have to buy grains from the market. We need at least eight quintals of Jawar (sorghum) per year.

Watershed development means stopping the flow of the rainwater, so it percolates into the soil. As we have done contour bunding in the farms, water stopped flowing and we got good crops. On the hills, trenches were dug and trees are planted; contour bunds were put in and so rainwater slowly percolated to the wells and streams. Since trees were planted in trenches their growth is better. And since trees were planted on contour bunds, we have got firewood and fodder for cattle.

The watershed development committee consists of 11 members and meets each month. Meetings of the watershed committee are open for all. In the meetings, discussions are held on what work is to be done and where, e.g. trenches, contour bunding etc., depending on the season. The village has made certain rules, such as not to cut the trees, and not to graze animals wherever trees have been planted. If anyone breaks the rule they are fined. This has proved successful. Even the number of goats has gone down very much. Washing clothes in check dams is forbidden so also nobody can lift the water. Villagers have contributed free labour for the construction of three *nala* bunds and repaired the road. This year, people contributed Rs.8000 towards digging the well for drinking water. We have built a temple of Biroba worth Rs.400 000 by giving donations. Some have given from Rs.500 to 700.

Formerly, I remember that there were no trees on hills and in the forest area. But today there are about 500 000 trees. In the past, as there was no ban, trees were cut mainly from the forest and also from the farms of farmers. Farmers used to cut trees like *babul, neem* and bushes like *tarvad* for firewood and to build fences. But now people are aware of the importance of trees so no one cuts trees. Formerly there were no trees in the fields but now trees are growing on bunds; there's lots of shade and this has made a big difference.

The VWC, which until now was informal, has now registered itself and will be taking up watershed work for a neighbouring village. The youth group is establishing a public trust with the intention of opening a high school in the village. The schoolchildren have a weekly lesson on the environment (as part of the curriculum) and have been involved in tree planting in the village.

To date, Kasare has been visited by at least 2000 people, from high-ranking dignitaries to farmers, from both near and far. In fact, Kasare is a major demonstration and farmer-to-farmer extension centre of the Indo-German Watershed Development Programme – a state-wide programme implemented in over 50 000ha involving 19 NGOs[4]. Moreover the members of the Kasare VWC are often called by other villagers to assist them in the setting up of their own VWC. On seeing the impact in Kasare, eight nearby villages comprising a gross area of over 5000ha have begun implementing a WS programme and another two (2300ha) are in the process of doing so. When asked by outsiders, 'Who implemented the programme?', the spontaneous response of the villagers is, 'We did it!' – an indication of their ownership of the programme. In fact one cannot but be struck by the air of hope and confidence the people exude even though, at the time of writing, Kasare was experiencing its third consecutive year of drought.

Barring unforeseen circumstances, this confidence and sense of proprietorship offers perhaps the best hope that the lessons learnt during programme implementations – that self-help and group efforts aimed at mobilizing and conserving resources, both ecological and social, are the only path to sustainable development – will continue to guide the people for a long time to come.

Kasare has indeed become a beacon of hope to many poor and ecologically fragile villages.

---

[4] At the time of publication, this now stands at 92 000ha, involving 51 NGOs.

20
Scaling-up Soil and Water Conservation Efforts in Chotanagpur Plateau, Eastern India

JAYA CHATTERJI, PRASHANT KUMAR DAS, SANDEEP CHAKRAVARTY, HARDEEP SINGH and R. P. AGARWAL

Introduction

A SIGNIFICANT PROPORTION of Indian farmers cultivate lands that suffer from inadequate and/or untimely rains. They practise rainfed agriculture which is highly prone to the vagaries of the monsoon. These areas have been mostly bypassed by the Green Revolution, which covered the flat, well-endowed and irrigated lands of the country.

Recognizing the need to undertake soil and water conservation on these lands, the government has spent millions of dollars over the years in soil and moisture conservation works. However, few of these works are now visible on the ground. Either the technology was wrong, or it was poorly implemented and hence short lived.

The Society for Promotion of Wastelands Development (SPWD) is a national NGO set up in 1982 to provide technical, managerial and institutional support to grassroots NGOs working to develop degraded wastelands. It is SPWD's firm belief that the people for whom development is being undertaken have to be involved in planning, designing and implementing the programme. The best techniques are those that combine the scientific knowledge with the traditional knowledge of the people. Furthermore, people must also contribute whatever they can towards implementing the programme so that there is real commitment to the programme.

This chapter documents one SPWD-partnered project where this philosophy was used with a certain degree of success.

Chotanagpur Plateau

Eastern Plateau Region, also known as Chotanagpur Plateau, cuts across the districts of South Bihar, the western part of West Bengal and North Orissa in Eastern India and covers about 0.88 million hectares. It consists primarily of uplands. Most of the population is tribal and about 80 per cent depend on agriculture, forestry, fishing and animal husbandry. In the upland areas a single crop is grown during the monsoon season, from June to December. The area receives an average annual rainfall of 1200mm.

259

However, it is erratic and its inter-temporal availability is poor because of a high run-off rate.

Rice (paddy) is the staple crop of the region. Although the average size of land holdings is small (about one hectare), there are significant differences between farmers in terms of the quality of the land cultivated. The indigenous soil classification systems indicate that these correspond to topography and the location of the land within the village. The best lands are the low lands (locally known as *Bahal* or *Kanali*), followed by the middle-level lands (known as *Baid*), and the most unproductive lands are the uplands (or *Tanr*). Most households have all three types of land. Land holdings are highly fragmented. Many households have lands in different micro-watersheds and at different levels of the slopes within the village. However, there is a concentration of small and marginal farmers in the middle-level lands.

Soils in the Chotanagpur region are mostly sandy, and hence their water retention capacity is very low. The run-off from the uplands and middle-level lands is high, leaving them to suffer moisture stress when rainfall is erratic. These lands are cultivated mostly by the poor farmers, who suffer high losses of production if there are long dry spells in the monsoon seasons.

SPWD's intervention

The grassroots NGO, Sevabrata, is a joint forum and federation of about 20 local youth clubs[1] working in 20 villages in Purulia District of West Bengal State. It has taken up a wide range of development activities since 1986. It is supported by Professional Assistance for Development Action (PRADAN), a professional NGO providing support for the development of people's institutions around natural resource management in Purulia District. In 1989, Sevabrata approached SPWD through PRADAN to provide support for development of a low-cost, location-specific, labour-intensive technological package to meet the challenges of a drought-prone, monocropped economy.

The project was initiated in 1989 in three villages. It consisted of a two-pronged strategy:

o to make the large stretch of uplands (40 per cent of the geographical area) productive by bringing it under a suitable tree-grass-crop combination

o to develop a technological package for uplands that would maintain the moisture regime and assure normal paddy production in medium-level and low lands.

---

[1] A significant resource in this region is the youth club. These are clubs formed at the village level mainly for social, cultural and sporting activities. Recently, they have also taken up non-formal education, tree planting and development works. They enjoy a great deal of trust and confidence from the village people.

260

Drawing on SPWD's previous experience, they selected what technological approach to take. The idea was to establish trees that would provide a habitat for lac insects (*Laccifera lacca*) which could provide a regular source of additional income[2]. Intercropping of grasses, pulses and vegetables was also proposed in between the host trees of lac insects to maximize efficiency of land use.

However, when PRADAN and SPWD staff started interacting closely with Sevabrata, the youth club and the farmers, it became evident that cultivation of vegetables and lac host trees was not a top priority for the local people. The people prioritized drought as their major problem and water as their major need, which would save their crops from regularly occurring moisture stress. SPWD reoriented the technology development process at this stage.

Participatory technology development and adaptation process

The village-level micro-watershed is the current unit of planning. Although the village boundary and the boundaries of the watershed may not coincide, the micro-watershed approach is adopted because it is socially acceptable. Within the village boundary, all the high elevation points are identified and the ridge lines that drain out water into different areas are demarcated. On the basis of such demarcation, the village lands are divided into various sub-micro-watersheds. Land treatment is started from the highest ridge line. It is site specific and involves differential treatments based on topography (Figure 20.1).

The higher uplands

The conventional technique followed by the Soil Conservation Department of the Government in the region was contour bunding. However, the farmers who had seen and experienced the technique were critical, and rejected it because:

○ Poor calculations during construction of the bunds meant that many bunds were breached by run-off water. The breach of one bund led to a series of breaches and to gully formation.
○ Where land holdings are small and fragmented, bunds on contour lines do not match the boundary of the holding and fragments them further.
○ During periods of continuous rainfall, water accumulates along the bunds, damaging leguminous and oilseed crops.

---

[2] *Laccifera lacca* is an insect that dwells on specific trees. Its resin (known as lac) has higher super-conductivity than artificial resin and is a less harmful coating than chemical coatings. It is used for various commercial purposes such as polishing, drying, decoration, resin and medicine. India is still the major primary producer of natural lac and most of the supply comes from the Chotanagpur area.

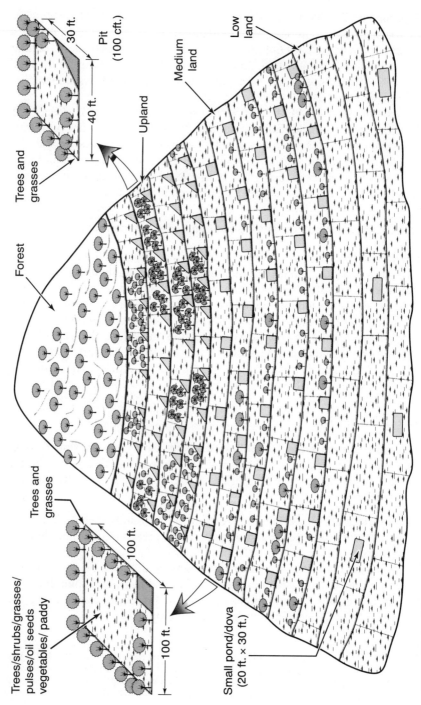

Figure 20.1: Micro-watershed after treatment and biomass introduction

Low land

Medium land

Upland

Forest

Trees and grasses

30 ft.

Pit (100 cft.)

40 ft.

Trees and grasses

Trees/shrubs/grasses/ pulses/oil seeds vegetables/ paddy

100 ft.

100 ft.

Small pond/dova (20 ft. × 30 ft.)

An exposure visit was organized to the Society for Hill Resource Management School in Daltonganj in Bihar (another project partner of SPWD) for key members of Sevabrata and local PRADAN professionals. The joint team of farmers and professionals decided to experiment with the tie-ridge method of harvesting water *in situ*, seen to be effective in areas with rainfall and topography similar to Purulia district.

From this visit, and from the analysis of local needs and the involvement of farmers and NGOs alike, a technology was developed known as the tie-ridge-cum-collection pit (TCP) (see Box 20.1). PRADAN had a significant role to play in this. The local people modified the technique to give it a practical shape. The role of SPWD was as a catalyst, being flexible and willing to experiment with new methods.

Box 20.1:   The evolution of the tie-ridge-cum-collection pit

The tie-ridge method practised in Daltonganj used small tie ridges of 2m × 2m. This was rejected by the farmers of Purulia as they felt that intercropping activities could not be taken up with such a small tie ridge. In consultation with the farmers, the size of the tie ridges for experimentation was increased to 4.5m × 4.5m.

Increasing the surface area meant that the size of the lower bund would have to be increased to hold the maximum likely rainfall. However, increasing the size of the bund would mean that a considerable amount of land would be lost. As trenches help to trap and conserve moisture, it was decided to use a trench in the tie ridge to reduce the pressure on the lower bunds. This allowed the size of the tie ridges to be increased to 9m × 12m (108m² of land area). They were arranged in a staggered manner to achieve the dual objectives of minimizing erosive water flow and maximizing moisture conservation.

One collection pit was dug in every tie-ridge, preferably at one corner at the lower end of each plot. The plots followed a staggered pattern as per the arrangement of tie ridges. Pits are shaped as right-angled triangles, which makes ploughing with country ploughs easy. These areas can be put under any of the following production systems, according to the available soil depth and soil profile – tree and grass or perennial pigeon pea (*arahar*), any legume and oilseed; vegetable or upland paddy.

Farmers have made some interesting adaptations to these pits, such as making compost in them.

The middle lands

Monitoring the TCP technology adaptation process revealed that there was poor uptake by farmers in the upper slopes. The small and marginal farmers who owned these uplands were involved in wage labour within and near the village, so were unable to find the labour to create these structures. TCP technology also needed an element of community mobilization to work. This required development of resource management systems to ensure that there is no free riding, development of rights, duties, regulations and their enforcement. This component did not evolve satisfactorily, leading to some laxity in protection, maintenance and supervision.

Thus the focus of the project was shifted because the most disadvantaged groups were located in the medium uplands. The challenge now was to develop an appropriate technology for these lands cultivated largely by small and marginal farmers. This led to the development of the Five Per Cent Farm Pit technique (Box 20.2).

Box 20.2: The Five Per Cent Model

Paddy cultivation in the uplands starts with a heavy shower, in the month of June or July, when the transplanting of paddy takes place. The traditional variety of paddy cultivated in the area takes four to five months to mature. The water requirement of such paddy is about 50mm of water every week. Thus over five months, the water required is 1000mm. However, an analysis of weekly rainfall data for the last 10 years reveals that the rainfall in September tends to fall below the monthly requirement and inflicts the greatest damage to the paddy crop. The third week of September is particularly problematic since the average rainfall is 28mm, whereas the requirement is 50mm. Conserving 100mm of rainwater in a pit will provide irrigation for at least two weeks. The pits are 100 cubic feet in volume and can conserve sufficient rainfall to improve the sub-soil moisture content.

Five per cent of the land area is demarcated at the lower slope of the plot and a 1m deep pit excavated. The pits are positioned in a staggered manner to allow uniform seepage and distribution. Earth excavated from the pits is used to strengthen the field bunds. The farm ponds are also used as compost pits using leaf litter. Not only do these pits harvest rain water, but they also contain seepage from the trenches and pits of TCP from the upper slope, thus increasing the sub-surface moisture regime. It is possible to achieve not only an assured crop of paddy withstanding drought, but also an early *rabi* (winter) crop of mustard and linseed (oilseed) in many cases.

The lowlands

Moisture level of the lowlands is maintained throughout the monsoon. This leads to prevention of moisture stress and rapid increase in paddy production. Farmers in the lowlands in Chotanagpur have wells that are used during the *rabi* (winter) vegetable cultivation when sufficient water is available. With the above treatment, the wells continue to hold water during winter and enable vegetable cultivation in the winter and early summer seasons.

The process of technology generation was not a smooth one, and required an interactive trial and error process seeking constant feedback from different stakeholders including the community, Sevabrata, PRADAN and SPWD and adapting to technical problems such as termite and other pest attacks and unanticipated excessive rainfall. The key element in technology evolution was flexibility and a willingness to learn.

Economic, social and environmental impacts

Data have been collected from a number of villages in Purulia and Bankura districts of West Bengal, where the programme has been implemented. Information was collected from households through group discussions and with individuals.

Impacts on productivity

The moisture conservation and harvesting technologies practised by the farmers have resulted in a 25 to 50 per cent increase in productivity of paddy. The yields have increased from 600 to 900kg per acre. This increase in yield is accompanied by a shift in the paddy varieties cultivated from short duration low yield upland varieties (*Bhubmiri* with 90 days maturity) to longer duration high yielding varieties for middle or low lands (*Asanlaya* with 115 days maturity). The farmers are experimenting and have started shifting to other longer duration varieties like *Baid Kalam Kothi*, with a maturity period of 120 days in Purulia District.

It has been possible for many farmers to produce a second crop of oilseeds like linseed and sesame utilizing the residual moisture as a result of moisture conservation technologies. There has been a significant increase in grass cultivation (*Dinanath*) and fodder production as a result of the TCP technology, with a significant increase in net income from these lands.

Changes in the trends of resource degradation

The adoption of TCP and Five Per Cent Pit techniques have led to a great increase in moisture conservation and reduction of moisture stress for paddy cultivation. The programme began with 20 hectares of land treated with moisture conservation measures in 1991 in one district. By 1996, 725 hectares had been treated in three states. The increase in moisture conservation and paddy production has been accompanied by development of agroforestry for rainfed paddy fields. The bunds have been utilized for

265

growing fruit trees, *Leucaena*, lac host trees, *Eucalyptus* and *Dinanath* grass, resulting in additional income and stabilization of the conservation works. The increased moisture conservation has led to healthy growth of trees and grasses. The ponds are also used for composting, resulting in soil enrichment and fertility improvement. The leaf litter from trees has also been used as a mulch in the fields.

Many farmers indicated that the lands that had the characteristic of being *tanr* (upland, barren) before treatment were becoming *baid* (middle lands), indicating improvement in land quality according to the indigenous soil classifications.

Contribution of farmers to technology adaptation and multiplication

The techniques described earlier are not rigid models. No single technique is appropriate in all micro-situations and socio-economic conditions. Continuous improvisation and adaptation are necessary to fit the local conditions. The essential feature of the approach is a pit on bunded fields. Yet utilization of the pits and the bunds varied from plot to plot according to the enthusiasm and innovations of the cultivator. When water was standing, some farmers used pits for fish farming. Pits were also used for making compost when dry. The bunds around the pits were sometimes planted with horticultural trees to exploit the better moisture regime. Plantation of field bunds also varied widely.

The size, shape and the location were often modified by the farmers. In one case, a farmer who had adjacent land holdings decided to dig one common pond straddling both the plots so that he could use it for fish farming. Another farmer decided to divide his plot and make two farm ponds in anticipation of the future division of the land between him and his brother. Another farmer made a triangular-shaped pond because of the shape of his land holding.

Retained ecosystem functions

The technology package takes an integrated approach to the available land and water resources in a village micro-watershed. The critical resource of rain water is harvested and distributed equitably to make it accessible to all the categories of landowners, on all lands. It facilitates a production system where there is diversity of produce – ranging from timber, fuel, fodder, nitrogen-fixing green manure, pulses, oilseeds, vegetables, paddy, and even fish. The constructed pits hold water for six months at most, from June to November. In some cases fingerlings are raised and fish are reared in the farm ponds during these six months. The farm pond also creates a micro-system favourable to amphibian creatures like crabs, frogs and snakes, which assist in biotic control of pests.

266

The assessment carried out indicates that the technologies used have enabled an increase in the inter-temporal availability of water. They facilitate percolation of rainwater equitably over the area. During dry spells, although the surface dries up, crops obtain their moisture through capillary action. The moisture stress due to dry spells during critical periods of crop growth has been significantly reduced. When the TCP technology is adopted over a wide area, there is a widespread recharge of the soil profile. Standing water has been visible in the collection pits even when there has been no rainfall for 20 days at a stretch. The positive impact on lands in the medium paddy terraces and lowlands is evident from the successive increase in productivity over the years.

Changes in local resilience and vulnerability

Diversity of agricultural and other products farmed. The cropping pattern has evolved taking into consideration the ecological features and the consumption and cash needs of the farmers. The diversification also aims at spreading economic returns from a variety of products spread over a larger part of the year compared to the highly monocropped production system in the past.

The private lands have been put under a combination of trees, grass (on the bunds), pulses (legumes) and oilseeds. Some vegetables are also being raised. These include tomato (marketed), okra, cowpea (marketed) and pumpkin. A little lower down the slope, where soil depth is relatively better, upland paddy, maize and pigeon pea are grown as a mixed crop.

The moisture conservation technologies introduced have led to double cropping on many cultivated lands and have facilitated development of a production system involving diverse products other than paddy, including timber, fuel, fodder, nitrogen-fixing green manure, pulses, oilseeds, vegetables, and even fish. These meet a variety of the community's needs and spread the availability of produce throughout the year, thus providing some cushion in case of crop failure.

Livelihood security. The increased paddy production, coupled with diversification of on-farm livelihood sources, has resulted in a reduction of involuntary out-migration for most households and the end of dependence on migration in some cases. This has enabled people to invest more time and resources in their lands.

Increase in savings base and access to credit. As part of the programme implementation, most village residents are contributing towards a village fund. These funds are being used in some cases for initiating community development activities and small-scale credit programmes managed at the village level. In the village of Rampur in Bankura District, for example, the village savings fund is being used to give credit to 40 farmers for purchasing

267

fertilizers. In the village of Brajrajpur, farmers have been given credit by the local commercial banks to take up moisture conservation activities on their lands, encouraged by the impact observed on the production and income of the initial set of farmer experimenters.

Building self-reliance in groups and communities

Building local capacity and skills. The programme is managed by local youth clubs and their federation, Sevabrata. Most techniques developed are simple, labour-intensive and not dependent on uncertain and costly external resources. SPWD, PRADAN and Sevabrata have made conscious efforts to organize competence-building workshops and training programmes for farmers experimenting and managing the programme. Sevabrata has been able to mobilize external resources in grants and credit from external institutions based on their experience so far. The programme has led to an increase in self-confidence and self-esteem among the participating families, and other multiplier social benefits such as a reduction in alcoholism.

Willingness of local people to participate. In the initial phase, many farmers did not experiment readily with the moisture conservation technologies, because they expected financial inducements analogous to other government development programmes. SPWD provided limited financial assistance to the initial experimenters. However, as the impacts of the technologies become evident, the second phase of the technology development process and extension is increasingly being funded with internal resources. Many local institutions are initiating experimentation without any external support.

One of the conditions laid down by SPWD for work on private land development is a contribution from the land owners. This contribution may be in the form of free labour or in cash. SPWD insists on a 50 per cent contribution for privately owned lands. It must be noted that the government always extends full wage support, i.e., no contribution is expected for land development works. When the landowner contributes his or her labour or forgoes wages he or she ensures that the quality of work is good and the assets created are maintained. This enables sustainability of the technology.

Effectiveness of local resource management groups and promotion of equity. The TCP technology was adopted in the privately owned uplands, which had either been lying fallow or producing little. The organization of development works and distribution of benefits was influenced by the approach adopted by the Society for Hill Resource Management School in Bihar. In this model, the output from the pooled private wastelands that were developed, was shared equally between the landowners, the workers and the village community. SPWD and Sevabrata laid down a pre-

268

condition that employment from developing these wastelands would be made available only to the village residents.

In the SPWD-supported intervention in Purulia, development resources were routed through the youth clubs of the villages; the constituent members of Sevabrata. After negotiations and discussions with the bigger landowners owning wastelands on the upper slopes of the uplands, some of them agreed to give them to the youth clubs on a 10-year lease for development. The TCP technology was used and the land put under grass and trees, with some intercropping. The landowners agreed to share the output from these lands with the youth club and workers equally.

Mostly the large farmers find it feasible to lease uplands to the youth clubs. In return for giving degraded fallow land, they get a one-third share of the output, besides having their lands reclaimed. Poorer farmers benefit from the employment generated and also get a one-third share in the produce. However, the amount of employment generated for a household is not large as the plots are small, and significant labour input is required only in the first year. This institutional arrangement is not adopted readily by poor farmers who depend on their smallholdings and are not able to acquire one-third of the produce from the developed lands. However, the unemployed youth members of the youth club, who are generally landless, have benefited from the current institutional arrangement.

The process of negotiation involving discussions between various groups of farmers has led to the revival of community action. This has manifested itself in the development of communal systems of protection of trees and grasses on private and community lands, and the operation of village savings funds.

Change in operating procedures of support institutions. When it became apparent that the people gave higher priority to solving the problem of moisture stress and hydrological drought, SPWD changed its programme. SPWD has now developed a more flexible approach to supporting the grassroot agencies for wasteland development and believes in an interactive and iterative approach to programme development.

The participatory process followed by SPWD enabled the identification of the people's perceptions and enabled the farmers to contribute the indigenous knowledge to develop technologies for conserving moisture and water. The participation of all key stakeholders, SPWD, Sevabrata, youth clubs and PRADAN in the technology development process has facilitated the technology adaptation, increasing its sustainability in the long run.

Replication and scaling up

Replication through NGOs and voluntary agencies. By 1991, farmers in nine villages had experimented with TCP technology over an area of 30 hectares. The feedback from the participating farmers indicated that this technology could be replicated and adapted in the upper regions of uplands in Chotanagpur Plateau on a wider scale. SPWD decided to talk to the district administration to encourage inclusion of the adapted technologies in their soil and moisture conservation programmes. However, there was an absence of mature and experienced voluntary agencies (VAs) in the region with the technical and managerial capacity to handle replication on a wider scale and influence the district and block development programmes. Hence, PRADAN and SPWD decided to help smaller community groups in different parts of the Chotanagpur Plateau (Purulia, Singbhum, and Bankura districts) to set up experimentation clusters to scale up the process.

Accordingly, a competence-building programme was developed and supported by SPWD, and implemented in the field by the Regional Management Team of PRADAN, stationed at Purulia. Twenty agencies from Chotanagpur Plateau region participated and provided a rich forum for synthesizing and developing the technological and institutional approach. These included participating agencies from three states in Eastern India. Voluntary agencies, local co-operatives and *panchayats* also participated in the competence-building programme. It consisted of a survey of the resources of the area, village-level micro-planning and development of a field methodology for undertaking it. Workshops and on-field discussions were organized to discuss and explain the concept of integrated development and technical aspects of on-farm experimentation.

It was emphasized that the kind of work undertaken with Sevabrata in Purulia was of an experimental nature and the TCP technique that evolved could not be viewed as a fixed model or 'the answer'. In the Chotanagpur area there is a wide variety of land and water problems, and any rigidity in applying a single solution would have serious consequences. The techniques had to be location-specific and evolve through a participatory and iterative process. In this context, SPWD focused its efforts on building the capability of the voluntary agencies to undertake the village-level microplanning process.

After participating in the competence-building exercise, the NGOs experimented with these technologies in their areas. PRADAN catalysed experimentation in Hazaribag and Dumka districts of Bihar State. It was introduced to Keonjar District of Orissa state through the SPWD professionals who had earlier worked in the Chotanagpur Plateau.

The technology experimentation process started in 1991 through Sevabrata and PRADAN in one district in Eastern India over an area of 20 hectares. By 1996, 15 institutions were participating in three states covering an area of 725 hectares. Due to their track record, Sevabrata and the youth clubs have been provided support by NWDB (National Wastelands Development Board – a central government sponsored programme) for expanding the TCP technology on 252 hectares of upland. In addition,

CAPART supported the development of Five Per Cent Farm Pit Technology on 264 hectares of upland in 1992–93. Many new youth clubs are coming forward to implement the programme.

Self-replication without NGO involvement. Many villages surrounding the initial experimenting villages showed a keen interest in participating in a technology experimentation programme supported in the region (Box 20.3).

External financial support for replication and scaling-up. The central government sponsored agencies like NWDB and CAPART have been extending funding support to implement these techniques. However, they route these funds through the field-level NGOs. The scaling-up is then limited by the capacity of the NGOs to manage the programme. The NGOs in Chotanagpur Plateau Region are by and large small NGOs working in limited geographical areas. It is not easy to build the technical and managerial capacities of a very large number of NGOs to cover effectively the Chotanagpur Plateau region where these techniques can be applied.

The State Government, with its well-established administrative system, could effectively supplement the efforts of the NGOs and cover a large area. Funds from the State Government or *panchayats* have not yet been tapped for this programme. It is hoped that this study will be used to persuade the State Government and the *panchayats* to adopt the technology package evolved and accepted by the people. If the State Government could be persuaded to adopt this programme with all its features, including flexibility, the coverage of the programme would be greatly expanded.

Acknowledgements

This study has been a learning experience for those who have authored it. Grateful acknowledgement is made to the International Institute of Environment and Development, London, for making this documentation possible. SPWD hopes to use the study for wider dissemination of the processes and technologies employed in the study area, and to initiate informed discussions on it. The guidance and inputs of Mr. Arvind Khare, Executive Director, Society for Promotion of Wastelands Development (SPWD) in the study was of critical importance. We also acknowledge the valuable suggestions made by Mr. S.S. Rizvi, Adviser, Forestry, SPWD, on the draft of the study. The co-operation, insights and time given by the concerned communities and implementing NGOs made this study possible. We are indebted to them and hope that this study will, even in some small way, contribute to future improvements in their lives.

Box 20.3: Locally-initiated adoption

Village Brajrapur is about 25km from Purulia. In 1992–93, Sri Haldhar, a worker at Hindustan Fertilisers Limited, organized the village community and took them on an exposure visit to Sevabrata and Hensla Harparvati Club, Purulia. The people saw the work related to moisture conservation and had intensive discussions with the landowners and the functionaries of Sevabrata and Hensla Harparvati Club. No external fund was available to initiate the work in the village. However, the people were keen to initiate technology experimentation.

The 46 households in the village organized themselves into four groups – three of *Adivasis* (tribals) and one of *Mahatos* (Scheduled Castes) on the basis of proximity of lands. These groups decided to work on each other's lands on a group basis and covered over four hectares each.

One of the group members, Jit Lal Soren, owns a little less than one hectare of land. His land, along with other *Adivasis* group members, was treated with Five Per Cent Farm Pond technology. This treatment enabled him to sow the paddy seeds on time, while others who had not treated their lands could not do so due to erratic rainfall during that period. Soren obtained 13.125 quintals of paddy per hectare, which was 16 per cent more than the output on untreated lands, using a traditional variety of seed. He expects a higher level of production using improved seeds. The food security of his family of four has been extended by one month with this increased production. After harvesting paddy, Soren took an early *rabi* crop of linseed and introduced perennial pigeon pea using the residual moisture in the field. He obtained 60kg of linseed and 54kg of perennial pigeon pea. His field bunds were sown with *Dinanath* grass, which yielded feed for two cows. The water from the pits was also supplied to adjacent plots, where treatment was not done, to transplant paddy.

Following this experience, the Bank of Baroda has decided to extend loans for implementing the Five Per Cent Farm Pit technology. On request of the village people, an amount of Rs. 200 per *bigha* (one-third of an acre) is being sanctioned as a loan to the participating landowners. Fifteen households from the village of Brajrapur have availed themselves of this loan from the bank.

21
Matching Participatory Agricultural Development with the Social Landscape of Northeast Brazil

IRENE GUIJT and PABLO SIDERSKY[1]
based on work with Luciano Marçal da Silveira, Maria Paula
C.L. de Almeida, José Camêlo da Rocha, and Manoel
Roberval da Silva

Introduction

THE MOVE TOWARDS more participatory environmental action seems to be greatly preoccupied with developing the 'right' methods and encouraging the 'right' attitudes (cf IIED. *PLA Notes*, 1995; Chambers, 1994). The simple message of participatory watershed development that is appearing is: with a technical 'best-seller' and the 'right' method or approach, massive participation and fantastic results will ensue. But is collective action straightforward once the right method or approach has been identified? And if such action does not spread spontaneously between communities, then are the methods, attitudes, or approaches perhaps incorrect?

The promise of participatory watershed development is based on several assumptions about the social landscape in which it takes place, but which are not universally applicable:

o Existing communication channels and social groups are both the starting point and the route for scaling up environmental rehabilitation. Mediating organizations or individuals play a key role in this process. But what happens when there are no viable channels, groups, or mediators?

o Community-wide participation leads to collective decisions which are implemented through collective action, thus bringing quick results. But what if the local tradition has always been one of individual action?

o The resource management innovation that is to deliver the quick results over wide areas must be more or less at hand, or there has to be an easy route or a willing partner to develop it. But what if there is no accumulation of technical understanding of local agricultural systems, either with farmers or external organizations, that can help identify the technical 'best-seller'?

---
[1] Pablo Sidersky is the director of AS-PTA's northeast programme, and overall manager of Projeto Paraíba. The Project is generously funded by ICCO (the Netherlands), Kellog's Foundation (USA), MLAL (Italy) and the Biodiversity project (Crocevia/EEC).

The experiences of AS-PTA (*Assessoria e Servicos a Projetos em Agricultura Alternativa*) show that the social context in which participatory development occurs, and not just 'the right approach', strongly influences the impact. In northeast Brazil the social context is not favourable for the type of collective action on which participatory watershed development is based. A weak sense of community and few mediating structures that can effectively act as an amplifier for the NGO input mean that participatory watershed development must take on a different form than those described elsewhere in this volume.

This chapter describes the work of Projeto Paraíba, one of AS-PTA's projects in northeast Brazil, its participatory strategy, and first results. While promising, these results are not yet overwhelming, either in terms of their geographic scale or local impact. Could these results have been better had a different participatory approach been followed? This is discussed in the final section, which raises questions about how the social landscape is perceived in participatory watershed development, and the limitations posed by existing social processes and players in the Brazilian context.

AS-PTA and Projeto Paraíba

Projeto Paraíba started in 1993 and is a local agricultural development pro-gramme run by the Brazilian NGO, AS-PTA. Since the mid-1980s, AS-PTA has been working with agroecology, family agriculture and sustainable de-velopment. Its activities focus around field research and the extension of appropriate technology for small-scale producers, networking, and advocacy.

Projeto Paraíba's work focuses on the municipalities of Solânea and Remígio. Project activities are carried out by a team of five agricultural professionals, in partnership with '*animadores*' (motivators) who are active members of the municipal rural trade unions, the STRs[2]. The STRs are crucial to the sustainability of the work, as they will carry on the agri-cultural activities once AS-PTA moves on to other municipalities. Besides the unions, farmers' experimentation groups are increasingly involved. These have no formal structure as yet, but meet to discuss specific agri-cultural innovations, such as integrated pest management in banana stands or pigeon pea intercropping. Project staff also interact infrequently with the local university, EMATER (the state-level agricultural extension ser-vice), and other NGOs in the region.

Smallholder agriculture in Solânea and Remígio

The Brazilian northeast is a huge tropical region, of more than 1.5 million km[2], ranging from the vast sugar cane estates along the coast to the semi-

---

[2] *Sindicato de Trabalhadores Rurais*, Rural Worker's Unions, are membership organizations, active at the municipal level, and federated at state and national levels in Brazil.

arid interior. In between lies the relatively unknown Agreste, home to Remígio, Solânea, and Projeto Paraíba. As elsewhere in Brazil, the land is concentrated in large holdings, yet the majority of farmers are smallholders, more than three-quarters of whom depend on less than five hectares (see Table 21.1).

The Agreste zone is characterized by its immense environmental diversity. While the average rainfall is around 1000 mm/year in the east, it drops to about 400 mm in the west, just 40km away. This variation has created both a diverse natural flora and widely differing agricultural systems. In 1994, AS-PTA's environmental survey with farmers identified 10 environmental micro-zones (Petersen, 1995). Furthermore, Projeto Paraíba staff identified six production sub-systems: annual cropping, permanent cropping, livestock, homegarden, extractivism[3], and small-scale irrigated agriculture. Each micro-zone, therefore, comprises several types of family farms, each with specific bottlenecks that hinder economic viability and agricultural sustainability.

In these diverse micro-zones, most farmers grow maize, common bean, and cassava. Minor crops include: lima bean, sweet potato, banana, and potato. A very short rotation cycle is common, sometimes giving way to permanent cultivation, with occasional use of organic fertilizers and even rarer use of other agro-industrial inputs. Small-scale livestock is an important supplement to diets and incomes. Despite the enormous diversity, practically all smallholders face the same basic problems: intense pressure on scarce natural resources, particularly soil, vegetation, and genetic diversity; and a large drop in agricultural income with the disappearance of cash crops. The latter is everyone's first priority.

Projeto Paraíba's strategy and activities

The Project has two strategic goals:

o conservation and regeneration of natural resources – focusing on soils and biodiversity

Table 21.1:   Land distribution in Solânea and Remígio

Solânea 32 750 people spread over 368km = 89 perkm
Remígio 17 155 inhabitants spread over 553km = 31 per km

Property size	Total area	Number of properties
< 5 ha.	5785 ha.	3623
5–50 ha.	13 035 ha.	1066
> 50 ha.	45 383 ha.	203
Total	64 203 ha.	4892

[3] Gathering or collecting in areas with natural vegetation, for construction and fuel wood, fodder, and fruit.

275

o revival of household income – focusing on diversifying cash crops and reintroducing old cash crops.

The main priority is improving current production systems, with future plans to address processing and marketing the produce. Four types of activities are pursued by the team: innovation development[4], dissemination, institutional support, and permanent planning.

As local autonomy of sustainable agricultural innovation is fundamental, Projeto Paraíba has sought to work through local partnerships from the onset and opted for STR. The rural trade unions operate at the municipal level and are the most accepted democratically chosen body that represents smallholder agriculture in Brazil. However, the STRs have traditionally not dealt with concrete agricultural problems, so the partnership requires them to change their focus and build capacities.

As farmers will be the managers of ongoing innovation and change, they are also involved in the process of technological development and implementation. Yet the team recognizes that not all farmers are equally interested and/or able to participate in all aspects of agricultural innovation. Therefore, Projeto Paraíba is working with three levels of farmer participation:

o A nucleus of about ten farmers, affiliated with the STR, is involved in strategic planning, data analysis, monitoring and evaluation. This group is also responsible for most dissemination and monitoring work in the field, and are the *'animadores'*.
o The second level of farmer participation involves about 80 farmers, men and women. It includes community association leaders and individual farmers engaged in joint experimentation. Practically all are also involved in key events of monitoring, evaluation and planning.
o The third level includes activity-specific collaboration with the general farming 'public' and community associations, covering 30 communities and over 500 farmers who are keen to adopt particular measures.

Farmer involvement started from the first step in 1993 with a participatory agro-ecosystems appraisal with 30 farmers and STR representatives to analyse the regional agricultural crisis and local coping strategies. This process identified distinct micro-zones and a programme of prioritized activities per micro-zone. The analysis was discussed with 40 communities (1450 farmers) using slide shows developed with, and facilitated by, STR. From 1994 onwards the partnership has pursued a permanent participatory planning process. Planning seminars are held annually, with about 40 farmers, to review progress and reassess priorities. Outputs from farmer-based monitoring and annual evaluations provide essential planning inputs.

---

[4] This does not always involve a technical change in agricultural practices as it also includes, for example, establishing community seed banks.

Initial results

From a modest beginning in 1993, Projeto Paraíba is now making a difference for almost 500 families. More importantly, there is continual emphasis on cultivating local capacity to sustain the work. From an initial focus on only one institution, Projeto Paraíba is expanding the partnership to include other groups and agencies (Table 21.2).

Table 21.2:   Main achievements of Projeto Paraíba

1993	1994	1995	1996
o established office and technical team o established a presence among smallholders and trade unions o started understanding diversity of problems for smallholder agriculture o started working with team of STR *animadores* o overall objectives clarified to focus on addressing disappearance of cash crops and tackling natural resource degradation	o deepening insights into local problems and potential o reached greater number of farmers o many adaptations to experiments such as density of planting, planning of seed distribution, the need to avoid labour-intensive innovations o independent functioning of *animadores* at more and different types of events o initial attempts at more structured farmer experimentation (maize varieties, aniseed production, green manures, millet and sorghum) o beginning of structured monitoring and evaluation	o own demonstration farm operational, Centro Sao Miguel o jump from 21 active communities with 210 families in 1994 to 32 communities with 500 families (mainly through seed banks) o steady consolidation of existing dissemination o more systematic approach to experimentation based on agricultural sub-systems o increasing diversity of experimentation (9 topics) o first group-based technology development, rather than individual farmers o development of wide range of self-produced training material	o more focus on developing proposals and technologies o new approach to experimentation via farmer groups o accepting need to expand partner organizations o more openness of STR and farmers towards agricultural alternatives o increased contact with universities and researchers due to visibility of initial results o formal collaboration with EMATER in Remígio o expanding work to third municipality, Lagoa Seca o focus on improving the quality of existing work, rather than expanding scale

AS-PTA has had a range of impacts with Projeto Paraíba (AS-PTA, 1997). Most are related to a more sustainable use and conservation of natural resources through developing and disseminating less destructive agricultural practices. There have been simultaneous improvements in raising social sustainability through better livelihoods and better forms of social organization and collective action. Some results include the following:

○ Contour planting and related soil conservation techniques have led 73 farmers to protect over 200 hectares of agricultural fields. Apart from greater soil and water conservation, which the farmers greatly value, initial monitoring data from their fields indicates that average productivity of beans doubled on protected plots (Guijt et al, 1997).

○ Community-based bean seed banks have guaranteed a minimum amount of seed at the right time for a large number of smallholders (just over 500 in 1995 and about 420 in 1996). The novelty here is not technical but a new form of social organization. The result is mainly economic (reduced costs) and institutional (the existence of the seed bank itself). Since late 1996, some banks have started diversifying their stock, thereby increasing biodiversity.

○ Banana weevil control has been adopted by just over 40 families in seven communities in the more humid areas. Monitoring with participatory mapping in three communities indicated that 30 per cent of banana growers were using this technique. Individual interviews showed that farmers noted a wide range of positive effects in their banana stands, including production increases, which they attributed to weevil control.

○ The yam[5] seed bank was started in 1996. It has helped a group of 26 farmers to diversify production with a relatively profitable crop. Despite the modest start, this activity has sparked intense curiosity due to its great potential to raise incomes. Nevertheless, even if yam can increase agricultural stability, it is a high-input crop and requires much work to make it more environmentally sound.

○ There have been at least 17 other technical proposals: agroforestry techniques, new ideas for livestock feeding in the dry season, etc. The shift from about 15 experimenting farmers in 1995 to about 80 in 1997 is a big change, especially as the new approach also builds the basis for dissemination at a later stage with a large long-term multiplier effect.

○ There has been steady progress in establishing contacts and collaboration prospects with different government rural development agencies (mainly research and extension).

○ Greater skills and knowledge have been acquired about participatory methods and appropriate local processes, notably the seed banks and the farmer experimentation groups.

---

[5] *Dioscoreia cayanensis* var. rotundata

o Greater capacity-building has developed, with much progress in the comprehension and capacities of STR (mainly Remígio) in more sustainable resource management and development.

Overall, the team feels convinced that it is on the right track with its participatory approach, without which progress would be much slower. However, the impact to date is insufficient to ensure sustainability of the changes, either agriculturally or socially. The main problem is that, despite growing farmer participation, proposal development is proving to be a very slow process and there is no organization or social channel to scale-up the impact. The results with the trade unions and other farmer organizations are also far from perfect, as is discussed in the next section.

Questioning the social landscape

Why, given the thorough and participatory nature of AS-PTA's approach, is there no spontaneous social combustion of technological improvement whizzing through the Paraíban countryside? This section discusses three aspects of participatory development that are seldom discussed, yet are crucial for understanding likely impacts: the effect of existing social structures, the role of collective versus individual action, and the absence of previous reference points for the technological innovations that are necessary.

How do existing social structures influence participatory development?

Participatory watershed development, as discussed in this volume, is not a spontaneous local initiative. It is initiated by an external organization and, when successful, evolves into a locally sustained process (and structure) of planning and implementation. In the short and medium term, mediation between communities and the outside world of resources and information is necessary (cf. Blauert and Zadek, 1998). And even in the long term, collaboration with other permanent formal structures is necessary to sustain improvements.

Participatory development depends on being able to identify accurately partners who will sustain the work. But an accurate reading of the social landscape in a new context requires skill and time. Key players are not always obvious, and those who seem to be logical partners in the beginning are not necessarily the most effective or interested in the longer term.

In northeast Brazil, the most obvious partner for widespread agricultural development would seem to be the farmers' associations.[6] But

---

[6] These community associations are not present everywhere. In the region we work in a rough estimate is that about half the smallholders belong to some kind of formal association.

these are grafted institutions, culturally foreign to most communities, and are not a traditional power centre. Associations are not genuine community organizations, as most were founded by EMATER or local politicians, as channels for government funding. Local councillors, keen to get votes during elections, encouraged the establishment of these associations, which subsequently often remain associated with that person and his or her allies.

So what other formal and informal organized structures exist? Rural Paraíba is organized around *sítios*, *comunidades*, and municipalities. And as described above, AS-PTA is trying to create 'farmer experimentation groups' as another channel for rural improvement. With which of these social units do farmers have ties that could form the basis of participatory watershed development?

The smallest rural settlement is the *sítio*, a cluster of homes forming a neighbourhood. It may encompass from two up to more than 100 houses, covering from a few hectares to more than 500ha. Members of the same *sítio* may be relatives, but this is by no means a necessity. In some cases, a *sítio* is the place where the workers of a single large landholding, or *fazenda*, live. Although *sítios* include people with leadership qualities, they are not a structure for representation, power, or decision-making.

Comunidades (or communities) sometimes overlap with a *sítio*, but are usually larger and differ mainly because they were established after externally-induced interaction (meetings, mass, etc.) between neighbouring families. In recent times, the Catholic Church has carried out grassroots work in the region, formally establishing *comunidades*[7] in the process. The government extension services have made a more half-hearted attempt to promote a similar community level of meeting and extension. These artificially created 'communities' provide some reasonably regular social interaction and an informal discussion forum but without a 'heart' or decision-making structure. Although *comunidades* are more likely than *sítios* to undertake some collective action, they are not widespread. Of the estimated 200 settlements in the municipalities of Remígio and Solânea, only about 20 per cent call themselves a *comunidade*.

The municipality is the real focus of economic and political life, and even of social events, although the ties with rural dwellers are loose. Most marketing transactions take place in the town centre, where the church, the government rural extension agency, and the banks are located. As the smallest administrative unit in Brazil, the municipality is also the stage for much political life. The most influential people, who are interested only in the votes and not in the lives of rural dwellers, are keen to keep municipal power in their hands so do not form good partners for Projeto Paraíba.

---

[7] This work was very intense in the 1980s, when many *Comunidades Eclesiais de Base* (Grassroots Church Communities) were established all over Brazil.

280

Nevertheless, the most effective type of farmer organizations act on a municipal basis: the STR.

How did this social vacuum arise? The social structure in Paraíba used to centre around the large landholding, the *fazenda*, a cohesive social and production unit despite its extremely inequitable nature. The 'patron-client' relationship with the *fazendeiro* (large landowner) is crumbling with the intruding global economy and the new social relations (labour and land tenure laws, and the corresponding claim possibilities) that have increased the incidence of expulsions from the land. The social vacuum has been filled, to varying degrees, by the church, by party politics, by governmental rural development projects, and most importantly by the market. However, no unit of social organization that has furthered sustainable smallholder production has taken root socially, economically or environmentally.

Much participatory development starts with a small venture, via a local social group or entry point, from where the work spreads. In some cases, the original partner is phased out or loses interest, and others take over. In English villages, a pub might be the social gathering point but this does not mean that the community works together on a collective activity. In Australia, the Landcare movement has created a sense of social identity, but started operating initially in a relative social vacuum (Campbell and Wood-hill, this volume). Social interaction was created. There is not always an obvious existing social entry point (structure, person, leader) for the external development agent around which collective mobilization can easily be focused. Where structure and leadership coincide, the impact can be large. Where neither exist, social relations need to be created.

These mediating structures mentioned above play three roles, which will evolve over time:

o they help shape the message of participatory watershed development (which technologies are appropriate for the local physical and socio-economic situation)
o they extend the message, through demonstration and training and joint research with farmers, and thus have to have sufficient outreach to amplify the impact
o they undertake advocacy work to ensure the message gains wider support in society, and therefore have to have sufficient political 'punch'.

Such a structure should be able to reach large numbers of smallholders, be willing to perform this role, have a formal structure that makes it a viable organization, and be considered a legitimate voice by the smallholders. These could, in theory, be a government agency or NGO (as is sometimes the case in Bangladesh or India), a federation of associations, or solid community-based organizations.

Which groups or structures could take on this mediating role in Paraíba? The most obvious choice, EMATER (the state agricultural extension agency) is understaffed, focuses on only a few cash crops, and has no inclination towards, nor likelihood of, becoming a representative of small-holders. AS-PTA has few staff and no likelihood of expanding, and believes that this is not its most appropriate role in rural Brazil.

Projeto Paraíba is therefore investing much effort in strengthening the more viable of the existing organizations, the STR, some associations and informal groups in the more active *comunidades*, and the new farmer experimentation groups. The STR has a large rural membership[8] which it is used to representing, and has a formal, albeit shaky, structure. For AS-PTA, it means helping an old institution take on a new role. Hitherto, the STR resolved pensions, organized state health insurance, and even used to have an in-house dentist. The more active branches dealt with land tenure issues or crisis mobilization (e.g. during severe drought). Asking it to resolve practical agricultural bottlenecks means building new analytical and practical skills. It also means motivating the STR to take on a more practical role that requires even longer hours on the road. Faced with these new demands has made many STR leaders opt for the *status quo*.

Dealing with agricultural production issues has also increased the handling of money (credit, small loans, revolving funds, etc.). Despite the militant face within politically quite radical organizations, such as the STR, altruism is not necessarily recognized as a virtue[9]. Lack of a tradition of financial accountability only adds to the temptation of corruption. Relying exclusively on the self-sacrificing actions of the trade union representatives is not proving a sound basis for partnership. Therefore, greater accountability will be needed if the new orientation of STR is to continue.

The lack of viable and appropriate social structures has implications for the role of external organizations committed to participatory agricultural development. Given the need for skills in organizational support and social awareness and facilitation, how can this best be balanced with the necessary technical agricultural skills? Relying on one partner for all activities, while an appropriate and essential starting point, is clearly no longer effective for Projeto Paraíba. Project staff are starting to identify other groups that can offer higher quality input. For example, there are clearer ideas on how to work with the farmer experimentation groups and the stronger community associations. EMATER is increasingly interested in collaboration, with one senior technician officially working with the team for one day a week. Pursuing a wider range of strategic alliances, however

---

[8] Large membership is a relative concept. For example, before 1993, the Rural Trade Union of Remígio had only 52 members. Now membership stands at 800 which, although representing a 15-fold increase, still includes only some of the 2000 farmers (Guijt, 1996).

[9] In Brazil, there is a strong sense of hierarchy as the natural social order. People do not expect leaders to work altruistically on participatory development, for no extra personal benefit. Therefore, what some would consider to be an abuse of power is acceptable in rural Paraíba.

imperfect potential partners may appear at first glance, will provide Projeto Paraíba with more continuity in local experimentation and dissemination, and thus more chances at scaling-up the impact.

What is the role of collective decision-making and action in participatory development?

Participatory development assumes that collective action offers greater and different benefits from individual action. It also assumes that local channels exist for collective decision-making, and that once such decisions are made they are then implemented collectively. The common picture (or carica-ture) of participatory watershed development is one of large community meetings in which people unanimously decide to plant trees or dig ditches and then run out together to do this. But making decisions in a public forum does not necessarily mean that collective action has been negotiated. Nor can it be assumed that the will and structure for collective decisions exist in the first place. Are farmers interested in collective action, for which issues, and for how long, and where do they make such decisions?

If decisions are made in a legitimate forum, they are more likely to be implemented. Each issue has an appropriate forum for making decisions. In Brazil, dealing with increased pest incidence or trees on farms will be discussed in a family forum; deteriorating roads perhaps in a *sítio* meeting; religious education is discussed within a *comunidade*. Where there is no traditional forum for collective resource management decisions, as in northeast Brazil, creating a legitimate decision-making body is one altern-ative, such as the village institutions by AKRSP (see Shah and Kaul Shah, this volume). Another approach is to encourage existing bodies to take on responsibility for this new type of collective environmental decision (see Lobo and Palghadmal, this volume). But for STR or the associations to take on such authority would require the unlikely scenario of farmers recognizing such new powers.

Collective decisions and action occur when there is an incentive. This commonly exists when there is a strong focus or need, such as in degrada-tion of, or conflict over, communal land. Another incentive occurs when there are sufficient resources that can support a structure of field facilita-tors, grants, etc. to encourage collective action.

In Paraíba, there are no communal lands and the only history of collect-ive action is the land tenure movement. Even in the case of the Movimento Sem Terra (Landless Movement, which based its work on collective action to claim land rights), the lack of previous social cohesion has meant that many a group has disbanded after the initial success of gaining formal ownership. There are no collective management traditions of, for example, forests or waterways, that can be revived. There is also no state regulation of environmental or agricultural issues that could act as an incentive for collective action. And AS-PTA certainly has no resources to set up a large network of facilitators.

Projeto Paraíba has found no tradition of, and few signs of interest in, collective resource management. Decisions about resource management are made by farmers and their immediate family. The team has organized numerous large events to discuss different resource management problems and alternatives, such as erosion and contour planting. But farmers never spoke of collective decisions or actions on these occasions. Experiences in 1996 with the first farmer experimentation group of legume intercropping strengthened this cautious stand. The group met only eight times in one year, for a total of about 24 hours. Yet when evaluating the first year, all the farmers said there had been too many meetings, taking precious time away from other farming tasks.

In Paraíba, not only are collective decisions about environmental rehabilitation difficult to make due to the lack of appropriate forums, but such decisions do not automatically lead to collective action. This does not mean that there is no need or scope for collective action. For Projeto Paraíba it will simply take a different form and relate to different issues from those commonly associated with participatory watershed development. Perhaps, in the short term, efforts are better invested in creating many smaller initiatives. There is some level of collective decision and action that can grow in the farmer experimentation groups, the community seed banks, and the municipal yam seed bank. At the moment they involve loose meetings of interested farmers who share their experiences. A greater sense of group purpose can be stimulated by more collective planning of experiments and group-based monitoring. In the meantime though, it is best not to assume that development in a watershed is best channelled through large-scale collective efforts.

Who identifies or creates the necessary technological innovations in participatory development?

Quick and widespread participatory watershed development hinges on dissemination of appropriate technical innovations. Many projects that produce rapid results do so because they are able to tap previous research experience, with relatively little need to 'shape the message'. It is fairly obvious that if one is to expect brilliant results in record time (the promise of participatory watershed development!), the 'message' has to be more or less ready at hand. In *Two Ears of Corn* (1983), Roland Bunch stresses the importance of finding one or two proposals that bring spectacular benefits for farmers with which to woo them for other forms of collective resource management. But where are these 'best-sellers'? What happens in the absence of existing reference points for innovation?

Projeto Paraíba could have much greater impact if it had greater capacity to generate more answers to the problems of smallholders. Only three of the 20 possibly significant technical innovations that farmers and the team have identified are being disseminated widely. The team has not yet found a single 'best-seller' that can increase incomes and is popular with farmers. Several potential innovations with wide applicability will require a long gestation period, such as agroforestry and pigeon pea intercropping.

The presence or absence of the basis for technological innovation is closely related to the social landscape. For example, in southern Brazil there is now considerable experience and information on the use of short-cycle green manures that can be offered to smallholders. This was possible only after two decades of intense and well-resourced research. In several experiences in this volume, rediscovering lost practices provided that essential body of knowledge and innovation. In Solânea and Remígio, only three innovations have some historical precedent on which to build – all others need thorough research to adapt them and to identify them in the first place. AS-PTA is starting from scratch, with at best, some international literature to guide them.

Paraíba is virtually barren in terms of research for smallholders. Not only are there few technical staff among state agencies but the topics are not relevant for most farmers. EMBRAPA, the agricultural research branch, has no impact in the region. The nearest EMBRAPA research centre focuses on cotton, a crop that no longer exists in the region. EMEPA[10] focuses on replicating the Green Revolution model and spends its resources sporadically training technical staff in the use of agrochemicals. EMATER takes its cue from research and assumes that lack of credit is the bottleneck. But instead of focusing on beans and maize, the local staples, credit focuses on potatoes for farmers without reliable cold storage[11]. With only two EMATER staff to deal with the 2000 smallholders in Remígio, a mere 170 to 220 farmers are reached each year. However, the EMATER office in Remígio has become increasingly involved with Projeto Paraíba.

Projeto Paraíba will continue to be limited in its capacity to generate popular innovations because of insufficient staff (and no immediate scope for expansion) and the lack of alternative agencies or organizations to do the necessary research. Furthermore, the great biophysical diversity of the Agreste means that any potential best-seller must be more finely tuned to local conditions than would be necessary in more homogenous environments. Due to the many micro-zones, any single solution is likely to be relevant for only a limited group of farmers operating in a small area, as

---

[10] Paraíban Agricultural Research Company
[11] One EMATER technician reported that only 20 loans were approved for potato production in the past year, and none for beans or maize.

285

conditions in neighbouring areas will need other responses. This diversity calls for very careful selection of the topic or ecosystem to address in any given round of experiments and dissemination of recommendations. With only four technical staff on hand to devote themselves to solving these problems, progress will be slow. This reinforces the need for new alliances, as it presents a route to speed up progress.

Implications

Participatory watershed development works best when there is a reasonable degree of social organization and local groups through whom the necessary critical mass of collective action can be organized and technical innovations generated. Where this social reality does not exist, it has to be created. Yet it takes time for new social structures to emerge and for a new ethic to take hold. Shaping the technical innovations of participatory watershed development does not happen overnight.

In northeast Brazil, there is no easy social entry point for participatory development and no organizational or social structure for quick diffusion. A society that is based more around individual than collective action begs a different approach. Where there is a relative knowledge vacuum, as in the northeast of Brazil, research about sustainable alternatives must precede any effort to implement such alternatives on a large scale. These are huge challenges for small organizations committed to pursuing a participatory mode of development, such as AS-PTA. Under these circumstances, it cannot reach many people quickly, nor be as participatory as it would like to be. It does not have the resources for extensive research on a technological best-seller or to fund a concerted effort of on-site catchment facilitators, as is being carried out in Santa Catarina by EPAGRI (de Freitas, this volume).

That social change of the kind AS-PTA espouses best occurs through farmer participation is clear. But the form that this participation takes is not easy to identify or create. A catchment approach is not an obvious choice for Projeto Paraíba, however attractive it might be in theory. Catchments are artificial units in the physical and social reality of Paraíba, which is composed of people devoted to individual action. As discussed throughout this volume, participatory watershed development is not as simple as finding the 'right' method or attitude. The chance of success will be greatly influenced by how a rural area is organized socially. To be effective, an approach must be based on careful consideration of the following questions:

○ What is the local history of collective resource management?
○ What is the scope in the area for collective decisions and action in resource managment?

286

- What social units are the most appropriate for participatory resource management, in terms of decision-making and implementation?
- What is the most effective social entry point (structure or person) for an external development organization?
- Is collective action going to be more effective for watershed development than many individual efforts?
- What are the existing references or most likely sources of technological innovation?

LOCAL CAPACITY AND
INSTITUTIONAL INNOVATION

Overview
Local Capacity and Institutional Innovation

From Individual to Collective Action

FOR AS LONG as people have engaged in agriculture, farming has been at least a partially collective business. Farming households have worked together on resource management, labour sharing, marketing, and a host of other activities that would be too costly, or even impossible, if done alone. Local groups and indigenous institutions have, therefore, long been important in rural and agricultural development.

These may be formal or informal groups, such as water management committees, water users groups, neighbourhood groups, youth or women's groups, housing societies, informal beer-brewing groups, farmer experimentation groups, burial societies, church groups, mothers' groups, pastoral and grazing management groups, tree-growing associations, labour-exchange societies and so on. These have been effective in many ecosystems and cultures, including collective water management in the irrigation systems of Egypt, Mesopotamia and Indonesia; collective herding in the Andes and pastoral systems of Africa; water harvesting and management societies in Roman north Africa, India, and south-west North America; and forest management in shifting agriculture systems. Many of these societies were sustainable over periods of hundreds to thousands of years.

The success of watershed development depends not just on the motivations, skills and knowledge of individual farmers, but on action taken by local groups or communities as a whole. This makes the task facing agriculture today exceptionally challenging. Simply letting farmers know that watershed development can be profitable to them, as well as producing extra benefits for society as a whole, will not suffice. Increased attention to community-based action through local institutions is also vital.

The uniting factor in the following six case-studies is that they have in common the prevalence of face-to-face interpersonal relationships, which are more frequent and intense within small groups. The fact that people know each other creates opportunities for collective action and mutual assistance, and for mobilizing resources on a self-sustaining basis. People feel more mutual rapport and a sense of obligation at these levels than at district or sub-district levels, which are really political constructions. At the household or individual levels, decisions and actions oriented towards

291

watershed development are not likely to be long lasting unless they are co-ordinated with what other households are also doing.

The perils of ignoring local institutions

Throughout the history of modern agricultural development, it has been rare for the importance of local groups and institutions to be recognized. Development professionals have tended to be preoccupied with the individual, assuming that the most important decisions affecting behaviour are made at this level. As a result, the effectiveness of local groups and institutions has been widely undermined. Some have struggled on. Many others have disappeared entirely.

Without realizing it, governments have routinely suffocated local institutions during agricultural modernization. Local management has been substituted for by the state, leading to increased dependence of local people on formal state institutions. Local information networks have been replaced by research and extension activities; banks and co-operatives have substituted for local credit arrangements; co-operatives and marketing boards have been replaced by input and product markets; and water boards have replaced local water users' associations.

Just as bad as ignoring existing local institutions is the imposition of new ones without the participation of local people. Outside interventions are liable to warp and weaken local institutions. There are dangers that the state will suffocate local initiative and responsibility, or capture and harness local initiatives and resources for other purposes. Local politicians may seek to take over local successes or gain reflected glory from them. As has been indicated above, not all initiatives are seen by local people as legitimate.

In the Tarbela-Mangla case, for example, Shahid Ahmad and Javed Ahmed attribute many of the problems to the failure of the programme to work with local communities: 'no evidence exists in any catchments of sustained community or group activity . . . There are no committees or farmer organizations for co-operative action . . . Some farmers are motivated to do soil conservation works and they approach the department to seek help . . . However, there is no concerted effort made by the project authorities for integrated catchment development'.

Establishing self-reliant groups

Studies of agricultural development initiatives are increasingly showing that when people who are already well organized, or who are encouraged to form groups, and whose knowledge is sought and incorporated during planning and implementation, they are more likely to continue activities after project completion. If people have responsibility, feel ownership and are committed, then there is likely to be sustained change.

292

The process of establishing self-reliant groups at local level must be an organic one, and so should not be forced or done too quickly. There are four essential elements of any self-supporting farmers' organization. They should have developed a financing capacity with resources of their own. They should have a structure for electing farmer representatives. They should have obtained recognition as a legitimate voice of farmers. They should have developed self-reliance for planning, for management, and for the provision of effective services.

Al Fernandez describes the way institutions develop in southern India: 'such institutions do not spring up overnight; they evolve over a period, during which members agree on their rights and responsibilities and on sanctions on those who do not abide by the accepted norms'.

Key impacts and scaling up from local capacity

Recreating a sense of community

When groups are established for the first time, or resuscitated, then one of the universal benefits expressed is the renewed sense of community. In Australia, members of farmer and community groups commonly state the important benefits of membership are not so much yield improvement and economic returns, but more the pleasures of problem-sharing, friendship and enjoyment of others' company. This has been a particularly notable effect of the Landcare programme in Australia, where typically independent and 'frontier-spirited' farmers have, in coming together in groups for the first time, achieved significant environmental and social changes.

Farmer-to-farmer extension and exchanges

There is growing experience in farmer-to-farmer extension, visitation and peer-training as mechanisms to support watershed improvement. Most common are farmer exchange visits, in which farmers are brought to the site of a successful innovation or useful practice, where they can discuss and observe benefits and costs with adopting farmers. Professionals play the role of bringing interested groups together and facilitating the process of information exchange. During the visits, participants are stimulated by the discussions and observations, and many will be provoked into trying the technologies for themselves. For farmers 'seeing is believing', and the best educators of farmers are other farmers themselves (see Shah case-study).

Community monitoring

When people are engaged in gathering information locally, they become more interested in finding out what it means. The transition from information to capacity to act upon it is important. In Western Australia, the slogan in the community-based water quality monitoring programme is 'measurement quickly becomes management' (West Hume case).

Credit groups

It has long been assumed that poor people cannot save money. Because they are poor and have little or no collateral, they are too high a risk for banks, and so have to turn to traditional money lenders. These inevitably charge extortionate rates of interest, and very often people get locked into even greater poverty while trying to pay off debts. Recent evidence is emerging, however, to show that when local groups are trusted to manage financial resources, they can be more efficient and effective than external bodies such as banks. They are more likely to be able to make loans to poorer people. They also recover a much greater proportion of loans. In a wide range of countries, local credit groups are directly helping poorer families both to stay out of debt and reap productive returns on small investments on their farms. The work of the NGO MYRADA has been at the forefront of this revolution, and the impacts on local groups and equity within communities has been substantial (see Fernandez case). Both AKRSP and SPEECH have credit management as vital components of their successful watershed development in Gujarat and Tamil Nadu, respectively.

Capacity to negotiate on own terms

As local groups and institutions become stronger, so they become better able to interact with external agencies on their own terms. John Devavaram and colleagues at SPEECH in Tamil Nadu, India, describe the impact in the community of Paraikulum: 'Paraikulum is clearly more resilient and self-reliant as a result of the five years of participatory watershed management. The community works together in a co-operative fashion; the agricultural system as a whole is more productive; and resources are more equitably spread. Villagers feel they can do things for themselves now, and now say "we don't want any outside contractors coming into our village – we can do everything ourselves".' SPEECH is no longer working in Paraikulum.

All these help in the process of scaling up from local capacity to have a wider impact. These six case-studies explore different aspects of how local institutions were developed and how they became stronger over time, serving as important mechanisms for both watershed and social development.

22
Equity, Local Groups and Credit: Lessons from MYRADA's Work in South India

ALOYSIUS P. FERNANDEZ

MYRADA'S INVOLVEMENT WITH the Participative Integrated Development of Watershed project (PIDOW) has already been described in relation to technology development in Chapter 7. In this chapter we examine the issues related to equity, local groups and credit. MYRADA's experience has shown that these three areas are closely related.

Equity: difficult to achieve, easy to pass by

Equity is perhaps the most difficult objective to achieve and sustain within the context of a watershed programme, especially in areas where resources are already scarce. It is even more difficult to assess the extent to which it has been achieved. Although this chapter raises more questions than it answers, it is an initial and limited attempt to focus attention on the issues related to equity which often tend to be treated last and hurriedly.

MYRADA's watershed projects have now generated enough evidence to indicate that if equity is not sustained, the pressures on the watershed's resources – and therefore on sustained productivity – tend to increase, diminishing returns in the long run. Thus it is an essential part of a sustainable watershed development strategy.

Who are the vulnerable in the watersheds?

Communities within watersheds are by no means homogeneous, and some of the vulnerable groups identified by MYRADA include:

○ the landless and marginal farmers, who have an economic base which cannot meet their livelihood needs
○ women, against whom gender relations are often biased and who traditionally have to perform major roles that can and should be shared, leaving them more time for nurturing responsibilities and self-growth, and
○ the tribals who tend to be marginalized by the existing economic and political system.

The physical structure of a watershed, by its very nature, can also contribute to inequity (Box 22.1).

Box 22.1:   A structural image of society

In the initial stages of the project, the author had a visual demonstration of the issues involved in relation to equity. A meeting was called of the families who lived and farmed in the Wadigera watershed. When all the people had gathered, a clear picture emerged of the class distinctions operating. On the floor, in front, sat those farmers with lands in the lower reaches of the watershed – the most fertile and benefiting from irrigation. Behind them sat or stood those farmers with lands in the middle reaches – slightly less productive and more vulnerable to dry spells, without the benefit of irrigation. The people on the periphery were mainly tribals and those with holdings in the upper reaches of the catchment. The landless hung around. There were no women present initially, but as the meeting went on they strolled in, more as interested bystanders than as participants.

The discussions were initiated and dominated by the farmers with holdings in the lower reaches (those sitting in the front). It was evident that if the marginalized groups were to be given an opportunity to participate effectively, they would have to meet in a different situation.

To 'liberate' these groups requires time and a multi-pronged strategy in order to:

o equip these vulnerable sectors with the skills required, such as literacy, numeracy and those skills necessary to manage their institutions
o improve their ability to manage resources, businesses and cottage industries
o support them to acquire the confidence to change public policies and influence political decisions in their favour
o increase their access to credit, raw materials and markets
o enable women to have access to, and control of, resources and to change attitudes that inhibit their growth and obstruct their rightful place in society.

In the following sections we describe some of these strategies in more detail.

People's institutions in watershed management

One of MYRADA's major strategies is to support the development of people's institutions for resource management. These institutions are the foundation for sustaining interventions on both private and community lands. They also have an important role to play in ensuring equity, as discussed below.

Such institutions do not spring up overnight; they evolve over a period, during which the members agree on their rights and responsibilities and on sanctions on those who do not abide by accepted norms. It takes time for the members to develop the skills required to hold meetings, to negotiate and motivate collaborative agreements, to establish priorities, to accept rejections and yet remain within the group, to solve conflicts and to raise needed resources. However, they are essential if sustainability is to be achieved.

The role of people's institutions in watershed development has been debated for several years. Initially the concern was restricted to the need to hand over responsibilities for a watershed after the interveners withdrew. The accepted approach was that there should be only one association covering the entire watershed under treatment, which was usually between 1000ha and 2000ha the size was mainly conditioned by programme focus and budget constraints.

A case-study of Wadigera Micro-watershed Association (Box 22.2), together with experiences in other MYRADA Watershed projects, indicates that there are several social and economic factors that must be taken into consideration before forming a watershed association. A common and necessary feature of these groups is that they are homogeneous; their members stay together because of common ties or interests, without regular assistance and support from interveners.

MYRADA drew several insights from this and other experiences concerning the structure and role of Watershed Associations or Self-Help Groups.

The structure of self-help groups. It became clear that the official policy – that each watershed should have one association – was not viable. In other words, the social configuration of the association did not necessarily coincide with the geographical unit of a watershed.

MYRADA's experience indicated that groups larger than 15–20 tend to have in-built pressures to disintegrate. They are large enough to accommodate different interest groups as well as socially distinct configurations such as caste, blood, similar occupation, creed or origin. These large groups are not 'homogeneous'. To stay together they require constant intervention by outsiders like NGOs. Internal pressures go against the smooth functioning of the group, and interveners have to spend far more time and energy keeping these larger groups together than in actually helping them to acquire the skills required to manage resources (credit, watersheds, community plantations, forests etc.). It became clear, therefore, that the basic social grouping, even within a micro-watershed, had to be what MYRADA began to describe in 1987 as 'socially functional groups' or groups that do not require an outside intervener to stay together. These groups are usually small (less than 15–20 members), have common interests and are largely homogeneous in terms of caste, class, livelihood base, etc.

Box 22.2: Case-study of Wadigera Micro Watershed Association[1]

When MYRADA started the Gulbarga Project in the early 1980s, the area accepted as a unit of programme planning was called a sub-watershed, covering approximately 1500 ha. consisting of micro-watersheds, each of 200–300 ha. The official approach was that there should be one watershed association for the entire sub-watershed. When Wadigera Watershed Association was formed in 1987, despite being a micro-watershed of about 395 acres, the interveners decided that there would be just one watershed association, even though it was clear that the Watershed Association members were not a homogeneous group.

There were caste families and tribals; there were families with land inside the watershed who lived outside and who belonged to different social groupings; there were families living inside Wadigera but with lands outside the watershed, who had no major interest in the treatment activities in Wadigera micro-watershed since their lands would not benefit from these measures. Hence there were different levels of interest in, and commitment to, the development of the watershed's resources.

However, the Watershed Association did run well for two years, mainly because there was a large and dominant group belonging to the same caste in the Association. Yet the interests of the members did not coincide; conflicts arose and latent divisions based on social groupings surfaced, and eventually the Association collapsed.

During 1992, MYRADA staff studied the association. Of the 43 members, it was observed that only 27 members, who lived in Wadigera and who had lands in Wadigera, were attending meetings regularly. Those who were absent were those families that did not have lands in the micro-watershed although they lived there, and those who did not live in Wadigera but had land there.

The remaining 27 members were given training in the Self-Help Group (SHG) concept and in management, and members decided to take up community action programmes like road repairs, health, sanitation and soak pits. Many took out loans for buffalo, agricultural inputs, etc. A study done in 1994 indicated that the 27 members of the SHG had regained confidence and trust, and the group was working well.

---

[1] This case study was initiated by the author in 1990 to provide the basis for a learning experience shared by the staff.

Role of apex societies. Discovering the need for more than one SHG, however, immediately raises the issue that several people's groups in one micro-watershed would make the implementation and maintenance of an integrated treatment plan difficult to achieve. Moreover, since MYRADA's groups did not include large farmers, how could these be involved in watershed management?

In several micro-watersheds throughout the Gulbarga Project, more than one homogeneous group emerged. Maragutti micro-watershed for example, has seven such groups; Kalamandargi has four, others have three to five. There were also a few large farmers who did not join any of these groups but who were represented when watershed activities were discussed. To cope with this situation apex societies emerged; they were referred to in some places as watershed implementation committees (WICs) and in others as watershed management committees. These apex societies were formed by representatives from the small homogeneous groups, including representatives of farmers who had lands in the micro-watershed but did not live in it, and of large farmers. Apex societies were mainly involved in co-ordinating the implementation of the treatment plan and in dealing with outside interveners.

Credit as a tool for building capacity. To ensure that farmers continue to have access to, and control of, adequate resources once the interveners withdraw, MYRADA encourages these small homogeneous groups to establish savings, to convert grants from the project into loans recoverable to the common fund of the group. The management of the common fund of each group also helps the members to acquire the skills necessary to maintain records and accounts, to establish priorities, to apply sanctions and in general to establish a culture that supports common action and management of the watershed.

MYRADA also successfully changed banking policy to allow groups to obtain credit from banks. Loans are not given to individuals; they are allocated on the basis of the group's performance in terms of savings, loan disbursements and repayments, and in the maintenance of basic records. This linkage with banks provides the groups with access to resources that their common fund cannot provide. It also gives them adequate freedom to allocate these resources according to members' priorities.

The SHG members acquire considerable management experience while conducting the group's affairs. They learn to set priorities, to take decisions and risks, to draw up rules of behaviour to resolve conflicts, and to apply sanctions effectively for non-compliance. They learn the skills required to sustain co-operation and to set up and maintain the systems necessary (such as records) to make co-operation a regular feature. These skills and systems are absolutely necessary for managing the resources of a watershed. They cannot easily be acquired in a watershed programme that is heavily guided and influenced by interveners. The 'transfer of technology' approach, for example, leaves little room for local people's institutions to develop.

The SHG therefore provides a training situation, using credit as a tool or instrument. Credit is an appropriate tool because it is familiar to all and because it meets a felt need. Successful management of their common fund gives the group confidence that they can achieve certain objectives, provided they are willing to observe certain rules and create a culture that motivates people to support each other.

Linked to this, it is important for the project to remove the impression that the intervention is a total grant. The people need to have a stake in the investment in the watershed, if they are to maintain it. In Wadigera, for example, the watershed association decided to convert all the grants given by the government for agricultural inputs into loans returnable to the association. As a result, the common fund of the SHG was built up with recoveries from agricultural inputs amounting to Rs. 240 000.

Handling funds and decisions on the quality and quantity of work are crucial areas for effective and sustained participation of people; they must therefore be transparent and be seen to be just. In many areas where treatment measures had been undertaken previously, people suspected that outside contractors had been the major beneficiaries. Hence they viewed these measures more as a benefit to others rather than to themselves, and their commitment towards maintaining them was weakened.

Maintaining treatment measures

The small homogeneous SHGs have emerged as the appropriate institutions to maintain treatment measures. For example, it is the SHGs that have entered into agreements with farmers to regenerate and maintain their fallow lands. In Gulbarga over 35 such agreements have been negotiated (Box 22.3). This strategy has converted lands that were neglected and

---

Box 22.3:   Role of SHGs in regeneration of fallow lands

A women's SHG in Maramanchi Thanda watershed, Gulbarga, entered into an agreement with the Revenue Department under which about 25 acres of revenue waste land was leased out to them. They protected this block with a boulder wall. In 1993 the SHG paid its members a daily wage of Rs.10 to harvest grass from this area and later sold the grass as fodder for Rs.5000, leaving the group with a profit of approximately Rs.3000. and adequate dry fodder for the animals of all its members. The SHG has continued to manage the resource.

---

becoming eroded into regenerated areas that increased biomass and played a more effective role in managing soil erosion and water run-off than bunds.

The SHGs also have the financial resources from which an individual farmer can borrow to undertake maintenance work on the structures in his fields after the project ends. They provide ready access to finance for improvement and maintenance of treatment measures. Commercial banks and regional rural banks do not advance credit for such measures. The land development banks – where they exist and have resources – do have provision, but conservation measures on dryland are not considered viable investments. Further, the official specifications for treatment measures in terms of size, structure and location usually conflict with farmers' requirements and with what they can manage; this makes approvals of such projects difficult, and raises transaction costs.

Yet the farmer needs credit, either because he has to give up alternative wage employment to construct the treatment measures or because he has to hire bullocks, carts and labour. It is the SHGs that have provided this credit in small amounts as and when required, enabling the farmer to construct structures in stages according to the time available and depending on the opportunities for wage employment elsewhere. Where farmers have not gone in for conservation measures as extensively as expected, one of the major reasons is lack of credit without high transaction costs such as bank charges and processing costs. A recent study conducted by the National Bank for Agricultural and Rural Development indicates that the direct funding pattern to the SHGs has reduced transactions costs to individuals by 78 per cent and to the banks by 40 per cent. The transaction costs involved in providing loans to individuals under various subsidized systems are so high (between 30 per cent and 40 per cent of the amount sanctioned) that it discourages farmers from applying for credit for treatment measures, even though official interest rates are kept artificially low. If they are prepared to pay these costs, they prefer to apply for loans for income-generating projects where returns are high, or to use the loan and subsidy granted towards treatment measures for other purposes.

The exact role played by the SHG depends on the resource to be maintained:

○ If it is a common resource such as revenue waste land and private fallows that were protected and from which all the members derived benefits regularly, the SHGs have taken the initiative to organize, develop, manage and maintain it. The cost of efforts to acquire this common resource is shared by the SHG and the interveners. The SHG usually contacts the owner of the private fallow land and negotiates an agreement, while the NGOs can lobby the government for the release of revenue lands. The activities involved in developing this resource (boulder walls, planting,

301

gap filling, etc.) have been funded by the interveners with the SHG organizing the work and contributing labour at rates lower than those prevalent in the area. The SHG takes on the management when the members are confident that they have access to, and control of, the produce and adequate protection from cattle. Where the boundary walls do not offer full protection from cattle, the SHG is reluctant to manage the resource since stray cattle grazing in the area would cause conflict.[2] The SHG also prefers to develop areas where the rights to land, both in terms of ownership and use, are clear.

○ If the measure is on private land or on lands over which individual farmers have control and from which only the farmer benefits, like gully plugs or silt traps, the SHGs have agreed to advance loans to the farmer both to construct and maintain the structure. No grants have been given to individual farmers yet, but interest-free loans have been advanced by SHGs in some areas on the condition that repayments of these loans were given priority.

○ If the structure is large, such as weirs constructed with cement, the SHGs have not agreed to maintain them. Their position is that they do not have the resources and skills required to maintain such structures. MYRADA staff however, are of the opinion that if people place a cash value on water collected in weirs which is used by domestic animals for drinking and wallowing, as well as for washing clothes, adequate revenue can be mobilized to pay for maintenance. In Kadiri Project one farmer has entered into an agreement with the SHG (which supervised the building of the weir and manages it) to lift water for irrigation. The amount he pays to the SHG depends on the crop he grows and the area under irrigation. Water for animals and domestic purposes, however, especially in drought-prone areas where MYRADA's projects are located, is considered a basic need. To levy a charge, therefore, can hardly be considered. To expect farmers in the valley, whose wells have been recharged significantly due to water conservation measures in the upper reaches, to pay for the extra water available has not yet come within the range of possible sources for resource mobilization; sub-soil water is a common resource and will remain so in the foreseeable future.

In later watershed programmes, both in Gulbarga and elsewhere in MYRADA, the watershed associations decided to motivate farmers to contribute both in cash and in kind. They listed the various treatment measures and established priorities; the contribution from each farmer varied depending on the value he or she placed on each measure. For example, farmers tend to contribute much more to activities from which they expect immediate returns, like silt traps; while measures involving cement and

---

[2] The productivity consequences of this are discussed in Chapter 7.

concrete get lower priority, and hence lower contributions. The community is also not willing to contribute to works that benefit an individual farmer entirely, although in several cases the SHG has advanced loans to these farmers to implement measures from which they benefit exclusively.

The scale and impact of Gulbarga's self-help groups

As a result of the above strategy, at the end of 1993 there were 103 SHGs in the Gulbarga Project area, and more in the surrounding villages where people had come forward to start SHGs on their own. Of these 103 groups, 58 were composed of socially or economically marginalized groups like tribals and scheduled castes. Women's SHGs numbered 40, of which 20 were tribal groups.

Each of the 103 SHGs had a common fund, which the members managed according to rules they had decided upon. The total fund of all the SHGs amounted to Rs 2.6 million in December 1993. The total amount lent totalled Rs 4.2 million, while the overdues were only Rs 260 000.

There is a great deal of evidence to show that these SHGs provided an opportunity for the marginal groups to gain confidence in managing their affairs and to attain a higher level of self-reliance, since they no longer had to depend on money lenders (usually the larger farmers in the watershed) for loans. Several groups have taken up income-generating activities on their own. Three groups of women have undertaken the responsibility of managing a watershed – the group's common fund would benefit from the savings mobilized as a result of supervising and implementing the work themselves instead of hiring in contractors. These groups now play a major role in planning, budgeting and implementing watershed treatment. They are no longer passive spectators or content to remain on the margin when issues concerning their lives are being discussed.

Tribal SHGs have also taken a much greater role in watershed planning and implementation through their SHGs, and have asserted their rights through lobbying for infrastructure such as roads connecting their villages, and for bus services. They also decided to form an apex association of all the tribal SHGs and to put candidates forward for the local elections.

Supporting the landless

The landless tend to be marginalized in watershed programmes since most investments are on land. The NGO involved has a major role to ensure that this does not occur, and needs to take a view broader than simply invest-ment in land. During the implementation period, the landless do get work and income; but this must be sustained. In some watersheds this has been achieved by giving the landless a stake in the increased biomass and by increasing their capacity to earn, through training and support to start small businesses or cottage industries. They also become members of the credit groups and have access to credit. The marginal farmers and those with lands of low productivity on the upper reaches also fall into the same category as the landless, as they are not able to provide all their needs from the output of their farms. Hence these groups too must receive special attention in terms of investment and provision of skills for non-farm activities if equity is to be achieved.

The landless in Gulbarga, however, are still largely marginalized. Efforts were made by MYRADA to persuade large absentee landlords to lease land to landless families, but these have not been successful, mainly due to existing laws that favour the tenant. However, the landless are all members of SHGs. In Wadigera they availed themselves of loans for business and to purchase livestock for which fodder was available due to their access to regenerated areas. As areas under cash crops also grew (today almost double what it was in 1987), this has helped to provide the landless and marginal farmers with increased labour opportunities. However, while they are much less dependent on larger farmers than before, they are still not in a position to bargain for higher wages, which continue to remain below official rates.

Equitable distribution of benefits: a condition for co-operation

Some soil and water conservation structures or technologies, although technically sound, do not always provide equal benefits to all farmers (Box 22.4). Failure to take this into account can be a real obstacle, especially where the measure requires co-operation among farmers. For example, contour bunding requires the co-operation of all the farmers, as they cross private farm boundaries. It was clear that people were reluctant to co-operate, even though the benefits were accepted by most. Some refused to co-operate at all, because they felt contour bunds would exacerbate their situation. These were farmers who owned lands at the end of contour bunds which they expected would be flooded and be more prone to erosion. Others were concerned that contour bunds would mean they would lose the clear demarcation of their property, or that they would have to co-operate with their neighbours, when friction already existed between them.

The project discussed these problems with farmers, and decided that boundary walls should be integrated with contours whenever possible. Farmers would also be compensated in kind for conservation structures that they had built on their own fields, even if they did not meet the approved (official) dimensions.

The lesson learned from this experience was not to impose a technology that demands a level of co-operation that people are unwilling to offer, and much less to sustain, since they know that the benefits would be unequal.

Box 22.4: Traditional practices that undermine equity

Traditional practices can also undermine equity. For example, the traditional practice in drought-prone areas is to harvest silt, rather than to prevent erosion. The larger and more powerful farmers have lands in the lower reaches where silt can be harvested, and also tend to have the resources to invest in silt harvesting measures.

The traditional measure of diversion drains to protect fields from flooding is partially motivated by the objective of harvesting silt lower down, even though it deprives the upper reaches of the potential to collect water through protection measures. There were cases where larger farmers with land in the lower reaches objected to conservation measures higher up, since they suspected that their silt harvest would decline.

The trickle-down effect favours the comparatively better-off

It was also evident to people with holdings in the upper reaches of the catchment that they would not benefit as much from SWC measures as would those lower down. The trickle-down effect, in this case, would favour the better-off sections.

However, for a number of reasons, it is often easier for a project to introduce measures in the middle and lower reaches than in the upper reaches. Titles to land here are clearer, for example. In the upper reaches, the land has often been encroached upon; or they are degraded forest lands and it takes time to involve the Forest Department in any strategy of joint forest management; or the land belongs to the Revenue Department and there is no access to it.

These are major constraints in a strategy for watershed management that is attempting to foster equity. MYRADA has lobbied the government and Forest Department effectively to treat the upper reaches and to evolve a more equitable and participatory management system. Where the lands belong to the Revenue Department, several watershed groups have taken the initiative to approach the government to allow them to regenerate these lands and use the biomass (Box 22.3). Farmers in the middle reaches have been supported to excavate shallow open wells along streams to provide protective irrigation.

However, farmers in the upper reaches have still benefited less from watershed treatment when compared to those lower down. For example, experience from several watersheds after treatment indicates that:

○ productivity of farms in the upper reaches hardly increased, while the increase was significant (20–100 per cent) in the lower reaches after two

305

or three years. Farmers in the upper reaches were also reluctant to use hybrids

○ farmers in the upper reaches did not shift to cash crops: only the farmers in the lower and middle reaches took that risk
○ experiments with tree growing in the upper reaches were unsuccessful: this was due to lack of water for irrigation during the summer; the priority that farmers gave to food crops; and the fact that people suspected that if large areas were brought under tree crops, the Forest Department would have a stronger claim to recover encroached lands
○ in the case of encroached land, people hesitated to invest time and labour on treatment measures on lands over which they have no clear title.

The strong message that emerges from this experience is that the project must invest in improving the depth and quality of the soil in the upper reaches. This requires a higher level of investment than for lower reaches, and would also require new measures that are not accepted in the official guidelines for watershed treatment.

New relationships also need to be negotiated between people who depend upon encroached areas belonging to the Forest Department, and these officials. Could a win-win strategy be evolved that would meet the Forest Department's objective to green the area, as well as people's interest in experimenting with tree crops? This would depend on people's short-term food needs and user rights to the land not being eroded. The policies incorporated in the Joint Forest Management strategy provide spaces for such a win-win solution to evolve, but it still has to be implemented outside specific project areas.

Women and equity

In this section we attempt to analyse whether the interventions made in the watershed have benefited women.[3] We focus more on women's *material condition* (i.e., whether they have increased access to credit, biomass, wages, to opportunities for income-generation and transport to markets, and to better drinking water and health and education) rather than on the *position* of women in society.

However, it is worth pointing out that the original objectives of the PIDOW Gulbarga project did not specifically include improving women's condition.

Women's self-help groups

Evidence from various studies of the watershed have confirmed that the SHGs have created a social space for women over which they have control;

---

[3] We do not distinguish between women in poor families and those belonging to better-off groups.

they are able to discuss their problems, work towards solutions and meet their credit needs through these groups (Vasudevan and Ramaswamy, undated). There has also been a gradual shift in the nature of the activities that women desire to pursue (Box 22.5).

Box 22.5: The growing confidence of women

Initially kitchen gardens, soakpits and so on, were discussed in the women's SHGs. Now many of the SHGs have graduated into discussions about flour mills, milch animals and mini-water supplies. One woman's SHG has taken up trading fertilizers, jowar and ragi by using Rs 5000 that they saved as a group. This was highly appreciated by the village because it came when the village was hit by drought. The same group now wants to take independent charge of 120 acres of the watershed. There is even a case of a woman who has taken a loan to buy a plot of land. There are also a couple of instances of groups giving house loans to the homeless.

Source: (Vasudevan and Ramaswamy, undated).

There is also evidence that women have used loans for purposes that support their well-being and that of their children – particularly in the areas of health care and daily sustenance. These are areas that men tend to neglect.

Criteria to assess whether equity is being achieved

In conclusion, the role of the intervening NGO in striving to promote and sustain equity in watershed development can be guided partially by considering the following:

○ Do these vulnerable groups have access to credit for their consumption needs as well as for small income-generating initiatives? The credit groups in all MYRADA projects have provided this resource base; but in several instances, intervention was necessary to ensure that members of these groups, especially the landless, were included. A regular analysis of the lending pattern is also required to ensure that the landless receive a fair share of loans without undue restrictions or patronage. The NGO also has to intervene to form and support women's groups that manage credit, as well as to tackle problems that primarily affect them.
○ Are the landless and marginal farmers given access to the increased biomass in the watershed? For example, are they given priority to harvest and sell or use grasses that have regenerated on private fallow or common lands, even if they have to pay for this right in cash or kind?

○ In projects where the treatment activities are supported by grants, do the larger farmers get a major portion of investments? Is this the impression given, even if there is evidence to the contrary? If so, the intervention will acquire an image of a strong bias towards the rich, which will increase the feeling of alienation among the poor.

○ When treatment activities are organized, is priority given to employ the vulnerable sections living in the watershed, or are they implemented at times convenient to the interveners (government and NGOs) and through contractors who bring in labour from outside?

○ Is adequate priority given to the provision and upgrading of skills and other support services required for the landless and marginal farmers to diversify and extend their productive base to include small business and industries, besides animal husbandry?

○ Is there a strategy to cope with the marginalization of tribal groups? In Gulbarga they opted to join other tribal groups rather than non-tribal groups in their own micro-watershed. Tribal groups first need to build confidence and often prefer to build up wider support through associating with other tribal groups before joining the non-tribals. Care should therefore be taken to ensure that the pressure to build watershed associations does not result in institutions in which the tribals will not be able to participate effectively; such institutions would not strengthen equitable relationships.

○ Is there a strategy to support a shift to more equitable gender relations? In some cases counselling services were required in homes when men reacted negatively to their wives' participation in meetings. Are interveners equipped to provide this service? Apart from this, the formation of credit groups of women helps to give them access to, and control of, resources as well as certain time and space of their own. Are these groups formed and functioning effectively? Do these groups have any role in the management of the watershed's resources? How are wage rates assessed for men and women? These are some issues that interveners need to address.

○ Are these vulnerable groups gaining importance in watershed institutions such as credit groups and watershed development associations? Are they emerging as office bearers of these new institutions? Have any of their leaders been supported by the watershed institutions as candidates for elections to local bodies?

23
Institutional Strengthening for Watershed Development: The Case of the Aga Khan Rural Support Programme (AKRSP) in India

PARMESH SHAH and MEERA KAUL SHAH

AKRSP IS A non-governmental organization established in 1985. Its aim is to stimulate improved rural livelihoods based on productive natural resource management and income-generation through participatory approaches and strengthened village institutions.

This case-study describes AKRSP's alternative approach to watershed management, acting as a facilitator and catalyst, and building on the local knowledge base. Much initial time is invested in enabling village communities to participate in appraisal and planning, technology generation, adaptation and diffusion. The focus is on developing and strengthening institutions responsible for the sustainable and productive development of the watershed. What this approach means for the communities and support institutions involved are considered in detail.

AKRSP's approach

AKRSP works with village communities in three districts of Gujarat – Bharuch, Surendranagar and Junagadh. Watershed management and SWC is one of their main priorities. AKRSP approaches watershed development through a number of steps:

Participatory appraisal and planning

As a first step, people inventory their resources and technologies and appraise them for their development potential. This process is critical to ensure that the analytical capacity, the existing indigenous knowledge and the innovations carried out by the watershed inhabitants are the basis for planning the watershed programme. The appraisal process consists of mapping, walking transects, conducting well-being rankings, holding focus group discussions and finally prioritizing possible locally derived solutions. It leads to a simple proposal being generated by the community, which is shared with external agencies such as AKRSP, the government, banks, etc. This village natural resource management plan also becomes a future reference for monitoring and evaluating the programme.

Understanding existing village institutions

However, it is not enough merely to inventory technologies – they are only one part of the solution. It is also necessary to understand existing informal and formal group mechanisms and community institutions for watershed management on both private and common lands. The external support institution could usefully build on groups that have already developed a process of joint decision-making. Where group interaction is low, the support institutions need to work more intensively on developing group interaction and informal institutions before giving technical management or financial support.

Forming and supporting village institutions

After conducting these appraisals, if the village shows interest in developing its watershed and has a history of group or community action, it is asked first to form a village institution. This village institution should comprise more than 70 per cent of the watershed inhabitants and landholders, and must include all the upland smallholders. This village institution (VI) is expected to take responsibility for the functions of appraisal, planning, implementation, conflict resolution, group action, extension, monitoring and evaluation of the programme. The VI is asked to suggest areas of expertise available at the village level and those for which the community would require external support. The community is also asked to suggest mechanisms to be used for the development, management and effective protection of the community land.

Selecting and supporting village para-professionals

The VI nominates a group of two or three extension volunteers (EVs) from among the villagers. These volunteers are selected based on their interest in, and knowledge of, the traditional SWC practices in their village, their track record of innovation and experimentation and their willingness to promote extension and technology adaptation in the village. These volunteers are expected to serve as a bridge between the support institution, the VI and its members.

The extension volunteers are exposed to participatory methods, and practise these by carrying out simple observation and appraisal exercises in their villages. This is followed by a training programme ('experience sharing' would be a better description) in one of the villages. All the volunteers from different villages make a presentation about their village

310

based on the participatory appraisal they recently conducted. Training does not start with lectures by the outsiders, but instead involves outsiders as listeners. Discussion among various volunteers is encouraged and in some cases is facilitated by the outsiders. This enables the volunteers to articulate their viewpoint and develop capacity and capability for analysis and discussion.

Each session is followed by a discussion and presentation by the participants about what they found useful for their village. They are further able to contribute and add to the ideas communicated in these sessions. Based on these discussions, possible options – technical, financial and managerial – are evolved for the problems identified and are presented by the volunteers to each other.

Village-managed technology diffusion and extension system

The group of EVs then manage the extension process at the village level on behalf of the VI. They perform the following functions:

o acquiring a combination of technical and managerial skills
o becoming a link between the external support team and the VI
o maintaining contact with farmers through regular visits to their fields, developing individual treatment plans with them, aggregating these treatment plans and presenting them to the village institutions for their approval
o providing guidance to farmers for implementing these treatment plans. If the volunteer is not able to answer the queries of the farmer satisfactorily he is able to contact other farmers, volunteers and the members of the external support team
o organizing exposure visits of farmers within the watershed to facilitate networking and experience sharing
o facilitating the process of technology adaptation (Box 23.1).
o motivating farmers to adopt low-cost SWC techniques such as contour ploughing and planting vegetative strips
o collecting data on runoff and rainfall after going through a simple training programme for understanding its importance and its use
o observing the main waterflows and performance of structures during rains. The EVs also collect feedback on the technical guidelines for incorporation into next year's programmes.

In the long term, their role will also evolve to include:

o providing an interface with local and other external research, extension and technical institutions to enable more on-farm research, monitoring and development of adaptive technologies that build on the indigenous technical knowledge of the farmers

311

o providing a local manpower base for extension for the watershed management programme on a larger scale in the region. Each EV is capable of working on 400 hectares for aggregate watershed treatment work. One hundred such volunteers have the potential of working on 40 000 hectares of the watershed over a period of five to seven years.

At the village level the EVs work in teams of three or four, with one volunteer concentrating on the SWC activities, another on dryland farming

---

Box 23.1: Supporting and disseminating innovations

The EVs ask farmers to make sketches of the innovations they are trying out. Farmers are good at making such sketches and line diagrams of these techniques. Extension volunteers collect these drawings and present them to other farmers to encourage further discussion.

All these experiences are shared, and their impacts assessed. Discussions are held with the help of the diagrams to suggest modifications. Sometimes local solutions are more effective than the solutions evolved or suggested by the outsiders. At other times local solutions are inadequate or have considerable scope for improvement.

Discussions are now held with the farmer facing the problem in the field, and his reactions to the diagram are sought. Farmers suggest specific changes and thus contribute to the technology evolution process. Finally, technologies (adapted and evaluated on farmers' fields) are compiled in the form of technical guidelines. These guidelines are converted into manuals in a very simple form that can be understood and used by the EVs. These technical guidelines become raw material for the technology diffusion process.

The extension volunteers follow the experimentation process with the farmers again in the field during the experimentation phase and finally the results are observed. The advantage of this approach is that the extension volunteers and the farmers both become more observant and are dynamically engaged in developing and adapting technologies and experimenting with them. They do not stick to a blueprint technology. They are also able to discern between various technologies suggested by the outsiders, and learn to experiment with them. It becomes a learning process in which innovations are constantly encouraged.

At the end of the agricultural or the rainy season, feedback sessions are held with the farmers and technologies they have tried out are evaluated through impact analysis. The data are presented in the form of a diagram to farmers and the volunteer groups.

---

and rainfed agriculture and the third on the credit and other commercial activities of the VI.

The VI is responsible for monitoring the performance of the EVs. One of these volunteers, who has relatively better skills in accounting and financial matters is nominated as the co-ordinator of this group and also acts as the secretary of the VI.

Although EVs were initially volunteers, the sacrifices they were making in terms of time and income forgone led to a decision by the village institutions to compensate them. Furthermore, the fact that most of the EVs provided a better quality of service and coverage than the existing village functionaries, aided this decision. Village institutions decided to pay the volunteers Rs 10 per acre of the land treated under the watershed. On average an EV is able to earn Rs 5000 per annum for the services rendered. This is a significant amount of money compared to the prevailing wage rates in the area. EVs are also paid on the basis of their performance, and similar incentives are offered to them, based on either the savings on cost of operations or the resultant increase in income, for providing community services such as community ploughing, community plant protection and credit.

Some EVs with higher commitment and aptitude have gone beyond their narrow role of provider of services and have shown initiative in taking up community extension beyond their villages, and in some cases beyond their watershed. These EVs have been designated master extension volunteers (MEVs). This has greatly reduced the dependence on AKRSP staff for planning, execution and monitoring the programme.

Some of these MEVs have performed better than some of the support institution team members. AKRSP decided to use their services as a team member of the support institution and to pay them incentives based on their performance. This might lead to the development of a local support institution, which would be spearheaded by these MEVs and represent all the VIs. It is also possible that a small group of these village professionals would like to move out to a new area and start similar processes in other neighbouring regions facing similar problems. This would still leave behind a fairly strong VI to work on managing and upgrading the watershed.

There is a strong possibility that this network of volunteers will remain after the withdrawal of the support institution. AKRSP is now working towards developing a federated support institution of these volunteers, which will take on the functions of the support institution after it withdraws.

Participatory monitoring and impact analysis

This has proved to be a very useful tool for people to explain, in their own terms, the linkages between investments in the watershed development process and the resulting benefits. Our experience shows that farmers can carry

313

out impact monitoring exercises effectively using field sketches, maps and diagrams related to an area, the watershed or an activity. The process starts with farmers preparing a baseline map that depicts the pre-project status of different resources. Information collection starts with individual farmers, or a group of farmers, and is aggregated and presented in a meeting where the information is cross-checked and verified before finalization by the villagers.

Mapping exercises are carried out with different social and economic sections in the village. Equity mapping is also done to assess the impact of an intervention on the poor, and can be done with the poorer sections of the community. Sensitive issues, such as the power of certain castes in cornering all the benefits of the programme, can more easily be dia-grammed, allowing people to discuss them without feeling intimidated.

Aggregated findings of the impact maps are presented to the community for verification and discussions on:

○ investment and returns
○ technologies tried out – which worked and under what conditions, which did not and why
○ what are the local variations and diversities
○ what is the range of options to choose from
○ bottlenecks in implementation
○ generation of technology innovations and adaptation for the village
○ what next?

This process of participatory monitoring involves monitoring the institu-tional aspects, as well as the technical and the economic aspects of the programme. Indicators for performance, participation and equity in a VI have been developed and are being monitored by the village institutions.

Performance indicators and impacts

What are the impacts of this approach? AKRSP measures the performance of the programme according to a number of criteria (Table 23.1), and has compared these with the outcomes of more conventional, top-down approaches.

Investment in watershed management

In the initial stages the process of facilitation and institution-building is intensive and should be treated as an investment. In subsequent years higher investments are made by the community in the support institution. AKRSP withdraws some of its staff, where communities take respons-ibility, and uses them to facilitate similar processes in other areas.

The capacity of extension volunteers has improved considerably and they are now in a position to triple the expenditure and investment in the watershed. It should be noted that this increase in investment has been accompanied by a large increase in the community's contributions (Table 23.1), building the local stake in the programme. Yet government is giving a 100 per cent subsidy for similar programmes in the area. This reinforces the argument that local communities invest more of their internal resources in the programme if they are supported through a facilitating institution once their local capacities are strengthened.

Cost effectiveness

The unit cost of watershed management, including soil and water conservation structures and planting, and all the management costs, is about Rs.1340 per hectare. Government watershed management programmes can incur costs of from Rs 3000 to 7000 per hectare. This demonstrates that when the community is given responsibility for planning and implementation, they can develop viable and cost-effective approaches.

Not only are the costs lower under this approach, but the community and the village institutions are also able to generate resources locally to pay for the services rendered by the extension volunteers. This has implications for initiating large-scale extension programmes dependent on the outside

Table 23.1: Indicators for performance of AKRSP-supported watershed development programme in Gujarat, India

Performance indicators	1988–89	1989–90	1990–91
Number of villages covered (cumulative)	3	29	36
Area developed each year (ha)	240	852	2146
Investment made (Rs)	78 515	663 603	2 862 560
Contribution by community (Rs)	36 372	321 395	1 445 046
Overheads as a percentage of the total programme cost	29%	14%	5%
Cost of preparing treatment plan per acre (in Rs)	130	45	10
Cost of arranging community ploughing per acre (in Rs.)	50	30	5
Area of watershed covered per professional (Ha)	40	150	220
Net income increase effected by each professional (in Rs.)	44 000	165 000	242 000
Number of extension volunteers trained	38	83	77

professionals. One of the reasons why locally managed and administered extension systems have become popular with the farmers, and that they are ready to pay for them, is because the existing system is not client-oriented and is largely ineffective.

Efficiency of the support institution

The efficiency of the support institution can be assessed by the capacity of its professionals to facilitate investments in the watershed by the village institution, physical coverage of the watershed and the ability to effect income increase for the watershed inhabitants. A good example is training costs, which decreased significantly after the villagers became trainers. It takes AKRSP 50 to 60 person-days to train a group of 20 village extension volunteers. AKRSP professionals have first to change their attitudes, learn from local people, facilitate the process of experience-sharing and remove their biases. When EVs take the training role the process can be completed efficiently in 10 person-days. They know the situation, they facilitate the process better, they are familiar with local classifications and are able to generate responses without bias and in the absence of outsiders.

Productivity and income generation

Table 23.2 demonstrates the impact on productivity and income in the watersheds in which AKRSP is working. This shows a significant increase in the productivity of various crops and profitability of the investments made. The impact of long-term flows from common property resources have not been taken into account in these computations. These data are no different from any other watershed management project. They have been

Table 23.2: Productivity changes for major crops in the watershed in Bharuch District, Gujarat

Crop	Average productivity in kg per ha		Increase in productivity
	1987	*1991*	
Paddy (lowland)	90	228	153%
Pigeon pea	63	140	122%
Paddy (upland)	400	750	88%
Cotton	153	234	53%
Ground nut	355	498	40%
Sorghum	205	282	38%
Sorghum (local)	166	194	17%
Nagli*	333	366	10%

* Local coarse grain

316

presented to show that participatory facilitator institutions can also effect significant increases in productivity and income generation.

Multiplier benefits and additional investment in the watershed

Additional benefits that multiply the productivity and sustainability of the watershed have also accrued due to strengthening village institutions. For example, the VIs have been able to mobilize local savings, initiating savings-based group credit and pooled marketing of the produce. These VIs, with a savings base of Rs 0.5 million (collected over a period of five years), advanced credit worth Rs 1 million and marketed a turnover of about Rs 4 million jointly in 1996, a performance better than most VIs working with irrigated farmers in the same area.

This process not only improves the viability of watershed management as an activity but also helps further to strengthen village institutions as they are able to build a capital base, enabling members to take risks that they would never have taken in the watershed, even if physical development had taken place.

Sustainability: environmental, economic and institutional

The sustainability of an approach can be commented on only after a significant time span, but some initial indicators include:

○ On average, about 30 metric tons of soil is saved per acre for the watersheds where AKRSP has been working.[1] It should be noted that in a number of these watersheds the inhabitants were earlier mining the common lands by taking cartloads of top soil. On average, 30 cartloads of top soil are saved from the common land per acre of land treated. This, coupled with SWC, grass seeding and plantation on the common lands, is beginning to allow natural regeneration.

○ Productivity increases have been sustained over a period of three years, despite variations in rainfall in all the different eco-regions. However, the data for a drought year would have to be monitored to study the impact on productivity in a stress year.

○ In Surendranagar District (a semi-arid area) farmers stated that in the last low rainfall year the moisture retention was good and helped save the crop in the treated area.

○ The investments made by farmers on their private lands increased by more than 50 per cent after initiating the watershed management programme. The village community has also taken up a number of community operations such as ploughing, plant protection and use of

---

[1] Soil loss has been measured through run-off plots and studying deposition profiles.

317

implements and post-harvest equipment, coupled with credit and pooled marketing of the agricultural produce. This shows that the village institution is becoming a conduit for higher economic investment and diversification. This is also reflected in the confidence of the financial institutions to advance credit to these institutions, despite a large membership of small farmers with rainfed holdings. These were earlier considered a high risk group by the bankers.

o These watersheds had a high degree of migration before the VIs initiated watershed management activity. There is a dramatic drop in the migration rate, leading to sustained livelihoods for the community. This has resulted in higher school enrolment, improved nutrition and health standards.

o Finally, the development of village institutions with a local pool of professionals and volunteers and their federations will help ensure that the development process is sustainable.

Equity. The initial planning approach ensures that all types of land are covered and that landless families have a significant role in the development of the common lands. Areas are selected that have a large proportion of small rainfed farmers, and AKRSP is also working with the Harijan and the Maldhari communities resettled from a forest sanctuary to make way for the Gir Lion. During the village interactions, the community is encouraged to treat the land at the top of the watershed where most of the land belongs to the poorest sections of the village community.

Developing local capacity and scaling up. In a short time-frame, developing local capacity and scaling up development programmes are not compatible. However, if the external support institution takes the role of a facilitator and spends enough time on the participatory process, the programmes are cost effective, result in more effective use of the resources, can be scaled-up by the local institutions without high overheads and lead to village institutions taking up activities having multiplier effects, like credit and savings. But this takes time.

Implications for policy and practice

Our limited experience indicates that participatory watershed programmes will require major reversals of the existing policies of research and extension, organizational processes, resource allocations and evaluation procedures and, most importantly, the attitudes of professionals. These reversals are possible in public systems and bureaucracies and are not necessarily happening only in NGO-supported projects. These implications are illustrated below.

318

Design and operation of implementing institutions. In the process described above, there is a strong emphasis on building local capacity and local institutions *before* substantial financial investments are made. Initially, therefore, the implementing organization could start on a smaller scale with a few committed professionals, who gain intensive experience and become trainers for the new staff joining the organization. Major staff recruitment and expansion of the organization would take place only *after* local capacity for analysis and appraisal is created and people are able to articulate the areas in which they need support from outsiders.

The external organizations would have to function in a way that allows learning from the people and promotes capacity development and institutional building as the strategic objectives in the initial phase of the programme. Corresponding skills in professionals and operating procedures would have to be evolved.

This would also mean some loss of hierarchy and more team-work in these institutions. The team leader would have to use less authority and more communication skills. Initially the structure would have to be in a loose form allowing for flexibility, initiative, innovation and failure. Once programmes are evolved after a consultative process and building of human resources, some more formal organizational aspects need to be incorporated to ensure effective management.

At present the bureaucracy of many support institutions stifles innovation and initiative. The programme leadership has an important role to play in ensuring that learning takes place in an enabling environment. Field work by staff members needs to be encouraged and there should be freedom regarding field trips and visits for learning and carrying out consultations with villagers. Field trip reports and learning should be shared in departmental forums to encourage discussion and analysis.

The staff performance evaluation procedures would have to be radically different from the conventional programmes. The emphasis should be on what the staff have learnt and what processes have been initiated in the communities. The leadership should actively conduct reviews and ask staff members to make presentations on the new learning and the process. This process has been used in the watershed management programme being implemented by the Dryland Development Board in Karnataka and the West Bengal Social Forestry Programme in India, and has shown positive results in the long run.

A related issue concerns the tenure of officials involved in the programme. The core group of trainers needs to be involved and retained in the programme for longer compared to the other technical and implementing staff. This would ensure that the aspects of institution-building and creating local capacity are strengthened in the initial phase of the programme, resulting in long-term sustainability.

Project cycle. The conventional project cycle framework would also have to be modified to include learning, capacity-building, institution-building and development of human resources as the initial stages in the programme. This could be followed by the conventional stages of planning, implementation, and evaluation. For watershed management projects the emphasis in the first two years could be on the preparation of watershed treatment plans by the community, creating institutions for them, encouraging small experimentation networks of the farmers to evolve technologies specific to their watershed, and ensuring that financial resources are earmarked for the plan. Once these are ready the project cycle could involve construction and extension activities.

In the last phase, the role of the support institutions is to work towards building federated support institutions for these villages, which can not only sustain the development of watersheds in their own watershed areas but also take up the responsibility in neighbouring areas or regions. The external support institution also helps the local support institution in developing linkages with the donors and with government. This ensures financial support for such institutions on a sustained basis in the initial stages. The support institution could then diversify into providing other commercial services in the watershed on an on-going basis, and also take up new activities on behalf of the watershed inhabitants for upgrading the watershed. Processing, credit, input supply and marketing activities are increasingly being taken up by these support institutions.

The project cycles need to be longer, and the technical and management objectives of the project could be evolved after the initial phase of capacity-building and assessment of the institutional and local capacity. The performance assessment procedures and the criteria for assessment would also need to change, with innovation and learning becoming important indicators for performance assessment.

Evaluation indicators. Project performance is rarely evaluated in terms of local capacity-building and institution-building. New approaches and indicators need to be developed to measure institutional performance and the institutional capacity to perform the functions for the management and maintenance of the projects. There is a need to evolve evaluation methods that recognize that material benefits, and those from institution-building, occur in tandem. This would make assessment of performance in different stages of the project cycle easier and more effective.

Financial implications. As demonstrated in the earlier sections of the chapter, there are compelling economic reasons for participatory approaches to watershed development. The present overhead costs of the soil and water conservation programmes are very high in proportion to the programme cost since state technical and extension bureaucracies are trying to perform functions which they are incapable of doing cost effectively and efficiently. If para-professionals and local institutions are trained and partnerships are developed with them for the implementation of the watershed management programmes, the costs of these programmes could decrease considerably and the programme would tend to be more efficient and client-responsive. Also, the bureaucracies would be more effective in more suitable roles. The speed and the scale of the programmes could be considerably enhanced through this process. This is different from the common assumption that participatory approaches are feasible only on a small scale and are difficult to scale up.

Using para-professionals for scaling up. It has been demonstrated earlier in this chapter that para-professionals take on a number of functions previously fulfilled by bureaucracies. With village-level extension functionaries managed by village institutions, client groups can decide financial compensation packages for these functionaries. The size of extension bureaucracies would in this way be reduced.

The role of the external professional would be reformed to one of creating confidence in the local community about their capacity, promoting building and strengthening local institutions, participating in creating that capacity by training and networking and providing technical choices, options and support when asked for by the village institutions. The para-professionals over time would develop relationships with research stations and offer collaborative partnerships to these institutions to carry out on-farm research in their area.

Extension process and technology adaptation

To fit into this approach, the extension process would have to undergo a reorientation. The emphasis in extension needs to be on involving people in the analysis of problems and ensuring that the existing knowledge, innovations and experimentation in the watershed are made accessible to the inhabitants in the watershed.

Subsequently, the extension process would also involve the interaction of the village volunteers with the research and extension wings of the support institutions to present the client viewpoint. Extension wings of the external support institution would play the role of information providers and facilitate the interaction of the research wing with the village institution extension functionaries. The technology generation process could take place at the farm level, and villagers would be inclined to adopt and adapt technologies evolved at the local level. Such a process should provide feedback to the external research institutions for the research agenda in the watershed and create an internal laboratory for experimentation in the watershed.

Research management

The present research system focuses mainly on off-farm trials. Such research is important and is still relevant for relatively well endowed and irrigated areas where the farming systems are simpler. However, complex, risk-prone and diverse rainfed areas require a significantly higher component of on-farm research than is now being undertaken. The present research institutions have made some efforts at undertaking on-farm research but have failed because of the professional attitudes and the lack of sustained experimentation and facilitation at the village level. The villagers do not own these experiments, and participate mainly to get financial incentives such as supply of seeds. Also, these experiments do not plug into the existing network of experimenters in the village. The existing indigenous experiments involve reducing risks and trying to get higher returns through change in practices without significant additional investments in cash.

The access to the village institutions and their functionaries could increase the capacity of the research institutions to do effective research and get rapid feedback on the performance of the new technologies and practices introduced. This will also help in evolving location-specific technologies. If the farmers and their institutions are roped in as effective collaborators in the research process and take an active part in deciding the research agenda of the research institutions, the subsequent process of technology diffusion and adaptation would also happen more effectively and smoothly.

Training

Training is one of the most critical inputs for creating local capacity for extension and management of the village institutions. Most training would have to be done through field exercises and on-the-job learning; not in classroom situations. Trainers would themselves first have to move out, spend substantial time in the field learning about the problems and, above all, develop skills of active listening, facilitation and the use of participatory methods for group work. Building the skills of farmers as trainers also needs to be explored. This availability of good trainers is likely to be a limiting factor in the spread of participatory programmes.

Decentralization and democracy

At present, most development and watershed plans are drawn up by the technical and other bureaucrats in the district office. This does not promote decentralization and participation in decision-making by either formal or informal institutions, in spite of the rhetoric of Five-Year-Plans and government policy documents. Community participation is hampered by people's knowledge that they would never have a real say in decisions about their watersheds. If communities are enabled to develop and implement their plans they would be encouraged to develop local institutions and capacity by making higher contributions than they normally do, and take more risks. The quality of their participation is considerably enhanced. The experience has also indicated that their participation in the decision-making of formal institutions like Panchayats, and forums like the Gram Sabha, also becomes more effective and leads to changes in the attitude of the bureaucracy and the political environment. The leadership pattern changes in favour of functional leaders (para-professionals and active members of the village institution, who are leaders by virtue of their performance) over traditional leaders (who are there by virtue of lineage, patronage, muscle power and social hierarchy). This could have long-term implications for the improvement in the quality and functioning of local democracy.

24
Watershed and Community Development in Tamil Nadu, India

JOHN DEVAVARAM, ERSKINE ARUNOTHAYAM,
RAJENDRA PRASAD and JULES N. PRETTY

Rural life in Tamil Nadu

THERE ARE MORE than 45 000 villages in the state of Tamil Nadu. Most people rely for a significant part of their livelihoods on the natural resource base, yet this is under increasing pressure. Growing population, inappropriate external interventions, the breakdown of traditional resource management systems, and deep socio-economic divisions all contribute to this pressure.

Although agriculture is the predominant occupation of rural people, many have little or no access to productive resources. Set against a background of poverty, communal riots, religious rituals, land disputes and conflicts with government schemes, the challenges for improving the resource base together with people's welfare are particularly great.

The Society for People's Education and Economic Change (SPEECH)

SPEECH is a non-profit voluntary organization primarily concerned with improving people's livelihoods through self-help and local capacity development. Established in 1987, the organization works mainly in Kamarajar District, a region known for its acute droughts, erratic monsoons, poor services and entrenched social and cultural divisions. SPEECH's central belief is that sustainable development cannot be achieved without the full participation and involvement of local groups and communities. The empowerment of people to control their own resources and take their own decisions is seen as the fundamental principle and goal.

This people-centred approach contrasts strongly with the conventional approach to rural development. Most government and many non-governmental agencies make plans and act with no local involvement. Many speak of participation, but still participation tends to mean local people participating in what external agencies want to do. As a result, enormous amounts of money and effort have been wasted. In addition, dependency on external systems has increased, and the gap between the 'haves' and the 'have-nots' has also grown.

None the less, there have been changes in recent years, with an increasing number of programmes and projects aimed at building on local knowledge, and enhancing local people's capacity to work together for welfare improvements.

SPEECH's approach has been to help build and strengthen groups and institutions in 45 villages of Kamarajar. The initial involvement is through the establishment of non-formal education classes. Following discussions, local people choose their own village animators, who then receive training in basic teaching methods, participatory learning methods (such as PRA), conflict resolution, songs and stories. They also receive a small honorarium, but essentially remain as farmers or labourers. The animators visit every house, raising awareness of the common problems faced and the need for effective organization and participation to resolve them. After a period of discussion, plays and other forms of interaction, local people form a *sangha* or village committee.

Sangha leaders, elected by the members, then attend a 30-day training course spread throughout the year. Key personnel from government organizations and banks are invited to attend and meet the *sangha* leaders. As *sanghas* become more confident, they begin to develop their own capacity, providing for health care, roads, credit and so on. Representatives are elected to a cluster-level governing council, an independent society that provides a platform for local groups to address emerging concerns.

The village of Paraikulum

Paraikulum is one of Tamil Nadu's typical villages, where there are all types of socio-economic, cultural and caste imbalances. There are some 100 households, of which only 20 are landless. In the past, farmers cultivated both rainfed and irrigated lands fed by seasonal rainfall that collects in the village tank. There are some 98ha of village land, of which 32 are rainfed. The landless had to rely on work on farms during the four-month agricultural season, but have to migrate out of the community during the rest of the year. Many farming families, too, have had to rely on out-migration during the summer season to guarantee a source of income.

The community is remote, the only access being a two-kilometre walk along a railway line. Consecutive monsoon failures in the late 1970s-1980s led to farmers abandoning rainfed land to concentrate just on the tank-feedable wetlands. The upper watershed of some 32ha became increasingly degraded, losing its topsoil through gully and sheet erosion. The land was over-grazed, and with increased run-off during the rains, less and less water was percolating to groundwater. The community was caught in a downward spiral.

There had been attempts by government to rehabilitate this land in 1986, but the process was a complete failure. As part of a wider land development programme, government contacted local leaders with a plan for soil and water conservation. A group of small farmers had tried to delay the work so that they could learn about what was planned, and so influence the choice of measures and technologies, but they were ignored. Within a few weeks, agricultural engineering experts were in the community constructing contour bunds and waterways, gully plugs, concrete outlets and new channels.

The SWC technologies led to many new conflicts, with bunds crossing land ownership boundaries, with enforced tenurial changes, with crop losses because of inappropriate drainage, and with wage losses for many landless families. Shortly after the government officers left the community, farmers gradually dismantled the structures and returned to their original system of management. At this point, officials accused farmers of not co-operating and even of deliberately obstructing the work, and so denied them any follow-up support. This whole approach induced great cynicism and bitterness among the community about 'outsiders'.

However, in 1991 the women's *sangha* of Paraikulum approached SPEECH to request their support for redeveloping this now barren land of the upper watershed. SPEECH decided to initiate a community planning process using PRA methods to ensure that any plans were developed by the community on their own terms.

The participatory process of planning and action

With the help of the village animator (extension volunteer) and the women's *sangha*, SPEECH initiated a process of participatory planning using a wide range of PRA methods. The whole process of community analysis, dialogue and planning took about three months.

Timelines and trend change analysis

Discussions were held with older members of the community in small groups of different social and class groups. These produced a clear historical view of Paraikulum in terms of water resources, grazing, cropping patterns, leadership structures, land use, animal populations, women's status, education, health practices and resource management over a 60-year period. When these findings were presented and discussed in wider community meetings, it was the youth who said that they learned most – for the first time having the opportunity to learn about their community's history.

Social and resource mapping

Various social and resource maps were constructed by both women's and men's groups to illustrate a wide range of geographic issues. These provoked great discussion within the community. When completed, these were redrawn by youngsters and left in the non-formal education centre for further discussion.

Seasonal calendars were prepared by various farmer groups to explore rainfall, cropping, migration and off-season employment patterns.

Focusing on inequity through wealth ranking

Criteria for well-being were developed from the social mapping, and five groups of villagers divided the 100 households into different wealth categories. The extension volunteer played a vital role in facilitation, helping eventually to consolidate all the groups' analyses. This eventually led to a long debate, during which the community was able to appreciate the particular needs of the poorest households. Problem and opportunity lists were then developed for each wealth category.

Prioritizing problems and opportunities

The next part of the process involved the community analysing and prioritizing these problems and opportunities. In the end, top priority was given to the issue of land rehabilitation of the 32ha of upper watershed. This was seen to be of benefit to small and marginal farmers and, with the increased demand for labour, also to the landless.

At this point, the community decided to organize itself into a new forum – the Paraikulum watershed community.

Field planning

The members of the forum then set about planning in the field. Groups led by local motivators spent time walking through the watershed observing and identifying problems. All groups walked throughout the whole watershed, giving them all a clear idea of the range of problems.

A few youngsters were encouraged to start depicting these on a large map, with each group then adding its findings. Gradually a watershed treatment plan was developed, with ideas for specific technologies identified according to location and landowner. This was then further developed by the whole community, with resources, responsibilities and roles allocated to each group in the community.

Treatment plan

The treatment plan included traditional soil conservation measures, treatment of gullies with earthen bunds, vetiver grass planting, contour ploughing, field bunds, well digging and tree planting. In addition, the plan included a system of raising dairy cattle using fodder to be grown on the rehabilitated land.

The fields would be cultivated with groundnuts and other legumes, with various fruit and fodder trees planted near the field boundaries. One innovation developed by farmers was that trees should be planted on only two boundaries of each field in an 'L' shape, so that neighbours would not come into conflict in future years. Trees were planted with alternate fruit-fodder/shade-fruit to discourage pests.

Another co-operative agreement involved the siting of the well. It was agreed that water would be needed on the watershed, and so all agreed that whoever's land was selected for the well would receive compensation from everyone else. The well was taken down to 10 metres depth and, with the construction of a side-bore, has been able to supply 9–10 hours of water daily.

The women's *sangha* established their own nursery to grow tree seedlings for the watershed. They also agreed a rota for watering the seedlings once planted.

Conflicts and innovations during implementation

The process of watershed development in Paraikulum has not been a straightforward implementation of the villagers' plan. New problems have arisen, which have needed innovative solutions from the community. The capacity to deal with emergent problems is an important element of watershed and community development. Some of the problems have been life-threatening; others a major challenge to the co-operative effort.

The most serious problems arose from a factional conflict with a neighbouring village. Seeing the successful rehabilitation, wealthy farmers from one particular political party claimed the land for themselves. This resulted in serious clashes, and the eventual cutting down of all the trees one night. Tension continued to rise, until the women's *sangha* was able to bring in a legal surveyor to make a binding decision. He decided to allocate 0.13ha to one of the non-Paraikulum farmers, and the Paraikulum community let the land go.

Another problem arose when two male farmers near the well decided in 1993 to cultivate paddy rice. They said it was a trial but, on getting very good yields, decided to expand rice cultivation much more. The women's group, however, said that this should not happen, as the rice consumed too much of the communal water. In the end, all farmers agreed to grow only finger millet, pulses, sesame and other vegetables.

Technology innovation and adaptation

The five years (1991–96) of watershed development in Paraikulum have been characterized by a wide range of innovations and adaptations.

Vegetable cultivation. After two seasons of growing groundnut and sesame, farmers diversified into vegetables in the third year, and now produce 50–60kg per day. Using only local resources, women have been able to develop a successful local system of vegetable management, particularly of lady's finger (okra) and squashes. Even in droughts, they still get some vegetables.

Adaptations to conservation practices. Vetiver grass was planted on the spill-ways at field boundaries to slow water flow. This was replaced by other grasses when it was felt that they could also be cut and carried for livestock feed. At first, the design for the spillways was for them to be equidistant, but farmers resited some over time according to the differences in slope and water flow.

Dairy management. As the landless families in the *sangha* were not directly benefiting from the land development, the women's group located a one ha plot of land owned by an absentee landlord. They bought the land for the whole group. Fodder is now grown, and is used by all the members. In the serious drought year of 1994–95, farmers in neighbouring villages had to sell all their animals. But in Paraikulum, everyone had sufficient fodder. Each household now has an average of two animals each. These animals are owned and managed entirely by the women.

Gully management. Check dams were first used for water flow manage-ment, but these were later supplemented with stone platforms, vetiver strips, stone-clad gullies and diversion dams to ensure water was fully diverted to the percolation ponds.

Trees. Guava, pomegranate, neem, mango and coconut were planted on field boundaries, with tamarinds on the edge of the watershed itself. The coconuts later failed, along with mulberry that had been planted near to the well as part of a government-subsidized scheme.

Fish in the irrigation tank. With the better water management, there is now water in the tank all year round. The women's group has deepened an area of the tank close to the village, and added a net to keep fish in. This has brought a new source of protein to the village.

Impacts in Paraikulum

Changes in productivity

There have been considerable impacts on agricultural productivity in the community. The 32ha on the upper watershed produces various beans, groundnuts, sesame, vegetables and livestock fodder. Groundnut and green gram yields have been of the order of four tonnes per ha. Vegetable production is roughly 50–60kg daily, and even in droughts some fresh vegetables are available for each family. As all households have dairy cattle, there is also the benefit of regular milk production. Each member of the group saves Rs 10 weekly for a revolving fund to benefit the whole group. The fish in the tank are now an important new protein source.

The greatest contribution, however, has come from better water management, which permits an extra crop of rice to be cultivated on the wetlands. This means that an extra 100 tonnes of rice are produced each year in Paraikulum.

The increase in cultivated area has meant an increase in demand for labour. Agricultural labourers used to receive Rs 12 per day – this is now Rs 18 daily. Now that they no longer need to migrate, this is seen as a positive social benefit to family life in the community.

Changes in resources

There have been many positive changes to the resource base:
o siltation has fallen, and is visibly being trapped by the various soil conservation structures
o the water level in the community well has increased, and the four wells in and around the watershed that used to dry up in summer are now permanently wet
o moisture retention in the soils has increased
o land value has increased from Rs 2000 to over Rs 22 000 per hectare
o leaves from the neem trees are used as a traditional medicine for the livestock.

Changes in resilience and self-reliance of the community

Paraikulum is clearly more resilient and self-reliant as a result of the five years of participatory watershed management. The community works together in a co-operative fashion; the agricultural system as a whole is more productive; and resources are spread more equitably.

Villagers feel they can do things for themselves now, and now say 'we don't want any outside contractors coming into our village – we can do everything ourselves'. SPEECH is no longer working in Paraikulum.

There are now three new groups in Paraikulum – the women's *sangha*, the landless group, and the watershed management group.

The greater land productivity is having a considerable social impact – no household in Paraikulum now needs to migrate to seek work and income, even during the severe drought of 1994–95.

Replication and spread

Much of the strength of the community of Paraikulum has been derived from the sense of common purpose developed by the 45 village groups.

These work together in an apex organisation called a cluster-level governing council. Lessons are shared among these communities, with one learning from another about problems encountered and innovative solutions developed.

Spread is beginning to occur, however, to communities not part of this structure. The people of the nearby village of Kottam, for example, have asked both Paraikulum villagers and SPEECH to help them rehabilitate some degraded land. A similar participatory planning process has occurred, with Paraikulum villagers helping to facilitate, plan and implement.

Impact on government agencies

The novelty of the participatory approach and its impacts has been recognized by government. A senior engineer of the Agriculture Department visited Paraikulum. He was surprised to learn about local maintenance, water management, profit-sharing and the involvement of women. He agreed that it was important to involve farmers before planning any project for them, and so persuaded the district collector to agree to a training programme in participatory appraisal methods. Now government has made participatory methods a part of their nearby large watershed project on 5000 hectares of land, and are paying village motivators from Paraikulum to help them.

Other projects have benefited too. The staff of a DANIDA-assisted soil and water conservation project, which is implemented by the Tamil Nadu Agriculture Engineering Department in Ramnad, have made several visits to the Paraikulum community and watershed. As a result, they have adopted the participatory appraisal and planning process in their approach to mobilize partner communities. This project is designed to protect 11 000ha of degraded lands – both private and public – in three districts: Kamarajar, Pasumpon Thevar and Ramanathapuram.

The greatest potential effects come following the recently-held *panchayat*[1] elections. Now that the *panchayat* elections are over in Tamil Nadu, almost all the local bodies have started functioning properly. In Kamarajar District, the elected local union bodies have adopted the Paraikulum approach as an appropriate model for making participatory plans at the union level. In this way, local capacity and institutions are seen as the base for widespread social development as well as for improvements to watersheds and the natural resource base.

---

[1] *Panchayats* are the lowest-level, most localized administrative unit within India.

25
The Impact of the Mangla Watershed Management Project, Pakistan

SHAHID AHMAD and JAVED AHMED[1]

Introduction

THIS CHAPTER DESCRIBES experiences over the past 30 years of implementing watershed development in the Mangla watershed in Pakistan. Drawing on the findings of a participatory impact study, it concludes that despite many approaches and efforts to encourage soil and water conservation within the watershed, the lack of community organizations to tackle catchment-wide problems, and the poor involvement of the community in the process of watershed development during the history of the project, has meant that the projects in the last 30 years have failed to provide sustained improvements in productivity. It recommends drastic changes to project management so that the communities' active participation can be fostered, and their skills enhanced.

A brief history

The Indus basin river system is the world's largest contiguous irrigation system. The rivers serving the Indus plains are the Indus and its tributaries: the Kabul, the Jehlum, the Chenab, the Ravi and the Sutlej. The Tarbela and Mangla dams provide about 85 per cent of the total storage facility available at present in the Indus basin system. The Mangla dam was completed in 1967 with a live storage capacity of 6.5 bm³ (WAPDA 1986). It cost Rs 3.172 billion to construct. Each year since it was built, the dam has lost about 0.04 bm³ in capacity, mainly due to siltation arising from watershed degradation in the upstream area.

The estimates of catchment areas and sediment load of the Jhelum river system above Mangla Dam reservoir are shown in Table 25.1. The population density in the catchment area ranges from 350 to 1000 persons per sq km of cultivated area, which is many times higher than the country's average population density.

---

[1] The authors are deeply indebted for the support provided by Dr M. Shafiq, Mr Zaheer-ul-Ikram and Mr Mohammad Aslam for conducting the participatory area appraisals and diagnostic analysis.

Table 25.1: Catchment area and sediment load of Jhelum River system above Mangla Dam Reservoir

River system	Catchment area (sq km)	Annual sediment ('000 tonnes)	Annual sediment (mm^3)*
Kunhar River	2436	3	2.56
Neelum River	7361	7	5.96
Kanshi River	1658	–	–
Upper Jhelum River	14 334	22	18.72
Lower Jhelum River	5002	14	11.91
Poonch River	4225	14	11.91

*mm^3: million cubic metres

Projects implemented

A wide range of watershed management practices have been implemented under various watershed projects of the Mangla Dam catchment. A pilot watershed management project began in 1966. In the beginning, the watershed management practices placed most emphasis on earthen dams with drop inlet arrangements. These were constructed using earthen bunds with prescribed slopes. The drop inlets were used to control the flow of water. In the case of earthen dams, compaction was followed by planting of *Cynodon dactylon* (Khabbal) grass, but rodent holes, animal grazing and lack of maintenance by the owners rapidly resulted in damage to the earthen dams. Subsequently, stone rubble or masonry structures, small dams, spillways, bed profiles etc., were designed and implemented.

There was a strong emphasis on planting pine trees, although fruit trees and other fast-growing forest trees were also introduced later. Planting on land not fit for cultivation was carried out by the project, while planting on field boundaries was left to the landowners.

The other biological treatments introduced in the Mangla Watershed Management Project included:

o groundnut, introduced because it provides a useful ground cover in the summer season, which receives high-intensity monsoon rains
o cyanogas pump and poisons were used on a large scale to eradicate rats
o napier millets were introduced for stall feeding
o sisal-agave was introduced on a large scale to control soil erosion.

Some plantations survived, but many were damaged as protection from free-grazing animals and maintenance of widely scattered patches of plantation could not be ensured (Ishaq, 1968). The conservation structures were successful where the siting of structures was correct and feasible. However, heavy monsoon rains and lack of maintenance damaged the stone structures after three or four years. Cyanogas poisons were used to

333

eradicate rats, but again success was only partial because of a lack of community participation and an area-based approach.

The first operational project was started in 1966 for a period of 24 years (1966/7 to 1989/90). After several evaluations and revisions, a new scheme was prepared for the period July 1983 to June 1988, which included a 'food for work' component by the World Food Programme. The evaluation wing of the planning commission reviewed the project in 1982 and the principal findings were that:

○ there had been a reduction in sedimentation from 63.6 to 42.2 million m³ per year, a reduction of 34 per cent, which meant an increase in useful life of the reservoir from 110 to 172 years
○ the project lacked proper management
○ there was no co-operation with or from local people.

The evaluation team recommended that watershed management should:

○ avoid piecemeal work and concentrate on contiguous areas
○ give priority to propagation of fruit plants that had not been given adequate attention in the past
○ give attention to the improvement of rangelands and cultivated areas.

It was also recommended that the project should not be transferred to the Provincial Forestry Departments, and that WAPDA should continue its operation.

Official achievements

The official achievements of the projects are recorded in the project document on Planning Commissions Performance. These indicate that 54 078ha were afforested, 401 000 stone check-dams constructed, 49 000 retaining walls constructed, 2656 silt traps and storage spillways built, and 1800ha of pasture was improved through levelling and bunding.

Problems identified

However, many problems were also encountered:

Absentee landowners. Because land-holdings are small, and income from agriculture is not sufficient to support families, many people take up employment and leave the land to tenants who are not interested in land improvement. Most owners who cannot take up employment through old age, also cannot do hard work to protect lands from erosion.

Grazing pressure. There is very heavy grazing pressure in the area. Overgrazing resulted in a loss of vegetation cover, which requires rehabilitation and management of rangelands.

Lack of co-operation and participation. Not all landowners in the area permitted project staff to carry out watershed works on their lands, and so coverage is fragmented. To overcome this problem, the project relied mainly on awareness campaigns through media, public meetings, celebration of watershed weeks, distribution of fruit/forest tree saplings free or at nominal prices, establishment of demonstration areas, and construction of public utility works like ponds, springs, etc. These activities are said to have raised awareness and improved co-operation over the project period.

Poor maintenance. After the areas were handed back to land owners, completed works, particularly afforested areas, were not protected, which resulted in greater degradation of the treated areas. To overcome this situation the project took on itself to maintain the engineering structures for two years, and afforestation for three to five years.

Impact study of Mangla Watershed Management Project

For the purpose of the case-study, the three catchments of Misa-Kaswal, Kahuta and Kotli-Sattian were selected for evaluation of the impact of the project activities during July-October 1994. These three catchments were selected to represent the wide variability of soil, topography, altitude, land forms, climate and cropping patterns prevailing in the project area.

Catchment characteristics

Soil erosion and loss of fertile topsoils are still the major issues affecting the productivity of these catchments. Farmers in these catchments are engaged mainly in subsistence agriculture and they supplement their income from off-farm sources. Women are generally engaged in bringing drinking water from springs/wells, collecting fuelwood, raising poultry, looking after livestock (both small and large ruminants), and harvesting crops – especially groundnut and vegetables. Specific characteristics of each catchment are outlined below.

Misa-Kaswal Catchment. The climate of the Misa-Kaswal catchment is humid in the summer season and semi-arid in the winter. The main seasonal rainfall is 500 to 600mm during the summer season, whereas it ranges from 250 to 300mm in the winter. The crop growth index, which is a function of growing degree days, is adequate in the summer season and moderately adequate in the winter season. Thus, primary productivity of the natural vegetation is dependent on the occurrence and distribution of rainfall. The soils in the area are loamy and clayey old terraces and loess of sub-humid zones. The relief of the area ranges from 300 to 600m from mean sea level.

335

Kahuta Catchment. The climate of the Kahuta catchment is humid in the summer season and sub-humid in the winter. The main seasonal rainfall is 600 to 700mm during the summer season, and 300 to 400mm in the winter. The crop growth index is adequate in the summer season and moderately adequate in the winter season. Thus, there is little or no limitation imposed on primary productivity of the natural vegetation by rainfall. Primary productivity of the natural vegetation is dependent on the occurrence and distribution of rainfall. The soils of the catchment are loamy eroded loess soils and shallow residual soils, with some badlands and some gullied lands. The relief of the area ranges from 300 to 1800m from mean sea level.

Kotli-Sattian catchment. The climate of the area is humid both in the summer and winter seasons. The rainfall during the summer ranges from 700 to 800mm, and varies from 300 to 500mm in the winter season. The crop growth index is adequate in the summer season and moderately adequate during the winter season. There is no limitation for primary productivity of the natural vegetation as compared to the other two catchments. The relief of the area is between 600 and 1800m above mean sea level.

Diagnostic analysis

A multi-disciplinary team was constituted, comprising of an agricultural engineer, soil scientist and a water management expert, to conduct a diagnostic analysis in the three selected catchments. A participatory approach was used with the communities, in which five to 15 farmers participated at each location – either a farm or a village. The framework of indicators provided by IIED (see Chapter 2) was used with some modifications, as outlined by Ahmad and Dawson (1994).

Summary of results

The data and information collected through PRA and diagnostic analysis were used to outline the impact of watershed management practices in the three selected catchments.

Changes in productivity

In all three catchments there were substantial changes to productivity (Table 25.2). Crop yields of maize, wheat, sorghum and groundnut have improved, along with natural biomass productivity. There are more trees on farms, and land values have increased, especially where there has been conservation. The increase in labour rates is due mainly to out-migration of labour in the past 10 years. There is heavy dependence on off-farm income, with many people serving in the army and civil sevice.

Table 25.2: Changes in productivity in three catchments

	Misa-Kaswal	Kahuta	Kotli-Sattian
Crop yields	Wheat, maize and groundnut up 100–140%	Wheat and sorghum up 30–75%	Wheat and maize up 50–100%
Biomass productivity	4–5x increase	2x increase	2–3x increase
Tree number (multi-purpose forest and fruit) on farms	up 20%	up 15%	up 15%
Land value increase due to conservation measures	up 5–6x	up 4–5x	up 6–7x
Labour rates	up 3–4x	up 3–4x	up 3–4x

Changes in resource degradation

The main changes that have affected resource degradation include the adoption of land terracing with local grasses planted on the bunds, land levelling with trees on boundaries, water disposal outlets and land reclamation (Table 25.3). Many non-adopters of technologies could not afford the cost of machinery, even though there is a government subsidy of 50 per cent of the structural costs of water disposal outlets and erosion control structures. Groundwater levels have increased in all three catchments due to better retention of rainwater, although the best improvement is in Misa-Karwal. Dug wells are being installed with diesel-operated pumping systems by a few resource-rich farmers.

It is estimated that soil loss has fallen in all areas from two- to five-fold.

Changes in local resilience and vulnerability

We investigated several aspects of resilience and vulnerability among local communities. The major sources of income in all catchments were livestock, wheat and maize. Due to diversification, farmers are now earning more income from pulses, groundnut, fuelwood/timber, vegetables and fruits.

Farmers in Misa-Kaswal catchment were aware of monthly meetings of extension agents and routine training activities of the provincial extension department.

Although credit facilities from scheduled banks are available, farmers are reluctant to take credit in all three catchments.

337

Table 25.3: Changes in resource degradation in the three catchments

	Misa-Kaswal	Kahuta	Kotli-Sattian
Proportion of farms with terracing	60%	40%	50%
Proportion of farms with land levelled and trees on boundaries	30%	10%	30%
Common land and pastures	Degraded	Degraded	Degraded
Groundwater levels	Substantial increase – from 30m depth 20 years ago to 10–20m	Small increase	Small increase
Proportion of catchment under tree-grass cover (other than state forest)	15–20%	10–15%	10–15%
Soil loss	Down 3–5x	Down 2x	Down 2–3x
Presence of private forest and fruit tree nurseries	Common	None	None

Changes in self-dependence of groups and communities

No evidence exists in any of the catchments of sustained community or group activity. However, communities do respond to efforts organized to consider their interests; for example, forest plantations, rodent control, etc. There is no improvement in group or community co-operative actions.

There are no committees or farmer organizations for co-operative action in any of the catchments.

Some farmers are motivated to do soil conservation work and they approach the line department to seek help for conservation plans, hiring machinery and construction of structures. However, there is no concerted effort made by the project authorities towards integrated catchment development, and farmers are supposed to visit 10 to 13 line departments for information or assistance.

Replication and operational procedures

There is some awareness of the watershed activities in neighbouring catchments, and some farmers in these catchments are terracing, planting eucalyptus on field boundaries, using better seeds of wheat and maize, and using fertilizers.

However, there is no integrated catchment development approach in these areas, and the replication is done only by individuals. It is only recently that a participatory catchment approach has been appreciated as an option for departments.

A major limitation is the lack of training for line department scientist/engineers and beneficiaries in integrated planning, design, implementation and monitoring/evaluation. The other shortcoming is the lack of a participatory approach.

Radio and television helped to engage the community to adopt new interventions, and the media played a significant role in the dissemination of technology.

The current approach lacks analysis between inputs, outputs and impacts. Most of the projects were designed using input/output concepts. The impact is directly related to attitudinal changes within the community. There is a need to use social and civic initiatives as an entry point, followed by productivity enhancement and income generation activities, and resource management interventions through a well-integrated strategy.

Looking to the future

No doubt the interventions introduced in the project area have had some impact on productivity, but farmers could not sustain levels of productivity because of the complete lack of community organizations. Most of the catchment interventions selected in the Mangla watershed management project, such as rodent control, grazing plans, afforestation and so on, require co-operative action to work effectively.

In summary, the watershed management approach followed in the last 30 years has failed to provide sustained improvements to system productivity, and so now considerable research and development efforts are required to test an integrated catchment approach using active community participation in identification, implementation and evaluation.

Changes are required in the management approach so that active participation and skill enhancement of the community can become an essential element. Furthermore, there is a need to link the community with line departments so that interventions are based on farmers' needs and perceptions. Technical backstop support is also required for the scientists/engineers of the project. For this purpose, linkages with national research institutions need to be developed to seek on-the-job consultancies and training of project personnel. Such linkages for dynamic interaction between research, education and extension do not exist. Institutional reform and adjustment will therefore be the key factor in improving these development programmes for soil and water conservation.

26
Local Conservation Action in Western Australia

ANDREW CAMPBELL, PHIL GRICE and JUSTIN HARDY

LANDCARE IS AN unstructured movement of about 3000 voluntary community land conservation groups in Australia.[1] Landcare groups operate co-operatively at a local or district level, usually with an initial focus on land degradation problems, evolving to broader considerations of developing more sustainable farming communities. The Lower Balgarup Catchment Group is a classic example of the original Landcare concept in action – a small group of farms defined by a surface water catchment, in which everyone is involved in co-operative efforts to tackle common problems, sharing meagre resources with minimal overheads.

This case-study of the Lower Balgarup Catchment Group is based on a survey of all group members carried out by Justin Hardy (the project officer funded by the National Landcare Programme to assist in the development and activities of Land Conservation Districts in the area) in 1994[2] The survey concentrated on how farming practices had changed in recent years, on the perceptions of group members of their land management problems and potential solutions, on the strengths and weaknesses of their farming systems in terms of production and water use, and on their attitudes to group-based farm planning, project implementation, and searching for new ideas. The survey of individual farmers was complemented by follow-up group discussions facilitated by Justin, at which he presented the initial findings of the survey and sought to stimulate further reflections and discussion.

Evolution of the Lower Balgarup Catchment Group

The Lower Balgarup Catchment is located 260 kilometres south west of Perth in Western Australia (WA). It enjoys a Mediterranean climate, with hot dry summers from October through April, usually with less than 50mm of rain over five months. Winters are cooler and wetter, and represent the growing season, during which annual pastures thrive, cereal crops are sown, and water run-off is captured in dams in readiness for the dry summer.

Geologically, Lower Balgarup is on the edge of the 2500 million years old Yilgarn Block, which underlies most of the agricultural areas in

---

[1] See Chapters 15 and 27 in this volume for more on the Landcare movement.
[2] Each farmer was interviewed for several hours, often together with other family members.

Western Australia. These ancient soils are deeply weathered, leached of nutrients, sandy and infertile. Weathering processes have given rise to a typical lateritic soil profile.

The impact of European settlement and European farming systems on the landscape of the Lower Balgarup catchment over the last hundred years has been extensive, rapid and severe. Eighty-six per cent of the catchment has been cleared of its native eucalypt forest, mostly since World War II. This has had a profound impact on catchment hydrology and on nature conservation, through sheer removal of most of the habitat, and through degradation of the remnants by grazing and introduced animals and plants. Clearing has, of course, been compounded by subsequent land management for agriculture:

○ introduced stock with their cloven hooves, quickly eating out the native grasses and herbs, compacting and eroding soils, contaminating watercourses
○ introduced pests such as foxes, rabbits and cats, predating on, or outcompeting, native marsupials, reptiles and birds, and grazing on native vegetation
○ introduced annual crops, pastures and weeds, incapable of using water outside their short growing season and thus contributing to salinity, waterlogging and erosion problems, and sometimes invading remnant bush
○ practices such as cultivation and burning stubbles, which have depleted an already impoverished nutrient bank and damaged soil structure, exacerbating erosion problems, soil acidity, waterlogging and salinity.

The Lower Balgarup Catchment Group is one of 18 catchment groups that formed following a public meeting and planning workshop held by the Kojonup LCDC[3] in February 1990. The group consists of 18 farms supporting 20 families (approximately 60 people) covering a catchment of 14 000 hectares. The farms range in size from 293 hectares to 1312 hectares, with an average of 776 hectares. Farm enterprises are based on various combinations of grazing (mostly sheep for wool, but with some beef cattle) and cropping (mostly cereals, but with increasing incorporation of grain legumes and oilseeds). Most land users are second or third generation farmers, and their land is private freehold.

Managing the group process

Compared with most Landcare groups, Lower Balgarup is small in both area and number of people. Its members are relatively homogeneous,

---

[3] Land Conservation District Committees were established by the State government to encourage greater involvement of farming and pastoral communities in land conservation. Catchment groups operate under the umbrella of LCDCs.

nearly all are full-time farmers, and know each other well.[4] The group was formed on the joint initiative of the Kojonup LCDC and Paul Ayres, a local farmer, with practical goals continuing to evolve from a down-to-earth beginning.

As group co-ordinator, Paul has an effective network for getting relevant information. He is able to promote the group's aims to the wider community and harness the necessary technical, financial, and institutional support. As a leader he is able to keep achievable objectives in perspective for the other members, while looking to the future. He is always conscious of involving everyone in decision-making and sharing the rewards. The 'involve everyone' philosophy from the start has been critical to the survival of the group.

The group has always invited members to bring along their wives and other family members to activities. The response has not been high, possibly because of the need for women to organize children with school and other activities, and the generally male-oriented culture of farmer groups in the WA wheatbelt (Box 26.1).

As the Lower Balgarup group progressed, they ensured that grants were shared equally among participating farmers. This was clearly very important for keeping the group together, but it is a departure from normal Landcare group practice. They receive government grants that are usually focused on demonstration sites, thus directly helping only a small number of members at any one time. When group members see a concentration of money on particular properties, there is a tendency for them to become disenchanted, particularly during economic crises. This situation demands skilled facilitation to manage resources creatively to keep everyone involved, not just those involved in the action generated by the grant. Paul Ayres and other group leaders made a conscious decision not to follow this route, but to divide all funding among all members, thus avoiding perceptions of inequitable allocation of grant moneys.

Lower Balgarup's group activities

The group really got going in 1991, with their first activity being a tour of their own catchment. The aim was to look at problem areas and any restoration work already done.

---

[4] This contrasts with the case-study on West Hume (see Chapter 27), which is a large, mature and active district group, covering a number of sub-catchments and local government areas. It therefore involves several rural communities, not all of which know each other, and necessarily acting in a more diffuse way involving a smaller proportion of the potentially relevant population. The scale of the group's operation and the resources it has attracted demand a more layered structure and professional staff, and the group is integrated into wider external networks. Given its proximity to the large regional centre of Albury-Wodonga, the West Hume Group also exhibits features characteristic of pluri-active groups, absentee landholders and a more heterogeneous membership.

Box 26.1: Women in Landcare

Involvement of women in the Lower Balgarup group seems to follow the general pattern for Western Australia, described in Campbell (1994). A survey of land conservation district committees in Western Australia, in 1991 found that women made up 17 per cent of the membership of these committees, and of these women, 35 per cent were secretaries (Duxbury, 1992). Anecdotal evidence from throughout Australia suggests that, as one travels further north and further away from the coast, the traditional gender roles of women in the home and men doing the farm work and going to meetings, become more entrenched. Where women are involved in Landcare groups in these areas, it is common that they are the secretary of the group and expected to provide the cakes and tea ('ladies bring a plate') after the meeting. Another survey found that 34 per cent of Landcare group members in Victoria are women, 47 per cent of group secretaries are women, but only 10 per cent of chairperson positions were occupied by women (Curtis et al., 1993). They found a significant positive relationship between female membership and group effectiveness.

Of course, many women on the land have always been intimately involved in discussions and decisions about land management, especially financial decisions. It is common in Australia that women on the land have more formal education than their husbands, so it is often the female farming partner who does the books. This may explain why women are often asked to be the secretary of Landcare groups (an onerous, unglamorous role, considering the paper warfare involved in Landcare funding and the amount of literature with which groups are bombarded). However, using the same logic one might expect there to be a disproportionately high number of women Landcare group leaders, which is not the case. People involved in Landcare should be asking why this is so. With rural economic decline and the difficulties of affording outside labour, many women on the land are now also doing more outside work (either on the farm or elsewhere for off-farm income) in addition to their work in the home (Bryant, 1992).

Each farmer then conducted a motorbike survey of their degraded areas (erosion, waterlogging, salinity) to quantify their land degradation problems. They found a total of 627ha (a range from three to 120ha per farm) affected by salinity and waterlogging; figures that were refined and mapped more accurately during the later farm and catchment planning exercises.

Since then, activities undertaken by the group have included:

○ field days to visit other farms where progressive steps have been taken to control degradation problems

○ revegetating degraded areas
○ monitoring water-table depth and groundwater quality using piezo-meters (see Chapter 27)
farm and catchment planning (see Box 26.2 for more details)
○ soils days to help farmers test their soils for texture, pH and structure
○ talks and visits by technical experts such as hydrologists, farm management consultants, soil scientists and economists.

Linking process to impacts

Establishing the impact of the Lower Balgarup Catchment Group was fraught with the same difficulties as the West Hume case-study (Chapter 27). As the group has been active for only about four years, it is too early for long-term impacts to show. Furthermore, many effects of the group are less tangible, such as changes in perceptions, knowledge and confidence, or growing personal networks as experienced by group members. Moreover, it is difficult to distinguish the impact of the group and the participatory approaches it employs from other changes in the catchment over the last five years, such as new technologies, fluctuating commodity prices, and state government rationalization of infrastructure and services.

The Natural Resource Base

It is too soon for many of the changes the group has made, and the works they have carried out, to be reflected in improvements in insidious problems that have developed over many years. But one can say that farmers' perceptions of these problems have changed dramatically since their initial survey of every farm.

Group members have changed many of their land management practices, as outlined more fully below. They have stopped clearing, minimized cultivation and now burn stubble only when there is no alternative. They are thinking more carefully about their crop/pasture rotations and cropping more to land type, thus ensuring land management linked to land capability. They are replanting trees and fencing out drainage lines and degraded areas. They are putting in erosion-control banks and investigating alternative farming systems.

Some changes on the ground are apparent visually, others are less obvious management changes such as stubble retention, improvements to pasture composition, better crop yields, adoption of new enterprises, and fencing and increased cropping. Noticeable changes in the landscape are tree planting, gully and problem area protection, contour banks and drainage work. Since its formation in 1991 the group has planted 220 000 tree seedlings and has direct-seeded 14 hectares of trees and shrubs; constructed 118 kilometres of new fencing to protect creeks, rivers and

344

Box 26.2: Farm and catchment planning

The development of farmer-directed farm planning is driven by a number of key assumptions (Campbell, 1991):

o that land degradation 'problems' are symptoms of inappropriate land management, and are most likely to be fixed if the required management changes benefit the land user. In other words, conservation and productivity must be complementary. Conservation works for their own sake are unlikely to be widely implemented.

o that any plan is ideally best prepared by the people who have to implement it, i.e. the farmers. This does not preclude the benefits of consultation with specialist technical advisers, family members, neighbours or consultants.

o that farmers are generalists who are used to integrating technical, financial and social information from diverse sources in decision-making, so the farm planning process must be capable of dealing with more than just the physical layout of the farm.

o a farm plan is not an ideal map of the farm, but simply an expression of the current state of a planning process that is dynamic, responsive, on-going.

An approved farm plan (the official term is now Property Management Plan) is now a prerequisite for Australian farmers to be able to claim tax deductions for land conservation works. Such a plan should comprise:

o an analysis of natural resources on the farm, divided into natural land management units based on an integration of soil type, slope, drainage, aspect and remnant vegetation

o identification and inventory of land degradation problems and 'best bet' management strategies for these problems

o strategies for nature conservation (particularly of ecological assets such as remnant native vegetation and wetlands) and creation of wildlife habitat where appropriate

o an implementation schedule, integrated into the farm budget; a monitoring, feedback and evaluation system

o ideally, some more radical consideration, brainstorming and discussion about what a sustainable farming system might look like, and how to get there.

Farm plans are usually based on large-scale aerial photographs, although a small but increasing number of people have access to GIS equipment through their Landcare group.

In the 1990s there was a natural scaling up from individual farm plans to group-based catchment plans, with the National Landcare Programme (NLP) encouraging Landcare groups to undertake catchment planning to develop a strategic approach to catchment sustainability. They were also a valuable exercise in developing group cohesion, while learning more about their problems and potential solutions, and accessing sources of technical support.

This strategic approach looks fine on paper, but in a rural economic crisis it can backfire. An increasing number of Landcare groups have spent several years meeting, learning, planning, mapping and estimating the cost of implementing their catchment plans, only to be confronted with figures of millions of dollars, well beyond the capacity of their current farming systems to pay. In the absence of skilled facilitation, this can be a demoralizing phase for a group, often leading to cynicism about Landcare in general, and government motives and sincerity in particular.

remnant bush from grazing; 68 kilometres of drains and banks to tackle erosion, waterlogging and salinity; and sown 25 hectares of perennial grasses and fodder shrubs to revegetate degraded land. By April 1994 the group estimated that they had spent $175 000 on the co-ordinated tree planting, including the cost of seedlings, some drainage and fencing. These obvious changes are very evident when compared to neighbouring catchments, particularly from an aeroplane.

Several members of the group admit that the accelerated revegetation work would not have taken place if the group had not existed. They knew something would need to be done eventually, but there were other priorities on individual farms. The opportunity to work together has made them reconsider the importance of conserving the productive potential of their farms. The involvement has stimulated them to try out innovations and change certain farm priorities. They have felt that taking small steps at a time as a group has maintained their enthusiasm and given more pride in their farm's appearance and productivity. Some members described this as 'wholesome competition'.

We need to keep this in perspective, however. The areas of revegetation are tiny in comparison to the whole catchment, for example 25ha of grasses for degraded land in a catchment of 14 000ha. The degradation of watercourses and remnant bush has yet to be halted, let alone reversed, and problems such as soil acidity are far from understood, let alone resolved. According to farmers' estimates,[5] drainage and contour bank work could cost $90 000; $400 000 is needed for liming to adjust soil acidity; $100 000 on tree planting to treat wind erosion; while fencing to land types and other management changes such as land conservation machinery, is likely to exceed $1 280 000.

There is a long way to go, but at least the land users in the catchment recognize these problems, and have their own institution, in the form of the Landcare group, for starting to reverse negative trends.

Nature conservation issues

The opportunity to plant trees was a key motivation for the group formation. However, it seems fair to say that the impetus for revegetation was to heal land degradation problems such as erosion, and to attempt to halt rising watertables. This activity had a production focus, rather than nature conservation per se.[6]

---

[5] Farmer estimates of costs are notoriously conservative because they rarely cost their own labour, either in terms of a market rate or as an opportunity cost.
[6] Although during the surveys in September 1994, one farmer drew attention to a rare and endangered plant known locally as Woolly Poison, which was found only on a short narrow section of road adjoining his property. The Department of Conservation and Land Management has since put a preservation order on the plants.

It will be interesting to see how this issue evolves. Conventional wisdom has it that behaviour change follows attitude change. However, research by Roger Wilkinson and John Cary (1992) with Landcare groups in Victoria suggests that it can also be the other way around: that attitude change follows behaviour change. For example, a farmer may be induced to change practices by financial incentives or regulation, only to find that the new practice is not so bad/hard/silly after all, and subsequently change his attitude towards that practice. It may be that, as Lower Balgarup farmers become more skilled and confident with revegetation, and as they see the results of their earlier plantings, they will plant or sow more trees of more species for more reasons, paying less heed to the apparent constraints that supposedly prevented them starting.

The group accepts that there are important ecological values from protecting remnant bush on farms. It has protected areas within streamlines, gullies and problem areas, which is where it has planted most additional trees. Protected creeklines have been set up as part of a corridor network. The group has had annual fox baiting and hunts to reduce fox numbers and allow smaller native animals to breed. It recognizes that native wildlife needs assistance. A small amount of local seed is collected for seedling replacements. However, biodiversity does not yet benefit from high enough recognition or concern for species to be protected for their intrinsic value. Individual interviews indicated that most protection of remnant vegetation is occurring mainly to stabilize the watertable, not to protect wildlife.

Productivity

It is not easy to ascribe changes in productivity to involvement in the group, but some generalizations can be made. Involvement in the group has exposed farmers to the farming systems and yields of their neighbours (Box 26.3) in a way that is rare in Australia outside specialist discussion groups.

Changes in land management practices

The group sees sustainability as including the protection and enhancement of farm lifestyles and the need to avoid harmful farming practices, such as the excessive use of chemicals. But the changes they have made so far to their farming systems are evolutionary, rather than revolutionary. Some members expect 'radical' ideas to come from the outside specialists, but their general approach to innovation is through experimenting, consulting with others and evaluating experiences through group meetings and field days. For some members, the concept of introducing new crops and farming to land types is itself a radical change.

Changes to land management practices include:

Box 26.3: Comparing yield notes

During group discussions, farmers considered the potential yields for certain cereal crops on each soil type. The broad range of farmers' desires to produce high-yielding crops was apparent. Some were surprised at others' ability to produce such high yields. For example, yields of oats ranged from 0.8 to 4 tonnes per hectare and wheat from 1.8 to 3 t/ha. Those farmers producing the higher yields consider that it is still possible to yield better by pursuing optimum water use efficiency (reaching for the potential yields for the rainfall).

Farmers' group discussions also exposed experience and knowledge within the group about optimizing productivity on each land type. They took place during a major slump in wool prices and for this reason there was more cropping taking place than normally. As canola, a high-value oilseed, had just been introduced to the district, even the cropping specialists were on a steep learning curve, generating much discussion about experiences and methods at group meetings.

Later personal interviews highlighted the influence on group members of being in the group. Farmers reported that they had gained information and confidence, which had helped them to implement changes such as taking on small areas of canola, growing other crops like barley, wheat or lupins as opposed to just low-input oat crops for feed, and being more adventurous with sowing larger areas.

It was clear that the opportunity to pick up this kind of free, locally-proven knowledge was a strong incentive to meet.

○ changing their cropping rotations. Other than the desire for a higher value cash crop, the move to more cropping was having a profound effect on improving pasture quality. In general, farmers increased the clover (*Trifolium* spp) content of the pasture through better grass control measures. Clover was recognized by group members as improving soil nitrogen status. Increases in crop yields and wool cuts per head were consistently attributed to changes in soil fertility. Those farmers cropping bigger areas had adopted longer rotations, attempting to capitalize on improved grass control and fertility.
○ minimizing tillage. The 'zero till' approach of drilling direct into the undisturbed and pre-sprayed soil surface is becoming the preferred method, but the rate of change is slow as it needs specialized and expensive machinery, including the spraying equipment.

o reduced burning – when burning of the last year's stubble was part of conventional land preparation. The use of chemicals and minimum tillage has reduced this burning and consequent erosion, and in the longer cropping rotations has better complemented grazing.

The most striking recent change has been the greater use of herbicides and insecticides. Nevertheless, this is accompanied by a healthy dose of caution. There has been increasing interest in soil testing and interpretation to ensure that appropriate fertilizer is used efficiently by plants, rather than leaking into groundwater and waterways. Fertilizer in cropping is generally applied closer to the time when the plants can use it, i.e. at seeding, rather than months before, as is often the case with pasture.

As cropping is still secondary to wool production, the use of chemical sprays is not yet heavy. Also, farmers see chemicals as necessary until a more environmentally friendly alternative can be identified for their farming system. Yet group members expressed concern about their increasing reliance on sprays and the potential threat of increased herbicide resistance. Furthermore, during the individual interviews four group members said that they were reluctant to adopt high-input cropping due either to the capital risks or the wish to remain strictly sheep farmers on smaller properties.

In line with a general tendency in Australian agriculture, the farmers in the Lower Balgarup catchment have been forced by declining terms of trade to look more carefully at what they produce, and how they produce it, for what market, according to what specifications. In both cereal and wool production, there is a trend towards growing more specific varieties for a particular quality and range of end uses, for on-farm use, for private sale, or for specific industry outlets.

Local resilience and vulnerability

Landcare group members feel that they are more in control of their destiny than before they joined the group. The group realizes that it has the ability to make things happen, that many people, agencies and resources are available to help if they ask in the right way and through the right channels. They have developed great trust in each other and have much respect for Paul Ayers. They have gained confidence that they can influence government policy, funding and advice.

However, it is difficult to say that the changes they have made to their farming systems actually make them any less dependent on commodity prices or less vulnerable to rising input costs. In the Lower Balgarup case, moving into more intensive cropping may be increasing (rather than decreasing) their vulnerability.[7] Real changes in resilience within current

---

[7] Apart from those people who formerly produced only wool, for whom it is a diversification.

349

farming systems are likely to come from value adding and/or innovative marketing, of either crops or wool, in an attempt to differentiate products and become more independent from the mass fluctuations in prices for raw commodities on distorted world markets. Despite the encouraging start made by the Landcare group, the demographic trend in this area is towards larger farms and fewer people, although in Lower Balgarup the trend is quite slow by comparison to farmland further away from the main service towns.

Autonomy of groups and communities

The Lower Balgarup group is a relatively autonomous Landcare group. It is small and compact, and is lucky to have a dynamic leadership team with someone keen enough to act as an unpaid co-ordinator. So their infrastructure costs are low, especially when compared with larger groups like West Hume, which have salaried staff, and they do not rely on government funding to stay afloat. Any grants they receive are shared evenly among the group, all moneys are spent directly 'on the ground', and are thus 'transparent'.

With their GIS-based farm and catchment planning and their instigation of monitoring processes, they are also becoming relatively autonomous in terms of seeking and using information. Nevertheless, as for Australian agriculture in general, technical breakthroughs and high quality research will be needed to overcome some presently intractable problems and to move to more sustainable farming systems. National investments, public and private, will be required to support this endeavour. It seems unfair, and unrealistic, to pass responsibility for all knowledge-generation down to the Landcare group level.

In terms of the momentum and sustainability of the Landcare group itself, Lower Balgarup appears to be in good shape. However, when one scales up from the small catchment group of 18 farms to the wider Kojonup community in which their children go to school, and which provides them with goods and services and social contact, it is very difficult to argue that the community has become more autonomous or self-reliant in recent years. The external forces of rural decline are simply overwhelming.

Replication

According to Justin Hardy, Lower Balgarup is leading the way for other catchment groups in the WA wheatbelt, particularly in the way it is using GIS as more than just a drafting tool to aggregate farm plans into a catchment plan. It has remained active since its formation, it has demonstrated that it is possible to share grant money equally among members and to carry out farm planning as a catchment group, that it can form strong linkages with other groups such as government agencies for group exchange of information and the experimentation of 'new' ideas on farms in the catchment. It has hosted visits from other groups and numerous supporting organization people. Some have been invited to offer their advice, others have come because of the opportunity to begin to see the potential of co-ordinating mapping and planning between farms in a catchment. The Department of Agriculture has assisted the group with trialing perennials, has carried out an extensive soil survey to investigate soil acidity trends, and more recently has nominated a farm to be part of a Wool Corporation-funded five-year on-farm pasture utilization study. Other farmer groups have gained the benefit of being inspired by these achievements to try managing change themselves. The group is seen as helping people to learn about local soil types, land degradation problems and the effect of different approaches. The use of GIS was also taken up by other groups for similar reasons, albeit more slowly than in the Balgarup group as these groups have not developed their farm plans as a group, and their completion has been more sporadic.

Support institutions and professionals

The growth in the number and enthusiasm of the land conservation district committees during the 1980s and the subsequent emergence of catchment groups under their umbrella in the 1990s was way beyond Western Australia government expectations, and has had a profound effect on the way the Department of Agriculture, in particular, goes about its business.

Globally, the department has had to change from individual to group extension, from providing individual specialist advisory services to group facilitation and integrated services across technical disciplines, and from disseminating knowledge and products to facilitating planning processes. These profound changes have taken place during an era of budget cutbacks, rationalization of services and organizational restructuring. This includes regionalization, moving away from a highly centralized decision-making structure and attempting to shed people from head office in Perth.

Thus it is difficult to distinguish between cause and effect, or between the changes forced by Landcare groups and those that would have happened anyway. But it is clear that the WA groups have greatly increased the momentum of land conservation and are engaged in many activities (extension, research, planning, monitoring) that used to be the province of government. There is a tendency for government to work through these groups, for example by asking them to comment on vegetation clearance applications, or by using Landcare groups to access NLP funds for projects that cannot be funded out of departmental budgets. This can be resented

351

by people who see themselves becoming submerged by bureaucracy, receiving only a tiny slice of the funding cake for spending where it has the most direct effect, i.e. 'on the ground'.

Justin Hardy exemplifies a new breed of extension staff employed and trained with an emphasis on groups and process, rather than individuals and content. His role involves facilitating the formation and development of groups, co-ordinating activities with groups, developing farm and catchment plans with groups and generally motivating groups.

Justin discovered that the most important learning from the evaluation of the Lower Balgarup group was the importance of responding to the whole group's needs, rather than to what he thought the whole group needed. He found that responding to the co-ordinator alone could be dangerous too, if the co-ordinator was not expressing the needs of the group.

The southern region of WA has since established a 'learning set' of those staff working with Landcare groups to be able to share experiences, particularly of group process and the resulting impacts, and to help resolve deficiencies in skills and resources.

Reflecting on the progress made

This evaluation has encouraged the Lower Balgarup Catchment Group to continue. It has empowered some of the group members through realizing several key points: that they have had an influence on the rest of the group; that they are needed; that as a group they can affect policy-making and the way institutions function; and that they can help the researchers and extension people with pioneering new technology and processes to develop better farming methods. They will continue to raise questions about how to improve the sustainability of their farming systems, and involve the external support people in a practical way to apply their knowledge on farms and learn with them.

Some of the key points that group members raised as learnings from this evaluation, and reflection after the New Horizons Bangalore workshop are:

○ the personal approach needs to be encouraged, with a farmer co-ordinator talking to the rest of the group members, especially in the group's formative stages
○ equal sharing of any incentive or grant and keeping the approach simple to ensure everyone's needs are taken into account
○ hasten slowly to build up motivation, rapport, trust, confidence and understanding between members before the more complex questions begin to unfold
○ encourage farmer evaluation and simple forms of reflection to review what they consider to be indicators of success

352

○ self-evaluations are very helpful for the co-ordinator to get feedback on how the group feel he (or she) is functioning and to identify new ideas for the future
○ groups need to set their own targets and indicators, not those that someone else outside the group is pushing
○ groups benefit when they compare with other groups and see if they can help or build a partnership
○ involve everyone in the group: male, female, community and government people.

The evaluation process is far from complete. This case-study report represents the end of the first phase of the evaluation. It will be presented to the farmers and will be the subject of further individual and group discussions, to explore in more depth the issue of what is a sustainable farming system in the Lower Balgarup Catchment, and what can be done individually and collectively to develop such systems. During these discussions, the role of the group and its relations with support institutions and external political and economic forces will be clarified further.

27
The Challenges of Change for the West Hume Landcare Group

JIM WOODHILL, JUDY FRANKENBURG, and PAUL
TREVETHAN

Introduction

THE WEST HUME LANDCARE GROUP (WHLCG) is located in southern
New South Wales in south-eastern Australia. The group was formed in
1989 in response to resource degradation that could not be overcome by
individual farmers. A catchment approach was needed to tackle a series of
pressing problems: rising water tables leading to water-logging and
salinization; soil acidification; decline of native vegetation; soil erosion; and
high silt, nutrient and salinity loads in run-off water.

The group has an official membership of 85 farm families, whose aim is
to encourage sustainable land management practices on all of the 160 farms
in the area. The group has been very active, highly successful in attracting
funds for its land care projects, and is widely cited as a fine example for
other Landcare groups, having generated over 75 separate items of publicity between 1990 and 1994. About Aus$500 000 has been invested in 17
different major land conservation projects. Over 240 group activities, such
as group meetings, field days, farm walks and discussion groups have been
organized by the group since it was formed.

In 1993, four years after starting its catchment work, the group had
reached the point where it was time to take stock of past achievements and
think strategically about future directions. Participatory rural appraisal
(PRA) was used to assess how group members and government agency
staff felt about the process and impacts of the Landcare approach (Box
27.1). Linked to this self-evaluation was a detailed economic study, carried
out by external consultants, of the capacity of landholders to fund the
necessary land and water conservation activities. This chapter describes the
outcome of these two evaluation processes.

Land, climate and the community

The total area covered by the Landcare group is 69 000 hectares, which
covers three relatively flat catchments: Majors Creek, Burrumbuttock
Creek and Long Plain Creek (Figure 27.1). The major soils are red and
yellow earths on the hills and slopes, and heavy brown and grey clays in
lower areas. Sands and sandy loams are more common nearer the River

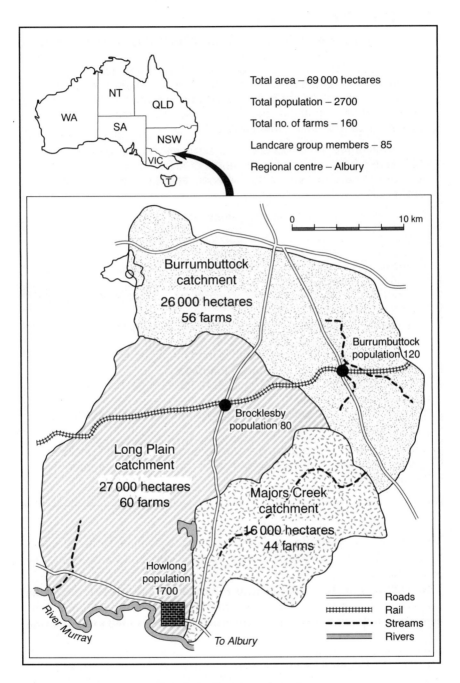

Total area – 69 000 hectares

Total population – 2700

Total no. of farms – 160

Landcare group members – 85

Regional centre – Albury

Figure 27.1:   West Hume Landcare Group catchment

355

Box 27.1: The evaluation process[1]

The intention of the PRA was to gather as much quantitative information as possible, as well as qualitative information, which was generated through interviews and focus group discussions with group members, local community members and government agency staff. The PRA was conducted in such a way as to maximize the involvement of group members and ensure that the outcome was considered to be truly their own assessment.

Ten focus group discussions and 20 family interviews, involving over 120 people from the community, conducted over a week, generated a large amount of interesting material, and were the core of the evaluation.

Other activities of the evaluation study included:

o gathering perceptions about Landcare in general, and the West Hume Landcare group in particular
o collating all available information about the group's history, activities and funding
o reports from government agency staff on the status of the area's natural resources
o an economic study of several local farms to investigate the conditions under which farmers can 'afford' landcare
o a questionnaire to ascertain which land management changes are being undertaken by individual landholders
o an assessment of suitable indicators for long-term monitoring of sustainable land use
o preliminary examination of the cost-benefit of some common local land conservation practices.

The study was managed by a core group of 15 people, including group members, Landcare co-ordinators and NSW government extension staff.

Murray, one of Australia's major rivers. Average annual rainfall varies from 550mm in the west to 650mm in the east, with concentrations in the winter months.

Nowadays, less than 1 per cent of the catchment is forested, following extensive clearing after settlement. Most trees are on private land, particularly in hills and rocky ridges, which are areas less suited to agricultural

---

[1] The West Hume experience with participatory evaluation is the basis of a forthcoming guide on participatory evaluation for wide distribution among Landcare facilitators and groups (Woodhill and Robins, 1998).

production. The only remnants of the natural understorey, which is severely depleted, occur on roadsides.

The area is typical of many rural communities in south eastern Australia. Agriculture is the main industry, supporting 2700 people. Farm sizes range from 40 to 1600ha. The community is relatively close knit, although there is considerable diversity in the background, financial wealth, educational qualifications, and types of employment of community members. Young people tend to leave the area due to the declining prosperity of rural communities, although proximity to the large regional centre of Albury has provided off-farm income for some.

Linking process to impacts

Addressing land degradation

The West Hume Landcare Group has put considerable effort into understanding its three subcatchments, the extent and severity of land degradation problems and confronting the possible consequences if current trends continue. Several grants have been used for catchment mapping, to look at land capability and suitability, groundwater depth and water quality and changes over time, distribution of salinity and also of remnant vegetation, and agricultural production by area.

Of the range of land degradation issues facing the catchment, the most severe is rising water tables and salinity. Rising water tables are a result of removing most of the original deep rooted vegetation, especially trees. The main options for dealing with salinity are tree planting, increased use of perennial pastures and drainage works, and these activities have been carried out by the Landcare Group.

As most of the land in the area is private land, the activities undertaken by individual landholders are fundamental for achieving land conservation in the area. The development of farm plans is the cornerstone of sustainable farming, allowing farmers to understand their resource base better, and is an important activity of all Landcare farmers. Developing the plans includes classifying land use types, identifying land degradation on the property, deciding where to plant trees and planning how to manage enterprises within the land's capability. Farm plans are often developed as a group exercise. The development of larger-scale catchment plans is a complementary and iterative process with the farm-scale planning[2].

Other activities pursued by the group include demonstrations of solutions to land degradation problems to farmers from outside the catchment,

---

[2] See Campbell (1994; 1992; 1991) and Chapter 26 in this book for more details.

357

group meetings, field days and farm walks, school activities, hosting visits, displays and farm planning workshops.

Managing the catchment group

The West Hume Group members, and the group itself, have become a major link between government extension services and local farmers. Staff from NSW Agriculture, and the Departments of Landcare Conservation and Water Resources regularly attend group meetings and work co-operatively with the group on a range of the projects it has chosen.

Managing the group activities well is an essential and time-consuming task. The group has been greatly assisted by a group co-ordinator – a young professionally-trained agriculturalist with good community facilitation skills, employed by the group with funding from the National Landcare Programme (see Chapter 26, this volume). The co-ordinator's role consists of:

○ networking both within the group and between the group and other organizations, providing a link between group members and sources of technical advice. The co-ordinator demystifies the technical side of land degradation control and provides ready access to straightforward, practical advice at the local level.
○ sustaining the momentum of the group, keeping members involved and ensuring that group plans are implemented
○ assisting voluntary group leaders to organize meetings, and taking an active role in planning and managing group projects
○ public relations and liaison work on behalf of the group
○ organizing farmer contributions to projects and organizing co-operative efforts between a number of farmers or with other groups.

The co-ordinator is seen as an independent person with an important liaison role between the group and government. Because the co-ordinator is usually local, their expertise tends to stay in the area for much longer than departmental advisory officers. These tend to be much younger and very mobile, as the promotion and reward systems within most state agencies make it very difficult for people to pursue a career within extension without having to re-locate regularly or move to a desk job.

While the West Hume group is a formal organization with a constitution and an elected committee, much group business is also undertaken informally when group members meet at other community functions or 'across the back fence'. Activities consist of numerous field days, discussion groups, farm walks, and social events. The involvement of people from all sectors of the community is encouraged, and the group aims to make Landcare a family affair. Women participate actively in the group, although men still hold most of the executive and committee positions (for more on women in Landcare, see Box 26.1, Chapter 26, this volume).

Assessing the impacts

Assessing the impact is difficult due to a lack of detailed monitoring of the group's activities and the status of the natural resource. Very little work exists on the environmental and economic consequences of a 'do nothing' scenario, which would have allowed for a better comparison. To argue for additional funding to convince the wider community about the benefits of supporting Landcare, and for the group to plan for the future, good monitoring and evaluation of projects is becoming increasingly important (Box 27.2).

A key issue in monitoring and evaluation is the development of appropriate sustainability indicators that are meaningful and workable at the local level, yet which provide useful aggregated data at catchment, state or national levels. How to do this effectively and efficiently is a challenge still to be faced by West Hume and other groups, and the institutions supporting Landcare[3].

The following analysis summarizes the achievements of the West Hume group and the issues it continues to face.

Community support

Landcare is viewed very positively by the whole community. People recognized that a high level of awareness has been raised by Landcare. Most significantly, it has brought people together and encouraged them to talk and think about better land management.

However, the jury is still out on what will be achieved in the long term. There was a feeling that despite the solid base of support, more substantial results will be needed in the future to maintain and increase this support. Some of the issues that may affect Landcare's longer-term local success include:

○ financial stress for farm families
○ the difficulty of encouraging more landholders to be involved
○ competition with people's time for family responsibilities and other community activities
○ a lack of clear and specific directions about what is needed to overcome land degradation problems
○ waning support from politicians and the wider community
○ the lack of clear monitoring and dissemination of achievements.

---

[3] A recent publication provides an interesting summary of over 200 efforts in community environmental monitoring throughout Australia, including by Landcare groups (Alexandra *et al.*, 1996). See Box 27.2 for several examples.

The main resource-conserving activities that have occurred over the last five years through Landcare include:

○ development of farm plans and catchment plans (approximately 50 per cent of farms have a farm plan)
○ tree planting (103 000 trees/200ha planted in the area)
○ stubble retention and minimum tillage practices
○ roadside vegetation surveys
○ drainage projects
○ re-fencing to land type
○ use of perennial pastures (15 per cent of area under perennial pasture)
○ soil conservation
○ liming soils to increase pH
○ several farmers introducing biodynamic practices
○ some enterprise diversification.

Revegetation. Restoring tree cover is a major plank in the West Hume strategy against land degradation. Tree planting is an excellent group activity for getting people involved in a common project and sharing knowledge and skills. Planting trees in agricultural areas formerly cleared by one's parents and grandparents is a richly symbolic act.

Nevertheless, revegetation is hard work and expensive. To overcome some of these problems, many individual farmers and Landcare groups have developed more efficient ways of establishing trees, and more sophisticated planning processes (Campbell, 1991, 1994), to ensure that the right trees are established in the right places for the right reasons, in the right way. Many of the 103 000 trees and shrubs planted by the WHLCG have been established either on rocky recharge areas, or to improve and increase linkages between remnant tree areas. As many people have been involved, it has increased awareness about the need for a serious revegetation approach.

Perennial pastures. Perennial pastures are advocated as a strategy to reduce waterlogging, soil acidity and salinity, while boosting productivity. However, they are not always seen as a sure bet by farmers, and the extent of the practice varies greatly between farmers.

It is currently unclear to the group what scale of revegetation or use of perennial pastures would be necessary to make a serious impact on rising water tables. There is no clear, reliable information on this that can guide the group in setting appropriate targets.

Drainage. One of the largest of the group's projects has been the Carroll's Lane drainage project. This has enabled improvement of drainage to prevent seasonal waterlogging and ground-water recharge over 1000 hectares of the Long Plain Catchment. Twenty-six properties have access to drainage, easing community tensions.

Roadside survey. In areas like West Hume, which have been extensively cleared for agriculture, roadside vegetation remnants are often the last refuges for indigenous plant communities. They are thus ecologically critical, both as habitat for birds, marsupials, reptiles and invertebrates, and as repositories of local genotypes that can be used for revegetation and improving the habitat value of other nearby remnant areas.

One of the most innovative projects carried out by the West Hume group was to map, record and assess remnant roadside vegetation throughout the catchment. The survey was conducted by 38 volunteers, helped by botanists. This type of survey is valuable for a number of reasons. From a 'land literacy' perspective (See Box 27.2), it enables land users to compare the ecology and diversity of the roadside vegetation with that of their pasture or nearby crop. Changes in soil fertility and structure, and, occasionally, water quality and hydrology, can also be appreciated in the contrast between farmland and the remaining islands of bush.

The outstanding level of participation stimulated broad awareness of both the parlous state and critical importance of the remnant roadside vegetation, and a dawning recognition on the part of the Shire of the importance of roadside management. Codes of practice in relation to stock movement along roads have been developed to help protect roadside remnants. A follow-up survey will be carried out to monitor and add to the original database.

The lack of benchmarking and monitoring makes it difficult to quantify in detail the impacts of activities such as those described above. However, it appears that the group has influenced the practices of its members. Tree clearing has stopped, stubble burning and overstocking have decreased dramatically. Farmers are reporting the ability to increase stocking rates from the use of perennial pastures and liming. There is significant potential for improving yield through better management. As in the Lower Balgarup case-study (see Chapter 26) and Australian agriculture generally, yields achieved on better-managed farms are significantly higher than average yields in the region.

However, some frustration was felt at the lack of progress that has been made in physical changes to the landscape. This needs to be balanced against the 200 years it has taken to create the problems now being faced. It also needs to be recognized that, despite the positive initiatives of government, the level of funding remains small relative to the scale of the problems.

Effectiveness of local resource management groups

Building local people's capacity to manage their land resources sustainably has been one of the major impacts of the West Hume Landcare Group.

Box 27.2: Land literacy: making the invisible visible

Many of Australia's land degradation issues are insidious and not readily apparent to unskilled observers. It is hard to get people excited about changing attitudes and practices if they cannot perceive the need. One of the key challenges, therefore, in tackling problems such as rising watertables, species extinctions and water quality decline is to make the invisible visible, so that people can appreciate the problem and also gauge their progress in fixing it.

A range of programmes designed to involve people in learning more about their landscape in a systematic, replicable way have emerged in Australia under the banner of Land Literacy – for example Saltwatch, Wormwatch, Streamwatch and Frogwatch (Campbell, 1994). The earliest example is Saltwatch, which began in 1987. By 1992, more than 900 schools and 50 Landcare groups were involved in gathering and analysing tens of thousands of water samples from creeks, rivers, reservoirs, irrigation channels and bores (White, 1992). Each school or community analyses its data and sends it to a central agency for processing, receiving in return a computer-generated overlay map of water quality in the district – displayed in the school and often the store or the hall. Data are stored on school computers as well as in government agencies, and groups are encouraged to look at trends over time within their district. The composite maps are used for interpretation, discussion and for planning further action such as excursions, rehabilitation projects and interpretative displays. Schools and community groups have access to education kits, manuals and curriculum materials, and training programmes for teachers have been developed over recent years.

The major value of land literacy programmes is the speed and effectiveness with which they transmit local environmental knowledge and teach people to observe and monitor the health of the land around them. Community groups and schools can gather more data from more sampling points than is conceivable for government agencies paying professional staff. People involved in gathering information are more interested in finding what it means, and taking it seriously. A slogan that emerged from a community-based water quality monitoring programme (with a focus on nutrient loads) in Western Australia was that 'measurement quickly becomes management.'

The roadside vegetation survey carried out by the West Hume group and the motorbike land degradation survey carried out by farmers of the Lower Balgarup group (see Chapter 26) are local examples of such programmes, in each case meeting a particular need, but they could certainly be replicated to monitor the extent of on-ground progress.

An important feature of a well-run land literacy programme is that the community trusts the data because they were involved in gathering it, they received some training as a group in knowing what to look for and how to measure, record and interpret it, and they need the information to assist with their own activities.

Box 27.2: (cont.)

There are other important spin-offs. Land literacy is more than just a learning exercise, as it tends to give people a feeling of having some control, that not everything is too remote, too large, too technical, too hopeless. Further, gathering 'real' data gives local communities some 'facts' of their own to fight with, a precious commodity in battles with unresponsive bureaucracies and a useful tool in the media. Quotes from the Peel-Harvey catchment cited in Campbell (1994) underscore this point:

'We didn't have to listen to people in the catchment very long to realise there was extreme unease about the monitoring data that had previously been presented. Most interested locals knew there had been a steady stream of people taking water samples for nearly ten years, and that these samples went into a 'scientific black box', which seemed to bear some resemblance to a scientific black hole. [Our monitoring] has shown up terrible problems with the government's monitoring programmes. Many of their statements were based on assumptions, not facts.'

The land literacy work that has been done in Australia to date is extremely encouraging, exciting, and it complements Landcare. But the potential of these programmes has hardly been scratched, and is in danger of being frittered away. There is a tendency to dismiss the data as not being 'real' or scientific, to see these programmes as mainly being for schools, a good way to get kids out of the classroom for a while. There are some grounds for this charge, as not all of these programmes have been rigorous in data collection or management.

Yet there is no reason why the information generated by land literacy programmes should not form the basis of society's knowledge of resource management issues, built in to the 'official' monitoring system. Where assessment techniques for a particular issue are considered too complex, or the technology too expensive or difficult for ordinary people to use, then there is obviously a role for science to develop simpler ways of making changes visible. Local groups will often do this anyway. For example, irrigators near the Murray River decided that piezometers are a good start, but watertable levels are still not easily observed, as one has to visit the piezometer and lower a tape measure into the pipe to gauge the depth to water. They came up with the idea of a bamboo pole with a float at the bottom, permanently floating in the piezometer, moving up and down with the watertable. The top of the pole is painted green, the middle orange and the bottom red, like a set of traffic lights, which can be seen from a passing vehicle without even entering the paddock. When only the green zone is visible, irrigators know that their soil is not saturated; a visible red zone spells danger, time to take remedial action; making visible the invisible.

There is enormous potential here to achieve several aims – increase aggregate knowledge of resource management issues, establish an ongoing capacity to monitor the health of natural resources, and broaden the political power base for resolving environmental problems.

The group has provided the motivation and the mechanism for encouraging local responsibility. The sheer scale of activities and projects that have been undertaken by the group illustrates the degree of autonomy, in a management sense if not financial, that has been generated.

There was no doubt in people's minds that local ownership is what makes landcare work. Sharing responsibility for understanding problems and developing solutions is what motivates people. Suspicion about who was driving landcare or perceptions that the group represented a particular clique were often quoted as reasons why people do not become involved.

Fundamental to the group's development has been the employment of the group co-ordinator. Several people commented that without this person the group would not have been able to achieve nearly as much. While the group's establishment and evolution has been quite clearly driven by local initiative, government funding has been very important to the group. Without this funding it is most unlikely that the same level of activity would have occurred.

The West Hume Landcare Group feels strongly about the fairness, equity and accountability of landcare funding. Having funds and being responsible for them is important to the group's success and motivation. However, there were different perspectives within the community about how equitably these funds were being used. Where government funds are used for landcare activities, all group members felt that there must be scrupulous accountability to ensure that scarce government funding be used in the most effective and efficient way.

Capacity to invest in Landcare

People spoke passionately about the severe economic, social and environmental challenges before them. Their whole way of rural life is under threat and the fabric of rural communities is breaking down. Clearly, land degradation cannot be dealt with separately from economic and social issues. Many people believed Landcare in general, and the local Landcare group, could have a broader role in helping to deal with these issues.

An economic study was conducted in an attempt to provide insight into the question 'Can farmers afford landcare?'[4]. A detailed case-study was conducted of four farms typical of different sizes and enterprise mixes, with a hypothetical financial analysis of two 'best practice' farms. The economic analysis, although developed from a small sample of farms using only one year's figures, raised issues that are significant for individuals, the Landcare group and broader Landcare policy.

In particular, it showed that the ability of landholders to 'afford landcare' depends largely on the structure of the farm unit and on the type of

---

[4] The study was carried out by Hassall and Associates Pty Ltd, a private agricultural consultancy firm.

improved land management practices. Farm size, level of equity, level of off-farm income and management capacity are key determinants of the financial surplus of a farm, and hence of the investment capacity of land-holders. The adoption of a particular landcare practice is affected by economic factors, including capital requirements, required management expertise, labour requirements, level of risk, and the time-scale and security of future financial returns.

Thus, larger, well-managed farms with a high level of equity are in a relatively strong financial position and should have little difficulty investing in landcare-related activities. Similarly, smaller farms with high equity and significant off-farm income should also be able to invest in landcare. Based on these criteria, it seems that 60 per cent of farms are financially so precarious as to severely restrict their capacity to invest in the long-term maintenance of their land and farm infrastructure. The issue is more than simply financial. Landcare requires personal time and energy – human resources that are often severely depleted when people are in financial strife.

The economic study concluded that:

o The range of landcare activities needs to be clearly defined and their benefits quantified to help landowners choose options that best fit their property and cash flow situation. Attention should be given to defining landcare programmes according to a profile of capital and cash flow impact.

o Landcare funding should be directed towards education and training to ensure that farmers have the necessary management skills to integrate land management practices and improve farm productivity objectives.

o It is possible in all farm business situations to improve farm performance. Landowners should be encouraged to develop and implement integrated landcare and farm productivity programmes.

The implication (see also Barr and Cary, 1992) is that the scale of land conservation activities will not be increased by focusing only on changing attitudes and promoting sustainable practices. Rather, farmers will need to be assisted to restructure their enterprise so that their financial situation allows them to invest in sustainable practices.

Supporting improved management

Management capacity is a key issue. Being able to manage a sustainable and profitable farm demands very complex skills in a world that is changing rapidly. Yet management is a sensitive issue, as nobody likes to feel or be told their management skills need improving.

Improving management capacity is clearly an area where the Landcare Group can continue to have an important impact. Discussion groups, farm walks, field days, presentation evenings by extension staff and newsletters all help. The need to pay more attention to good communication and adult education principles in the way the group organizes its activities, was raised by group members during the PRA impact assessment. However, who is involved, whether the activities are specific and detailed enough, and how well prepared individuals are to implement their new knowledge requires further analysis.

Impacts on support institutions and professionals

The landcare group has become central to the transfer of information and knowledge to many landholders in the area. This is the case for both land conservation and production-oriented information. The group has become a focus through which government extension agencies and other providers of information and expertise can operate.

The West Hume Landcare Group has evolved in tandem with a dramatic change in the culture of natural resource management agencies. Today the good partnership between agency staff and the Landcare group is clear, although there are still ambiguities about how the group and extension services interact. Although it is dangerous to oversimplify 'old' and 'new' approaches to extension, it is fair to suggest that landcare has brought about a change from a technology-centred one-to-one extension model, to a new model that places greater emphasis on community development, developing local self-reliance and working with community groups. Considerable training has occurred within government agencies to support this change. Whereas in the past there were only technical experts, there are now many Landcare facilitators and co-ordinators employed by government agencies. This change, however, has resulted in some polarization between technical roles and facilitation roles. It has become clear that the most effective agency staff are able to combine technical knowledge with good community facilitation skills.

Inadequate agency support for the group, particularly in terms of assistance with mapping and monitoring natural resources, remains a major constraint. Considerable stress is felt by agency staff who are trying to meet extraordinary demands with constantly diminishing resources. There have been reductions in funding for state government agencies, and concerns have been expressed that resources provided by the Commonwealth Government for landcare through the National Landcare Program end up being used for what should be core state government agency responsibilities. Thus, overall, government support has not increased to the extent suggested by looking at increases in Commonwealth expenditure on landcare.[5]

---

[5] Chapter 15 provides a policy overview of the evolution of Landcare.

Some clear points on extension emerged from interviews and group discussions:

○ The move to group extension activities and greater recognition of land-holders' 'local knowledge' that has accompanied the evolution of Landcare was welcomed by both landholders and extension staff.
○ Landcare is pulling in people who would not otherwise have contact with extension agencies.
○ Some landholders and extension staff noted that while group activities can give the general picture, it is often helpful for individuals to have individual extension advice regarding the specifics of what to do on their own property.
○ Landcare activity increases, rather than decreases, the need for extension services from state government agencies. Extension staff and group members were concerned about the inability of extension agencies to provide adequate support.

Where does the West Hume Landcare Group go from here?

Like so many of the other 2000 Landcare groups across Australia, the achievements of the West Hume Landcare Group are remarkable, and have occurred through the voluntary efforts of community members.

There is little question that the group has established a solid foundation. The awareness among people in the area about land degradation is very high, the group has strong community support, and it has been exceptionally successful in accessing funds for projects. The momentum of the group has been maintained over a five-year period and there is now considerable experience and understanding within the group about how to make things work. The group can also demonstrate its impact in terms of on-ground projects.

However, it is not plain sailing from here on. The group faces several challenges and must make decisions about the next steps. These decisions need to be addressed by the group members and by the government alike.

Increasing the scale of land conservation

A sobering reality is that despite the group's efforts, the scale of land conservation activities is not yet sufficient to stabilize land degradation, much less reverse it. Exactly how much more is needed, and how quickly, is not fully understood. However, looking at the revegetation efforts needed to address salinity (the major land degradation problem in the area) highlights the scale of the task. The Department of Conservation and Land Management estimates that a tree cover of at least 6 per cent should be aimed for. This is quite modest as it is generally recognised that farms can have 15 – 20 per cent tree cover without reducing productivity. Furthermore, much more than 6 per cent is likely to be needed for effective control of salinity. Yet, over the last five years (despite the planting of over 100 000 trees) the tree cover has been increased by only 0.3 per cent. In other words, to reach the minimum 6 per cent level over the next five years, efforts will need to be increased seventeen-fold.

This need to increase the scale of land conservation activities raises significant questions for the landcare group and government agencies. In particular, there is a need to focus on how this increase in scale can be achieved through innovation and greater levels of efficiency, given the economic reality that neither landholders nor government are able to increase expenditure on land conservation to the extent required.

The wider socio-economic environment

People of the West Hume area realize there is much they can do as a community and on their own farms. However, they also recognize the external forces that have a major impact on life at the local level. Government help is needed to adjust to these changes and to ensure that they are in the best interests of both rural communities and Australia at large.

Improving the management capacity of individual land managers was raised by many individuals as a key to the future. It was recognized that in today's world, agriculture is a highly complex business that requires many sophisticated skills, especially when trying to integrate productivity and sustainability goals.

People felt strongly that government assistance is required in the following three areas:

o funding for the implementation of group projects
o maintaining and strengthening the research and extension support structure
o incentives that would encourage and enable individuals to undertake more land conservation activities on their properties.

However, it was also recognized that the problems will not simply be solved by throwing money at Landcare. While many comments were made about the need for various forms of taxation and other incentives, the West Hume Landcare Group has no clear views about how to make these work and how to deal with issues of equity and environmental priorities. While the reasons for local resource degradation are in part due to external factors, local people cannot be expected to shoulder the full responsibility and financial cost of achieving sustainable land use. The scale of changes still required in the area is enormous. Technical, practical and financial support is required if these changes are to be achieved. Without this support from the wider community and government there is a high risk of burnout and loss of motivation of local landholders.

368

SUMMARY

28
Towards New Horizons: Implications for Joint Watershed Development and Challenges for the Future

THE CASES OF joint watershed management presented here have many important common elements, from which much can be learnt. All emphasized the use of locally-adapted resource-conserving technologies that provide immediate returns to farmers, rather than the use of externally-derived technologies. All focused on encouraging action by groups or communities at a local level, rather than working with individual farmers. All involved supportive government and/or non-governmental institutions working in partnership with each other and with farmers, rather than the more common mode of working in isolation.

The principal impacts were:

○ economic benefits, such as increases in land value and demand for labour; substantial increases in crop and livestock production (cereal yields doubled on average with no additional use of external inputs); and increases in fodder and fuel production. There were also increases in the diversity of crops grown. The overall result of these economic benefits was increased livelihood security through the diversification of livelihood sources.

○ social benefits, such as greater self-confidence and a sense of cohesion in communities; reduced conflicts over resources; reduced out-migration; attention to the needs of landless groups; and new rapport between local people and external professionals.

○ environmental benefits, such as recharge of aquifers and an increased supply of drinking and irrigation water; reduced soil erosion, salinity, and the use of fertilizers and pesticides. The numbers of trees have increased, and birds and other wildlife have returned.

Despite their many achievements, these cases are as yet only islands of success. They have generally been successful despite existing policies that tend to undermine sustainability. If these impacts are to spread further, then policies and practice must now be more directed towards these proven alternatives.

In November 1994 a workshop was held in Bangalore, India. This was a forum for the New Horizons case-study team members to meet and discuss the lessons learned from their studies and to suggest practical ways forward. Participants suggested some immediate implications for all existing

371

national and international institutions concerned with agricultural development, watershed management, and soil and water conservation. These are listed below with respect to five cross-cutting themes, namely technology, process and methods, impacts and indicators, inter-institutional arrangements and policies.

Technologies

Redirect incentives. Linking financial and food inducements to pre-selected conservation measures must cease. These encourage farmers to permit or engage in the construction of conservation measures that they neither agree with nor feel responsible for maintaining. When the incentives stop, so does the conservation. Instead, incentives should be increasingly directed towards institutional development at the watershed level. Incentives are effective only in certain situations when they are decided in consultation with communities for group management and institutional development. Access to credit for taking up productive enterprises and technologies should be increased, particularly for poorer households.

Innovation. The capacity of individuals and institutions to innovate and experiment must be actively encouraged. It is impossible to predict the technologies that may be appropriate in a particular time and place. Good technologies today will be superseded by others in the future. What needs to be made sustainable is the process of innovation itself.

Biological measures. A much greater emphasis is needed on adapting and applying biological measures for soil and water conservation, such as green manures, cover crops, mulching, composting and reduced tillage. These are favoured by farmers because they can improve productivity as well as reduce labour needs.

Participatory technology development and adaptive research should become an integral part of watershed management programmes. 'On-watershed' research would be an appropriate approach (using on-farm research as a model).

Process and methods

Farmer-to farmer extension and experimentation should be an integral part of watershed management programmes if they are to be sustainable and are to encourage scaling-up. The capacity of farmer and community-level organizations for experimentation and extension should therefore be strengthened.

372

Flexibility. External institutions must be flexible and responsive, and ready to learn with farmers. Every farm has its own signature. No one can predict what each farm requires and how needs will change over time. A thoroughly designed and pre-planned project is not a good project.

Confidence-building. The pace of programmes and projects must be slow in order to build motivation, confidence and rapport among all the groups involved.

Decentralization. The village-based management of programme funds and planning are important pre-requisites for sustainable watershed management.

Impacts and indicators

Adaptation versus adoption. Impact indicators should focus on adaptation of technologies and practices by farmers, rather than on adoption of technologies.

Equity. Much greater efforts are needed to address equity issues if the poorest and most marginalized in any society are not to be missed. This is, at present, largely left out, even of participatory programmes.

Self-evaluation enriches the learning process in institutions. It leads to greater honesty about what does and does not work, particularly if local people's measures of what constitutes success are used. What is needed is a widespread transition towards 'learning organizations', using impact analysis as the impetus for improvement.

Inter-institutional arrangements

Widespread training and competence-building is needed to encourage and sustain a participatory approach to joint watershed management, especially in bureaucracies and universities. There is a particular need for expanding training in participatory methods that focus on joint learning for action.

Joint approaches increase the contacts and linkages between farmers and external institutions, improving the likelihood of policies and practices emerging that satisfy all stakeholders. The case-studies highlighted many creative approaches to developing partnerships between farmers and extensionists, researchers, markets, private companies, local authorities and education systems.

Clear roles. There is a need to clarify the roles of the different institutions, such as governments and NGOs, involved in developing joint watershed management.

Inter-village federations. Sustainable watershed development requires the development of strong inter-village institutions or federations. These institutions can effectively manage a range of activities such as credit, marketing and the protection of common lands, with limited external support.

Policies

Policy reform. Most national and international agricultural and rural policies do not provide a favourable climate for the implementation of the approaches to watershed development described here. There is a need for widespread reform to create a more supportive and enabling policy environment.

Appropriate support. If authorities are to hand responsibility for complex, costly and conflict-ridden problems back to local people, this must be accompanied by adequate financial and institutional support.

Equity and livelihoods. The policy focus should not be solely on natural resource management, but should also encompass livelihood security, equity and institutional development.

Challenges for the future

Soil and water conservation practices based on imposed technological interventions have not delivered the environmental or economic benefits they promised. The practice of designing and implementing interventions without involving local people can succeed only with coercion. Such enforced responses may appear technically appropriate but are commonly rejected by local people when external pressure is removed.

A thorough reassessment and reorientation of existing soil and water conservation practices is needed, building on the experiences of participatory watershed programmes such as the New Horizons case-studies presented here. These experiences make no claim to perfection, but signal that changes to soil and water conservation programmes are both possible and positive. The challenge is to identify and encourage the conditions that will foster the further spread of these innovative efforts.

References

Chapter 1

Anderson, D. 1984. Depression, dust bowl, demography, and drought: the colonial state and soil conservation in East Africa during the 1930s. *African Affairs*, 321–43.

Bannister, M.E. and Nair, P.K.R. 1990. Alley cropping as a sustainable agricultural technology for the hillsides of Haiti: experience of an agroforestry outreach project. *Amer. J. Altern. Agric.* 5(2): 51–59

Beinart, W. 1984. Soil erosion, conservationism and ideas about development: a southern African exploration, 1900–1960. *Journal of Southern African Studies*, II, 52–83

Bennett, H.H. 1939. *Soil Conservation.* McGraw-Hill, New York.

Blackler, A. 1994. Indigenous versus imposed: soil management in the Mixteca Alta, Oaxaca, Mexico. Paper presented to Rural History Centre Conference, May 10, University of Reading.

Carnes, A. and Weld, W.A. 1941. A study of old farmer-built terraces. *Agricultural Engineering* 22, 361–366

Carter, J. 1995. *Alley Cropping: Have Resource Poor Farmers Benefited?* ODI Natural Resource Perspectives No 3, London.

Cerna, L.L., Moneva, L.A., Listones, W.M. and Gerardino, E.C. 1994. The impact of soil and water conservation practices promoted through farmer-based extension system on the development of a farmed watershed area: a case study from the Philippines. Paper for IIED Conference New Horizons: The Social, Economic and Environmental Impacts of Participatory Watershed Development, November, Bangalore, India.

Dogra, B. 1983. Traditional agriculture in India: high yields and no waste. *The Ecologist* 13, (2/3), 84–7

FAO. 1992. *The Keita Integrated Development Project.* FAO, Rome

Fernandez, A. 1993. *The Interventions of a Voluntary Agency in the Process and Growth of People's Institutions for Sustained and Equitable Management of Micro-Watersheds.* MYRADA Rural Management Systems Paper 18, Bangalore.

Fish, S. K. and Paul, R. 1992. Prehistoric landscapes of the Sonoran desert Hohokam. *Population and Environment: A Journal of Interdisciplinary Studies* 13 (4)

Gichuki, F. N. 1991. Conservation Profile. In: *Environmental Change and Dryland Management in Machakos District, Kenya 1930–90.* ODI Working Paper 56. ODI, London.

Haagsma, B. 1990. *Erosion and Conservation on Santao Antao. No Shortcuts to Simple Answers.* Working document 2, Santao Antao Rural Development Project, Republic of Cape Verde.

Hall, A. R. 1949. Terracing in the southern Piedmont. *Agricultural History* 23, 96–109

Hudson, N.W., Cheatle, R.J., Woods, A.P. and Gichuki, F.N. (eds) 1992. *Working with Farmers for Better Land Husbandry.* Intermediate Technology Publications, London.

375

Huxley, E. 1960. *A New Earth. An Experiment in Colonialism.* Chatto & Windus, London.

IFAD. 1992. *Soil and Water Conservation in Sub-Saharan Africa.* IFAD, Rome.

Jacks, G. and Whyte, R. 1939. *The Rape of the Earth: A World Survey of Soil Erosion.* Faber and Faber, London.

Kang, B. T., Wilson, G. F. and Lawson, T. L. 1984. *Alley Cropping: A Stable Alternative to Shifting Agriculture.* IITA, Ibadan.

Kelly, L. C. 1985. Anthropology in the Soil Conservation Service. *Agricultural History*, 59, 136–47

Kerkhof, P. 1990. *Agroforestry in Africa. A survey of project experience.* Panos Institute, London.

Kerr, J. 1994. How subsidies distort incentives and undermine watershed development projects in India. Paper for IIED Conference New Horizons: The Social, Economic and Environmental Impacts of Participatory Watershed Development, November, Bangalore, India.

Kerr, J. and Sanghi, N. K. 1992. *Soil and Water Conservation in India's Semi Arid Tropics.* Sustainable Agriculture Programme Gatekeeper Series SA34, IIED, London.

Lal, R. 1989. Agroforestry systems and soil surface management of a Tropical Alfisol. I: Soil moisture and crop yields. *Agroforestry Systems* 8: 7–29.

Marchal, J-Y. 1978. L'espace des techniciens et celui des paysans histoire d'un périmètre antiérosif en Haut-Volta. In: ORSTOM. *Maîtrice de L'Espace Agrarian et Développement en Afrique Tropicale.* ORSTOM, Paris.

Marchal, J-Y. 1986. Vingt ans de lutte antiérosive au nord du Burkina Faso. *Cahiers ORSTOM, Série Pédalologique,* XXII (2), 173–80.

Mndeme, K. C. H. 1992. Combatting soil erosion in Tanzania: The HADO experience. In Tato K and Hurni H (eds). *Soil Conservation for Survival.* SCS, Ankeny, Iowa.

Musema-Uwimana, A. 1983. La conservation des terraces au Rwanda. *Recherche Agricole* 16, 86–93.

Östberg, W. and Christiansson, C. 1993. *Of Lands and People.* Working Paper No 25 from the Environment and Development Studies Unit, Stockholm University, Stockholm.

Oxfam, 1987. *Soil and Water Conservation in Hararghe Region, Ethiopia.* Mimeo. Oxfam, Oxford.

PRAI. 1963. *Soil Conservation Programme in Village Sherpur Sarraiya (Etawah): A Case Study.* Planning Research and Action Institute Publ. No 307, Lucknow.

Planning Commission. 1964. *Study of Soil Conservation Programme for Agricultural Land.* Programme Evaluation Organisation, Planning Commission, Government of India, New Delhi.

Pretty, J. 1995. *Regenerating Agriculture: Policies and Practice for Sustainability and Self-reliance.* Earthscan, London.

Pretty, J. N. and Shah, P. 1994. *Soil and Water Conservation in the 20th Century: A History of Coercion and Control.* Rural History Centre Research Series No.1. University of Reading, Reading.

Reij, C. 1988. The agroforestry project in Burkina Faso: an analysis of popular participation in soil and water conservation. In: Conroy C and Litvinoff M (eds). *The Greening of Aid.* Earthscan Publications Ltd, London.

Reij, C. 1991. Indigenous soil and water conservation in Africa. Sustainable Agriculture Programme *Gatekeeper Series SA27.* International Institute for Environment and Development, London.

Rohn, A. R. 1963. Prehistoric soil and water conservation on Chapin Mesa, south-western Colorado. *American Antiquity*, 28, 441–455

Sampson, H. C. 1930. Soil erosion in Tropical Africa. *Rhodesian Agric. Journ.*, 33, 197–205.

Sanghi, N. K. 1987. Participation of farmers as co-research workers: some case studies in dryland agriculture. Paper presented to IDS Workshop Farmers and Agricultural Research: Complementary Methods. IDS, Sussex.

Shaxson, F. 1996. Conservation at the crossroads in tropical countries. *Journal of Soil and Water Conservation* 51(6), 471 (Nov/Dec).

Shaxson, T.F., Hudson, N.W., Sanders, D.W., Roose, E. and Moldenhauer, W.C. 1989. *Land Husbandry. A Framework for Soil and Water Conservation.* Soil and Water Conservation Society, Ankeny, Iowa.

Showers, K. B. 1989. Soil erosion in the Kingdom of Lesotho: origins and colonial response. 1830s-1950s. *Journ. Southern African Studies* 15: 263–86.

Showers, K. B. and Malahleha, G. 1990. Pilot study for the development of methodology to be used an historical environmental impact assessment of colonial conservation schemes. Paper presented at Workshop on Conservation in Africa: Indigenous Knowledge and Conservation Strategies. Harare, Zimbabwe.

SIDA. 1984. *Soil Conservation in Borkana Catchment. Evaluation Report.* Final Report, Swedish International Development Authority, Stockholm.

Stocking, M. 1985. Soil conservation policy in colonial Africa. *Agric. History*, 59: 148–61.

Trimble, S. W. 1985. Perspectives on the history of soil erosion control in the eastern United States. *Agric. History*, 59: 162–80.

UNEP. 1983. *Rainwater Harvesting for Agriculture.* UNEP, Nairobi.

Wenner, C. G. 1992. *The Revival of Soil Conservation in Kenya.* Carl Gosta Wenner's personal notes, 1974–81. Edited by A. Eriksson. RSCU/SIDA, Nairobi.

Wilson, K. B. 1989. Indigenous conservation in Zimbabwe: soil erosion, land-use planning and rural life. Paper presented to 'Conservation and Rural People' African Studies Association of UK Conference, Cambridge.

Worster, D. 1979. *Dust Bowl. The Southern Plains in the 1930s.* Oxford University Press, Oxford.

Chapter 2

Abbot, J. and I. Guijt. 1997. Changing Views on Change: Participatory Monitoring of the Environment. *SARL Discussion Paper No 1.* London: International Institute for Environment and Development.

Blackburn, J. with Holland, J. 1997. *Who Changes? Institutionalizing Participation in Development.* Intermediate Technology Publications, London.

Chambers, R. 1997. *Whose Reality Counts? Putting the Last First.* London: Intermediate Technology Publications.

Chambers, R. and Guijt, I. 1995. PRA – five years later. Where are we now? *Forest, Trees and People Newsletter* 26/27: 4–14.

Cornwall, A., Guijt, I. and Welbourn, A. 1994. Acknowledging process: Methodological challenges for agricultural research and extension. In Scoons, I. and Thompson, J. (eds) *Beyond Farmer First.* Intermediate Technology Publications, London.

Guijt, I. 1995. *Moving Slowly and Reaching Far.* London: International Institute for Environment and Development and Kampala: Redd Barna, Uganda.

Pretty, J.N., I. Guijt, J. Thompson and I. Scoones. 1995. *A Trainers' Guide to Participatory Learning and Action.* London: International Institute for Environment and Development.

RRA/PLA Notes (1988 - present). Sustainable Agriculture and Rural Livelihoods Programme. International Institute for Environment and Development, London.

Scherler, C., R. Forster, O. Karkoschka, and M. Kitz, eds. 1977. *Beyond the Toolkit: Experiences with Institutionalisation of Participatory Approaches of GTZ-Supported Projects in Rural Areas.* Eschborn, Germany: GTZ.

Thompson, J. 1995. Participatory approaches in government bureaucracies: Facilitating the process of institutional change. *World Development 23 (9)*: 1521–54.

Thompson, J. 1997. *Cooperation on the Commons: The Emergence and Persistence of Reciprocal Altruism and Collective Action in Farmer-Managed Irrigation Systems in Kenya.* Unpublished Ph.D. Worcester, MA: Graduate School of Geography, Clark University.

Thompson, J. and J.N. Pretty. 1996. Sustainability Indicators and Soil Conservation: A Participatory Impact Study and Self-Evaluation of the Catchment Approach of the Ministry of Agriculture, Kenya. *Journal of Soil and Water Conservation* (July/ August): 265–73.

van Veldhuizen, J.A. Waters-Bayer, R. Ramirez, D.A. Johnson and J. Thompson, eds. 1997. *Farmers' Research in Practice: Lessons from the Field.* Intermediate Technology Publications: London.

Chapter 3

Bunch, R. 1977. Better Use of Land in the Highlands of Guatemala. In Stamp, E. (ed.) *Growing Out of Poverty.* Oxford University Press, Oxford.

Bunch, R. 1982. *Two Ears of Corn, A Guide to People-Centred Agricultural Improvement.* World Neighbors, Oklahoma, USA.

Bunch, R. 1988. Guinope Integrated Development Programme, Honduras. In: Conroy and Litvinoff (eds.) *The Greening of Aid, Sustainable Livelihoods in Practice.* Earthscan Press, London.

Bunch, R. 1990. Low input soil restoration in Honduras: The Cantarranas farmer-to-farmer extension programme. *Gatekeeper* 23. International Institute for Environment and Development, London.

Bunch, R. 1993. *The Use of Green Manures by Villager Farmers, What We have Learned to Date.* Technical Report No. 3, Second Edition. CIDICCO, Tegucigalpa.

Bunch, R and Lopez, G. 1995. *Soil recuperation in Central America: Sustaining Innovation after Intervention.* Gatekeeper Series SA 55, IIED, London

Flores, M. 1991–96. Series of *Cover Crop Newsletters.* CIDICCO, Tegucigalpa.

Chapter 5

Bhat, M.K., 1991. *MYRADA Kamasamudram Evaluation Report (1985–90).* MYRADA, Bangalore, India.

Fernandez, A. 1993. *Analysis Of The Process In People's Effort To Manage Micro-Watershed In Lakennahalli Village (Myrada Kamasamudram Project).* MYRADA, Bangalore, India.

Chapter 9

Guijt, I. 1998. Assessing the merits of participatory development of sustainable agriculture: experiences from Brazil and Central America. In: Blauert, J. and Zadek, S. (eds.) *Mediating Sustainability.* Kumarian Press, Hartford, Conn.

Chapter 10

Admassie, Y. 1992. *The Catchment Approach to Soil Conservation in Kenya. Regional Soil Conservation Unit Report No. 6.* RSCU, Swedish International Development Authority, Nairobi.

Anderson, D. 1984. Depression, dust bowl, demography, and drought: the colonial state and soil conservation in East Africa during the 1930s. *African Affairs,* 321–43.

Beinart, W. 1984. Soil erosion, conservationism and ideas about development: a southern African exploration, 1900–1960. *J. Southern African Studies II,* 52–83.

Bennett, H. H. 1939. *Soil Conservation.* McGraw-Hill, New York. CIIR in association with James Currey, London.

Eckbom, A. 1992. *Economic Impact Assessment of Implementation Strategies for Soil Conservation. A comparative analysis of the on-farm and catchment approach in Trans Nzoia, Kenya.* Unit for Environmental Economics, Dept. of Economics, Gothenburg University, Sweden.

Figueiredo, P. 1986. *The Yield of Crops on Terraced and Non-Terraced Land. A Field Survey in Kenya.* Swedish University of Agricultural Sciences, Uppsala.

Grönvall, M. 1987. *A Study of Land Use and Soil Conservation on a Farm in Mukurweini Division, Central Kenya.* Swedish University of Agricultural Sciences, Uppsala.

Holmgren, E. and Johansson, G. 1988. *Comparison Between Terraced and Nonterraced Land in Machakos District, Kenya.* Swedish University of Agricultural Sciences, Uppsala.

Howell, J. (ed). 1988. *Training and Visit Extension in Practice.* ODI, London.

Hunegnaw, T. 1987. *Technical Evaluation of Soil Conservation Measures in Embu District, Kenya.* Report of a minor field study. IRDC, Swedish University of Agricultural Sciences, Uppsala.

Kiara, J.K., Segerros, M., Pretty, J.N. and McCracken, J. 1990. *Rapid Catchment Analysis in Murang'a District, Kenya.* Soil and Water Conservation Branch, Ministry of Agriculture, Nairobi.

Lindgren, B–M. 1988. *Economic Evaluation of a Soil Conservation Project in Machakos District, Kenya.* Swedish University of Agricultural Sciences, Uppsala.

Lundgren, L. 1993. *Twenty Years of Soil Conservation. SIDA Report No 9* Regional Soil Conservation Unit, Nairobi.

MOA. 1981. *Soil Conservation in Kenya. Especially in small-scale farming in high potential areas using labour intensive methods.* SWCB, Ministry of Agriculture, Nairobi, 7th edition.

MOA/MALDM. *passim.* Reports of Catchment Approach Planning and Rapid Catchment Analyses. Soil and Water Conservation Branch, Ministry of Agriculture, Livestock Development and Marketing, Nairobi, 1988–1993.

Moris, J. 1990. *Extension Alternatives in Tropical Africa.* ODI, London.

Mullen, J. 1989. Training and visit system in Somalia: contradictions and anomalies. *J. Internat. Development 1,* 145–67.

Pretty, J.N., Kiara, J.K. and Thompson, J. (eds). 1993. *The Impact of the Catchment Approach to Soil and Water Conservation: A Study of Six Catchments in Western, Rift Valley and Central Provinces, Kenya.* Soil and Water Conservation Branch, Ministry of Agriculture, Livestock Development and Marketing, Kenya.

Pretty, J.M. 1990. *Rapid Catchment Analysis for Extension Agents.* Notes on the 1990 Kericho Workshop for the Ministry of Agriculture, Kenya. IIED, London.

Raikes, P. 1988. *Modernising Hunger: Famine, Food Surplus and Farm Policy in the EEC and Africa.* Catholic Institute for International Relations in collaboration with James Currey, London, and Heinemann, Portsmouth, N.H.

Thompson, J. and J.N. Pretty. 1996. Sustainability indicators and soil conservation: a participatory impact study and self-evaluation of the catchment approach of the Ministry of Agriculture, Kenya. *Journal of Soil and Water Conservation* (July/ August): 265–73.

Thompson, J. 1995. Participatory approaches in government bureaucracies: facilitating the process of institutional change. *World Development 23(9)*: 1521–54.

Tjernström, R. 1992. Yields from terraced and non-terraced fields in the Machakos District of Kenya. In: Tato, K. and Hurni, H. (eds). *Soil Conservation for Survival*. Soil Conservation Society, Ankeny, Iowa, p 251–65.

Chapter 11

CTAE. 1992. *Annual Results of Technical Evaluation: Integrated Watershed Development (Plains) Project: Rajasthan Component*. College of Technology and Agriculture Engineering, Rajasthan Agriculture University, Udaipur, Rajasthan.

CTAE 1994. *Annual Results of Technical Evaluation: Integrated Watershed Development (Plains) Project: Rajasthan Component*. College of Technology and Agriculture Engineering, Rajasthan Agriculture University, Udaipur, Rajasthan.

Jodha, N.S. 1990. Rural Common Property Resources: Contributions and Crisis. *Economic and Political Weekly*, Bombay, India, June 30: A 65 – A78.

Korten, D. 1980. Community organization and rural development: A learning process approach. *Public Administration Review* 44(4): 480–511.

Rondinelli, D.A. 1983. *Development Projects as Policy Experiments: An Adaptive Approach to Development Administration*. Methuen, London.

Singh, V. Personal communication, July 1994. Analysis and results of an evaluative survey conducted in sample watersheds of Rajasthan.

Chapter 13

BTRT. 1992. *Mid-Term Evaluation of Begnas Tal/Rupa Tal (BTRT) Water Management Project – Final Report*.

Krishna, K.C. *et al*. 1978. *A Study of Farming Practices BTRT Watershed Management Project Area, Kaski, Pokhara, Nepal*.

Chapter 14

Bunch, R. 1982. *Two Ears of Corn*. World Neighbors, Oklahoma City.

Bunch, R. 1990. Low input soil restoration in Honduras: the Cantarranas farmer-to-farmer extension programme. *Gatekeeper Series* 23. International Institute for Environment and Development, London.

Campbell, C.A. 1994. *Landcare: Communities Shaping the Land and the Future*. St. Leonards, NSW, Australia: Allen and Unwin.

Central Soil and Water Conservation Research and Training Institute (CSWCRTI). 1989. *CSWCRTI: an Introduction*. CSWCRTI, Dehra Dun, India.

Chambers, R., Saxena, N.C. and Shah, T. 1989a. *To the Hands of the Poor: Water and Trees*. Oxford & IBH Publishing Co. Pvt. Ltd., New Delhi, and Intermediate Technology Publications, London.

Chambers, R., Pacey, A., and Thrupp, L-A. (eds.) 1989b. *Farmer First: Farmer innovation and agricultural research*. Intermediate Technology Publications, London.

Coase, R.H. 1960. The problem of social cost. *Journal of Law and Economics* 3:1–44.

Critchley, W. 1991. *Looking After our Land: Soil and Water Conservation in Dryland Africa*. Oxfam. Oxford, UK.

Fernandez, A.P. 1991. *The MYRADA Experience: alternate management systems for savings and credit of the rural poor*. MYRADA, Bangalore.

Fernandez, A.P. 1993. *The MYRADA Experience: The interventions of a voluntary agency in the emergence and growth people's institutions for sustained and equitable management of micro-watersheds*. MYRADA, Bangalore.

Fujisaka, S. 1989. The need to build upon farmer practice and knowledge: Reminders from selected upland conservation projects and policies. *Agroforestry Systems* 9: 141–53.

Gadgil, M. 1992. 'State Subsidies and Resource Use in a Dual Society.' in *The Price of Forests*. Centre for Science and Environment, New Delhi.

Gangi Reddy, P., Sriramappa, G., Katyal, J.C., Sanghi, N.K. and Kerr, J.M. 1994. Converting irrigation tanks into percolation tanks in South India: a case study of social organization leading to equitable development. Paper prepared for New Horizons: The economic, social and environmental impacts of participatory watershed development, Nov 28–Dec 2, Bangalore, India. IIED, London.

Government of India. 1991. *National Watershed Development Project for Rainfed Areas (NWDPRA): Guidelines*. 2nd Edition. Ministry of Agriculture, New Delhi.

Gulati, A. 1990. Fertilizer subsidy: is the cultivator 'net-subsidized'? *Indian Journal of Agricultural Economics* 45 (1) 1–11.

IFAD, 1992. *Soil and Water Conservation in sub-Saharan Africa: Towards sustainable production by the rural poor*. IFAD, Amsterdam.

Jackson, T., with Eade, D. 1982. *Against the Grain*. Oxfam, Oxford.

Kerr, J.M., Chandrakanth, M.G. and Deshpande, R.S. 1997. Economics of groundwater management in Karnataka. In: Kerr, J.M., Marothia, D.K., Singh, K., Ramasamy, C., and Bentley, W.R. (eds.) 1997. *Natural Resource Economics: Concepts and Applications to India*. Oxford and IBH. New Delhi.

Kerr, J.M. and Sanghi, N.K. 1992. Indigenous soil and water conservation in India's semi-arid tropics. *Gatekeeper Series* 34. IIED, London.

Lutz, E., Pagiola, S. and Reiche, C. (eds.) 1994. Economic and institutional analyses of soil conservation projects in Central America and the Caribbean. *World Bank Environment Paper 8*. World Bank, Washington DC.

Murray, G. 1994. Technoeconomic, organizational, and ideational factors as determinants of soil conservation in the Dominican Republic. In: Lutz, E., Pagiola, S. and Reiche, C. (eds.) 1994. Economic and institutional analyses of soil conservation projects in Central America and the Caribbean. *World Bank Environment Paper 8*. World Bank, Washington DC.

Parthasarathy, G. 1994. *Economic Impact of Women's Thrift and Credit Societies in Cuddapha District, Andhra Pradesh*. Institute of Development and Planning Studies, Visakhapatnam, India.

Patel-Weynand, T. 1997. Sukhomajri and Nada: Managing common property resources at the village level. In: Kerr, J.M., Marothia, D.K., Singh, K., Ramasamy, C., and Bentley, W.R. (eds.) 1997. *Natural Resource Economics: Concepts and Applications to India*. Oxford and IBH. New Delhi.

Pender, J. 1993. Farmers' irrigation investments in the presence of credit constraints: theory and evidence from South India. Brigham Young University, *Department of Economics Working Paper No. 93–16*. Provo, Utah, USA.

Pender, J. and Kerr, J. 1996. Determinants of farmers' indigenous soil and water conservation practices in India's semi-arid tropics. *EPTD Discussion Paper*. IFPRI, Washington, DC.

Pimbert, M. 1991. Designing integrated pest management for sustainable and productive futures. *Gatekeeper Series 29*. IIED, London.

Pretty, J.N. 1995. *Regenerating Agriculture: Policies and Practice for Sustainability and Self-reliance.* Earthscan, London; National Academy Press, Washington DC; Vikas Publishers and ACTIONAID, Bangalore.
Sanghi, N.K. 1987. 'Participation of farmers as co-research workers: some case studies in dryland agriculture'. Paper presented to IDS Workshop on Farmers and Agricultural Research: Complementary Methods. Institute of Development Studies, Sussex, UK.
Tiffen, M., Mortimore, M. and Gichuki, F. 1994. *More People, Less Erosion: Environmental recovery in Kenya.* John Wiley and Sons, Chichester.
Valdes, A. 1994. Economic analysis of soil conservation in Honduras. In: Lutz, E., Pagiola, S. and Reiche, C. (eds.) 1994. Economic and institutional analyses of soil conservation projects in Central America and the Caribbean. *World Bank Environment Paper 8.* World Bank, Washington DC.
World Bank. 1990. *Staff Appraisal Report, India: Integrated Watershed Development (Plains) Project.* World Bank, Washington, DC.

Chapter 15

Australian Bureau of Agricultural and Resource Economics (ABARE). 1992. Land management and financial conditions on Australian farms. *Outlook Conference.* ABARE, Canberra.
ABARE. 1991. *Australian broadacre agriculture 1990–91 and 1991–92.* Canberra, Australia.
Baker, R. forthcoming. Landcare policy, practice and partnerships. *Australian Geographical Studies.* 35(1). January 1997
Barr, N. and Cary, J. 1992. *Greening a Brown Land: An Australian Search for Sustainable Land Use.* Macmillan, Melbourne.
Bayliss-Smith, T.P. 1982 *The Ecology of Agricultural Systems.* Cambridge University Press, Cambridge.
Beale, B. and Fray, P. 1990. *The Vanishing Continent: Australia's degraded environment* Hodder and Stoughton, Sydney.
Bryant, L. 1992. Social aspects of the farm financial crisis. In: G.Lawrence, F.M.Vanclay and B.Furze Eds., *Agriculture, Environment and Society: Contemporary Issues for Australia.* Macmillan, Melbourne.
Campbell, A. 1992. *Taking the long view in tough times–Landcare in Australia* Third annual report of the National Landcare Facilitator. National Soil Conservation Program, Canberra.
Campbell, A. 1994a. *Landcare–Communities Shaping the Land and the Future.* Allen and Unwin, Sydney.
Campbell, A. 1994b. Community First–Landcare in Australia. In: I. Scoones and J. Thompson (Eds). *Beyond Farmer First – rural peoples' knowledge, agricultural research and extension practice.* IT Publications, London.
Carr, A. 1994. *Grass-roots and green tape: community-based environmental management in Australia.* PhD thesis, Australian National University, Canberra.
Cock, P. 1992. Cooperative land management for ecological and social sustainability. In: G.Lawrence, F.M.Vanclay and B.Furze (Eds). *Agriculture, Environment and Society: Contemporary Issues for Australia.* Macmillan, Melbourne.
Cocks, D. 1992. *Use With Care: Managing Australia's natural resources in the twenty-first century.* New South Wales University Press, Kensington, Australia.
Curtis, A., De Lacy, T. and Klomp, N. 1992. *Evaluating landcare in Victoria: an analysis of Landcare group annual returns 1988–89 to 1990–91.* Unpublished report. The Johnstone Centre of Parks, Recreation and Heritage, Charles Sturt University, Wagga Wagga.

Farley, R. 1996. Realising the Full Potential of Landcare. *Landcare Australia Yearbook 1996–97*. EM Pty. Ltd.
Farley, R. and Toyne, P. 1989. A National Land Management Program. *Australian Journal of Soil & Water Conservation*. II(2):6–9
Fisher, B. 1993. Prospects for Australian commodities. *Agriculture and Resources Quarterly* V(1):54–59.
Giddens, A. 1992. *Modernity and Self-Identity: Self and Society in the Late Modern Age*. Polity, Cambridge.
Hadler, R. 1996. A new Landcare vision. *Down to Earth: an analysis of environment issues by the National Farmers' Federation*. No 5, January 1996.
Lawrence, G. and Williams, C. 1990. The Dynamics of Decline: Implications for Social Welfare Delivery in Rural Australia. In: Cullen, Dunn and Lawrence (Eds.) *Rural Health and Welfare in Australia*, Centre for Rural Welfare Research, Charles Sturt University, Wagga Wagga, Australia.
Reeve, I., Patterson, R.A. and Lees, J. 1988. *Land Resources: Training Towards 2000*. Rural Development Centre, University of New England, Armidale, Australia.
Robinson, P. 1996. Local Government and Landcare. *Landcare Australia Yearbook 1996–97*. EM Pty. Ltd, Canberra.
Scarsbrick, B. 1996. Role of Landcare Australia. *Landcare Australia Yearbook 1996–97*. EM Pty. Ltd, Canberra.
Sher, J. and Sher, K. 1994. Beyond the conventional wisdom: rural development as if Australia's rural people and communities really mattered. *Journal of Research in Rural Education*, **10**(1): 2–43.
Woodhill, J. 1992. *Landcare in NSW: Taking the Next Step–Final Report and Recommendations for the Development of Landcare in NSW from the 1991 Landcare Review*. Faculty of Agriculture and Rural Development, University of Western Sydney, Hawkesbury.

Chapter 17

Jodha, NS. 1991. Rural common property resources: a growing crisis. *Gatekeeper Series 24*. IIED, London.
Karnataka Electricity Board (KEB). 1994. *Annual Report*. Bangalore, India.
Ludden, D. 1979. Patronage and irrigation in Tamil Nadu: a long term view. *Indian Economic and Social History Review* 16(3):347–65.
Palanisami, K., and C. Ramasamy. 1997. Conjunctive use of tank and well irrigation. In J.M. Kerr, D.K. Marothia, K. Singh, C. Ramasamy, and W.R. Bentley (eds). *Natural Resource Economics: Concepts and applications to India*. 1997. Oxford and IBH, New Delhi.
Von Oppen, M. and K.V. Subba Rao. 1980. *Tank irrigation in semi-arid tropical India*. Patancheru: ICRISAT.

Chapter 21

AS-PTA. 1997. 'Trajetória do Projeto Paraíba: Período 1993–1996'. Unpublished report. AS-PTA, Solânea.
Blauert, J. and S. Zadek. 1998. *Mediating Sustainability*. Kumarian Press, Hartford, Conn.
Bunch, R. 1983. *Two Ears of Corn: A guide to people-centred agricultural improvement*. World Neighbors, Oklahoma City.
Chambers, R. 1994. Participatory Rural Appraisal (PRA): Challenges, potentials and paradigm. *World Development* 22(10): 1437–54.

Guijt, I. 1996. *From the Outside Looking In: Reflections on Projeto Paraíba, AS-PTA*. Unpublished report. IIED, London.

Guijt, I. 1998. Assessing The Merits Of Participatory Development Of Sustainable Agriculture: Experiences From Brazil And Central America. In: J. Blauert and S. Zadek, eds. *Mediating Sustainability*. Kumarian Press, Hartford, Conn.

Guijt, I. and P. Sidersky. 1996. Agreeing on Indicators. *ILEIA Newsletter* 12(3), 9–11.

Guijt, I, da Silva, M.R. and da Silveira, L.M. 1997. *Monitoramento Participativo Da Agricultura Sustentável: Relatório Do Terceiro Encontro em Paraíba*. IIED and AS-PTA.

IIED. *PLA Notes*, 1995 (RRA Notes, 1988–95). Sustainable Agriculture Programme, IIED, London.

Petersen, P. 1995. *Diagnóstico Ambiental do Município de Remígio-PB*. AS-PTA, Recife.

Sidersky, P. 1993. Peasant Farmers, Participation and Impact in the Brazilian Northeast. Unpublished report written for IIED New Horizons workshop, Bangalore, India. December 1993.

Chapter 22

Vasudevan, B. and Ramaswamy, U. Undated. *Gender in PIDOW*. SDC-sponsored study. MYRADA, Bangalore.

Chapter 25

Ahmad, S. and Dawson, M.D. 1994. Diagnostic analysis for integrated catchment development of Barani areas. *A Handbook of Diagnostic Analysis for Programme Managers, Scientists and Engineers*. ABAD/ADB/IFAD/UNDP.

Akram, R.M. 1968. Mangla Watershed Management Kanshi and Poonch River Catchment. In *Proceedings of West Pakistan Watershed Management Conference*, Pakistan Forest Institute, Peshawar.

Ishaq, C.M. 1968. Mangla Watershed Management. Outline of Planning and Execution Problems Experienced. In *Proceedings of West Pakistan Watershed Management Conference*, Pakistan Forest Institute, Peshawar.

Qureshi, B.A. and Ahmad, M. 1968. An economic evaluation of Mangla Watershed Management Project. In *Proceedings of West Pakistan Watershed Management Conference*, Pakistan Forest Institute, Peshawar.

WAPDA. 1986. *Siltation in Reservoirs*. Water Resources Management Directorate, Lahore.

WASID. 1967. *Sedimentation Appraisal Report*. Lahore.

Chapter 26

Bryant, L. 1992. 'Social aspects of the farm financial crisis.' In: G. Lawrence, F.M. Vanclay and B. Furze (Eds.) *Agriculture, Environment and Society: Contemporary Issues for Australia*. Macmillan, Melbourne.

Campbell, A. 1991. *Planning for Sustainable Farming*. Lothian Books, Melbourne.

Campbell, A. 1994. *Landcare – communities shaping the land and the future*. Allen and Unwin, Sydney.

Curtis, A., Tracey, P. and De Lacy, T. 1993. *Landcare in Victoria: getting the job done*. The Johnstone Centre of Parks, Recreation and Heritage, Charles Sturt University, Albury, Australia.

Duxbury, L. 1992. 'Community Involvement in Waterways Protection in Denmark and Albany, Western Australia.' In *Proceedings of the Catchments of Green Conference*. Greening Australia, Canberra.

Wilkinson, R. and Cary, J. 1992. *Monitoring Landcare in Central Victoria*. School of Agriculture and Forestry, University of Melbourne.

Chapter 27

Alexandra, J., Haffenden, S. and White, T. 1996. *Listening to the Land. A Directory of Community Environmental Monitoring Groups in Australia*. ACF, Fitzroy.

Barr, N. and Cary, J. 1992. *Greening a Brown Land: An Australian Search for Sustainable Land Use*. Macmillan, Melbourne.

Campbell, A. 1991. *Planning for Sustainable Farming*. Lothian Books, Melbourne.

Campbell, A. 1992. 'Farm and Catchment Planning – steps towards sustainability'. In G. Lawrence, F. Vanclay and B. Furze (Eds). *Agriculture, Environment and Society – the Australian experience*. MacMillan, Australia.

Campbell, A. 1994. *Landcare – communities shaping the land and the future*. Allen and Unwin, Sydney.

Hassall and Associates, Pty. Ltd. 1994. Economic Study for the Review of the West Hume Landcare Group. Unpublished report.

White, T. 1992. 'Land Literacy'. In: *Proceedings of the Catchments of Green Conference*. Greening Australia, Canberra.

Woodhill, J. and L. Robins. 1998. *Participatory Evaluation for Landcare and Catchment Management Groups*. Greening Australia, Canberra.